Arkansas Atlas & Gazetteer™

Grid numbers refer to detailed map pages

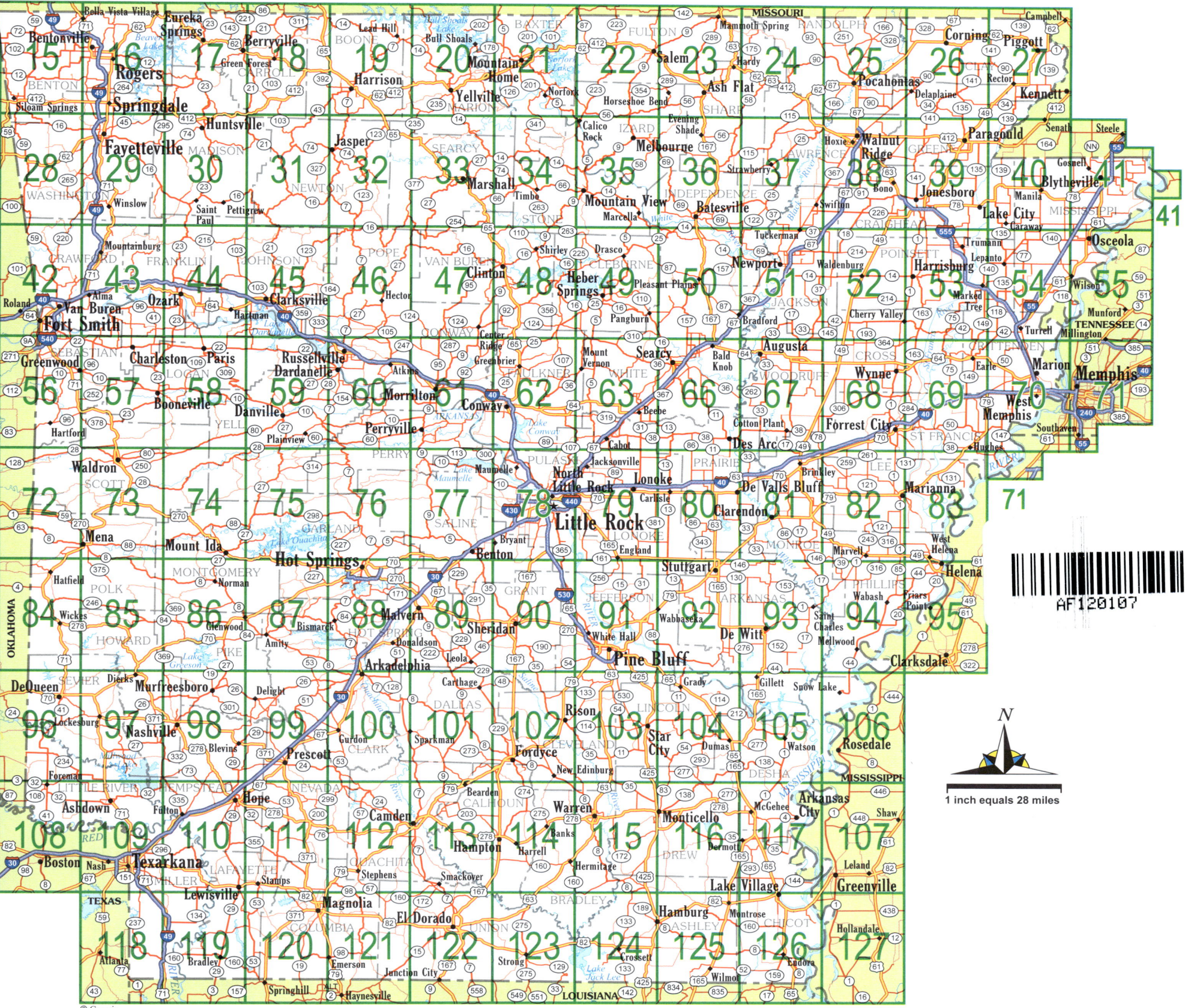

1 inch equals 28 miles

AF120107

© Garmin

No portion of this atlas may be photocopied, electronically stored or reproduced in any manner without written permission from the publisher.

Important Notices

Garmin has made reasonable efforts to provide you with accurate maps and related information, but we cannot exclude the possibility of errors or omissions in sources or of changes in actual conditions. GARMIN MAKES NO WARRANTIES OF ANY KIND, EITHER EXPRESS OR IMPLIED, INCLUDING THE WARRANTIES OF MERCHANTABILITY AND FITNESS FOR A PARTICULAR PURPOSE. GARMIN SHALL NOT BE LIABLE TO ANY PERSON UNDER ANY LEGAL OR EQUITABLE THEORY FOR DAMAGES ARISING OUT OF THE USE OF THIS PUBLICATION, INCLUDING, WITHOUT LIMITA- TION, FOR DIRECT, CONSEQUENTIAL OR INCIDENTAL DAMAGES.

Nothing in this publication implies the right to use private property. There may be private inholdings within the boundaries of public reservations. You should respect all landowner restrictions.

Some listings may be seasonal or may have admission fees. Please be sure to confirm this information when making plans.

Safety Information

To avoid accidents, always pay attention to actual road, traffic and weather conditions and do not attempt to read these maps while you are operating a vehicle. Please consult local authorities for the most current information on road and other travel-related conditions.

Do not use this publication for marine or aeronautical navigation, as it does not depict navigation aids, depths, obstacles, landing approaches and other information necessary to performing these functions safely.

California Prop 65 Warning

⚠ **WARNING:** Cancer and Reproductive Harm - www.p65warnings.ca.gov

SEVENTH EDITION. Copyright © 2025 Garmin Ltd. or its Affiliates. All rights reserved.
2 DeLorme Dr. Suite 200, Yarmouth, Maine 04096
www.garmin.com/DeLormeAtlas
Printed in Canada.

Table of Contents

From diamond mines to riverboat cruises, hot springs to music festivals, antebellum buildings to adventure parks, Arkansas is a treasure trove of historic, entertaining, and educational activities. The name derives from the French interpretation of the Sioux word "acansa," meaning "downstream place." It is the birthplace of President William Jefferson Clinton, and houses the Clinton Presidential Library.

Ozark National Forest encompasses more than a million acres of northwest Arkansas; it was established in 1908 by President Theodore Roosevelt. Most of the St. Francis National Forest, established by President Eisenhower in 1960, is in the state's hilly Crowley's Ridge section. The forests hold many threatened and endangered species, including bats, alligators, and bald eagles; vultures, turkey, bear and deer can also be spotted. There are almost 400 miles of hiking trails.

Ouachita National Forest covers 1.8 million acres in central Arkansas and southeast Oklahoma. The forest hosts wilderness management, timber and wood production, watershed protection, wildlife and fish habitat, minerals leasing and outdoor recreation—camping, fishing, trails, picnicking, shooting ranges and wilderness areas.

Mount Ida and Hot Springs play host to rock hounds from all over the world searching for quartz crystals. The Ouachita Mountain area was considered mystical by Native American tribes—a place of peace even for warring tribes.

Parkin Archaeological State Park is the 17-acre site of a Native American village once surrounded by a moat and log palisade (believed to be the village of Casqui visited by the expedition of Hernando de Soto in 1541). It now features educational programs, a museum, picnic and fishing areas and a visitor center. Toltec Mounds Archaeological State Park in Keo was built by the Plum Bayou society in the seventh-to-tenth centuries. Five of the original eighteen mounds remain, as well as remnants of earthworks, artifacts, interpretive programs and a visitor center.

Float trips down Arkansas' many rivers range from very easy to extreme. Find one to suit your level of expertise and enjoy a scenic paddle.

The Arkansas Post National Memorial in Gillett is the site of a trading post established in 1686 known as the birthplace of Arkansas. Later, it was host to both Revolutionary and Civil War skirmishes. It has a large archaeological site, hiking, picnicking and fishing.

The Trail of Tears National Historic Trail was the route of the forced relocation of Seminole, Chickasaw, Creek, Choctaw and Cherokee tribes to "Indian Territory" in Oklahoma in the mid-nineteenth century.

Old Washington Historic State Park in Washington is a preserved town established in 1824 as a stop along the Southwest Trail from St. Louis to Texas. Features include printing and weapons museums, blacksmith shop and a steam-powered cotton gin.

The Peel Mansion Museum and Historic Gardens in Bentonville is an 1875 Italianate villa with locally produced bricks, carved stonework, a walnut balustrade stairway and Victorian furnishings. Also on the site are gardens with heirloom roses and an antebellum log cabin.

Locate your favorite activities—and discover some new favorites—with the help of the Gazetteer.

RECREATION

Arkansas offers everything from rodeos to riverboat cruises, caves and caverns to auto racing, haunted hotels to natural spas, as well as wineries, microbreweries, golfing and a diamond mine. Activities for the whole family abound.

Hot Springs National Park surrounds the north end of the city; the hot springs have been used for more than two centuries for relaxation and treatment. Prehistoric Native American novaculite quarries are in the park.

The Clinton Presidential Library and Park is on the banks of the Arkansas River in the River Market District of downtown Little Rock. It contains an authentic replica of the Oval Office, a 30-acre city park, and the University of Arkansas Clinton School of Public Service, and is located in the renovated 1899 Choctaw Station.

See the Ozark Mountains from the inside—visit Blanchard Springs Caverns in the Ozark-St. Francis National Forest. Hike through water-carved passages or take a guided tour. Mystic Caverns in Dogpatch feature an 8-story-high crystal dome and a mineral museum. Cosmic Cavern in Maple has two underground lakes as well as gemstone panning.

Motels, campgrounds, beds and breakfasts are for ordinary travelers; spend the night at a converted service station with 1930s art deco styling—the Texaco Bungalow & Bungalette—or the Grand Treehouse Resort, both in Eureka Springs, or at the Beckham Creek Cave in Parthenon.

The Arkansas Air Museum in Fayetteville features functioning aircraft representing the history of flight, housed in a World War II-era hangar at Drake Field. Ride restored railway cars with stunning views of the Boston Mountains at the Arkansas and Missouri Railroad in Van Buren, or visit the Arkansas Railroad Museum in Pine Bluff. Also in Pine Bluff: the country's only museum dedicated to band instruments, the Band Museum, housed in an 1880s downtown building.

There are hundreds of miles of roadways and trails for all levels of bicycling, from the Backwoods Ozark Tour to the Fossil Flats Trail and Huckleberry Mountain Trails. Or, take a cruise on the *Belle of Hot Springs* riverboat on Lake Hamilton, or the *Belle of the Ozarks* on Beaver Lake from Eureka Springs.

The South Arkansas Arboretum in El Dorado displays native and rare flora of the state's West Gulf Coastal Plain region, as well as providing birdwatching, hiking, picnicking and guided tours.

Crater of Diamonds State Park located in Murfreesboro (sits above an eroded volcanic pipe from 95 million years ago) is the only world diamond-producing site open to the public.

For information on state and federal lands, contact the following agencies.

State of Arkansas
www.portal.arkansas.gov
(501) 324-8900

Arkansas Department of Parks, Heritage & Tourism
www.arkansas.com

National Park Service
www.nps.gov/state/AR

USDA Forest Service
www.fs.usda.gov
(800) 832-1355

National Wildlife Refuges, U.S. Fish & Wildlife Service
www.fws.gov/refuges
(800) 344-WILD (9453)

FISHING AND HUNTING

Find what you're looking for in the state's 12,000 miles of streams, 600,000 acres of lakes, and many bayous, creeks, sloughs, or the dozens of hunting areas. Arkansas game includes bear, elk, deer, mink, badger, turkey, waterfowl and frog. Fishing opportunities include catfish, bass, sunfish, crappie and trout.

Familiarize yourself with the local restrictions, regulations and licensing requirements and download maps by contacting:

Arkansas Game and Fish Commission
www.agfc.com
(800) 364-4263

TRAVEL

Find information about highway, bicycle, pedestrian and public transportation travel from the Arkansas State Highway and Transportation Department. Get the latest on road conditions, gas prices, road construction, maps and travel information centers by contacting:

Arkansas State Highway and Transportation Department
www.ardot.gov
(501) 569-2000

CAMPGROUNDS

The Ozark-St. Francis National Forests maintain 23 developed campgrounds, five wilderness areas, and six scenic byways. The Ouachita National Forest hosts 263 campsites in 16 campgrounds, as well as fishing, rock-hunting, scenic byways, shooting ranges, trails and wilderness areas. Find camping, cabins and lodges—or rent a tepee or furnished camp—at one of the state's 30 campgrounds or one of the many private campgrounds around the state.

Arkansas Department of Parks & Tourism
www.arkansas.com/outdoors/camping

State Parks of Arkansas
www.arkansasstateparks.com
(888) 287-2757

STATE FACTS

Admitted to the Union:
June 15, 1836; 25th state
Capital: Little Rock
Size: 52,068 square miles
Population: 3,088,354 (2024 estimate)
Nickname: The Natural State
Motto: Regnat populus ("The People Rule")
Bird: Mockingbird
Flower: Apple Blossom
Tree: Pine
Fruit and Vegetable: South Arkansas Vine Ripe Pink Tomato
Mammal: White-tailed Deer
Butterfly: Diana Fritillary
Insect: Honeybee
Soil: Stuttgart
Rock: Bauxite
Mineral: Quartz Crystal
Gem: Diamond
Songs: "Arkansas" and "Oh, Arkansas"
Name for Residents: Arkansans
Major Industries: Food processing, fabricated metal, machinery, paper and wood products, mining, poultry, cattle, hogs, agriculture (soybeans, cotton, rice, sorghum)

Major Cities (with population):
Little Rock	203,842
Fayetteville	101,680
Fort Smith	89,770
Springdale	88,324

Major Mountains:
Magazine Mountain	2,753 feet
Signal Hill	2,749 feet
Black Fork Mountain	2,661 feet
Blue Mountain	2,612 feet

Lowest Point:
Ouachita River	55 feet

Major Lakes:
Bull Shoals Lake	45,150 acres
Lake Ouachita	40,100 acres
Greers Ferry Lake	30,500 acres
Beaver Lake	28,370 acres

Major Rivers:
Mississippi River	2,320 miles
Arkansas River	1,460 miles
Red River	1,018 miles
White River	690 miles
Ouachita River	605 miles

Family Outings

ARKANSAS AIR MUSEUM – Greenland – 29 B4 Features functional airplanes representing history of flight. Early airliners and famous planes of the 1920s and 1930s such as Stinson Jr SM8, Douglas A-4 Skyhawk, TravelAir Mystery Ship and Bell UHI-H. Visitor center.

ARKANSAS ALLIGATOR FARM & PETTING ZOO – Hot Springs – 88 A2 Four ponds are stocked with 200 alligators measuring up to six feet long. Scheduled feeding times. Petting zoo features, emu, sheep and goats.

ARKANSAS & MISSOURI RAILROAD – Van Buren – 42 C3 Restored early-1900s railway cars traverse Ozark National Forest between Van Buren and Springdale. Trips cross three trestles and wind through 1882 Winslow Tunnel. Scenic views of Boston Mountains.

ARKANSAS ARTS CENTER – Little Rock – 78 B2 Founded in 1960, center displays works by modern and contemporary masters, including Pablo Picasso, Paul Cézanne, Georges Braque, Willem de Kooning, Georgia O'Keeffe and Alison Saar. Supports regional artists through changing exhibits.

ARKANSAS MUSEUM OF NATURAL RESOURCES – Smackover – 113 D5 Museum chronicles southern Arkansas oil boom of 1920s and its impact on area history. Oil well, pumping rig and three derricks in Oil Field Park demonstrate drilling methods and production techniques. Bromine extraction also documented. Interpretive events.

ARKANSAS POST MUSEUM – Arkansas Post – 105 B4 Life on and history of Arkansas' Grand Prairie and Mississippi Delta explored through complex of five exhibit buildings with furnishings, clothing, artifacts and documents dating from Colonial period to modern times.

ARKANSAS POST NATIONAL MEMORIAL – Arkansas Post – 105 B4 Trading post near the confluence of Arkansas and Mississippi rivers, known as the "birthplace of Arkansas," was established in 1686 by French lieutenant Henri Tonti. Large archaeological site features remains of early forts and territorial capital. Visitor center. Musket and cannon demonstrations. Guided tours.

ARKANSAS RAILROAD MUSEUM – Pine Bluff – 91 D5 Vintage buildings of Cotton Belt Railway feature the 368-ton Engine 819. Fourteen additional historic railroad cars include 1941 Lark, built by Pullman Standard, and 1950 Suscapejo, which sports stainless steel body and observation dome. Guided tours.

ARKANSAS SCENIC 7 BYWAY – Harrison to Arkadelphia – 19 D4 North-south route through Ouachita National Forest, Arkansas River valley and Ozark National Forest. 290-mile route features streams, spring wildflowers and colorful fall foliage. Highlights include panoramic views from Rotary Ann Overlook.

ARKANSAS STATE CAPITOL – Little Rock – 78 B2 Replica of US Capitol in Washington, DC, houses state government. Construction of neoclassical-style marble and limestone structure began in 1899 and was completed in 1915. Changing museum exhibits. Guided tours.

ARKANSAS STATE UNIVERSITY MUSEUM – Jonesboro – 39 C4 State's prehistory to present time chronicled in over 100 exhibits ranging from fossils and farming artifacts to quilts and toys. Period room illustrates turn-of-the-20th-century village life with dentist office and pharmacy. Exhibits highlight Native American history and animal species native to state. Special collections of glass and military wares round out diverse holdings. Guided tours.

BLUE SPRING HERITAGE CENTER – Eureka Springs – 17 A4 33 acres of informal gardens feature year-round botanical displays. Labeled flora includes bulbs in spring; azaleas, redbud and dogwood trees in summer; and pansies and ornamental cabbage in late fall. Pavilion overlooks Blue Spring, one of largest natural springs in Ozark Mountains.

BOONE COUNTY HERITAGE MUSEUM – Harrison – 19 D4 Former high school features three floors of exhibits on diverse topics of county history. Railroad memorabilia and Civil War and Native American artifacts.

CLINTON HOUSE MUSEUM – Fayetteville – 29 A4 Preserved home of 42nd US President Bill Clinton. Living room hosted marriage of Clinton to Hillary Rodham. Restored to 1975 condition. Clinton memorabilia.

DELTA CULTURAL CENTER – Helena – 95 A5 Restored 1912 Missouri-Pacific train depot and nearby visitor center feature exhibits on heritage and culture of Arkansas Delta. Displays focus on the Civil War, cultures of Native Americans and African-Americans, the Mississippi River and development of the region's music. Houses broadcast facilities for *King Biscuit Time*, the longest-running blues radio show in US history.

EUREKA SPRINGS HISTORICAL MUSEUM – Eureka Springs – 17 B5 1889 stone house chronicles history of town in photographs, documents, clothing, furnishings and artifacts such as switchboard from 1886 Crescent Hotel. Special exhibits highlight prominent local African Americans and women.

FORT SMITH NATIONAL HISTORIC SITE – Ft Smith – 42 D2 75-acre site of two frontier military forts established for peacekeeping during the years of westward expansion and government-enforced relocation of Native Americans from their homes to reservations. Features remains of fort in use from 1817-1824, barracks and jail known as "Hell on the Border." Courthouse presided over by "Hanging" Judge Isaac C. Parker for over 21 years. Reproduction of 1886 gallows. Museum. Visitor center. Guided tours.

GREAT RIVER ROAD – Blytheville to West Memphis – 41 C5 Road follows Mississippi River from Minnesota to the Gulf of Mexico. Northeast Arkansas portion begins in Blytheville, which offers a panoramic river view from Barfield Landing. 362 miles in state.

HAMPSON ARCHAEOLOGICAL MUSEUM STATE PARK – Wilson – 55 B4 Museum houses archaeological remains of Nodena site where farming-based civilization existed AD 1400–1650. 15 acre palisaded village on Mississippi River had three ceremonial mounds and plaza for religious ceremonies. Vessels, tools and weapons uncovered at site on display.

HEADQUARTERS HOUSE – Fayetteville – 29 A4 Greek Revival-style house built in 1853 by legislator and self-proclaimed Unionist Jonas Tebbetts. Occupied by both Union and Confederate forces during Civil War. Battle of Fayetteville occurred across the street, and holes from ammunition are still embedded in exterior doors. Restored rooms include dining room, parlor, library, bedrooms and entrance hall. Original furnishings include Tebbets' silver tea service. Smokehouse. Guided tours.

HISTORIC ARKANSAS MUSEUM – Little Rock – 78 B2 Exhibits Arkansas art and artifacts. Surrounding neighborhood dates to the early 19th-century. 1826 Hinderliter Grog Shop is the oldest building in city. Living history exhibits include 18th-century crafts, lifestyles and heirloom quilts. Guided tours.

HOT SPRINGS NATIONAL PARK TOUR – Hot Springs – 88 A2 Drive traverses the national park that surrounds the 19th-century resort city renowned for natural mineral springs and "curative" waters. 8-mile loop begins at Bathhouse Row, a line of elegant, restored establishments built to cater to health seekers. Hot Springs Mountain Drive accesses 216-foot-high observation tower offering views of Zig Zag Mountains.

JACKSONPORT STATE PARK – Jacksonport – 51 A5 Park interprets Jacksonport's role as a prominent 19th-century river port, county seat and strategically located Civil War headquarters. Restored 1872 brick courthouse features exhibits pertaining to area history.

KA-DO-HA INDIAN VILLAGE – Murfreesboro – 98 A2 Preserved archaeological site features 1,000-year-old remains of mud and straw houses built by ancient Native American society. Museum features jewelry, weapons and pottery, as well as exhibits on unique mound construction, ceremonies and customs. Designated area for arrowhead hunting. Guided tours.

LITTLE ROCK CENTRAL HIGH SCHOOL NATIONAL HISTORIC SITE – Little Rock – 78 B2 Site of landmark 1957 desegregation incident where nine African American students were escorted to class at all-white school by federal troops. Visitor center with historical exhibits chronicle event and history of desegregation.

LITTLE ROCK ZOO – Little Rock – 78 B2 More than 700 native and exotic animals roam 40 acres, including African giraffes, rhinos and zebras, South American jaguars and flamingos, and Serval cats.

LOGAN COUNTY MUSEUM – Paris – 58 A2 1903 Old County Jail building was the site of the last legal hanging in Arkansas, July 15, 1914. Museum exhibits in cells now display military artifacts from US wars since WWI. Exhibits also include coal mining, railroad and farming equipment, and Native American artifacts.

LOUISIANA PURCHASE STATE PARK – Blackton – 82 C1 Site where 1815 US land surveys of Louisiana Purchase began. Park encompasses 37.5-acre swamp representative of endangered eastern Arkansas environment, home to prothonotary warbler and rare swamp cottonwood tree. Guided nature trail along 950-foot-long barrier-free boardwalk.

LOWER WHITE RIVER MUSEUM STATE PARK – Des Arc – 66 D3 Museum dedicated to preserving and interpreting the history of Arkansas' navigable rivers from 1831–1931. Remarkable breadth of coverage emphasizes impact of river on all aspects of life along state's waterways. Reveals strategic importance for Union supply support during Civil War and economic importance of mussels for meat and button making. Guided tours.

MCCOLLUM-CHIDESTER HOUSE MUSEUM – Camden – 113 B4 1847 home of McCollum and Chidester families, prominent local entrepreneurs. Served as headquarters for Confederate General Sterling Price and Union General Frederick Steele. Contains original furnishings brought by steamboat from New Orleans in 1863. Replica carriage house contains reconstructed stagecoach and surrey. 1850 Greek Revival-style Leake-Ingham Building, Camden's first library. Scenes from TV miniseries *North and South* shot here.

MID-AMERICA SCIENCE MUSEUM – Hot Springs – 88 A1 Interactive museum allows visitors to push, pull, tug, twist and spin exhibits designed to make science fun. Flight parodied with flying machines such as that created for classic movie *Chitty Chitty Bang Bang*. The natural world comes alive with tornado "demonstrations" and freshwater aquarium. Nature trail.

MOUNT MAGAZINE SCENIC BYWAY – Web City to Havana – 58 A2 Route through Ozark National Forest ascends 2,753-foot-high Mt Magazine, highest point in the state, offering sweeping views of surrounding Arkansas River valley, Ozark Mountains to the north and Ouachita Mountains to the south. Travels through dense hickory and oak forest before winding into Petit Jean River valley. 45 miles.

MURALS OF PINE BLUFF – Pine Bluff – 91 D5 Walking or driving tour within "Arkansas' City of Murals" includes nine murals depicting town's history and notable citizens. Highlights include *Main Street, 1888*, by Robert Dafford; Michael Wojczuk's *Movie Mural*, which honors Freeman Owens, developer of sound-on-film technology; and Max "Bronco Billy" Anderson, first great cowboy star.

MUSEUM OF AUTOMOBILES – Oppelo – 60 C3 Ever-changing display encourages repeat visits to see fifty antique and classic automobiles dating from 1904. Features founder and late Arkansas governor Winthrop Rockefeller's 1951 and 1967 Cadillac Fleetwood 75s, rare Model A and 1923 Climber, built in Little Rock.

MUSEUM OF DISCOVERY – Little Rock – 78 B3 Emphasizes geology and ornithology as well as Native American and pioneer history of Arkansas. Features Arkansaurus, Imagination Station, live animal program and other hands-on exhibits.

MUSEUM OF THE ARKANSAS GRAND PRAIRIE – Stuttgart – 92 A3 Museum dedicated to preserving character of pioneer farming on Grand Prairie from 1880–1921. Restored Lutheran church, rustic prairie homes and waterfowl hunting exhibits illustrate period. Multimedia learning experience includes "cockpit" views of aerial crop dusters.

OLD DAVIDSONVILLE STATE PARK – Black Rock – 25 D4 Former site of Davidsonville, the small town established in 1815 along the Southwest Trail linking St Louis to Texas. Site of the state's first courthouse, post office and land office. Visitor center exhibits old tools, dishes and personal items uncovered at the archaeological site.

OLD STATE HOUSE MUSEUM – Little Rock – 78 B2 Greek Revival-style structure, completed in 1842, served as the state capitol until 1911. The oldest standing state capitol building west of the Mississippi River houses exhibits on state history. Collections include Arkansas political memorabilia, gowns of Arkansas first ladies, Civil War battle flags and quilts. Six period rooms, two restored legislative chambers.

OLD WASHINGTON HISTORIC STATE PARK – Washington – 98 D2 Preserved section of 1824 town includes twelve antebellum homes, relocated 1832 Williams Tavern and 1836 Hempstead County Courthouse, site of the Confederate State Capitol of Arkansas from 1863-1865. Features printing museum, weapons museum, blacksmith shop and 1883 Goodlett Cotton Gin. Guided tours.

OZARK FOLK CENTER – Mountain View – 35 C4 Folk Center dedicated to preserving heritage and way of life of Ozark people. Mountain village cabins nestled amongst misty hills create living history environment. Featured activities include music from fiddle, banjo, mandolin and dulcimer as well as weaving, blacksmithing, pottery and cooking.

OZARK HIGHLANDS SCENIC BYWAY – Boxley to Hillcrest – 45 B5 Route travels south through Ozark National Forest, taking in the scenic Boston Mountains and the headwaters of Mulberry River and Big and Little Piney creeks. Sandstone and limestone rock outcroppings and hardwood forests home to buzzards that roost along cliflines. 35 miles.

PARKIN ARCHAEOLOGICAL STATE PARK – Parkin – 69 A5 17 acre site thought to be village of Casqui, encountered by Spanish explorer Hernando de Soto in 1541. Village, occupied AD 1000–1550, was once surrounded by moat and log palisade. 1910 one-room schoolhouse and museum exhibits of uncovered artifacts. Guided tours.

PEA RIDGE NATIONAL MILITARY PARK – Pea Ridge – 16 A2 Site of March 7-8, 1862 battle that saved Missouri for the Union. Landmarks include Leetown Battlefield, where Confederate generals Ben McCulloch and James McIntosh were killed, and reconstructed Elkhorn Tavern, around which the battle was fought. Visitor center. Guided tours.

PEEL MANSION MUSEUM & HERITAGE GARDENS – Bentonville – 16 B1 1875 Italianate-style villa built by Civil War Colonel Samuel West Peel. Features locally produced bricks, carved stonework and turned woodwork such as walnut balustrade stairway. Victorian furnishings include a variety of replica lamps and chandeliers. Gardens feature heirloom roses and other native plants. Guided tours.

PIG TRAIL SCENIC BYWAY – Paradise to Brashears – 44 B1 Steeply graded route winds through 19 miles of dense Ozark National Forest, taking in dramatic views of sandstone cliffs and brilliant fall foliage. Crosses Mulberry River and 165-mile-long Ozark Highlands National Recreation Trail.

PLANTATION AGRICULTURE MUSEUM – Scott – 79 C4 Renovated 1912 general store houses museum documenting cotton agriculture and its impact on state's economy from statehood through WWII. Exhibits examine harvesting, implements (including rare cotton gin), labor and plantation life until early 1940s introduction of tractors signified beginning of mechanized cotton production.

POWHATAN HISTORIC STATE PARK – Powhatan – 37 A6 Restored 2 story courthouse built in 1888 served as county courthouse until 1963. Courtroom features original jury chairs, dumbwaiter to first-floor clerk's office, and pressed tin ceiling. Restored jailhouse of native limestone. Guided tours.

CRYSTAL MINES

CRATER OF DIAMONDS STATE PARK – Murfreesboro – 98 A2 World's only diamond producing site open to the public. Explore through the 37 acre diamond search area and keep what you find.

FIDDLER'S RIDGE CRYSTAL MINE – Mt Ida – 75 D4 Mine features veins of milky-white quartz crystal deposited during creation of Ouachita Mountains approximately 250 million years ago. Visitors may dig for quartz using own hand tools.

RON COLEMAN CRYSTAL MINE – Mountain Valley – 76 C1 Mine purchased by Ron Coleman in late 1980's. Ron's grandfather worked in the mine in 1946. Approximately 40 acres available for public mining at Old Coleman mine. Crystal washing stations.

WEGNER CRYSTAL MINES – Mt Ida – 86 A3 Three mines available for digging quartz crystals. Phantom Mine features phantom crystals, and Crystal Forest Mine offers clear gem-quality crystals. Salted Mine is suitable for children and seniors. Hand digging tools available with deposit.

Continued on page 4

PRAIRIE GROVE BATTLEFIELD STATE PARK – Prairie Grove – 28 B3 Re-created village at site of December 7, 1862 Union victory includes Borden House, burned after the battle and rebuilt in 1972 on the original site, and 1834 John Latta log house with springhouse and smokehouse. Schoolhouse, church, store and blacksmith shop moved to site to re-create 1800s village. Demonstrations. Visitor center. Guided tours.

ROGERS HISTORICAL MUSEUM – Rogers – 16 C2 Local history emphasized in exhibits spread over 3 buildings. The main attractions being the 1895 Hawkins House museum, furnished with period antiques and the Key building containing exhibits and children's activities.

ROSALIE TOUR HOME – Eureka Springs – 17 B5 Built in 1889 Eastlake-style home by entrepreneur J.W. Hill. Exterior features include gingerbread woodwork imported from New York and handmade bricks formed and fired on premises. Furnishings include period telephone switchboard similar to that used by Hill to conduct business. Guided tours.

SAUNDERS MUSEUM – Berryville – 17 B6 Museum dedicated to Berryville native and expert marksman C. Burton Saunders. Two of Saunders' passions, travel and firearms, illustrated by unique items such as guns used by outlaws Jesse and Frank James and Billy the Kid, markswoman Annie Oakley and Mexican revolutionary Francisco "Pancho" Villa. Other items collected on his travels include Sioux leader

Sitting Bull's war bonnet, knife belonging to Western showman William "Buffalo Bill" Cody and Arab sheik's tent.

SOUTH ARKANSAS ARBORETUM – El Dorado – 122 B2 13 acre site exhibits native and rare flora of Arkansas' West Gulf Coastal Plain region. Also displays azaleas and camellias. Birdwatching. Nature paths and hiking trails.

SOUTHEAST ARKANSAS ARTS AND SCIENCE CENTER – Pine Bluff – 91 D5 Center founded in 1968 to encourage practice and enjoyment of arts and science among citizens of southeast Arkansas. Activities include science exhibits, plays, concerts and films. Permanent collection dedicated to painting and sculpture by local artists.

ST FRANCIS SCENIC BYWAY – Marianna to Helena – 83 B4 Paved and gravel road runs 21 miles through St Francis National Forest along 100-200-foot-high Crowley's Ridge, a landform stretching from the northeast corner of the state to the Mississippi River. Route through hardwood forest parallels St Francis River and accesses Bear Creek and Storm Creek lakes.

SYLAMORE SCENIC BYWAY – Calico Rock to Blanchard Springs – 35 A4 Farmland turns to woodlands as 27-mile route enters Ozark National Forest. Road climbs limestone bluff overlooking gentle hills and White River before turning west on SR 14. Ascent to ridgetop offers panoramic views of Ozark Mountains. Terminates at Blanchard Springs Caverns, featuring underground crystalline formations.

TALIMENA SCENIC DRIVE – Mena to Oklahoma state line – 73 D4 54-mile route traverses ridge tops of the Ouachita Mountains. From Mena, road ascends 2,681-foot-high Rich Mountain, the highest point on the byway. Several overlooks provide commanding views of Ouachita River valley and Kiamichi and Winding Stair mountains in Oklahoma.

THE CLAYTON HOUSE – Ft Smith – 42 D2 1852 Victorian home of district attorney William Henry Harrison Clayton. 1882 addition in Italianate style. Restored and furnished in period decor, with hand-carved black walnut staircase, restored 1852 Italian ceiling fresco and original Clayton belongings.

TINY TOWN – Hot Springs – 88 A2 Miniature indoor mechanical display features representative scenes from across US, including farmland, Wild West, Native American reservation, Niagara Falls, Pennsylvania Dutch country and Mt Rushmore. Planned and built by single family over 60-year period.

TOLTEC MOUNDS STATE PARK – Keo – 79 C4 One of the largest mound-builder sites in lower Mississippi River valley built by Plum Bayou society circa AD 600–1050. Five of original eighteen mounds, which served as religious and social centers, still remain. Visitor center with artifacts. Guided tours.

TURPENTINE CREEK WILDLIFE REFUGE – Eureka Springs – 17 C5 460-acre ranch home to neglected or unwanted large animals, including lions, tigers, cougars and bears.

WAL-MART MUSEUM – Bentonville – 16 B1 Sam Walton's original 1945 variety store that began the enterprise known as Wal-Mart. Timelines, videos and electronic narrated map trace development and enormous success of America's giant discount retail chain. Walton's office, pickup truck, awards and memorabilia displayed.

WILLIAM J. CLINTON PRESIDENTIAL CENTER – Little Rock – 78 B3 Exhibits on life and legacy of 42nd US President Bill Clinton. Replica Oval Office and Cabinet room. Interactive Clinton Administration timeline. Exhibits on campaign and Clinton's post-presidential career. Changing exhibits. Photo gallery. Library.

WOLF HOUSE – Norfork – 21 D5 Hand-hewn house built 1809–1825 by Major Jacob Wolf, settler, blacksmith and member of pre-statehood Territorial Council. Thought to be the state's oldest surviving log structure. Over 400 antique tools, furniture pieces and other artifacts dating to 1700s. Guided tours.

Campgrounds

NUMBER, NAME, LOCATION	PAGE & GRID	RV SITES	TENTING
4000 Almost Home RV Park, Walnut Ridge	38 A2	27	
4004 Anglers White River Resort, Mountain View	35 B4	100	●
4009 Arrowhead Cabin &Canoe, Caddo Gap	86 B3	11	●
4015 Barnes RV Park, Bald Knob	66 A2	75	
4016 Beaver Lake Hideaway Campground, Rogers	16 C3	100	●
4018 Big Pine RV Park, Waldron	73 A5	16	
4022 Blue Heron Campground	20 C3	37	●
4024 Blue Sky RV Park, Mountain View	35 C4	52	●
4025 Brinkley Motel & RV Park, Brinkley	81 A6	34	
4027 Buffalo Camping & Canoeing, Gilbert	33 B5	15	●
4029 Buffalo River Campground, Harrison	19 D4	22	
4033 Byrd's Adventure Center, Beach Grove	44 A2	47	●
4036 Caddo Valley RV Park, Caddo Valley	88 D2	55	●
4042 Cloud Nine RV Park, Hot Springs	76 D3	45	●
4046 Copper John's Resort, Bull Shoals	20 B3	50	●
4048 Country Living Park, El Dorado	122 B2	36	
4051 Dad's Dream RV Park, Lamar	45 D5	35	
4054 Dogwood Springs Campground Resort, Jasper	32 B1	18	●
4060 Eureka Springs KOA, Eureka Springs	17 B4	60	●
4063 Ft Smith–Alma RV Park, Alma	43 C4	58	●
4066 Golden Pond RV Park, Shirley	48 B2	50	
4069 Green Tree Lodge & RV Park, Eureka Springs	17 B5	24	●
4072 Greentree RV Park, Siloam Springs	15 D4	37	●
4074 Harris Brake Lakeside Resort, Perryville	61 D4	38	●
4075 Harrison Village Campground & RV Park, Harrison	19 D5	74	●
4078 Heart O' the Ozarks Campground, Bull Shoals	20 B2	26	●

NUMBER, NAME, LOCATION	PAGE & GRID	RV SITES	TENTING
4079 Herber Springs RV Park, Herber Springs	49 C5	50	
4081 Heritage Inn & RV Park, Brinkley	81 A6	30	●
4085 Hide-A-Way on The White River RV & Tent Campground, Old Joe	21 D6	20	●
4090 Hot Springs National Park KOA, Hot Springs	88 A2	63	●
4091 Hot Springs RV Park, Hot Springs	88 A2	58	
4093 Into the Woods RV Park & Campground, Yellville	20 C2	23	
4096 JB's RV Park/Campground, Benton	89 A5	44	●
4099 Kettle Campground & Cabins, Eureka Springs	17 B5	41	●
4100 Lake Hamilton RV Park, Hot Springs	88 A1	81	
4102 Lake Shore RV Park, Luna	117 D6	70	
4111 Lewisburg Bay RV Park, Morrilton	61 B4	19	
4114 Little Rock North KOA, North Little Rock	78 B2	80	●
4115 Lucky Camper RV Park, Jonesboro	39 D4	73	
4117 Many Islands Camp, Mammoth Spring	23 B6	150	●
4120 Memphis KOA, James Mill	70 A2	75	●
4123 Mill Pond Village RV Park, Hot Springs	88 B1	21	
4126 Miner's Camping & Rock Shop, Murfreesboro	98 B2	33	●
4130 Mockingbird Mountain Resort, Edgemont	48 B3	50	
4132 Monte Ne Beaver Lake Camp Resort, Monte Ne	16 C2	70	
4135 Morrilton RV Park, Morrilton	61 B4	53	●
4141 Mountain View RV Park, Mountain View	35 C4	39	
4144 Oaks Corner Campground, Concord	42 C3	12	
4147 Outdoor Living Center RV Park, Russellville	60 A1	50	
4150 Overland RV Park, Van Buren	42 C3	50	
4151 Ozark Canopy RV Park - Springdale, Springdale	16 D1	48	
4153 Ozark RV Park, Mountain View	35 C4	73	●

NUMBER, NAME, LOCATION	PAGE & GRID	RV SITES	TENTING
4156 Ozark View RV Park & Campground, Burlington	18 B3	55	
4162 Pecan Grove RV Park, Lake Village	126 A2	104	●
4177 Riverside Resort, Mammoth Spring	23 B6	50	
4180 Rogers/Pea Ridge Garden RV & Campground, Pea Ridge	16 A2	60	●
4181 Rustic Pines RV Park, Batesville	50 A2	33	●
4183 Shadow Mountain RV Park & Campground, Mena	84 A3	64	●
4186 Shady Oaks Campground & RV Park, Elmwood	19 D4	34	●
4189 Shearin's RV Park, Lemsford	41 C5	52	
4192 Shell Lake Campground, Shell Lake	69 B6	57	●
4195 Sherwood Forest RV Park & Campground, Yellville	20 D2	23	●
4198 Silver Leaf Camp Park, Winslow	29 D5	15	
4201 Southfork Resort, Saddle	23 B5	22	●
4204 Southland Village, Sheridan	90 C1	24	
4210 Spring River Oaks, Mammoth Springs	23 B6	110	●
4213 Sunrise RV Park, Texarkana	109 C6	119	
4222 Tom Sawyer's RV Park, West Memphis	70 C3	138	●
4223 Trails End RV Park, Maumelle	78 A2	50	
4225 Treasure Isle RV Park, Hot Springs	88 A1	65	
4228 Wagon Circle RV Park, West Pangburn	49 C6	65	●
4231 Wanderlust RV Park, Eureka Springs	17 B5	88	
4237 White Buffalo Resort, Buffalo City	21 D4	35	●
4240 White River Campground & Cabins, Cotter	20 C3	48	
4243 Whitewater RV Park, Mountain View	35 C4	50	
4246 Wiederkehr Village RV Park, Wiederkehr Village	44 C2	20	
4255 Winn Creek RV Park, West Fork	29 C4	25	●
4258 Young's Lakeshore RV Park, Hot Springs	88 A1	43	

Type of Access Legend

- P = pier
- W = walk-in access
- B = barrier-free access
- D = developed boat launch site (trailerable)
- U = undeveloped boat launch site (hand-carry)

Species columns (across): CHANNEL CATFISH · BLUE CATFISH · FLATHEAD CATFISH · TIGER MUSKELLUNGE · BASS (LARGEMOUTH, SMALLMOUTH, SPOTTED, STRIPED, HYBRID STRIPED, WHITE, ROCK) · SAUGER · SUNFISH (BLUEGILL, REDEAR, WARMOUTH) · CRAPPIE · TROUT (BROOK, BROWN, CUTTHROAT, LAKE, RAINBOW) · WALLEYE

Number, Name	Page & Grid	Acreage/Mileage	Type of Access
1000 Arkansas River	61 C6	328	D
1003 Bear Creek Lake	83 C4	625	PB
1006 Beaver Fork Lake	62 B1	640	D
1009 Beaver Lake	16 B3	28,220	D
1012 Beaver Lake Tailwaters	17 B4	1.5	—
1015 Belcoe Lake	105 B5	240	—
1018 Belknap Lake	93 B6	10	—
1021 Bennett Lake	62 A2	33	—
1024 Big Belle Lake	67 B4	6	U
1027 Big Hurricane Lake	67 A4	33	U
1030 Big Island Chute	94 C1	5	—
1033 Big Lake	40 C3	6,500	D
1039 Big Piney Creek	45 A6	66	U
1042 Black River	37 D5	160	D
1045 Blue Mountain Lake	58 C2	2,910	D
1046 Bois d'Arc Lake	110 B2	650	D
1048 Bragg Lake	112 A2	160	D
1051 Brewer Lake	61 A6	1,165	D
1054 Brooks Bayou	93 D6	7	—
1057 Buffalo River	32 B3	137	U
1060 Bull Shoals Lake	20 B2	45,440	D
1063 Burnt Cane Lake	69 D4	240	D
1066 Cache River	67 B5	142	D
1069 Caddo River	86 B3	70	U
1072 Cadron Creek	61 B6	69	U
1075 Calion Lake	122 A3	500	D
1078 Cane Creek Lake	104 B1	1,700	DPB
1081 Champagnolle Creek	113 D6	38	U
1082 Cargile Lake	61 A4	143	W
1084 Cossatot River	97 A4	82	U
1087 Cove Creek Lake	76 A2	42	—
1090 Cove Lake	58 B3	160	D
1093 Cox Creek Lake	89 D5	350	D
1096 Cox Cypress Lake	92 C2	250	D
1099 Craighead Forest Lake	39 D4	677	—
1102 Crooked Creek	20 C1	83	—
1105 Crystal Lake	15 B5	60	D
1108 Current River	25 B6	39	D
1111 Dacus Lake	70 B3	1,000	—
1114 De Gray Lake	88 C1	13,400	D
1117 De Queen Lake	96 A2	1,680	D
1120 Dierks Lake	85 D5	1,360	D
1123 Driver Creek Lake	47 C5	30	—
1126 Dry Fork Lake	76 A1	90	—
1129 Eleven Point River	25 C4	39	D
1132 Essex Bayou	93 D6	14	—
1135 First Old River Lake	110 C2	240	D
1138 Flint Creek Lake	15 C4	530	—
1141 Fourche LaFave River	74 A3	143	D
1144 Gillham Lake	85 D4	1,370	D
1147 Grand Lake	126 C3	900	D
1150 Greers Ferry Lake	49 C4	31,500	D
1153 Gurdon Pond No 1	100 C1	60	D
1156 Harris Brake Lake	61 D4	1,300	DP
1159 Hickson Lake	81 A5	30	D
1162 Holowell Reservoir	92 C2	600	D
1165 Honey Lake	67 B4	20	U
1168 Horsehead Lake	44 B3	100	D
1171 Horseshoe Lake	37 B6	20	U
1174 Illinois Bayou	46 C3	19	U
1177 Illinois River	15 D5	46	U
1180 Island Forty Chute	70 A3	350	—
1183 Kate Adams Lake	117 B6	160	D
1186 Kingfisher Lake	60 C1	100	D
1189 Kings River	17 D6	89	W
1192 L' Anguille River	82 B3	104	D
1195 LaGrue Bayou	93 D6	7	—
1198 Lake Ashbaugh	25 C6	500	D
1201 Lake Atalanta	16 B2	60	—
1204 Lake Atkins	60 B3	752	P
1207 Lake Austell	69 B4	64	D
1210 Lake Bailey	60 C3	64	PBW
1213 Lake Bald Knob	50 D2	200	D
1216 Lake Barnett	63 B5	245	D
1219 Lake Bentonville	16 B1	10	—
1222 Lake Bob Kidd	28 B3	200	D
1231 Lake Catherine	88 A3	1,940	DP
1234 Lake Charles	37 A6	650	DP
1237 Lake Chicot	126 A2	5,300	DP
1240 Lake Columbia	120 A2	3,000	DPB
1243 Lake Conway	62 D1	6,700	DP
1246 Lake Dardanelle	59 A4	34,300	W
1249 Lake Des Arc	66 D3	350	D
1252 Lake Dunn	69 B4	68	D

Number, Name	Page & Grid	Acreage/Mileage	Type of Access
1255 Lake Elmdale	16 D1	200	U
1258 Lake Enterprise	125 C5	350	D
1261 Lake Erling	120 C1	7,000	—
1264 Lake Frierson	39 B4	335	P
1267 Lake Grampus	125 A6	350	U
1270 Lake Greenlee	81 A6	320	D
1273 Lake Greeson	86 D2	2,500	D
1276 Lake Hamilton	88 B2	7,460	D
1279 Lake Hindsville	16 D3	20	U
1282 Lake Hinkle	72 A3	960	U
1285 Lake Hogue	52 B2	280	P
1288 Lake Jack Lee	124 C1	15,000	D
1291 Lake Maumelle	77 A6	8,900	—
1294 Lake Ouachita	75 D5	40,000	D
1297 Lake Paradise	117 C6	7,200	—
1300 Lake Pine Bluff	91 C5	500	P
1303 Lake Poinsett	53 C4	600	DP
1306 Lake Roosevelt	60 C3	11	—
1309 Lake Sequoyah	29 A5	500	D
1312 Lake Sylvia	77 A4	82	P
1315 Lake Wallace	116 C3	350	D
1318 Lake Wedington	28 A2	102	—
1321 Lake Wilhelmina	72 D3	300	U
1324 Lake Winona	76 B3	715	—
1327 Lee Creek	42 A3	35	U
1330 Little Bear Lake	76 A1	42	—
1333 Little Missouri River	98 A2	81	—
1336 Little Missouri River	99 C6	49	—
1339 Little Red River	50 C1	81	—
1342 Little River	97 D4	76	D
1345 Lower Brock Creek Lake	47 C4	30	—
1348 Luther Lake	60 C1	20	W
1351 Mallard Lake	40 C3	300	P
1354 Mellwood Old River Lake	94 D2	1,000	—
1357 Mercer Bayou	118 B3	800	D
1360 Midway Lake	83 A6	1,000	—
1363 Millwood Lake	97 D6	29,200	D
1366 Mississippi River	95 A5	477	D
1369 Moon Lake	94 B1	173	—
1372 Mountain Fork of Little River	84 A2	21	—
1375 Mulberry River	44 A1	69	U
1378 Nimrod Lake	60 D1	3,550	D
1381 Norfork Lake	21 B6	22,000	D
1384 North Fork Lake	74 D1	70	—
1387 North Fork of White River	21 D6	5	DPB
1390 Old River Channel	60 B2	5	—
1393 Old Town Lake	94 B3	900	DPB
1396 Ouachita River	88 B3	28	—
1399 Ouachita River	113 C5	181	—
1402 Overcup Lake	61 B5	1,025	DPB
1405 Ozark Lake	43 C5	10,600	D
1408 Petit Jean River	58 C3	70	U
1411 Prairie Bayou	93 D6	6	—
1414 Pullen Pond	60 C1	400	D
1417 Red River	110 D2	151	D
1420 Robe Bayou	81 A5	4	D
1423 Saline River	89 B5	177	—
1426 Saline River	102 C3	33	—
1429 Shady Lake	85 B5	25	D
1432 Shirey Bay	37 B6	60	D
1435 Shores Lake	43 A6	82	D
1438 Siloam Springs Lake	15 D4	35	D
1441 South Fork of Little Red River	47 B6	37	—
1444 Spring Lake	59 B5	82	D
1447 Spring River	23 C6	57	—
1450 St. Francis River	69 A5	245	U
1453 Storm Creek Lake	83 D5	420	D
1456 Strawberry River	36 A2	105	—
1459 Sugarloaf Lake	56 C2	334	D
1462 Table Rock Creek	18 A3	43,100	D
1465 Taylor Old River	104 A3	360	—
1468 Tommy Sproles Lake	79 A4	350	—
1471 Tri-County Lake	102 D2	280	D
1474 Upper Brock Creek Lake	47 C4	30	—
1477 Wapanocca Lake	54 D2	1,800	D
1480 War Eagle Creek	17 D5	57	—
1483 White Oak Lake	112 A1	2,560	D
1486 White River	35 A4	49	—
1489 White River	36 D2	162	D
1492 White River	81 C5	243	—
1495 Wilson Brake Lake	125 B6	150	D

Outdoor Adventures

HIKING

ATHENS–Big Fork Trail – Athens – 85 A6 Strenuous trail follows century-old former mail route. Rugged, 10.5-mile track crosses Big Tom, Brush Heap and Brushy mountains in Ouachita National Forest. Streams, waterfalls, wildflowers, lush forests and views from rock outcroppings provide relief from arduous terrain.

BATTLEFIELD TRAIL – Pea Ridge National Military Park – 16 A2 Trail offers natural features as well as historical interest. Path crosses Winton Spring and traverses forests, cedar thicket and bluffs, with views of Civil War battlefield and distant Boston Mountains. Leetown Battlefield cannons, Ford Cemetery and Elkhorn Tavern, site that marked beginning and end of 1862 Battle of Pea Ridge. 7-mile loop.

BEAR CREEK LAKE NATURE TRAIL – Marianna – 83 C4 Peaceful, self-guided path winds through woodlands of Crowleys Ridge in St Francis National Forest. Follows creek bottoms and crosses several bridges. Flowering dogwood, cucumber tree, winged elm, sassafras and black cherry. 1-mile loop.

BEECH RIDGE TRAIL – White Oak Lake State Park – 112 A1 2-mile loop provides an example of the transitional ecosystem of Gulf Coastal Plain, winding through hardwood and pine forest, bottomlands and sandhills. Armadillos, beavers, osprey, great blue herons and vultures, as well as southern twayblade orchids and jack-in-the-pulpit may be seen from boardwalks and bridges. View of White Oak Lake from overlook.

BONA DEA TRAILS – Russellville– 60 A1 Network of barrier-free trails through Prairie Creek floodplain designed as multi-use system for hiking, fitness and nature watching. Paths go through wildlife sanctuary where white-tailed deer, Canada geese, herons and bitterns are commonly seen. Benches and feeding stations dot way. 5.6 miles.

BUFFALO RIVER TRAIL – Woolum – 32 B3 Traverses bluffs overlooking river. Strenuous, 15-mile trail begins by crossing Richland Creek, which can be deep at times. Passes old homesteads and several sinkholes, indicating presence of caves.

BUFFALO RIVER TRAIL – Boxley –31 B5 One of the longest trails in state follows upstream segment of nation's first national river. 36-mile route features outstanding scenery, including rocky bluffs, waterfalls, farmsteads, hollows and panoramic river and valley views. Moderately difficult.

CANEY CREEK TRAIL – Athens – 85 B5 Trail traverses the length of Caney Creek Wilderness, taking in a variety of scenic elevations. Rock outcroppings and mountain ridges offer views of countryside with lush, grassy flats and forests of oak, beech and pine. Creek crossings and springtime wildflowers. 9.5 miles.

CEDAR FALLS TRAIL – Petit Jean State Park – 60 C3 Steep stone stairway descends 200 feet into Cedar Creek Canyon. Difficult 2.25-mile trail follows creek upstream to magnificent Cedar Falls, cascading 95 feet to canyon floor. Lichen-covered boulders, rock glaciers and large pines and oaks dot trail.

CRANE-FLY TRAIL – Logoly State Park and Natural Area – 112 D1 Trail crosses boardwalk and dam while circling pond. Woodland streams and rolling hills provide habitat for Gulf Coastal Plain flora and fauna such as hoary bats, flying squirrels, forest ferns and giant, centuries-old southern red oak. Wildflowers and butterflies. 0.75-mile loop.

CROWLEYS RIDGE STATE PARK TRAILS – Walcott – 39 A4 Four trails feature scenic hardwood-forest beauty. Hilly Dancing Rabbit Trail crosses two swinging bridges. Wild turkey, pileated woodpeckers and Carolina chickadees populate area around Spider Creek Trail. Partially barrier-free Lake Ponder Trail follows marshy, fern-lined lakeshore. Walcott Lake Trail features blue heron, kingfisher and a "condominium" that houses approximately 500 mosquito-controlling brown bats. 3.6 miles.

DOGWOOD TRAIL – Bull Shoals Lake Project – 20 B3 Nature trail winds for 3 miles through the hardwood forests of the Ozark Plateau above Bull Shoals Lake. Points of interest include Fossil Rock, Gall Tree (covered with bacteria- or fungus-caused growths) and Cedar Glade. Tags on trees denote species. Limestone bluffs afford views of lake and dam.

KNAPP TRAIL – Toltec Mounds State Park – 79 C4 Paved, self-guided trail takes in archaeological remains of Plum Bayou community that occupied site AD 600–1,000. Remnants of defensive embankment and several mounds, possibly used for religious or political purposes, are visible. Bald cypress seen from boardwalk. 0.9-mile loop.

LAKE CATHERINE STATE PARK TRAILS – Diamondhead – 88 B3 Three trails of varying levels of difficulty offer views of Ouachita Mountains. Falls Branch Trail, the shortest and easiest, crosses Little Canyon Creek and encounters a scenic waterfall. Horseshoe Mountain Trail features rock outcroppings, wildflowers and mosses on steep path. Dam Mountain Trail passes streams and cascades, and offers scenic views of Lake Catherine and Ouachita range from Narrow Mountain. 8 miles.

LAKE WEDINGTON TRAIL – Wedington Woods – 28 A2 Trail winds through Ozark National Forest, past small waterfall and unique rock formation known as Twin Knobs, to banks of the Illinois River. Moderately difficult 18-mile route crosses ridge top and bluffs covered with ferns, mosses and abundant wildflowers.

LOUISIANA PURCHASE BOARDWALK – Louisiana Purchase Historic State Park – 82 C1 950-foot-long barrier-free boardwalk culminates at granite monument marking point from which survey of 1803 Louisiana Purchase began. Unique swamp ecosystem is one of the last remaining in eastern Arkansas. Rare swamp cottonwood, bald cypress and water tupelo trees preserved. Wildlife include prothonotary warbler, pileated woodpecker, heron, wood duck and reptiles. Wayside exhibits.

LOVERS LEAP TRAIL – Queen Wilhelmina State Park – 72 C2 Loop begins by crossing tracks of miniature railroad, which encircles park. Steep and rocky in sections, trail passes rock gardens on way to the top of Rich Mountain. Summit features windblown trees and spectacular view of Ouachita Mountains. 1.3 miles.

MILITARY ROAD TRAIL – Village Creek State Park – 69 B4 Relatively easy, 2-mile loop. Portion of trail follows 1829 Old Military Road, first improved route from Little Rock to Memphis, Tennessee. Echo Point provides the opportunity to shout and take in view of Village Creek. Scenic views of Lake Austell.

MT MAGAZINE TRAIL – Paris – 58 B3 Trail winds among the cedars and wildflowers of Ozark National Forest on the way to summit of Mt Magazine, the highest peak in Arkansas at 2,753 feet. Streams, ponds and rock garden line the way as path steepens. Beyond summit, Mossback Ridge offers views of Petit Jean Valley to south. 9 miles.

MT NEBO STATE PARK TRAILS – Dardanelle – 59 B6 Hiking trails traverse Mt Nebo and 1890s summer resort area. Rim Trail circles mountaintop and features panoramic views of Lake Dardanelle and Arkansas River. Bench Road Trail circles mountain on natural sandstone shelf below summit. Trails connecting Rim and Bench Road trails offer strenuous, nearly vertical hikes to Nebo Springs, Fern Lake, Gum Springs and seasonal waterfall. 14-mile network.

OUACHITA NATIONAL RECREATION TRAIL – Queen Wilhelmina State Park – 72 C2 Ridgetop trail traverses 192-mile length of Ouachita National Forest. Diverse scenery includes views from rugged Ouachita mountaintops ranging from 600 to 2,600 feet high, hardwood and pine forests, lush hills, wide valleys, streams and springs. Numerous spur and loop trails for day hiking.

OZARK HIGHLANDS TRAIL – Mountainburg – 43 A5 Broadly considered among the most scenic trails in US. Trail begins in western Arkansas, crosses entire Ozark National Forest and ends at Buffalo National River. 207-mile route passes through remote forested areas and mountainous terrain, taking in rock outcroppings, waterfalls, clear mountain streams and Hare Mountain, the highest point on trail at 2,360 feet.

PEDESTAL ROCKS/KINGS BLUFF TRAILS – Ben Hur – 46 A2 Two trails form 4.3-mile loop that features ancient geological formations in Ozark National Forest. Pedestal Rocks Trail follows bluff line above Illinois Bayou, taking in weathered limestone columns, caves and shelters formed by centuries of erosion. King's Bluff Trail provides fantastic views of sandstone bluffs and one of the highest waterfalls in the Ozarks. Trails are steep and close to bluff line.

PINNACLE MOUNTAIN STATE PARK TRAILS – Pinnacle – 78 A1 Scenic base trail winds among cypress trees along Little Maumelle River. West Summit Trail to top of Pinnacle Mountain offers panoramic views of Lake Maumelle, Arkansas River, Ouachita National Forest and Little Rock metropolitan area. Extremely steep East Summit Trail descends rock face to Base Trail. Strenuous 2.75 miles.

POST BAYOU NATURE TRAIL – Arkansas Post National Memorial – 105 B4 Unpaved trail winds through forested peninsula that divides Arkansas River and Post Bayou. Takes in site where fort was established in 1686, beginning fort's long military history. Path follows edge of bayou to Civil War rifle pits. Wildlife includes white pelicans, bald eagles and alligators. 2.3 miles.

RIVER TRAIL – Crater of Diamonds State Park – 98 B2 Trail winds through lowland pine and hardwood forest, following creek to Little Missouri River. Footbridges cross streams and labels identify tree species. Area home to deer, turkey, migratory songbirds, hummingbirds, wood ducks and herons. 1.3-mile loop.

ROBINSON POINT TRAIL – Norfork Lake Project – 21 B6 Trail follows shoreline before ascent to Robinson Point. 3.3-mile path loops atop high bluff, offering views of the Ozark Mountains and Norfork Lake. Old twisted cedar trees, springtime wildflowers, rock garden and seasonal waterfalls.

RUSH HIKING TRAILS – Buffalo National River – 33 A6 Trail network through Rush Historic District provides a glimpse of Rush's glory days, when 1880s discovery of zinc ore created a boomtown. Morning Star Trail passes ruins of Morning Star Mine, including blacksmith shop, 1886 smelter and residences dating from 1899. Links to Rush Hiking Trail, which passes Hicks Store, Boiling Springs and several mine entrances. Traverses ridge overlooking Rush Creek, Clabber Creek and Buffalo River. 2.5 miles.

SEVEN HOLLOWS TRAIL – Petit Jean State Park – 60 C3 Trail alternately climbs bluffs and descends into hollows, showing off great diversity of natural formations and scenic beauty. Hardwood forest of wildflowers, moss and fern contrasts with desert-like rock formations. Passes grotto and natural stone bridge. Strenuous, 4.5-mile loop.

SHORES LAKE–WHITE ROCK TRAIL – Fern – 43 A6 Creek drainage trail begins on lakeshore and crosses Bliss Spring Hollow, several creeks and waterfall on trek up White Rock Mountain. Summit noted for views of surrounding Ozark National Forest. Steep hillside descent. Difficult, 13-mile loop.

SUGAR LOAF MOUNTAIN NATIONAL NATURE TRAIL – Greers Ferry Lake WMA – 48 B3 Nature trail located on island in Greers Ferry Lake accessible only by boat. Wildflowers at lower elevations yield to lichen-covered sandstone formations and dwarf English elm higher up, as well as caves and sandstone crevices. Summit ridge features panoramic views and huckleberry, wild azalea and prickly pear cactus. Lake swimming. 2-mile loop.

SUNSET TRAIL – Hot Springs National Park – 88 A2 Gentle grade traverses crests of Blowout, Music, Sugarloaf and West mountains. 12-mile loop offers views of mountains and valley below from rock outcroppings. Short spur trail leads to Balanced Rock, believed to be remnant of Native American quarrying activity. Trail crosses SR 7, joins Dead Chief Trail to downtown Hot Springs and picks up west of town returning to trailhead.

WATERFOWL WAY TRAIL – Millwood State Park – 109 A6 Trail follows Millwood Lake shoreline and winds through bogs and forests. Early morning and evening best times to view blue heron, white egret, bald eagles, active beaver dam and alligators. Picnic area. 1.5-mile loop.

WHITE ROCK RIM TRAIL – Mulberry – 43 A6 Path traces White Rock Mountain bluff line taking in views of Ozark National Forest and Salt Fork to Potato Knob Mountain and beyond. 2-mile loop features moss- and lichen-covered rocks and ferns clinging to sandstone bluffs. Four stone shelters provide rest and viewing opportunities. Trail runs very close to edge and has no guardrails.

BIKING

BACKWOODS OZARK TOUR – Jasper – 32 B1 Challenging touring loop through the northern section of Ozark National Forest and along the Buffalo River. Visits towns of Jasper, Boxley and Swain on SRs 74, 21 and 16. Last 3 miles are downhill returning to Jasper. Strenuous, 58-mile route.

BEAR CREEK TRAIL – Daisy State Park – 86 C2 Rough, rocky, 31-mile motorcycle trail through mature hardwood forest is open to mountain biking. Follows north shore of Lake Greeson, past Kirby Landing, ending at Laurel Creek Campground. Steep in places. Heavy use at times.

BENCH ROAD TRAIL – Mt Nebo State Park – 59 B6 Level, well-used doubletrack forms "bench" below 1,350-foot-high summit of Mt Nebo. 4-mile loop features scenic vistas of Arkansas River valley and Lake Dardanelle, as well as the Ozark and Ouachita mountains. Side trips lead to seasonal waterfall and historic sites.

BUFFALO GAP TRAIL – Ouachita National Forest – 76 B1 Marked gravel trail through Ouachita National Forest begins on FR 771. Offers scenic vistas of forest and Buffalo Gap, where, in pre-settlement times, buffalo were rounded up in narrow area and easily hunted. 9-mile loop offers colorful spring and fall foliage.

DELTA HERITAGE TRAIL – Barton – 82 D3 42 mile Biking/Hiking trail on old Union \Pacific railbed. Wildlife viewing. Will eventually stretch 85 miles to Arkansas City

FOSSIL FLATS TRAIL – Devil's Den State Park – 29 D4 Level, singletrack trail popular with bikers of all skill levels. 6-mile dirt trail accesses four homesites and a sawmill dating to the early 20th century. Fossils common along Lee Creek. No bridge at either of two creek crossings. 2 loops.

HOLT ROAD LOOP – Devil's Den State Park – 29 D4 Dirt trail along abandoned road and doubletrack winds through the densely wooded Boston Mountains of Ozark National Forest. Moderately difficult, 10-mile loop features 250-foot ascent. Accesses old homesites from mid-1800s, as well as a few from the 1930s. Side trails lead to waterfall and cave.

HUCKLEBERRY MOUNTAIN TRAILS – Havana – 58 B3 System of marked, multi-use trails around Mt Magazine and through Ozark National Forest traverses deep valleys and mountain bluffs. 37-mile network of gravel logging roads, forest roads and dirt trails comprise 12-mile-long Apple Loop and more challenging 18.8-mile-long Huckleberry Mountain Loop. Use caution when crossing Shoal Creek at high water levels.

MOCCASIN GAP TRAIL – Simpson – 46 B2 Marked, multi-use trail system offers four major loops through Ozark National Forest. 36-mile network accesses waterfalls, streams and scenic vistas from surrounding ridge tops. Abundant wildflowers in spring.

POSSUM KINGDOM TRAIL – Jessieville – 75 C6 Popular marked trail composed of series of loops on paved county and gravel forest roads begins on FR J-47. Travels through pine and hardwood trees of Ouachita National Forest near scenic Lake Ouachita and Richardson Bottoms. Prime wildlife viewing area. 17 miles.

WOLF PEN GAP TRAIL – Dallas – 85 A4 Gravel and dirt multi-use trail consists of a number of loops through Ouachita Mountains southeast of Mena. 42-mile network of doubletrack features high mountain vistas, pine and hardwood forests and an abandoned mine shaft. Accesses scenic Gap Creek and Board Camp Creek.

Outdoor Adventures, *continued*

WOMBLE TRAIL – Story – 75 B4 Multi-use singletrack dirt trail begins on FR 149 and winds through 37 miles of Ouachita National Forest and along the bluffs of Ouachita River. Accesses several float camps along river. Trail becomes steep in places. Well used in summer.

PADDLING

BIG CREEK – Wilburn – 49 C6 Cypress trees line bluffs along remote tributary of Little Red River. Swift rocky chutes, Class I-II rapids and deep pools. 15-mile route passes through Big Creek Natural Area. Camping. Put-in at low-water bridge. Takeout at old iron bridge.

BIG PINEY CREEK – Treat – 46 B1 Challenging run features flat gravel bars interspersed with Class II-III whitewater rapids such as Roller Coaster and Cascades of Extinction. Willow strainers, boulders and rock shelves. Put-in at access near FR 1805. Takeout 15 miles downstream at SR 164 bridge or midway at Long Pool Campground.

BIG PINEY CREEK – Fort Douglas – 45 A6 Scenic paddle along clear mountain stream in Ozark National Forest. Easy, Class I-II rapids link a series of pools. Willow thickets. Camping. Put-in at SR 123 bridge. Takeout 8 miles downstream near Treat Run.

BUFFALO RIVER – Ponca – 31 B5 Scenic, 25-mile section of river features Class I-II whitewater rapids, 225-foot-high waterfall at Hemmed-In Hollow, numerous caves and the highest bluffs in the Ozark Mountains. Swimming and camping. Put-in at SR 74 bridge. Takeout at SR 7 bridge.

BUFFALO RIVER – Jasper – 32 A1 Flatwater float along the banks of the country's first national river. High bluffs and numerous gravel bars. Easy, 99-mile stretch suitable for families and beginning paddlers. Takeouts, camping, and facilities along way. Put-in at SR 7 bridge. Takeout at SR 123 bridge.

CADDO RIVER – Norman – 86 A2 Intermediate, Class I-II rapids give way to a slow float through Ouachita National Forest. 24-mile stretch features a swinging footbridge, rock gardens, gravel bars and a natural hot spring. Camping. Put-in at ramp in Norman. Takeout at SR 182 bridge.

CADRON CREEK – Greenbrier – 62 A1 Scenic run features creek's highest bluffs. Ice formations in winter and waterfalls in summer. Class I-II rapids, boulders, pinnacles, caves and shoals. Camping. Put-in at US 65 bridge. Takeout 10 miles downstream at SR 285 bridge.

CADRON CREEK – Guy – 62 A1 Short, 3.5-mile run along rugged part of remote stream. Rocky shoals, flat pools, willow strainers and canyon-like bluffs. Camping. Put-in at access off of Pinnacle Spring Road. Takeout at US 65 bridge. Class I-II.

COSSATOT RIVER – Vandervoort – 85 B4 Narrow, fast-paced run down one of state's roughest whitewater streams. Rugged wilderness scenery. Camping. Put-in at SR 246 bridge. Takeout 3 miles downstream at Ed Banks Bridge. Class II-III.

COSSATOT RIVER – Wickes – 84 B3 Short, steep run drops 60 feet in 2 miles. Constant, heavy, Class II-III whitewater rapids with boulders, eddies, hydraulics, culverts and rock-filled flumes. Camping. Put-in at Ed Banks Bridge. Takeout above falls.

COSSATOT RIVER FALLS – Wickes – 85 B4 5-mile stretch of lively, Class III-V rapids, 6-to-8-foot drops and strong crosscurrents. Native American name means "skull crusher." Dangerous east bank portage. Camping. Put-in at access above falls. Takeout at SR 4 bridge.

CROOKED CREEK – Pyatt – 20 C1 Rural paddle along popular fishing creek. Class I-II riffles, fast chutes, gravel bars and willow thickets. Put-in at access off of US 64. Takeout 25 miles downstream at SR 14 bridge or at two midway takeout points.

ELEVEN POINT RIVER – Birdell – 25 C4 Secluded, 12-mile paddle along spring-fed wilderness stream. Old stone dams and frequent islands create challenging run during high water Camping. Put-in at US 62 bridge. Takeout at confluence with Black River.

ILLINOIS BAYOU – Hector – 46 C3 Fast-moving whitewater stream features standing waves, willow shoals and natural slalom course with hydraulics. Camping. Put-in at SR 27 bridge. Takeout 5 miles downstream at SR 164 bridge. Class I-II.

ILLINOIS BAYOU; MIDDLE FORK – Hector – 46 B3 Lively run of continuous, Class II-III whitewater drops 20 feet per mile. Technical rapids through narrow channels, boulder gardens and hardwood forested banks. Camping. Put-in at confluence with Snow Creek. Takeout 2 miles downstream at SR 27 bridge.

ILLINOIS BAYOU; NORTH FORK – Ben Hur 46 B2 – Fast-paced, 10-mile run through the dense tree cover of Ozark National Forest. Narrow channels and tricky, Class II-III rapids. Series of caves and limestone columns known as Pedestal Rocks. Camping. Put-in at confluence with Dry Creek. Takeout at old SR 27 bridge.

KINGS RIVER – Marble – 17 D6 Peaceful, 54-mile float through clear waters. Deep pools interspersed with occasional Class I-II rapids. Fishing and camping. Put-in off of US 412. Takeout at SR 143 bridge.

LITTLE MISSOURI RIVER – Langley – 85 C6 Ouachita Mountain stream claims Class I-III rapids and some of the biggest standing waves in state. Steep ridges and twisted rock strata. Camping. Put-in at SR 84 bridge. Takeout 11 miles downstream at SR 70 bridge.

LITTLE MISSOURI RIVER HEADWATERS – Albert – 86 B1 Whitewater run with technical, Class I-IV rapids through 8.5 miles of spectacular Ouachita Mountain scenery. Scouting is advised. Camping. Put-in at access on SR 369. takeout at SR 84 bridge.

LITTLE RED RIVER – Heber Springs – 49 C5 Calm, 29-mile float through the Ozark foothills becomes swift and dangerous during dam releases. Narrow shoals lead to deep pools. Fishing and camping. Put-in at Greers Ferry Dam. Takeout at SR 305 bridge. Class I-II.

MULBERRY RIVER – Cass – 44 A1 Long, deep pools characterize lower section of Class I-II whitewater stream in quiet, remote area. Scouting is advised. Camping. Put-in at SR 23 bridge. Takeout 28 miles downstream at SR 215 access area or midway at Milton Ford.

MULBERRY RIVER – Beach Grove – 44 A2 Whitewater stream winds through 7 miles of tree-lined bluffs. Large boulders and twisting turns create turbulent Class I-II rapids. Camping. Put-in at FR 1504 bridge. Takeout at SR 23 bridge.

MULBERRY RIVER – Yale – 44 A3 Springtime whitewater run with dangerous willow thickets, rock gardens and standing waves. Class II-III. Summer offers a calm float and swimming. Camping. Put-in at access on SR 215. Takeout 11.5 miles downstream at FR 1504 bridge.

OUACHITA RIVER – Board Camp – 73 D5 Lively bluff-lined float through 17 miles of Ouachita National Forest. Tight channels, shallow pools, overhanging branches and logjams. Class I-II route is best after rainfall. Camping. Put-in on CR 68. Takeout at access east of Pine Ridge.

OUACHITA RIVER – Pine Ridge – 74 D1 Pleasant, 33-mile float past bluffs and through the unspoiled Ouachita National Forest. Narrow turns, deep pools and rolling, Class I rapids. Camping. Put-in off of SR 68. Takeout at access south of Gibbs.

SALINE RIVER – Benton – 77 D6 Backcountry paddle along one of the last undammed streams in area features long pools with few riffles. Rare gravel bottom and slow current. Camping. Put-in off of SR 5. Takeout 120 miles downstream at Stillions access area.

SALINE RIVER; NORTH FORK – Salem – 77 C5 Fast-paced run along 6.5-mile, forested stream flowing from foothills of the Ouachita Mountains. Brush piles and willow thickets. Frequent portages due to deadfalls. Camping. Put-in at access off of Steel Bridge Road. Takeout at SR 5 bridge. Class I-II.

SPRING RIVER – Mammoth Spring – 23 A6 Popular paddle down clear, cold river fed by Mammoth Spring. 17-mile route features Class I-II rapids and waterfalls. Fishing and camping. Put-in at access off of US 63. Takeout at SR 62 bridge.

STRAWBERRY RIVER – Evening Shade – 36 A2 Remote paddle past forested banks and sandy beaches. Frequent downed trees and willow snags. Portages. Camping. Put-in at US 167 bridge. Takeout 22 miles downstream at SR 58 bridge.

WHITE RIVER – Bull Shoals – 20 B3 9-mile stretch of usually calm, Class I river. Depth and speed of crystal-clear water varies due to dam. Fishing and camping. Put-in below Bull Shoals Dam. Takeout at SR 933 access.

Unique Natural Features

BAKER PRAIRIE – Baker Prairie Natural Area – 19 C4 71-acre area last remnant of vast tallgrass Osage prairie that covered most of Boone County prior to settlement. Among native species are wildflowers such as rare royal catchfly, and animals and insects including prairie mole cricket, ornate box turtle and grasshopper sparrow.

BIG LAKE NATURAL AREA – Big Lake National Wildlife Refuge – 40 C3 6,400-acre landmark tract of forest and wetland within one of the oldest inland refuges in US. Illustrates extension of southern swampland and hardwood forest into Mississippi embayment. Virgin cypress and tupelo swamp surrounds lake. Area supports variety of wildlife, including many endangered bird species.

BLANCHARD SPRINGS CAVERNS – Ozark National Forest – 34 B3 Series of subterranean caves provides opportunity to see Ozark Mountains from inside. Discovery Trail winds through water-carved passages used by early cave explorers; deep, young cave system still active. Less strenuous Dripstone Trail traverses older, more ornate chambers featuring crystalline flowstones, towers and stalactites. Guided tours.

BULL SHOALS CAVERNS – Bull Shoals – 20 B3 Caverns once provided natural shelter for Native Americans and, later, Ozark explorers and mountaineers. Cathedral and Diamond Chapel rooms showcase live formations with well-lit paths. Concrete walkway features underground trout stream, rivers and miniature lake with falls. Guided tours.

COSMIC CAVERN – Maple – 18 A1 Series of show caves features spectacular rock formations and two large underground lakes. Silent Splendor cave, discovered in 1993, contains nearly transparent formations such as pristine white "soda straws" and helictites. Gemstone panning. Guided tours.

HEMMED-IN HOLLOW – Buffalo National River – 31 A6 Wooded hollow reveals 210-foot-high waterfall. Located on Buffalo National River between Steel Creek and Kyles Landing. Accessible only by river or steep Ponca Wilderness Area hiking trail; no road access. Paddling, fishing and camping allowed on river; no camping near waterfall.

LAKE WINONA RESEARCH NATURAL AREA – Ouachita National Forest – 76 B3 Site known for forest containing 150–200-year-old virgin stand of shortleaf pine that once covered most of state. Hardwood species interspersed with pine include black oak, hickory, dogwood, white oak, black gum and southern red oak.

MAGAZINE MOUNTAIN – Ozark National Forest – 58 B3 Highest peak in state at 2,753 feet one of the richest habitats for rare plants and animals. Both north and south sides of the mountain support species at extremes of their range. Primarily rocky forest of oak, sassafras, hickory and undergrowth. Best views at Cameron Bluff. Hiking trails.

MAMMOTH SPRING – Mammoth Spring State Park – 23 A6 Spring flows underground and out through cavern at base of limestone bluff to form 64-foot-deep head pool and source of Spring River. Third largest spring in Ozark Mountains maintains average water flow of 9.78 million gallons per hour and constant temperature of 58 degrees Fahrenheit.

OLD SPANISH TREASURE CAVE – Gravette – 15 A5 according to legend, gold was buried in cave by Spanish soldiers in 18th century. Features a variety of formations, including Heart of the Cave and Land of a Thousand Lakes. Guided tours.

ONYX CAVE – Eureka Springs – 17 A5 Abundant stalactites and stalagmites adorn still-forming cave. Formations include Onyx Elephant, Friendly Dragon and Witches Fireplace. Trail from cave leads to Cedar Creek Valley overlook and picnic area. Museum. Guided tours.

ROARING BRANCH RESEARCH NATURAL AREA – Ouachita National Forest – 85 B6 272-acre site contains only known significant-sized virgin white oak and oak–pine forests in Ozark and Ouachita mountains. Forested 600-foot-deep ravine of beech, basswood and umbrella magnolia represents relict outlier forest common to Indiana, Kentucky and Tennessee. Roaring Branch Creek runs through area.

WAR EAGLE CAVERN – War Eagle – 16 C3 Secluded cavern within unspoiled wilderness of Ozark Mountains along Beaver Lake used by Native Americans prior to European settlement. Named for Hurachis the War Eagle, Osage chief who signed treaties with US government in 1820s. Trail leads to natural entrance, domes and underground stream. Average year-round temperature 58 degrees Fahrenheit. Abundant fossils. Guided tours.

WHITE RIVER SUGARBERRY NATURAL AREA – White River National Wildlife Refuge – 106 A1 Wilderness area contains virgin timber and three bottomland hardwood forest types: overcup oak–water hickory, sweetgum–Nuttall oak–willow, and sugarberry–American elm–ash. Wildlife species include songbirds, deer and black bear.

Name	Page & Grid	Acreage	Alligator	Bear	Deer	Elk	Furbearers	Rabbit	Squirrel	Crow	Quail	Turkey	Waterfowl
Bald Knob NWR	66 A3	15,022			●		●	●	●		●	●	●
Bayou Des Arc WMA	66 D3	953			●		●	●	●	●	●	●	●
Beaver Lake WMA	16 D3	5,827		●	●		●	●	●	●	●	●	
Bell Slough WMA	62 D1	2,040		●	●		●	●	●	●	●	●	●
Benson Creek Natural Area WMA	67 B5	1,386			●		●	●	●	●	●	●	
Beryl Anthony/Lower Ouachita WMA	124 D1	7,500			●		●	●	●	●	●	●	●
Big Creek WMA	82 B1	290			●		●	●	●	●	●	●	●
Big Lake NWR	40 B3	11,038			●		●	●	●	●	●	●	●
Big Lake WMA	40 B3	12,320			●		●	●	●	●	●	●	●
Big Timber WMA	99 C6	36,464		●	●		●	●	●	●	●	●	●
Blevins WMA	99 C4	128			●		●	●	●	●	●	●	●
Blue Mountain WMA	58 C2	8,200		●	●		●	●	●	●	●	●	●
Brewer Lake/Cypress Creek WMA	61 B6	1,200			●		●	●	●	●	●	●	●
Brushy Creek WMA	52 D2	208			●		●	●	●	●	●	●	
Buffalo National River WMA	32 B3	87,154		●	●	●	●	●	●	●	●	●	●
Cache River NWR	81 B5	56,000			●		●	●	●	●		●	●
Camp Robinson WMA	78 A3	26,675		●	●		●	●	●	●	●	●	●
Caney Creek WMA	85 B5	85,000		●	●		●	●	●	●		●	
Casey Jones WMA	124 C2	51,242			●		●	●	●	●	●	●	●
Cattail Marsh WMA	26 D1	72			●		●	●	●	●	●	●	
Cedar Creek WMA	74 B1	99			●		●	●	●	●	●	●	
Cherokee Prairie Natural Area WMA	43 D5	553						●			●		●
Cherokee WMA	47 D4	62,203		●	●		●	●	●	●	●	●	●
Chinquapin Mountain Walk-In Turkey Hunting Area	76 A3	8,011										●	
Cove Creek Natural Area WMA	62 A1	226			●		●	●	●	●	●	●	
Crossett Experimental Forest WMA	124 C2	1,595			●		●	●	●	●	●	●	
Cut-Off Creek WMA	116 C3	8,285			●		●	●	●	●	●	●	●
Cypress Bayou WMA	63 D6	1,413			●		●	●	●	●	●	●	●
Dardanelle WMA	45 D4	54,060			●		●	●	●	●	●	●	●
Dave Donaldson Black River WMA	26 C1	24,008			●		●	●	●	●	●	●	●
Deckard Mountain Walk-In Turkey Hunting Area	76 B1	7,400										●	
DeGray Lake WMA	87 C6	29,298		●	●		●	●	●	●	●	●	●
Departee WMA	50 D3	430			●		●	●	●	●	●	●	●
Departee Creek WMA - Estep Unit	51 D4	115			●		●	●	●	●	●	●	
Devil's Knob Natural Area WMA	35 B4	722		●	●		●	●	●	●	●	●	
Dr Lester Sitzes III Bois D'Arc WMA	110 B2	7,244	●		●		●	●	●	●	●	●	●
Earl Buss Bayou DeView WMA	52 B2	4,250		●	●		●	●	●	●	●	●	●
Ed Gordon Point Remove WMA	61 A4	8,317		●	●		●	●	●	●	●	●	●
Ethel WMA	93 C6	166			●		●	●	●	●	●	●	●
Falcon Bottoms Natural Area WMA	111 C5	2,914			●		●	●	●	●	●	●	●
Felsenthal NWR	123 B6	65,000			●		●	●	●	●	●	●	●
Fort Chaffee WMA	57 A4	60,887			●		●	●	●	●	●	●	
Fourche Mountain Walk-In Turkey Hunting Area	75 A5	3,162										●	
Freddie Black Choctaw Island WMA/ Deer Research Area	117 B6	10,688			●		●	●	●	●	●	●	●
Frog Bayou WMA	43 C4	707			●		●	●	●	●	●	●	●
Galla Creek WMA	60 B2	3,128		●	●		●	●	●	●	●	●	●
Garrett Hollow Natural Area WMA	28 D2	701			●		●	●	●	●	●	●	
Gene Rush WMA	32 C2	17,652		●	●	●	●	●	●	●	●	●	
George H Dunklin Jr. Bayou Meto WMA	92 C1	33,832			●		●	●	●	●	●	●	●
Greers Ferry Lake WMA	48 C3	18,984			●		●	●	●	●	●	●	●
Gum Flats WMA	108 A3	14,829			●		●	●	●	●	●	●	●
H. E. Flanagan Prairie Natural Area WMA	43 D6	249						●			●		●
Harold E Alexander Spring River WMA	24 C1	12,787			●		●	●	●	●	●	●	●
Harris Brake WMA	61 D4	2,653		●	●		●	●	●	●	●	●	●
Henry Gray Hurricane Lake WMA	67 B4	16,584			●		●	●	●	●	●	●	●
Hobbs State Park–Conservation Area	16 C3	11,471			●		●	●	●	●	●	●	
Hogan Mountain Walk-In Turkey Hunting Area	58 D1	7,800										●	
Holla Bend NWR	60 B2	7,000			●		●	●	●	●	●	●	●
Holland Bottoms WMA	79 A4	5,275			●		●	●	●	●	●	●	●
Hope Upland WMA	98 D3	2,115			●		●	●	●	●	●	●	
Howard County WMA	85 D4	25,295			●		●	●	●	●	●	●	
Howard Hensley–Searcy County WMA	33 B5	178		●	●		●	●	●	●	●	●	
Iron Mountain Natural Area WMA	84 A6	256			●		●	●	●	●	●	●	
J Perry Mikles Blue Mountain Special Use Area	58 C1	4,000			●		●	●	●	●	●	●	●
Jamestown Independence County WMA	50 A1	964		●	●		●	●	●	●	●	●	
Jim Kress WMA	49 B6	14,527		●	●		●	●	●	●	●	●	
Jones Point WMA	20 A2	1,173		●	●		●	●	●	●	●	●	●
Jordan Tract WMA	84 D3	300			●		●	●	●	●	●	●	
Lafayette County WMA	119 C6	13,696		●	●		●	●	●	●	●	●	●
Lake Greeson WMA	86 D1	35,382		●	●		●	●	●	●	●	●	
Leader Mountain Walk-In Turkey Hunting Area	85 B6	9,925										●	
Lee County WMA	83 A4	209			●		●	●	●	●	●	●	●
Little Bayou WMA	116 D3	1,246			●		●	●	●	●	●	●	●
Little River WMA	110 A1	597			●		●	●	●	●	●	●	●
Loafers Glory WMA	33 A6	2522		●	●		●	●	●	●	●	●	
Maumelle River WMA	77 A6	8046		●	●		●					●	●
McIlroy Madison County WMA	17 D5	13,672		●	●		●	●	●	●	●	●	
Millwood Lake Project	97 D6	25,600			●		●	●	●	●	●	●	●
Mike Freeze Wattensaw WMA	80 A3	18,702			●		●	●	●	●	●	●	●
Moro Big Pine Natural Area WMA	114 D1	15,261			●		●	●	●	●	●	●	●
Mount Magazine WMA	58 B3	110,178		●	●		●	●	●	●	●	●	
Muddy Creek WMA	74 B2	150,000		●	●		●	●	●	●	●	●	
Nacatoch Ravines Natural Area WMA	110 A1	1565			●		●	●	●	●	●	●	
Nimrod Lloyd Millwood WMA	59 D5	20,660		●	●		●	●	●	●	●	●	●
Norfork Lake WMA	21 C6	46,979		●	●		●	●	●	●	●	●	
Overflow NWR	125 C5	13,000			●		●	●	●	●	●	●	●
Ozan WMA	98 C2	580			●		●	●	●	●	●	●	
Ozark Lake WMA	43 C6	16,208			●		●	●	●	●	●	●	●
Ozark National Forest WMA	32 D1	630,641		●	●		●	●	●	●	●	●	
Palmetto Flats Natural Area WMA	108 A3	1,764			●		●	●	●	●	●	●	
Petit Jean WMA	59 C6	14,276			●		●	●	●	●	●	●	●
Pine City Natural Area WMA	81 D6	892			●		●	●	●	●	●	●	
Piney Creek WMA	46 A1	176,000			●		●	●	●	●	●	●	
Poison Springs WMA	112 A1	17,604			●		●	●	●	●	●	●	
Pond Creek NWR	97 C4	27,000			●		●	●	●	●	●	●	●
Prairie Bayou WMA	80 C1	418			●		●	●	●	●	●	●	●
Provo WMA	97 B4	10,757			●		●	●	●	●	●	●	●
Railroad Prairie Natural Area WMA	80 B2	207			●		●	●	●	●	●		
Rainey WMA	46 D3	458		●	●		●	●	●	●	●	●	
Rex Hancock Black Swamp WMA	67 C5	5,681			●		●	●	●	●	●	●	●
Rex Hancock Black Swamp WMA- Lee LeBlanc	67 D5	380			●		●	●	●	●	●	●	●
Rex Hancock Black Swamp WMA- Wiville Unit	67 B5	333			●		●	●	●	●	●	●	●
Rick Evans Grandview Prairie WMA	98 D2	4,885			●		●	●	●	●	●	●	●
Ring Slough WMA	26 A3	81			●		●	●	●	●	●	●	●
River Bend WMA	61 C4	63			●		●	●	●	●	●	●	●
Robert L Hankins Mud Creek Upland WMA	25 B4	992			●		●	●	●	●	●	●	
Roth Prairie Natural Area WMA	92 A2	39			●		●	●	●	●	●		
Sandhills Natural Area WMA	118 B2	208			●		●	●	●	●	●	●	
Scott Henderson Gulf Mountain WMA	47 B5	12,303		●	●		●	●	●	●	●	●	
Seven Devils WMA	116 B2	6,000			●		●	●	●	●	●	●	●
Sharptop Mountain Walk-In Turkey Hunting Area	87 A4	11,275										●	
Sheffield Nelson Dagmar WMA	81 A5	7,976			●		●	●	●	●	●	●	●
Shirey Bay-Rainey Brake WMA	37 B6	10,711			●		●	●	●	●	●	●	●
Slippery Hollow Natural Area WMA	20 B1	703			●		●	●	●	●	●	●	
Smoke Hole Natural Area WMA	80 C2	438			●		●	●	●	●	●	●	
Spring Bank WMA	119 C4	512			●		●	●	●	●	●	●	●
St Francis National Forest WMA	83 B4	20,946			●		●	●	●	●	●	●	●
St Francis Sunken Lands WMA	53 A6	27,279			●		●	●	●	●	●	●	●
Stateline Sand Ponds Natural Area WMA	26 A2	82			●		●	●	●	●	●	●	
Steven N Wilson Raft Creek Bottoms WMA	66 C3	3,878			●		●	●	●	●	●	●	●
Sulphur River WMA	118 B3	16,000			●		●	●	●	●	●	●	●
Sylamore WMA	34 A3	160,660		●	●		●	●	●	●	●	●	
Terre Noire Natural Area WMA	100 A1	456			●		●	●	●	●	●	●	
Trusten Holder WMA	105 A5	17,587		●	●		●	●	●	●	●	●	●
Two Bayou Creek WMA	113 B4	1,266			●		●	●	●	●	●	●	
University of Arkansas Pine Tree Experimental Station WDA	68 C2	11,850			●		●	●	●	●	●	●	●
W E Brewer Scatter Creek WMA	26 D2	3,846			●		●	●	●	●	●	●	●
Wapanocca NWR	54 D2	5,485			●		●	●	●	●	●	●	●
Warren Prairie Natural Area WMA	115 B5	4,037			●		●	●	●	●	●	●	●
Wedington WMA	28 A2	25,487			●		●	●	●	●	●	●	
White Cliffs Natural Area WMA	97 D5	520			●		●	●	●	●	●	●	
White River NWR	105 A6	160,000			●		●	●	●	●	●	●	●
White Rock WMA	44 A1	291,629		●	●		●	●	●	●	●	●	
Whitehall WMA	52 C3	109			●		●	●	●	●	●	●	●
Winona WMA	76 A3	160,000		●	●		●	●	●	●	●	●	
Wittsburg Natural Area WMA	69 B4	146			●		●	●	●	●	●	●	

Index of Placenames and Map Features

ABOUT THE INDEX

This index contains almost 5,000 features shown on the maps on pages 15–127. Names are listed alphabetically along with map page(s) and grid coordinates to help locate them. The grid coordinates correspond to the letters (A–D) and numbers (1–6) along the top and outside edges of all map pages.

Guidelines for using this index:

- Placenames appear in boldface type, such as **Rogers** 16 B1
- Drainage names (e.g., lakes, reservoirs, rivers, creeks, springs) appear in italic type, such as *Alligator Lake* 105 A6
- All geographic features (e.g., mountains, canyons, hollows, valleys) appear in regular type, such as Hog Island 40 C3

A

1916 Cut-off Lake 110 C2
1927 Cut-off Lake 110 C2
Aa Junction 38 A2
Aaron Branch 49 B4
Abb Creek 31 C5
Abbot Mountain 74 B1
Abbott 57 C4
Abco 89 B4
Aberdeen 81 D4
Abernathy Spring 85 A6
Abernathy Springs 85 A6
Ables Creek 103 C6; 104 C1;D1,2; 116 A3
Accident 16 D2
Achmun Creek 59 C6
Acklin Gap 62 B2
Acorn 73 C4
Ada Valley 60 C3
Ada 60 C3
Adams Bayou 93 A5
Adams Branch 121 D6
Adams Creek 109 D5
Adams Cut-Off Lake 110 B1
Adams Mountain 46 C2
Adamson Creek 56 B3
Adcock Creek 116 B1
Adeline Hill 35 C6
Adkins Creek 31 D4
Adler Cave 36 C2
Adler Hill 36 C2
Adona 60 C3
Advance 21 D5
Aetna 37 B4
Aetna 39 C5
Agnos 23 C4
Ain 90 D2
Airport Village 51 A6
Akers Reservoir 80 D3
Akins Creek 47 A6
Alabam 17 D5
Alamo 87 A4
Albert 86 B1
AlbertPond 93 D6
Albion 50 D1
Alco Mountain 34 C1
Alco 34 C2
Alcohol Spring 19 C6
Alder Creek 66 A1; 85 A6
Alder Gap 59 C4
Alewine Branch 60 A3
Alexander Cave 34 B2
Alexander Mountain 43 A6; 78 D1
Alexander 78 D1
Alf 86 A1
Alfrey 81 B6
Algoa 51 C6
Alicia 38 C1
Alix 44 D2
Allard Mountain 30 D1
Allbrook 98 D1
Alleene 96 D3
Allen Bayou 69 C4,5
Allen Branch 111 B4; 84 C3
Allen Creek 74 B1;C2 ; 109 A4;B4
Allen Hill 50 A2
Allen Knob 30 C3
Allen Lake 26 C1
Allen Peak 75 A4
Allendale 81 B5
Allens Creek 77 B5
Allgood Creek 102 A3
Alligator Bayou 70 B1
Alligator Lake 105 A6
Allis Mountain 78 C2
Allis 115 B6
Allison 35 B4
Allport 80 D1
Allred Creek 24 C3
Allred Lake 26 A3
Alma 43 C4
Almond Creek 84 D3
Almond 49 A6
Almus Knob 34 A1
Almyra 93 B4
Alneta Lake 77 B6
Alpena 18 C3
Alpha 59 C6
Alpine 78 C1
Alpine 87 D5
Alread Hill 47 A4
Alread 47 B5
Altheimer 91 C6
Alto 54 B1
Altus 44 C2
Alum Cave Canyon 47 A5
Alum Cave 48 C2
Alum Fork Saline River 76 B2,3; 77 C4;D4,5
Aly 75 B4
Amagon 51 B6
Amanca 70 C2
Amason Creek 122 A3
Amboy 78 B2
Ames 111 B6
Amith Addition 51 A5
Amity 87 C4
Amos Bayou 104 C3; 105 D4,5
Amos 20 B3
Amy 113 A4
Anders Branch 49 D6
Anderson Bay 93 B6
Anderson Creek 46 C3
Anderson Flat 33 A4
Anderson Knob 29 C6
Anderson Mountain 28 D2
Anderson Tully 53 C5
Anderson 73 A5
Andrews 66 B2
Angle Ditch 38 D2
Angling Creek 76 C2
Angling Pinnacle 76 B3
Angora Mountain 34 D1
Anna Branch 114 A2
Annieville 24 D2
Anthony Brake 92 A1
Anthony Lake 122 A3; 125 B5
Anthony Switch 111 B6
Anthonyville 70 C1
Antioch Creek 88 C2
Antioch 25 B4
Antioch 39 C5
Antioch 61 D4
Antioch 63 B6
Antioch 88 C2
Antoine River 86 C3; 87 D4; 99 B5
Antoine 99 A5
Apalco 111 D4
Apex 56 D2
Aplin 60 D2
Apperos Creek 69 A4
Apple Hill 63 C5
Apple Spur 16 B1
Appleby 29 B4
Appleton 46 D3
Applewhite Cutoff Lake 108 B3
Apt 39 D4
Arbaugh 31 D4
Arbor Grove 38 B1
Arbuckle Island 43 C5
Arcadia 99 C4
Archer Island 107 C4
Archer Lake 107 D4
Archey Creek 47 A4,6; 48 B1
Archey Valley 47 A4
Archey Valley 47 A5
Ard 59 B6
Arden 108 A3
Ark Slough Ditch 38 C3
Arkadelphia 100 A2
Arkana Station 21 D5
Arkana 21 C5
Arkansas City 117 B6
Arkansas Post Canal 105 B5
Arkansas Post 105 B4
Arkansas River 104 A3; 105 B4,5;C6; 106 D1; 42 D1; 43 C6;D4; 44 C1;D1,3; 45 D5; 59 A6; 60 B1; 61 B4;C5;D6; 62 D1; 78 A1;B2;D3; 91 A4;D6; 92 D1
Arkapola Bluff 81 B4
Arkawana 21 B4
Arkinda 96 D2
Arkmo 40 B2
Arkola 56 C3
Arlberg 34 D1
Arm Lake 51 D4
Armorel 41 C6
Armstead Mountain 47 B4
Armstrong 24 B2
Arnett 29 C5
Arnold Bend 33 B4
Arnold Branch 35 D6; 36 C1
Arnold Creek 75 D5; 91 C4; 99 D4
Arrington Brake 104 D2
Arrington Creek 31 B5
Artesian 114 D1
Artex 110 D1
Arthur Branch 123 C4
Arthur 61 A5
ArtificialLake 113 D6
Artist Point 43 A4
Ash Branch 121 C6
Ash Creek 84 D2
Ash Flat 109 A6; 126 C1
Ash Flat 23 D5
Ash Reservoir 92 B3
Ash Slash 93 A6
Ash Slough 70 C2
Ash Spread Ditch 52 A1
Ashdown 109 A4
Asher 30 B1
Ashley Bayou 79 C4
Ashley Creek 58 B2
Ashley Hollow 28 D2
Ashley Point 83 B6
Ashlock Hill 34 D3
Ashton 126 A1
Ashworth Hill 99 A5
Asia Point 32 C1
Atcheson Creek 59 D5
Atheistan 54 A2
Athens 85 C6
Athye Brook 24 A2
Atkins Lake 91 D6
Atkins Lake 91 D6
Atkins Slough 105 B4
Atkins 60 A3
Atkinson Branch 120 A2
Atlanta 121 C5
Attica Hill 25 B4
Attica 25 B4
Atwood Creek 102 C3
Atwood 97 A5
Aubrey 82 C2
Augsburg Mountain 45 D6
Augsburg 45 D6
Augusta 67 A4
Aunt Lucy Hillt 25 B5
Aurelle 123 C4
Aurora 30 B2
Austin Ridge 47 C4
Austin 47 C4,6
Austin 63 D5
AustinBrake 116 A3
Auvergne 51 C5
Ava 75 A6
Avant 75 C5
Avery Brake 104 B2
Avery Spring 18 A2
Avery 104 C2
Avilla 77 C6
Avoca 16 B2
Avon 96 A3
Aydelotte Washer 36 C1
Azor 111 B5

B

B B Junction 81 D6
Babb Lake 113 D6
Baber Creek 98 D1
Back Gate 105 B4
Back Valley 86 B2
Backbone Mountain 56 B2; 58 B1
Backbone Narrows 57 B5
Backbone Ridge 48 A3; 63 D4; 66 A1
Backer Hollow 15 C4
Bacon Creek 98 A1
Bacon Lake 100 D3; 67 A4
Bad Luck Creek 63 A5
Badders Creek 49 D4
Bailey Branch 121 A5; 22 A2; 59 C4; 62 B3
Bailey Cole Creek 32 D3
Bailey Creek 35 A4; 50 B3; 116 C2
Bailey Cut-off 108 A1
Bailey Falls 50 A1
Bailey Gap 62 B2
Bailey Hollow Creek 48 C2
Bailey Lake Hill 66 B3
Bailey Mountain 50 B1; 62 B2
Bailey 50 B3
Baily Branch 76 C2
Baker Bend 109 A6
Baker Bluff 24 C3
Baker Branch 104 D1; 121 B4; 37 D4
Baker Creek 53 A4; 85 C4
Baker Den Creek 24 A3
Baker Den Hill 24 A3
Baker Ford 23 B5
Baker Hill 36 A2
Baker Hollow 33 C5
Baker Knob 30 C1
Baker Mountain 85 A4
Baker Spring Branch 33 A4
Baker Springs 85 C4
Baker 111 C4
Baker 24 C1
Baker 33 C6
Bakers Bayou 79 B-D5;B4
Bakers Creek 24 A3; 46 D1; 58 C3
Balch Addition 36 D2
Balch 52 C1
Bald Dave 21 B4
Bald Hill 49 C6; 62 B2; 24 B3
Bald Jesse 20 D2
Bald Knob 24 D2; 25 A4; 33 C4; 34 C2; 46 C1; 46 A1; 50 B2; 58 D1; 85 A4; 42 A3
Bald Knob 66 A2
Bald Mountain 35 A5; 48 B1;86 B1;88 A3
Bald Scrappy 35 B4
Bald Spring 23 B5
Baldon Branch 98 B3
Baldwin Creek 30 D2
Baldwin Hill 33 C6
Baldwin 29 A5
Baldwin 91 C4
Ball Creek 30 C1
Ball Hollow 24 C1
Ball Lake 66 C3
Ball Mountain 77 B6
Ball Point 83 A4
Ball Spring 100 C2; 58 B2
Ball 42 C3
Ballard Branch 121 A5
Ballard Creek 28 B1,2
Ballard Hill 62 C3
Ballard 23 C5
Ballinger Branch 33 C5
Bancroft Hill 34 D3
Band Mill Creek 22 D2
Band Mill 22 D2
Bandy Creek 85 D6
Bandy Branch 120 C1
Bane Creek 66 D1; 80 A1
Bangs Slough 113 D6; 114 D1; 123 A4
Bankhead Creek 100 C2
Banks 114 B2
Banner Mountain 48 B1
Banner 49 A6
Bar House Branch 32 A2
Barbaree Branch 111 C4
Barber Creek 59 B4
Barber 57 C5
Barberry Creek 31 C6
Barbers Lake 66 B3
Barcelona 42 B2
Bard 40 A1
Bardstown 54 C3
Bare Stone 50 D2
Barfield Landing 41 C6
Barfield Point 41 D6
Barfield 41 C6
Barger Ridge 60 C1
Barham Branch 111 A6; 112 A2
Barham Lake 111 A6
Barham 112 A2
Bark Camp Island 40 A1
Barkada 115 A6
Barker Creek 53 A4
Barker Gap 42 A2
Barker Knob 30 C3
Barkley Branch 80 A3
Barling 56 A3
Barlow Branch 120 A3
Barlow Christian Mountain 32 C2
Barlow Creek 101 C6
Barmes Pond 110 D3
Barn Branch 58 B2
Barn Hill Creek 102 A1
Barn Hill 58 B1
Barnes Bay 20 A2
Barnes Branch 23 D6
Barnes Creek 24 B1; 74 D3; 80 A2;B2; 90 A3
Barnes Lake 69 A5; 81 A4
Barnes 44 A1
Barnett Creek 36 C2
Barnett Lake 91 C6
Barney Chute Old River 54 C3;D2
Barney Chute 54 C3
Barney 62 A3
Barnhart Creek 75 A5
Barnum Landing 40 B3
Baron Creek 44 A1
Baron Fork 28 C2
Barr Mountain 33 C6
Barren Hollow 33 B6
Barren Creek 21 C4; 84 B2,3
Barren Fork Creek 36 B1
Barren Fork 18 B3; 19 B4; 21 C6; 22 C1; 33 A5
Barren Hollow 33 B6
Barrentine Corner 63 C5
Barrettsville 80 A1
Barringer 100 C1
Barrow Bend 69 A5
Barson 68 B1
Bart Lake 107 A4
Barton Lake 100 D2
Barton 82 D3
Barum Branch 25 A4
Basement Point 49 A5
Bashaw Mountain 87 A4
Bashe 56 A2
Bashum Creek 45 B4
Basin Creek 115 A5; 73 C4; 89 A4
Basin Hollow 73 C4
Basin Spring 18 C2
Baskin Creek 60 C1
Bass Creek 62 C3; 93 B6
Bass Gap 62 C2
Bass Island 27 A6
Bass Mountain 47 C5
Bass 32 C2
Bassett Cave 29 C5
Bassett 54 B3
Bat Cave 16 C3; 37 C4
Bat House Cave 32 A2
Bat Knob Hill 35 B6
Batavia 18 C3
Bateman Bend 51 B5
Bates Creek 24 C2
Bates Knob 46 B1
Bates Lake 25 C4
Bates Mountain 28 B1
Bates 72 A2
Batesville Creek 48 D2; 62 A1
Batesville Mountain 48 D2
Batesville 36 D2
Batson 44 B3
Battle Axe Bend 37 D5
Battle Creek 110 D3
Battle Lake 119 A5
Battle Springs 44 B1
Battlefield 110 B2
Baucum 79 C4
Bauxite Junction 77 D6
Bauxite 77 D6
Baxley Creek 90 A1
Baxter Hill 36 C2
Baxter Spring 36 C3
Baxter 116 C3
BaxterPoint 45 B4
Bay Bayou 105 A4
Bay Creek 22 A2;A3; 24 A3
Bay Ditch No 1 39 C6
Bay Plantation 67 D4
Bay Village 53 C4
Bay 39 D5
Bayless 81 B5
Bayou Bartholomew 103 A5;B6; 104 B1;C2;D3; 116 A-D3; 125 A5,6;B6;C5; 91 C4;D5
Bayou de Loutre 122 B2;C3
Bayou Dee 88 B3
Bayou des Arc 63 A5;B6; 66 B1;C1,2;D3
Bayou DeView 52 A2;B2;D1; 52 C1; 67 A-C6;D5; 68 A1; 81 A5;B5
Bayou Dorcheat 111 C5;D5; 120 A1,2;C2
Bayou Macon 117 A4;B-D5; 126 A2;B-D2
Bayou Meto 104 A3; 105 A4; 62 D3; 78 A3; 79 A4;B5,6;C6; 80 C1;D1,2; 92 A-C2;A1;D3
Bayou Meto 79 C6
Bayou Meto 92 D3
Bayou Mountain 62 B3
Bayou Narrow 91 B4
Bayou Two Prairie 63 D4
Bayou Two Prairie 79 A4,5;B6; 80 B1;C1;D2
Beach Branch 100 B3; 114 D2
Beach Grove 44 A2
Beacon Addition 16 B3
Bean Bluff 21 A6
Bean Lake 66 D3
Bean Mountain 31 C6
Bear Bayou 117 D4; 41 D5; 92 B1;D3
Bear Brake 125 A6
Bear Branch 101 D4; 45 A4; A2; 49 D5; 50 B1; 63 B5
Bear Creek Lake 83 C4
Bear Creek Mountain 76 A1
Bear Creek Springs 19 C4
Bear Creek 19 A5;B4; 22 D2; 31 A6;D5; 33 B5;C4,5; 36 A2; 45 A5,6; 46 A1; 47 A4; 56 B3; 66 D2; 68 B3; 75 B5;D6; 76 A1;B1;D1; 83 C4; 86 C2; 87 A6; 90 B3; 96 A3;B2; 100 C2; 113 D4; 119 C6; 121 A6; 122 C1,3; 123 C5
Bear Creek 33 D4
Bear Den Mountain 75 B4; 86 A1
Bear Head Mountain 75 B4
Bear Lake Slough 51 C5
Bear Lake 51 C5; 94 D1
Bear Mountain 33 D4; 49 B4; 57 C6; 59 B5; 75 D5; 85 A5; 86 A3
Bear Pen Creek 34 A3;B2
Bear Pen Falls 34 D2
Bear Ridge 49 B6
Bear Slough 51 D4; 67 A4;C4;D4; 92 A2
Bear Spring Gap 35 B5
Bear Waller Spring 59 A4
Bear Wallow Prong 74 C3
Bear 75 D6
Beard Branch 90 A2
Beard Hill 24 C2
Beard Lake 109 A6
Bearden Mountain 86 A1
Bearden 113 A6
Beardon Mountain 86 B2
Beardy Branch 47 C5
Bearhouse Creek 116 C1;D2; 125 A5
BearLake 105 D5; 109 B6
Bearskin Lake 79 C4
BearSpring 15 B5
Beasley 54 C1
Beaton 87 C6
Beaty Branch 28 B2
Beaty Creek 15 B4
Beaty Lake 69 C4
Beaty 15 A4
Beauchamp Creek 88 B3
Beauchamp 72 B3
Beau-O-Rama 16 D2
Beautiful Lake 53 D6
Beaver Bayou Ditch 94 A3
Beaver Bayou 67 D4
Beaver Brake 104 A1
Beaver Creek 33 C5; 48 D3; 86 C2; 99 C6; 100 C3; A4; 122 C1
Beaver Dam Lake 93 A6
Beaver Dam Slough 92 C2
Beaver Fork Lake 62 B1
Beaver Fork 62 C2
Beaver Lake 16 B3; 29 A5; 69 D5; 126 A3
Beaver Pond Creek 101 D6
Beaver Pond Mountain 77 B4
Beaver Pond 123 A4
Beaver Shores 16 C2
Beaver Slough 99 C6; 103 D5
Beaver 17 A5
Beaverdam Bayou 91 A4
Beaverdam Creek 62 D1
Beaverdam Slough 89 D6
Beck Bayou 71 d5
Beck Mountaint 86 A3
Beck 110 D2
Beck 71 d5
Beckette Mountain 62 A3
Beckham Creek 31 B5
Becks 68 D3
Becton 67 C5
Bed Creek 57 D6
Bee Basin 109 A6
Bee Bayou 94 D1,2; 109 A6
Bee Bluff 34 D2
Bee Bluff 45 D5
Bee Branch 34 A2; 48 C2; 99 C5
Bee Branch 48 C1
Bee Creek 17 A5; 23 C6
Bee Knob 74 B2
Bee Mountain 57 D6; 58 A1; 85 A4
Bee Ridge 45 A5
Bee Rock 44 A1
Bee Rock 66 A1
Bee Suck Creek 74 B3
Bee Suck Mountain 74 A3
Bee Tree Slough 51 C5; 53 D5
Beebe 63 C6
Beech Branch 100 C2
Beech Creek Crossing 124 A2
Beech Creek 111 D5
Beech Creek 31 A6;B5;C4; 86 A1; 97 A6; 100 C2;D2; 101 B5; 102 A1;C1; 110 D1; 111 D5; 112 C2;D3; 114 A1;C3;D3; B4;C4; 119 A4; 120 A2; 121 A6;B4,5; 122 C1; 124 A2,3; 125 B5;C5
Beech Fork 49 A4,5
Beech Grove 102 D1
Beech Grove 26 D1
Beech Hurricane Creek 30 D3
Beechwood 31 B5
Beedeville 51 D6
BeeLake 119 B4
Beene Creek 121 D5
Begley Creek 33 C6
Beirne 99 C6
Belcher Lake 80 D2
Belcher 66 C2
BelcoeLake 105 B5
Belden Spring 19 B5
Belfast 90 B1
Belk Corner 61 C6
Bell Bluff 98 B3
Bell Branch 77 A4; 80 A3; 109 A5
Bell City 27 C6
Bell Creek 25 C5; 87 D6
Bell Gully 93 D5; 105 A5
Bell Hill 36 C2; 63 D6
Bell Island 127 A4
Bell Lake Brake 37 D5
Bell Lake 37 D5
Bell Mountain 28 B1
Bella Vista Lake 16 B1
Bella Vista Village 16 A1
Bella Vista 16 B1
Bellah Creek 84 D3
Bellah Hills 24 A3
Bellaire 117 C4
Bellaire 98 C1
Belle Mead 83 A6
Bellefonte 19 D5
Belleville Ridge 59 C5
Belleville 59 C4
Bellhammer Slough 54 D2
Bellknap Lake 93 B6
Bells Bayou 105 A4
Bells Chapel 60 B2
Bellville Creek 97 B4
Bellville 19 A5
Bellville 97 B4
Belly Creek 99 A6
Belton 98 B2
Belview 35 A5
Bemis 68 B1
Ben Branch 32 B3
Ben Cove 59 A4
Ben Davis Lake 113 D5
Ben Hill 32 B3
Ben Hur 46 A2
Ben Lomond 97 D5
Ben West Mountain 35 B5
Ben 49 A5
Bench Creek 37 A5
Bend Hill 44 A1
Bend Lake 123 B6
Bend 45 D5
Ben-Gay 36 B3
Bengel 51 C5
Benjamin Lake 123 A5
Bennett Branch 51 B4
Bennett Lake 62 A2
Bennetts Bayou 21 A6
Bennetts River 21 B6; 22 A2;B1
Bens Branch 32 B2
Bens Creek 23 D4
Benson Lake 92 C2
Benson Slash Creek 67 D5
Benton 77 D6
Bentonville 16 B1
Benwood Lake 70 A1
Benzal 105 B6
Berea 116 D1
Berg Lake 112 B3
Bergen Lake 51 A5
Berger 78 C2
Bergman 19 C5
Bergren Cave 34 A3
Berkley Bluff 51 A4
Berks Branch 114 A1
Berlin 125 C4
Bernice 60 A1
Berry Branch 30 A2; 49 B6
Berry Creek 115 B4
Berry Gap 62 C2
Berryville 17 B6
Bert Creek 121 B6
Bertha 46 A1
Bertig 40 A1
Beryl 62 C2
Bethany 97 A5
Bethel Branch 85 C5
Bethel Chapel 84 B3
Bethel Creek 121 A6
Bethel Heights 16 D2
Bethel 39 B5
Bethel 59 B6
Bethel 99 B6
Bethel 103 D5
Bethel 111 D5
Bethesda 35 D6
Bethlehem Spring 100 A3
Bethlehem 61 A6
Betsy Gill Creek 35 D6
Bettis Creek 49 D4
Beulah Island (Island No 74) 106 D1
Beulah 115 C6
Beulah 81 A4
Beurknob Mountain 58 D2
Beverly 43 D5
Bevis Corners 79 C5
Bexar 22 C2
Bice Bend 33 A6
Biddle 78 C2
Bidville 29 D6
Biene Creek 66 D3
Big Baptize Lake 81 C5
Big Barn Creek 24 B1
Big Bayou Canal 117 B4
Big Bayou Slough 117 B4
Big Bayou 117 C4;D4; 126 A1;B1
Big Bear Cave 32 B1
Big Bear Lake 69 B4
Big Bell Lake 67 B4
Big Bench 32 C3
Big Bluff 31 A5
Big Bottom Slough 50 A3
Big Branch 42 A3; 48 A2; 62 B2; 75 C5; 76 B3; 77 A4; 99 A4; 111 D4
Big Brushy Creek 74 C1; 75 A6; 90 B2; 124 B1,2
Big Brushy Lake 81 B4
Big Buck Lake 67 D4
Big Cane Creek 26 A3
Big Cedar Creek 74 B1,2;D2; 86 A2
Big Clifty Creek 17 C4
Big Corney Creek 121 B5
Big Cornie Bayou 121 C6
Big Cornie Creek 121 A4;B5
Big Cove Creek 76 A1
Big Creek Corner 82 C2
Big Creek Narrows 57 B4
Big Creek Site 15 Reservoir 39 B4
Big Creek 21 C5;D5; 22 B1;B2; 23 A6; 25 B5; 26 C2,3; 27 B4; 32 B2;C2;D1; 33 B6; 34 A1;B1; 39 B4; 43 D4; 49 A-D6;D5; 50 A3;C1;D1; 53 B4; 54 D1; 57 A5;B5; 59 D5; 60 C2; 66 D3; 68 C1;D1; 72 B2;C3; 74 C3; 77 D5; 80 A2; 81 D4; 82 A1;B1;C2;D2,3; 89 B5;C5; 90 B1;C2;D3; 93 B5;D6; 94 A2,3;B1,2;C1; 103 A-C4; 111 C6;D6; 120 A3;B2,3
Big Cypress Creek 37 A5; 82 C3;D1; A1
Big Cypress Swamp 39 B6
Big Devils Fork 32 D2
Big Dickinson Lake 78 C2
Big Dixon Lake 113 A4
Big Eagle Lake 81 D5
Big Eddy 69 C4
Big Elam Lake 67 B6
Big Flat 34 B1
Big Foot Branch 44 A1
Big Fork Creek 85 A6; 73 D6; 85 A6
Big Fork 85 A6
Big Grassy Brake 92 D2
Big Gravel Slough 66 B3
Big Green Tom Lake 67 A4
Big Greenbrier Hill 66 C2
Big Gum Lateral 26 D1
Big Hill Creek 73 D6; 86 A1
Big Hill 114 A1
Big Horseshoe Brake 113 D6
Big Horseshoe Lake 51 C5; 94 C1
Big Hunting Slough 26 A3
Big Hurricane Creek 35 A5
Big Hurricane Lake 67 A4
Big Island Chute 93 C6; 94 C1
Big Island 39 C6; 40 A1;C3; 94 C1; 105 C6; 106 C1
Big Johnson Lake 113 C5
Big Lake 40 C3
Big Lake 40 C3; 53 D6; 69 D5; 70 B1; 78 D3
Big Lick Hill 24 D2
Big Middle Ridge 32 C2
Big Mingo Creek 50 D3; 66 A3;B3
Big Music Creek 20 B1
Big Onion Creek 30 A3
Big Piney Creek 31 D5,6; 45 B6;D5,6; 46 B1;C1; 59 C4; 81 B6; 82 B1
Big Point 32 D3
Big Pond 80 A1
Big Rabbit Bayou 69 C6;D6
Big Ridge 77 C6
Big Robe Bayou 81 A5
Big Rock Hill 78 A3
Big Rock 56 B3
Big Round Lake 105 A6
Big Round Top Mountain 74 C3
Big Running Water Creek 25 D5; 37 B6;C6; 38 A1
Big Sandy Bayou 94 D2
Big Sandy Mountain 30 A3
Big Sawyer Creek 45 B6
Big Shoal Creek 59 B4
Big Slash 67 B6; 81 C6;D6
Big Slough Ditch 27 B5;D5
Big Slough 115 B5; 97 D5
Big Spring Branch 23 D6
Big Spring Mill 36 D1
Big Spring 15 C5; 18 D2; 28 C3
Big Springs 34 C2
Big Springs 34 C2
Big Taylor Lake 26 B2
Big Telico Creek 68 C3
Big Tom Mountain 85 B6
Big Twin Lake 67 D4; 81 B4; 81 B4; 83 A4
Big Weidmann Lake 81 C4
Big White Lake 93 C6; 94 C1
Big York Lake 67 C6
Bigelow 61 D5
Biggers Hill Cave 23 C6
Biggers 25 B6
Bigsby Creek 86 C3; 87 C4
Bilbo Lake 123 A5
Bill Hill Peak 32 C2
Bill Hill 50 A2
Bill Hunt Mountain 73 A6
Bill Young Bayou 126 A1
Billcol Mountain 56 B3
Billingsleys Corner 96 C2
Billottis Slough 125 C5
Bills Bayou 69 C5; 105 A4
Billstown 98 B3
Billy Goat Hill 62 D3
Billy Hall Bend 108 B1
Biltmore Siding 35 C6
Bingen 98 B1
Bingham 78 D2
Birch Pond 66 A2
Birchfield Creek 112 D2
Birchfield Mountain 42 B2
Bird Creek 36 A2
Bird Point 37 D5
Birdell 25 C4
Birdeye 53 D4
Birdsong Mountain 21 C5
Birdsong 54 C2
Birdtown 61 A6
Birmac 92 D2
Birmingham Gap 62 C3
Birta 60 D1
Biscoe 81 B4
Bishop Branch 24 B2
Bishop Creek 97 A6
Bismarck 88 C1
Black Bayou 91 A5;C5
Black Bois D'Arc Creek 98 D2
Black Branch 88 C3; 100 B1,2; 101 A4; 108 A2; 110 B3; 112 B1; 121 C5
Black Creek 66 B2; 99 C5; 111 B6
Black Diamond 118 C3
Black Fish Bayou 70 D1
Black Fork Fourche La Fave River 73 B4
Black Fork L'Anguille River 52 D2
Black Fork Mountain 72 C2
Black Fork Poteau River 72 B2,3
Black Fork 62 A2;B2
Black Fork 72 B2
Black Island 51 A5
Black Jack Mountain 63 B5
Black Jack Ridge 57 C4
Black Lake 80 A3; 105 B6; 113 C6
Black Mountain 44 A1; 47 B5
Black Oak Ridge 46 B1
Black Oak 29 B5
Black Oak 40 C1
Black Oak 53 C6
Black Pond Slough 117 B4;C4
Black River 25 C5,6;D4; 26 A3;B2;C1; 37 A6;B6; 37 D5; 51 A4
Black Rock 38 A1
Black Slough 101 C5
Black Springs 86 A2
Black Ward Ridge 48 C1
Blackburn Creek 16 C3; 29 D4; 42 A3
Blackburn 29 D4
Blackfish Bayou 69 A-C6;D5; 83 A5
Blackfish Lake 69 B6
Blackfish 69 C5
Blackfoot 82 D3
Blackjack Corner 16 A1
Blackjack Knob 33 B6
Blackland Branch 99 B4
Blacks Branch 97 D5
Blacks Lake 62 C2
Blackton 81 C6
Blackville 51 C6
Blackwater Creek 113 C5
Blackwater Lakes 113 C5
Blackwell 61 B4
Blagg Cave 36 A3
Blagg Ridge 74 B2
Blair Creek 28 C3
Blakely Creek 88 B2,3
Blakely Mountain 76 D1
Blakely 76 C2
Blakemore 79 D6
Blakes Branch 24 D1
Blakey Branch 49 D4
Blakey Creek 103 D4,5
Blanchard Creek 122 D2
Blanchard Spring 34 B3
Blanchard Springs 122 C3
Blanchton 124 A1
Blanco 33 C4
Bland 16 B3
Bland 77 C5
Blaney Hill 62 C1
Blann Creek 114 C1
Blansett 73 B4
Blanton 70 B3
Blatz Lake 25 C5
Blaylock Creek 85 B6
Blaylock Knob 32 C3
Blaylock Mountain 85 B6
Bledsoe 83 A5
Blendsoe Bend 83 B5
Blevens Hollow 18 B3
Blevins 98 C3
Blick 47 D5
Bliss Mountain 48 A3
Blocher 76 C3
Block Bend 69 A4
Blockade Hill 51 D5
Blocker Creek 75 C6; 86 B1;C1; 98 A3
Bloomer 57 A4
Bloomfield 15 C4
Blossom 82 A1
Blowing Cave 33 B5; 36 C1; 50 A1
Blowing Spring 19 B6
Blowing Springs 16 A1
Blowout Mountain 74 C2; 76 D2; 84 A3
Bloyd Mountain 29 C4
Blue Ball 58 D2
Blue Bayou 97 B6
Blue Bayou 97 B6;C6; 126 A3
Blue Branch 48 D3; 63 D4; 121 C6
Blue Cane Island 27 D5
Blue Creek 36 D2; 36 D2; 51 C4; 86 D1; 87 A5; 90 A1; 96 B3
Blue Eye 18 A2
Blue Hill 63 A4; 78 A2
Blue Hill 78 A2
Blue Hole Branch 50 A1
Blue Hole Creek 99 A6
Blue Hole 36 A3; 46 C3; 81 A4; 105 B4; 119 C4
Blue John Creek 20 D3
Blue Lake Slough 67 D4
Blue Lake 67 C4;D6; 80 B3; 83 A4
Blue Lake 70 D1; 113 B4; 123 B6
Blue Mountain Knob 34 C2
Blue Mountain Lake 58 C2
Blue Mountain 33 C6; 35 D5; 73 C5
Blue Mountain 58 B2
Blue Ouachita Mountain 75 B6;C6
Blue Point Ditch 80 C1
Blue Ridge 36 C1
Blue Spring 17 A4; 18 A1; 36 D1
Blue Springs Village 16 D3
Blue Springs 114 B2
Blue Springs 76 C1
Bluebaugh Hill 45 D5
Blueberry Hill 57 D5
BluePoint 60 C3
Bluff Branch 86 B1
Bluff City 112 A1
Bluff Creek 85 D5; 97 A5; 98 A1
Bluff Lake 110 B1
Bluff Mountain 63 A4
Bluffton 74 A3
Blythe Branch 76 A1
Blythe Ridge 57 B5
Blytheville 41 C5
Boar Tusk Mountain 85 A4
Board Camp Creek 85 A4,5
Board Camp 73 D5
Boardtree Branch 77 C5
Boat Creek 21 D4
Boat Gunwale Slash 81 C6;D6
Boat Mountain 32 A2
Boat Ridge Island 48 B2
Boat Run 53 C5
Boatright Creek 31 A4
Bob Barnes Branch 59 B4
Bob Bates Fork 46 C1
Bob Neal Branch 60 D3
Bob Williams Lake 81 A4
Bobo Creek 18 C2
Bobs Blue Hole 107 A4; 117 A6
Bobtail Creek 32 D3
Bobtail Lake 105 C6
Bodcau Branch 111 C4
Bodcau Creek 111 B-D4; 119 A6; 120 A1
Bodcaw 111 B5
Boen Gulf Branch 31 C5
Boeuf Brake 123 B6
Boeuf River 126 A1;B1;D1
Boeuf 126 B1
Bog Springs 84 C2
Boggins Branch 105 A4
Boggy Bayou 70 D1; 91 D4; 117 A5
Boggy Creek 73 D5; 99 C6; 118 A3; 119 A4; 122 B3
Boggy Slough 92 C1; 96 D3
Boggy 119 B4
Bohannan Mountain 30 A1; 33 D5
Bohannon 33 D4
BoilingSprings 100 C1
Bois D'Arc Bayou 109 B6;C6; 110 C1
Bois D'Arc Creek 110 A-C2
Bois D'Arc Lake 110 B2
Bolan Creek 73 D6
Bolding 123 C6
Boles 73 B5
Bolin Slough 100 D2
Bolivar Creek 53 B4
Bonair 68 D3
Bonanza 56 A2
Bondsville 54 A2
Bone Hill 49 A6
Bone Town 36 A1
Bonnerdale 87 B5
Bono 38 C3
Bono 62 A1
Booker 70 A1
Booker 78 B3
Boone Branch 63 C4
Boone Mountain 30 D1
Boone 19 A5
Booneville Lake 57 B5
Booneville Mountain 57 B6
Booneville 57 B6
Booster 33 D5
Boot Creek 77 C5
Booth Creek 24 C1
Boothe 57 C5
Bordeaux Island 83 B6
Boss Island Creek 88 A3
Boston Creek 73 B6
Boston Mountains 31 D5
Boston 30 C3
Boswell Lake 99 A6
Boswell 35 A4
Boswell 99 A6
Bothersome Creek 35 D5
Botkinburg 47 A6
Bott Spur 68 B3
Boughton 99 C5
Boulder Mountain 35 B4
Boundary Mountain 47 C5
Bovine 124 B3
Bowen Creek 44 A3
Bowen 99 B4
Bowery Hill 34 D3
Bowles Gap 43 A6
Bowles Mountain 43 A6
Bowman Hollow 45 A6
Bowman Hill 24 C1
Bowman 117 C5
Bowman 39 D6
Box Elder 40 B2
Box Factory Bend 38 A1
Box Spring Branch 59 B5
Box Spring 15 D4
Box Springs 120 A2
Boxley 31 B5
Boyce Creek 47 A6
Boyce Hill 50 D3
Boyce Lake 109 D6
Boyd Branch 115 A5
Boyd Creek 101 B6; 102 B1; 103 C6; 104 D1
Boyd Hill 110 C2
Boyd Hill 110 C2
Boyd Mountain 30 A1; 43 B6; 61 A4
Boyd Point Cutoff 91 C5
Boyd 109 D6
Boydell 116 D3
BoydPoint 91 C5
Boydsville 27 B4
Boyer Ridge 49 A4
Boynton 40 B2
Bracy Mountain 36 D1
Bradberry Hill 63 B5
Braden Mountain 32 A1
Bradenberg 35 B4
Bradford Knob 42 A3
Bradford 50 D3
Bradley Bayou 93 D6
Bradley Branch 31 A5; 47 B6; 90 A3
Bradley Creek 24 C3; 46 C3
Bradley Gap 84 B3
Bradley Lake 119 A5
Bradley Slough 91 B6
Bradley 119 C5
Bradshaw Creek 99 A6
Bradshaw Mountain 31 A4
Bradshaw Narrows 57 B5
Brady Mountain980 ft 75 D6
Bragg City 112 A2
Bragg Lake 112 A2
Bragg Mill Creek 112 A2,3
Brakebill 25 A5
Branch 57 A6
Branchville 103 C6
Brandenburg Mountain 35 B4
Brandon 115 A5
Brandywine Chute 54 D3
Brandywine Island 54 D3
Brannon Mountain 29 C6
Brannon 29 D6
Branscum Spring 34 A3
Brantley Mountain 74 B3
Brantley Ranch Creek 74 B3
Brasel Creek 31 B6; 32 B1
Brasfield 81 A4
Brashears 30 D1
Braswell Br 18 B1
Braswell Spring 18 B1
Bratton Creek 33 B6
Brawley 72 A3
Bray Branch 22 C2
Bray Hill 36 B3
Bray Spring 58 B2
Bread Creek 76 B2
Bread CreekPinnacle 76 B2
Bredlow Corner 79 D4
Breedlove Lake 108 A1
Brentwood 29 C5
Brewer Branch 78 D2
Brewer Hill 36 D2
Brewer Lake 51 B6; 61 A6
Brewer Spring 34 B2
Brewer 48 A3
Brian Creek 35 D6
Briar Branch 44 A2
Briar Creek 21 A5; 25 B6; 58 B2; 98 A1
Briar Plant Lake Two 98 A1
Briar Ridge 93 D6
Briar 98 A1
Briarcliff 21 C5
Briark 70 B3
Brice 70 C1
Brickey Hollow 47 B6
Brickeys 83 A5
Brickyard Creek 86 D1
Bridal Veil Falls 49 C4
Bridewells Lake 110 B3
Bridge Creek 62 D2; 78 A3; 96 B3; 97 C4; 98 D1; 39 C4; 103 D4; 110 A1,2; 112 C3;D3; 120 B2; 122 C2
Bridge Junction 70 B3
Bridges Bluff 102 C3
Brier Branch 49 D4
Brier Creek Mountains 85 B6
Brier Creek 49 A6;D6; 50 D1; 85 B6
Brier Lick Branch 78 D1
Briery Creek 72 B2
Briggsville 75 A4
Bright Lake 51 C4
Bright Star 97 D6
Bright 111 D5
Brighton 40 A1
Brightstar 118 C3
Brightwater 16 B2
Brindley Creek 61 A6
Bringle Creek 77 A5
Brinkley Lake 81 A6
Brinkley 81 A6
Briscoe Branch 58 D2
Brister 121 B4
Brittain 78 C2
Britton Hill 23 B6
Broad 124 A1
Brock Creek Lake 47 C4
Brock Creek 47 C4
Brock Mountain 50 A1
Brockett 25 B5
Brockington Corner 62 D2
Brockwell 22 D2
Brodie Creek 78 C1
Brogan Creek 75 A5
Brogden Hollow 46 A3
Broken Rock Mountain 75 D5
Brookings 26 C1
Brookland 39 C5
Brooks Bayou 93 D6
Brooks Branch 79 A6; 80 A1
Brooks Creek 101 B6; 115 B4
Brooks Gap 86 C2
Brooks Hill 36 C1
Brooks Mountain 86 B2
Brooks 78 D1
Broom Lake 67 B6
Broomfield 46 C2
Brother Reservoir 80 D3
Brougham Lake 69 A6
Brown Bayou 55 A4
Brown Cave 20 C1
Brown Creek 35 B6; 76 A3; 77 A4; 115 C6; 116 C1
Brown Lake 25 D4
Brown Mountain 29 C6; 45 B6; 46 A3
Brown Spring 23 A6; 58 B3
Brown Springs Branch 88 D3
Brown Springs 88 D3
Brown's Creek 101 B5
Browning Creek 103 C5
Brownings Branch 66 D2
Browns Bend 83 C4
Browns Branch 66 D1; 80 A1
Browns Creek 24 C2; 59 D5
Browns Lake 118 A2
Browns Shanty Lake 93 A6
Browns 70 C1
Brownstown 97 D5
Brownsville Branch 79 B6
Brownsville 49 B4
Brownsville 57 B6
Brownsville 79 B6
Bruce Creek 20 B3; 21 B4
Bruce Mountain 73 B5
Bruins 71 d5
Brumett 80 D2
Brumley 62 C1
Bruno 20 D1
Brush Creek 15 D6; 16 D1;D3; 17 A6
Brush Creek 19 D5; 23 B6; 29 A6; 30 A1; 33 B5;C5; 34 A1; 48 A3; 49 D4; 63 D6; 74 A1; 75 A6;B6; 89 D5
Brush Creek 89 D5
Brush Heap Mountain 85 B6
Brush Lake 37 D4
Brush Mountain 77 B5
Brushey Lake 52 C2
Brushy Branch 24 B2; 36 C1; 114 A2; 120 C3; 121 B4
Brushy Cr Mountain 74 C1
Brushy Creek 19 A4; 22 D1; 24 D3; 52 D2; 57 C6;D4; 68 A2; 74 C1; 76 C2; 77 B5; 85 B4;D6; 87 D6; 88 D3; 89 A5;B5; 90 A1;B2; 97 B5; 98 C1,2; 99 A5;C4; 100 A2;C1,3; 101 B4;C4; 103 B4; 111 B6;C5; 113 A5;D4
Brushy Fork 20 C2; 47 B4
Brushy Hollow Creek 76 A2
Brushy Island 78 B3
Brushy Knob 73 C6
Brushy L' Aigle Creek 115 B4; 114 C3
Brushy Lake 67 A4;B5;C6; 69 D4; 81 C5; 83 D5; 93 A5,6; 104 A2; 109 B5
Brushy Lakebed 106 A1
Brushy Mountain 33 C6; 44 A2; 58 A1; 73 A4;B6; 74 C3; 75 B4; 76 B1; 77 B4; 86 C2
Brushy Point 33 C5
Brushy Ridge 35 A5;45 A4
Bruton Ridge 73 B5
Bryan Mountain 33 C4
Bryant Creek 101 B6; 102 B1
Bryant Woodland Heights 36 D2
Bryant 36 D2
Bryant 77 D6
Bryant 78 D1
Bryanville 82 A2
Bubbling Slough 92 C1
Bubbling Spring 24 C1
Buchanan Creek 24 D3; 75 A5
Buck Branch 32 D1; 48 D3; 86 C1; 89 C5; 125 A4
Buck Creek 80 B1; 47 D6; 80 A2;B1; 86 D1; 87 D6; 97 A4; 98 A1
Buck Island 35 B4
Buck IslandNo 53 71 D5
Buck Knob 57 D6; 73 C6
Buck Knob 73 C6
Buck Lake 69 B6; 93 B6; 123 B6
Buck Mountain 46 D2; 86 B2
Buck Point 32 A1;33 B4
Buck Range 98 C1
Buck Ridge 23 D6; 58 D1; 61 A6; 74 B2
Buck Snort 39 C4
Buckalew Hill 35 B6
Buckaloo Creek 122 C2
Bucker Gap 34 A1
Buckeye Mountain 46 C3; 85 B5
Buckeye 29 A6
Buckeye 40 B2
Buckhead Creek 114 C3
Buckhorn Slough 124 D1; 123 D6
Buckhorn 82 C1
Buckingham Flat 92 D2
Buckley Lake 67 A4
Buckley Spring 19 B5
Buckman Lake 59 C4
Buckner 111 D4
Bucksnort 102 C1
Bud Brown Hill 48 A2
Budd Creek 49 B4
Budd Creek 49 B4
Budd Kidd Creek 28 B3
Budd Kidd Lake 28 B2
Buell 56 A2
Buena Vista 112 C3
Buffalo City 21 D4
Buffalo Creek 31 C5; 50 A1; 67 B6;C5; 73 B5; 84 B2; 99 B4
Buffalo Gap 76 B1
Buffalo Head Slough 38 B3
Buffalo Hump 48 A2;D3
Buffalo Mountain 73 B5
Buffalo River 31 A6;B5;C5; 32 A1;B2; 32 B3; 34 A1
Buffalo Slough 92 A2
Buford Station 21 D4
Buford 21 C4
Bufram Creek 72 C2
Buie 89 B6
Bull Bayou 76 D1; 88 A1
Bull Bottom Bluff 20 A1
Bull Branch 111 A4; 109 B4
Bull Creek Hill 63 B4
Bull Creek 44 A3; 62 C3; 63 B4,5;C4,5,6; 66 C1; 73 A4
Bull Lake 60 D3; 81 A4
Bull Mountain 61 A5; 63 B4; 100 C2
Bull Shoals Lake 19 A6; 20 A1;B3
Bull Shoals Mountain 20 B2
Bull Shoals 20 B3
Bull Spring 18 C2
Bullard Mountain 77 B6
Bullerton Towhead 55 A4
Bullfrog Valley 45 C6
Bullneck Brake 79 C4
Bullock Branch 50 C3
Bullpen Creek 22 C3
Bulltown 67 B6
Bunce Gap 44 A1
Bunker Hill 26 A3; 59 A6;C5
Bunker Hill 61 C5
Bunn 102 B1
Bunney 54 A1
Bunyard (Banyard) 29 D4
Burchette Spring 29 B6
Burdell Branch 111 B5
Burdette 41 D4
Burg 85 C5
Burgiss Knob 46 A1
Burke Creek 97 A4;B4
Burks 93 C4
BurksPond 113 A4
Burlesons Pond 80 A1
Burlington 18 B3
Burna 56 C3
Burnett Cove 60 A3
Burnett Creek 47 B4
Burnett Spring 58 B3
Burns Creek 37 D5
Burns Hill 23 D4
Burns Lower Bend 37 C6
Burns Pond 121 B6; 122 B1
Burnt Bayou 81 B4
Burnt Cane Crossing 69 D5
Burnt Cane 69 D4
Burnt Cypress Lake 93 A5
Burnt Hill 39 C6
Burnt Lake 93 D6
Burnt Mill Bluff 69 C4
Burnville 57 B4
Buroak 33 C4
Burrell Mountain 30 D1
Burrell Spring 44 B1
Burris Branch 79 A5;B5
Burt Creek 45 C4
Burton Bluff 45 D5
Burton Creek 27 B4
Burton Hill 35 C5
Burton Mill 119 B6
Burton Point 35 D6
Burton 41 C5
Burtsell 99 B6
Busch 17 A4
Bush Brake 37 D5
Bush Creek 16 B1; 28 C2
Bushart Mountain 29 B6
Bushy Creek 98 A1
Bushy Lake 69 C4; 71 D5; 110 B2
Bussell Branch 23 A5
Bussey 120 B1
Busted Mountain 46 D3
Butcherknife Creek 85 A6
Butler Branch 101 A4
Butler Creek 15 A4; D5; 17 A4; 47 B6
Butler Hollow 49 A4
Butler 55 B4
Butlers Knob 57 A4
Butlerville 63 D6
Butterfield 89 B4
Buttermilk Springs 86 B3
Buttermilk 46 D3
Butts Hollow 44 A2
Buzzard Bluff 19 A6; 20 A2; 31 A6; 58 A1; 110 C1
Buzzard Cave 37 C4
Buzzard Lake 67 D6
Buzzard Mountain 77 B6
Buzzard Roost Mountain 34 C1; 50 D3
Buzzard Roost 35 A4
Buzzards Rock 59 A4
Byran 57 D4
Byrd Lakes 38 A2
Byron 22 C2

C

Cabanal 18 C1
Cabin Creek 20 D3; 24 C1; 45 C5
Cabot 63 D5
Cache Bayou 67 B4;C4
Cache Fork 36 C3
Cache Lake 26 C2
Cache River Main Canal 26 D1
Cache River 25 D6; 38 A3;C2;D1; 51 B6;D6; 52 A1;B1; 67 A-C5;D4; 81 A4;B5
Caddo Gap 86 B3
Caddo Gap 86 B3
Caddo Mountains 86 B2
Caddo River 86 A1,2;B3; 87 C4,5; 88 D2
Caddo Valley 88 D2
Cades 104 B2
Cadron Creek 48 D3; 49 C4;D4; 61 A6;B6; 62 A1
Cadron Gap 62 C1
Cadron Ridge 61 C6; 62 C1,2
Cadron Valley 62 B2
Cages Lake 113 D5
Cagle Spring 114 B2
Cagles Eddy 80 A3
Caglesville 46 D2
Cagnes Creek 35 C5
Cahill Bend 53 B6
Cain Lake 71 D5; 83 A6
Cain 43 B4
Cairo 121 B6
Calamine 37 B4
Caldron Creek 48 D2
Caldwell Mountain 36 D3
Caldwell 68 C3
Cale 111 B6
Caledonia 122 C2
Caley Hill 48 D2
Calf Creek 33 B-D4
Calfneck Bend 61 D4
Calftail Cut 31 A5
Calhoun Junction 121 A4
Calhoun 104 C1
Calhoun 121 B4
Calico Bluff 35 A4
Calico Creek 22 D1; 58 A2
Calico Mountain 58 A2
California Branch 114 C3
California Point 31 A5
Calion Lake 122 A3
Calion 122 A3
Call Creek 86 A1
Callagahan Creek 78 C1
Callahan Gap 58 D3
Callahan Knob 58 D3
Callahan Mountain 16 D1
Callens Br 18 B2
Callie Lake 105 D6
Calmer 103 B4
Calumet 41 B4
Calvin 38 B1
CalvinCr 72 D2
Camark 113 B4
Camden 113 B4
Cameron Creek 24 B3
Cammack Village 78 B2
Camp Bayou Canal 125 D6
Camp Bayou 125 C6
Camp Branch 49 D6
Camp Creek 23 B4; 25 B4; 84 B3; 85 D5; 87 D4; 88 D3; 89 D4; 90 C2; 102 C2; 111 B4; 113 D4; 114 B3; 121 A6; 122 A1
Camp Ground Creek 20 D2
Camp Ground 39 A5
Camp Lake 117 D6
Camp 23 B4
Campbell Bayou 90 A3
Campbell Brake 104 C1
Campbell Creek 32 C1
Campbell Hollow 72 A2
Campbell Ridge 20 B1
Campbell Station 51 A5
Campbell 34 C1
CampbellPoint 19 A6
Campbells Brake 104 D2
Campground Branch 93 D5
Campground Creek 101 B5
Canaan 33 C5
Canaan 82 A3
Canada Creek 102 B2
Canadian Reach 41 D6
Canady Branch 47 D4
Canale 119 C4
Candler Lake 119 A5
Candlestick Creek 49 D5
Candlestick Knob 35 B4
Candy Creek 82 A3

Cane Bottom Bluff 20 A2
Cane Branch Hills 32 B3
Cane Branch 32 B3
Cane Creek Lake 104 B1
Cane Creek 20 C2; 44 D3; 45 D4; 63 B6; 66 C1; 69 B4; 72 A2; 74 A3; 78 D3; 84 D2; 90 A2;B2; 96 A2; 103 A4;B6
Cane Creek 90 A2
Cane Hill 123 A5
Cane Island Slough 59 C6
Cane Island 20 B3; 39 C6; 59 C6
Cane Lake 69 A6
Canehill 28 C2
Caney Bayou 90 B3; 91 C4; 93 C5; 105 A5; 123 A4;B5,6; 126 B2;C2;D1
Caney Branch 114 D3; 116 A2
Caney Cave 33 A5
Caney Creek 36 A1; 37 C4,5; 49 A6; 50 A1,2; 52 D2; 57 A6; 58 A1; 61 B6;D5; 62 B3; 63 A4;B4; 67 A4;C6;D6; 68 B3;C1; 74 A3; 75 B6;D5; 77 B6;C5; 79 C6;D6; 82 C3; 83 D5; 84 B3; 85 A6;B5;D5; 86 B3;D3; 87 B-D4; 88 C2;D1; 89 A4; 90 D2; 96 C2; 97 A5; 98 C1,2;D3; 99 D6; 100 B1;C2;D1; 102 D1; 104 C2; 110 A3; 111 B6;C6; 112 A1; 113 B5,6; 114 A3;B2; 116 D2; 118 A3;B3; 121 C6; 125 A5
Caney Hollow 33 A6
Caney Lake 57 A6; 58 A1; 108 A1
Caney Marais Bend 123 B6
Caney Slash 81 A6
Caney Slough 37 C5; 39 A4
Caney Valley 87 C4
Caney 33 A5
Caney 62 C1
Caney 88 C1
CaneyPoint 93 D6
Canfield 119 B6
Cannon Creek 29 C6
Cannon Creek 29 C6; 123 B5
Canoe Creek 49 B5
Cantley Branch 111 A6
Cany Creek 122 B3
Cap Fork 34 B2
Capitol Hill1160 ft 21 B4
Caple Creek 90 A1
Capps Branch 118 D3
Capps 19 C4
Caraway 40 D1
Carbon City 58 A1
Carden Bottom 60 B2
Carden Bottoms 60 B2
Carden Creek 60 D1
Cardiff 73 A6
Cardin Branch 62 B3
Carely Mountain 74 B3
Cargile Lake 61 A4
Cargile 122 B2
Carlisle 80 B1
Carlock Mountain 30 A2
Carlton Creek 96 D2
Carmel 115 B4
Carmi 40 C2
Carmichael Creek 115 B4
Carmichael Gap 62 C3
Carnes Creek 57 C4
Carney Creek 34 B2
Carnis 57 A4
Carolan 57 C6
Caroline Chute 126 D3
Caroline Gap 34 A2
Carpenter 115 D6
Carrion Crow Mountain 60 A3
Carroll Ridge 45 A4
Carroll Slough 124 B1
Carrolls Corner 54 A2
Carrollton Hollow 19 A5
Carrollton 18 C2
Carrolton Hollow Creek 19 A5
Carryville 27 B6
Carson Lake 55 B4
Carsons Slough 66 C1
Carter Bayou 105 C5
Carter Branch 37 C4
Carter Creek 37 D4; 51 A4; 59 D6; 73 D4; 85 A4
Carter Mountain 44 B2; 59 B5
Carter Point 25 C6
Carters Creek 84 D3
Carthage 101 A6
Cartney 21 D4
Cartwright Mountain 43 A4
Caruse Creek 99 D4
Carver Mill Creek 91 B4
Carver 32 B2
Carver 89 D5
Cary 53 A4
Cas Creek 77 D5
Casa Massa Creek 100 A3;B3
Casa 60 D2
Cascade Gap 62 C3
Cascade Mountain 62 B3
Case Creek 90 B3
Case 25 D6
Casey 67 C6
Cash Bend 33 B4
Cash Brake 92 A1
Cash 38 D2
Casper Branch 116 A2
Cass 44 A1
Cassatot River 85 B4;C4
Casscoe 93 A4
Cassidy 53 B6
Castle Ridge 74 A3
Castor Bayou 92 C1
Cat Creek 35 A4; 82 B2;C2
Cat Island No 50 70 D2; 71 D6
Cat Island Towhead 71 D6
Cat Island 105 D6
Catalpa Bayou 41 D4
Catalpa 45 A4
Cataract Creek 34 A3
Catcher 42 D3
Catesville 122 C2
Catfish Pond 111 A4
Catholic Point 47 D6
Cato Point 62 D2
Cato 78 A3
Catron 94 C2
Cattail Creek 37 D6
CattoSpring 25 A4
Caulk Island 107 A4,6
Caulk Neck 117 A6
Caulk Point 107 A4
Caulksville 58 A1
Cauthron 58 B1
Cauthron 72 A3
Cavanaugh 56 A2
Cave Branch 59 A6
Cave City 36 B3
Cave Creek 24 B1; 32 B3;C2; 36 D2; 77 B5; 85 D4
Cave Creek 32 C2
Cave Creek 36 C2
Cave Hill 24 D2
Cave Mountain Cave 31 B5
Cave Mountain 31 C4
Cave Point 35 C5
Cave Spring 33 C5; 35 B5; 36 C2
Cave Springs 16 C1
Cave Springs 16 C1
Cavell 67 A5
CC 79 C4
Cearley Creek 87 A6
Cecil Creek 31 A6
Cecil 43 C6
Cedar Bayou 110 C2
Cedar Bend 33 B5
Cedar Bluff 63 B5
Cedar Branch 49 C6;D6; 50 C1;D1; 60 D1; 62 A3
Cedar Cabin Mountain 74 C1
Cedar Creek 18 C1; 20 B2;D3; 21 A5;D4; 24 D3; 32 A2; 34 B1; 37 A4; 42 B2,3; 43 C6; 44 C2;D2; A5;D6; 46 A2;D3; 47 B5;D4; 49 A5; 57 D5; 58 C2,3; 59 C4; 60 B3;C2;D3; A6; 63 A4,5;B5; 72 A2;B2;D2; 73 C4;D5; 74 D2; 75 B5; 76 A2;C2,3; 88 A3; 109 C6
Cedar Creek 61 A6
Cedar Creek 74 B1
Cedar Falls 60 C3
Cedar Fourche Creek 75 C6
Cedar Grove 25 C5
Cedar Grove 37 C4
Cedar Grove 50 B1
Cedar Hill 48 A1
Cedar Hill 91 B4
Cedar Knob 56 A2
Cedar Mountain 35 D5; 47 C4; 72 D2; 76 D1
Cedar Piney Lake 59 C4
Cedar Ridge 62 D1
Cedar Scrappy 35 B4
Cedarville 42 B3
Centennial Bend 54 D3
Center Grove 90 C2
Center Hill 39 A5
Center Hill 63 A6
Center Point 44 C2
Center Point 63 C4
Center Point 72 D2
Center Point 80 A2
Center Point 97 B6
Center Point 100 B1
Center Point 110 C3
Center Ridge 47 D6
Center Ridge 49 C5
Center Valley 60 A1
Center 23 D6
Centerton 15 B6
Centerville 37 D5
Centerville 60 C1
Centerville 62 A2
Centerville 111 A4
Central City 56 A3
Central 100 A1
Central 68 A2
Central 88 C3
Central 96 C3
Cessions Towhead 106 A2
Chadwick Creek 62 D2
Chaffie Creek 112 C3
Chaffin Branch 120 B2
Chalk Bluff 27 A5
Chalybeate Creek 15 A4
Chalybeate Mountain 73 A4; 74 C3; 74 C2; 87 D5
Chalybeate Spring 75 C4
Chalybeate Springs 35 D5
Chalybeate Springs 58 D3
Chalybeate Spur 45 B5
Chalybeate Valley 87 D5
Chamberlain Creek 89 A4
Chambers Mountain 47 D5
Chambers Spring 28 A2
Chambersville 102 D1
Champagnolle Creek 101 D6; 113 C6;D6; 114 A1;B1
Champagnolle 122 A3
Chance Creek 103 C6
Chancel 32 D1
Chances Creek 73 D4
Chandler Creek 23 D5; 36 A3
Chandler 87 A6
Chaney Branch 49 D5
Chaney Creek 95 A4
Chaney Lake 94 C1
Channey Slough 81 B5
Chanticleer 126 A2
Chapel Creek 90 D1; 101 D4; 113 A4
Chapel Hill 36 C2
Chapel Hill 96 A2
Chapel Hill 98 B1
Chapelle Slough 113 D6
Chapman Spring 20 B1
Chapman 19 D5
Charivari Creek 114 D2; 123 A6
Charles Gap 62 C3
Charleston Lake 57 A5
Charleston 57 A5
Charley Creek 19 A4
Charlie Rollans Mountain 59 A5
Charlotte 37 D4
Charnnings Ferry 102 C3
Chase Reservoir 52 A3
Chasewood Landing 74 C2
Chastain Springs Branch 49 B5
Chatfield 70 D1
Chatman Creek 88 B3; 89 B4
Cheatam Lake 67 B6
Cheatham 96 A2
Cheatman Creek 19 B5
Cheek Lake 66 C1
Chelford 54 C2
Chemin-A-Haut Creek 125 A4-D4
Chenault Island 78 C3
Cherokee City 15 C4
Cherokee Creek 15 C4; 56 C3;D3
Cherokee Village 23 C6
Cherry Branch 60 D1
Cherry Creek 29 A6
Cherry Hill 60 D3
Cherry Hill 73 D6
Cherry Hollow Branch 23 B4
Cherry Knob 28 D3
Cherry Valley 52 D3
Chester 43 A4
Chick Creek 85 B6
Chickalah Creek 59 B5,6;C6
Chickalah Mountain 59 B4
Chickalah 59 B6
Chickasawba 41 C4
Chicken Bristle Mountain 29 B6
Chicken Creek 118 A3
Chicken Island 70 B3
Chicken Wilson Knob 33 D6
Chicot Bayou 117 A5;B5
Chicot Junction 126 B2
Chicot 126 B2
Chidester 112 A2
Chigger Creek 58 A1;B2
Childers 80 A3
Childress 40 B1
Chilson 52 A1
Chimes 47 A4
Chimney Rock Bluff 32 B1
Chimney Rock Mountain 30 D2
Chimney Rock 59 A6; 86 D2
Chimney Rocks 48 A2; 49 A6
Chinkapin Knob 42 A2
Chinkapin Ridge 47 A6; 49 D5
Chinn Spring 36 C2
Chinquapin Branch 99 A4
Chinquapin Creek 36 D1; 50 D2; 89 A5
Chinquapin Knob 32 C2; 46 A2
Chinquapin Mountain 76 A1; 77 A4
Chinquapin Ridge 44 B3
Chinquapin Spring 32 A3
Chismville 57 B6
Choate George Branch 59 C6
Choctaw Bar Island 117 B6
Choctaw Bayou 104 A2;B2;C3; 108 B2
Choctaw Creek 48 C1
Choctaw Island No 78 117 B6
Choctaw Lake 66 D3
Choctaw Pines 48 C2
Choctaw 48 C1
Chop Off Mountain 74 A2
Choppy Knob 48 A3
Chris Hill 36 C1
Christian Ridge 59 B6
Christies Branch 121 B4
Christmas Knob 57 A4
Christopher Mountain 86 A1
Chronister Store 45 C5
Chula Mountain 74 B3
Chula Ritter Creek 74 B3
Chula 74 B3
Churchill Ridge 49 C6
Cicalla 69 C5
Cincinnati Creek 28 A1;B1
Cincinnati 28 A1
Cisco 18 B1
City Park Lake 70 B2
City Rock Bluff 34 A3
Civil War Cave 15 B6
Clabber Creek 17 B6; 20 D2,3; 29 A4
Clantonville 16 A3
Clarendon 81 C5
Claret Branch 114 B3
Clark Bayou 78 C3;D3
Clark Branch 111 A6
Clark Corner Cutoff 69 C4
Clark Creek 31 B5; 74 B3; 80 A3; 101 A6
Clark Hill 19 C6; 35 C6; 36 C2
Clark Lake 109 C6
Clarkedale 70 A2
Clarkridge 21 A5
Clarks Corner 69 C5
Clarksville 45 C4
Claude 47 C6
Claunch 39 C6
Clay Bayou 117 C5
Clay Branch 63 A5
Clay Hill 83 A4
Clay 50 D1
Clayburn Point2142 ft 31 D5
Claypool Reservoir 52 B3
Clayton Branch 60 D3
Clayton Creek 37 A4
Clear Creek 16 D2; 17 C5;D4; 19 D6; 20 D1; 24 D3; 28 A3; 29 A4;D4; 32 A3; 43 A4; 44 A2;B2; 46 C3;D2,3; 57 D4; 58 B3; 60 A2; 62 A3; 63 A4; 74 D1; 76 D1; 78 D2,3; 84 A3; 89 C5; 90 A3; 96 B3;C3; 98 B3; 102 D1; 103 C5; 111 C5;D5; 115 B6;C5,6;; 121 C5
Clear Fork Fourche La Fave River 72 C3; 73 B4
Clear Lake 38 A1; 51 C5; 67 B4;C4; 81 D5; 90 C3; 91 A5; 105 D6; 109 C6; 110 C2; 124 D1
Clear Lake 41 C5
Clear Lake 90 C3
Clear LakeJunction 109 C6
Clear Point 16 C3
Clear Spring 37 A6
Clear Spring 99 A5
Clearpoint Creek 80 D2
Clearview Estates 36 D2
Clearwater Lake 89 A4
Clearwater 40 C2
Clegg Creek 90 D2
Clenny Branch 75 B4
Cleveland Knob 21 D4
Cleveland 47 D5
Clift Creek 89 A5
Clifty Canyon 34 A3
Clifty Creek 17 C4; 49 A4; 63 A4
Clifty Hollow 31 D4; 45 A5
Clifty 17 C4
Clinton Mountain 47 A6; 48 A1; 62 B2; 78 A2
Clinton 48 B1
Clipper 110 B1
Cloar 69 A6
Cloud Lake 81 D5
Clover Bend 37 B6
Clover Bend 38 B1
Clover Branch 85 C6
Clow 98 C2
Clubb Hill 45 D5
Clubhouse Spring Branch 36 C1
Clubhouse Spring 36 C1
Clyde 28 C2
CoahomaPoint 81 D5
Coal Creek 57 B6
Coal Hill 44 C2
Coal Ridge 57 A5
Coaldale 72 A2
Coatner Spring Branch 33 C5
Cobb Mountain 50 A1
Cobbite Branch 66 B1
Cobbs 79 D5
Cobeen Brake 113 D6
Coburn Brake 92 A1
Coca Cola Lake 109 D6
Cochran Branch 22 C2
Cochran Creek 21 D5
Cock Spurs 77 B5
Cocklebur Lakes 94 C1
Cockrell Creek 58 B3
Cody 83 A4
Coe Creek 110 D1
Coffee Bayou 125 D6
Coffee Creek 68 D2; 82 D2; 94 A2; 124 C1,2;D1
Coffee Prairie 124 C1
Coffeeville 51 C4
Coffman 38 A1
Coffman 39 A6
Coin 18 C2
Coker Creek 60 D1
Cold Branch 97 B4
Cold Spring Mountain 77 B5
Cold Spring 23 A6; 58 B2
Cold Spring 77 B5
Cold Water Creek 87 A4
Coldwater Creek 21 D5
Coldwater Spring 21 D5; 25 C4
Coldwater 53 D5
Cole Branch 22 A3
Cole Creek 31 C5
Cole Fork 34 A2
Cole Hollow 24 B1
Cole Mountain 61 A6; 77 B5
Cole Ridge 41 C4
Cole 109 A6
Coleman Creek 76 C2; 97 B6; 98 B1
Coleman Knob 46 A1
Coleman 104 D1
Coler 110 B3
Coles Brake 104 B1
Coley Knob 48 A1
Colfax 21 C4
College City 38 A2
College Heights Addition 36 D2
College Heights 115 B6
College Hill 111 D6
College Hill 46 D1
College Station 78 C3
Collegeville 78 C1
Collier Creek 86 B3
Collier Spring 86 A3
Collietown 35 C6
Collins Bayou 98 B3
Collins Branch 104 D1
Collins Creek 66 D1; 80 A1
Collins Hill 34 C3
Collins 116 C3
Colona 67 B5
Colony Mountain 45 C6
Colt 68 C3
Colton 53 D5
Columbia Hollow 15 B4
Columbus Lake 93 D6
Columbus 98 D1
Comal 20 C1
Combs 30 D1
Comet 109 A4
Cominto 116 B2
Compton 31 A6
Conant 66 B2
Concord 42 C3
Concord 49 A6
Cone Point 19 D4
Cone Point 32 A1
Congo 77 C6
Conley Bend 66 A2
Conley Creek 68 B1
Connells Point 94 B1
Conner 18 C1
Connerly Bayou 117 D5
Conway 62 C1
Cook Branch 111 C4
Cook Cave Hollow 19 B6
Cook Cave 19 B5
Cook Mountain 78 A1; 88 A3
Cooker Branch 101 B5
Cooks Brake 104 D2
Cooks Branch 61 A5
Cooks Creek 101 C6; 102 C1
Cooks Lake 93 A5
Cooks Pond 122 C1
Cooks Ramp 105 D5
CooksPoint 105 B4
Cool Easy Creek 96 B3;C3
Cooley Hill 25 B4
Cooley Lake 124 C1
Cooleyville 98 B2
Coon Bayou Brake 104 D3
Coon Bayou 105 D4; 117 A5
Coon Branch 30 B2
Coon Creek 15 C4; 20 B1; 25 D5; 36 C2; 38 A1,2; 50 C2; 84 C3; 99 A4
Coon Hollow 31 C5; 33 B6
Coon Point 94 C1
Coon Spring 20 C1
Coon Tail Creek 67 D6
Cooney 101 A6
Cooney 89 D6
Coono Brake 106 C1
Cooper Branch 53 C4; 59 A5
Cooper Creek 37 A5;B5; 53 D4; 88 B2; 96 C2
Cooper Island 92 D2
Cooper Lake 63 D4; 80 C2
Cooper Mountain 30 D2
Cooper Point 35 C4
Coopers Ridge 40 D1
Cooter Lake 93 A6
Copeland Lake 119 A5
Copeland Ridge Branch 100 B2
Copeland 47 A5
Copper Mine 16 B3
Copper Spring Hollow 47 C6
Copper Spring Mountain 47 A6
Copper Spring 49 A6
Copperas Gap 61 C5
Copperas Lake 70 C1
Coppers Knob 47 B6
Cord 37 D4
Cordell Creek 113 A6
Corinth 59 C5
Corinth 73 D4
Corinth 98 A1
Corinth 115 B5
Corley 58 B3
Corner Spring 15 C5
Cornerstone 92 D1
Cornertown 23 A4
Cornerville 103 C5
Cornfield Chute 126 B3
Cornie 122 C1
Corning Lake 26 B2
Corning 26 B2
Cornish Branch 119 C5
Cosgrove 126 A1
Cossatot Mountains 86 B1
Cossatot River 85 A4;B4;D4; 97 A-D4
Cotter Branch 22 A1
Cotter 20 C3
Cotton Belt 39 A6
Cotton Plant 67 D5
Cotton Town 44 D3
Cotton Town 60 C2
Cottondale 91 D6
Cottonmouth Creek 102 C3
Cottonwood Chute 126 A3
Cottonwood Corner 40 D1
Cottonwood Corner 54 A3
Cottonwood Corner 69 C4
Cottonwood Falls 23 B6
Cottonwood Point 94 B1
Cottonwood Slough 27 D4; 43 C5; 94 C2
Coulter Branch 97 D5
Coulter Lake 97 B5
Council Lake 83 B5
Council 83 A6
Countis Creek 73 B5
Countiss 94 C2
County Line Branch 23 B5
County Line Knob 31 D6
County Line 21 A6
County Line 22 A1
County Line 97 B6
Courthouse Slough 43 D5
Cousart Bayou 91 D5,6; 103 A6; 104 A1
Cove Branch 32 C1
Cove Creek Lake 76 A1
Cove Creek 18 D3; 28 C3;D2,3; 30 D1; 31 A6; 33 C6; 42 A2; 44 A1;B3; 48 C1;D1; 58 A3;B3; 60 A3; 62 A1; 88 A3; 89 A4
Cove Lake 58 B3
Cove Mountain 60 C2; 61 A6; 75 A6
Cove Prong 35 D4,5
Cove Spring 28 C2; 43 A5
Cove 84 A2
Covington Lake 94 C1
Covington Pond 113 A6
Cow Bayou 83 A4;B4
Cow Creek Mountain 72 D2
Cow Creek 21 D4; 31 D6; 32 D1; 43 A5; 45 A5; 73 B6; 84 C3
Cow Head Creek 102 A1
Cow Island 53 C6
Cow Mountain 34 C3
Cowan Creek 45 A4
Cowan Hollow 46 B2
Cowan Knob 31 D4
Cowan 20 D2
Cowden Spring 25 A4
Cowell 32 D1
Cowger Lake 59 C5
Cowhide Creek 86 D3
Cowlick Branch 86 C2
Cowlingsville 97 C5
Cox Creek Lake 89 D5
Cox Creek 43 D4; 87 C5; 89 D5,6; 99 D6
Cox Cypress Lake 92 C2
Cox Reservoir 92 B3
Cox Spring 86 A1
Cox Spring 86 A1
Coy 79 D6
Cozahome 33 A6
Crab Lake 93 A6
Crabtree 47 B6
Craft Creek 74 C2
Craig Creek 90 D3
Craig Hill 36 B1
Craigshead Point 55 A5
Crain City 122 A3
Cram 114 B1
Crane Island 60 B3
Crane Lake 94 D1; 103 D4; 113 D6
Cranenest Creek 18 A2
Craney 114 C3
Cravens Creek 43 B6
Cravens 43 B6
Crawford Mountain 19 D6
Crawford Point 44 B3
Crawford 19 D6
Crawfordsville 70 B1
Crazy Creek 15 C4
Creamery Package 54 B2
Creben Creek 61 A6
Creech 16 D2
Creely Bayou 69 D4
Creigh 94 A1
Cremer 124 C2
Crescent 56 A3
Crest 18 A3
Creswell Mountain 35 A4
Creswell 35 A4
Cricket Creek 18 A3;B3
Cricket 18 A3
Crigler 104 B1
Cripple Branch 44 B1
Crittenden 69 A6
Crocker Creek 58 B1
Crockett Lake 93 B6
Crockett 27 B4
Crocketts Bluff 93 A5
Croker 35 C6
Crooked Bayou 83 A6; 117 A4;B5;C4;D4; 126 A1;B1
Crooked Branch 33 D4; 111 D4
Crooked Creek 19 C5;C6;D4; 20 C1-C3; 25 C5; 32 A1; 66 C3; 78 D1; 79 C6;D6; 80 D1; 82 D2; 83 D4; 85 B6; 86 B1; 92 A1;B2; 111 C6; 120 B1;C2;D2
Crooked Lake Bayou 41 B6
Crooked Lake 41 C6
Crooked Slough Bend 123 A4
Crooked Slough 108 B3; 123 A4
Crosby 63 A6
Cross Bayou 54 C2; 79 D6; 92 C1;D3; 104 B2
Cross Creek Mountain 73 A4
Cross Creek 16 C1; 73 A4; 84 C2
Cross Current Brake 113 D6
Cross Current Slough 113 D6; 114 D1
Cross Hollow 16 C2
Cross Lanes 43 D4
Cross Mountains 84 B2
Cross Pond 79 D4
Cross Roads 29 A6
Cross Roads 87 B5
Cross Roads 90 D1
Cross Roads 94 B1
Cross Roads 96 C2
Cross Roads 113 D5
Cross Roads 114 B3
Crosses Creek 29 C6
Crosses 29 C6
Crossett 124 C2
Crosspond Bayou 81 A4
Crossroad 32 C1
Crossroad 66 D1
Crossroad 124 B2
Crossroads 22 D1
Crossroads 48 C3
Crossroads 51 B5
Crossroads 57 C4
Crossroads 59 B4
Crossroads 110 A2
Crosstie Slough 123 A6
Crouthers Bayou 69 D6
Crow Creek 37 A6; 58 C2; 68 C3; 69 D4
Crow Creek 69 D4
Crow Island 50 A3
Crowell Creek 58 B3
Crowell Mountain 47 B6
Crowell Pinnacle 47 B6
Crowfoot Lake 93 B6
Crowley 39 A5
Crowleys Ridge 26 D3; 27 B4; 39 A5;C4; 53 A4;D4; 83 C4;D5
Crown Lake 23 D4
Crows 77 D4
Crudington Creek 87 A6
Crump Creek 86 A2
Crumrod 94 D2
Crystal Mountain 87 A5
Crystal Hill 78 B1
Crystal Hill 78 B2
Crystal Lake 15 B5
Crystal Mountain 75 D5; 76 A3; 77 A5; 78 B1
Crystal Mountains 86 A3
Crystal Point 21 D4
Crystal Prong 76 A3
Crystal Springs 87 A5
Crystal Valley 78 C1
Cub Creek 32 D1; 76 B2
Cub Mountain 86 A1
Cuba Bottom 45 D4
Cubby Creek 123 C6
Culbertson Point 31 D5
Cullendale 113 B4
Culler 79 C6
Cullum Mountain 48 C1
Culotches Bay Slough 67 D4
Culp 34 A3
Culpepper Mountain 47 C6
Culpepper 47 C6
Culver Creek 26 D3
Cumi 21 B6
Cummings Springs 100 D1
Cummins 104 A2
Cunningham Corner 70 B1
Cunningham Creek 21 D4; 49 C4
Cup Bayou 69 D5
Curia Creek Ditch 37 C5
Curia Creek 36 C3; 37 C4,5
Curia 36 C3
Curl Creek 50 D1; 88 B1
Curley Branch 24 A3
Current River 25 B6;C6
Curtis Creek 31 D6; 45 B4
Curtis Mountain 75 B4
Curtis 100 B1
Cushman Junction 36 D1
Cushman 36 C1
Cut-Bluff Slough 93 A5
Cutoff Bayou 69 D6; 70 C1
Cut-Off Creek 66 A3; 116 A2;B2;C3;D3
Cut-Off Lake 109 B6
Cutoff Slough 66 B3
Cypert Mountain 35 B5
Cypert 94 A2
Cypress Bayou 62 C3; 63 C4-6;D6; 66 C1; 93 D5; 94 C1; 105 A5; 109 A6
Cypress Bend 117 A5
Cypress Brake 67 A4; 105 B4
Cypress Branch 78 A3
Cypress City Lake 110 D2
Cypress Corner 82 C3
Cypress Creek 37 B6; 47 D6; 50 C1; 61 A-C6;A5;C4; 62 C1; 68 C1;D2; 77 B4; 81 B6;C6; 96 D3; 104 A2; 100 C2,3; 101 A4;B4; 104 B3;C3; 105 C4,5;D5; 111 B5;C5; 112 A1;B-D2; 117 A5; 120 D3; 123 A4;C4
Cypress Lake 109 A6
Cypress Point 27 D5
Cypress Slough 66 A3; 97 C5
Cypress Swamp 67 D4
Cypress Valley 61 A5

D

Dabney Creek 30 C1
Dabney 47 B4
Dacus Lake 70 B3
Daggett 67 D5
Dagmar 81 A5
Daily Creek 73 B6
Daisy Creek 86 C2
Daisy 86 C2
Dalark 100 A3
Dale Creek 90 B3
Dale Place 56 C3
Daleville 100 A2
Daley Creek 75 C5
Dallas Creek 73 D4
Dallas Mountain 85 A4
Dallas 73 D4
Dalton Mountain 62 B3
Dalton 24 B3
Damascus 121 A5
Damascus 48 D1
Dan Heffley Creek 32 D1
Dan Henry Spring 23 C6
Daniel Mountain 32 C2
Daniels Creek 63 A4
Daniels Mountain 31 C5
Daniels Point 41 D6
Danner Creek 60 D3
Danner Lake 70 A3
Dansby 83 A4
Danville Creek 75 A5
Danville Mountain 59 C5
Danville 59 C5
Darby Lake 57 A5
Dardanelle Lake 44 D1,3
Dardanelle Mountain 60 A1
Dardanelle Rock 60 A1
Dardanelle 60 B1
Dare Creek 46 C3
Darling Spring 59 B6
Darst Branch 66 C2
Datto 26 B1
Daugherty Reservoir 93 A4
Dave Creek 48 B3
Dave 110 A1
Davenport Creek 22 B3
David D Terry Lake 78 C3
Davidson Hill 23 D4
Davidson 111 C6
Davidson 42 A2
Davis Branch 89 A6; 111 D4; 121 A5
Davis Creek 24 D3; 32 A2; 33 C6
Davis Ford 85 C6
Davis Hill 36 C2
Davis Hollow 30 D1
Davis Knob 31 D6
Davis Lake 62 D1; 105 B5
Davis Mountain 35 D5
Davis Slough 97 D4
Davis Spring 24 A1
Davis Spur 53 A5
Davy Crockett Mountain 33 A4
Dawn Hill 15 C4
Dawson Slough 93 A6
Day 23 C4
Dayberry Creek 24 C2
Days Creek 118 A3
Dayton Bayou 105 C4
Dayton 57 C4
De Ann Creek 98 D3
De Ann 98 D3
De Boer 63 C4
De Gray Creek 88 D1
De Gray Lake 87 C6; 88 C1
De Gray 88 D1
De Lisle Creek 88 C2
De Lisle Hills 88 C2
De Queen Lake 96 A2
De Queen 96 B3
De Roche 88 C2
De Soto Lake 94 D3
De Valls Bluff 80 B3
De Witt 93 C4
Dead Man Point 81 C5
Dead Mule Bend 51 A4
Dead Timber Lake 54 C1
Dead Tree Hill 36 C2
Deadman Bend 25 D4
Deadpecker Slough 124 C2
Deal Hollow 32 B2
Dean Brake 125 A6
Dean Branch 20 D2; 33 D5
Dean Island 54 D3
Dean Mountain 33 D5; 36 D1
Dean Point 33 D5
Dean Reid Knob 59 B5
Dean Springs 43 C4
Dean 18 D1
Deane 116 B1
Deans Branch 63 C4
Deans Market 43 C4
Deanyville 99 C4
Dearman 41 C4
Dearmond Gap 62 C3
Deberrie 60 D2
Deberry Branch 62 B2
Decatur Creek 15 B4
Decatur 15 B5
Deceiper Creek 100 A1,2;B2,3
Deceiper Lake 100 B2
Deckard Branch 76 B1
Deckard Mountain 76 B1
Decker Bayou 70 C2
Decker Hill 49 B6
Deckerville 54 C1
Deener Creek 66 A1
Deep Hollow 43 A6
Deep Bayou 91 D5,6; 103 A6; 104 A1; 106 A1
Deep Elm 117 C4
Deep Elm 81 D6
Deep Lake 105 D6
Deep Slough 52 A1; 99 D6; 123 B6
Deer Bayou 54 D1
Deer Creek 74 C3; 75 C4; 90 C1
Deer Creek 90 C1
Deer Lick Creek 25 A6
Deer 31 D6
Deerfield 106 A2
Deerlick Creek 77 A5
Deerwood 61 B5
Deevers Branch 45 C5
Degelow 40 D1
Deglow 40 D1
Deitrich Flat 33 C4
Delaney Branch 115 C6
Delaney Creek 29 D6
Delaney 29 C6
Delaware 59 A6
Deleware Creek 59 A5
Delfore 40 C1
Delight 99 B4
Dell 41 C4
Delmar 18 D2
Delpro 54 B3
Delta 111 C6
Deltic Farms Lake 77 A4
Deluce 93 D5
Democrat 69 D6
Dempsey Spring 19 C5
Denby Creek 87 A4
DenbyPoint 75 D4
Denim Hill 24 D1
Denmark 50 C2
Dennard 33 D6
Denning Creek 19 C4
Denning 44 D2
Dennis Slough 80 D2
Dennison Bottoms 36 D2; 50 A2
Dennison Heights 36 D2
Denny Mountain 29 D6
Denton Creek 72 B3; 73 B4
Denton Island 38 D1
Denton 37 A6
Denton 73 A4
Denver 18 B2
Denwood 54 C2
Departee Creek 50 B2,3;D3; 51 B4;C4; 67 A4
Depot Creek 77 D6
Dermott 117 C4
DeRoche Creek 88 B1;C1,2
Derrieusseaux Creek 90 C3;D3; 102 A3;B3
Des Arc Mountain 63 B6
Des Arc 66 D3
Deshield Fork 19 B6
Detonti 89 A6
DeView 67 B6
Devil Jump Hollow 45 A4
Devils Backbone Ridge 57 B4
Devils Backbone 33 C6
Devils Canyon 43 A5
Devils Creek 60 A3; 61 A4
Devils Elbow 51 A5; 54 D2
Devils Fork Little Red River 49 A5;B4
Devils Fork 37 C4; A5
Devils Gap 35 B4
Devils Knob 35 B4; 45 A5; 47 D4
Devils Neck 67 A5
Dew Spring 20 B3
Dewey Mill 54 C1
Dewey 117 C5
Dewey 50 D1
Dexter 91 C4
Dial Creek 81 C5;D6
Diamond Bay 21 C6
Diamond Cave 31 B6
Diamond City 19 A6
Diamond Creek 21 C6
Diamond Grove 57 A4
Diamond Lake 23 D4
Diamond Point 104 A3
Diamond Woods 83 B6
Diamondhead 88 A3
Diaz 51 A5
Dick Knob 32 C2
Dickey Junction 32 C2
Dickie Branch 116 B1
Dicks Creek 45 B5
Dicks Gap 85 B5
Dicks Point 66 C3
Dickson Branch 57 C4
Dicus 38 A2
Diera Mountain 30 A3
Dierks Lake 85 D5
Dierks 97 A6
Diffy Mountain 56 B3
Digman Lake 38 A2
Diles Creek 24 A2
Dill Branch 49 B5
Dillard Bend 119 B5
Dillard Creek 97 B6;C6
Dillen 46 A1
Dillon Ferry 69 C5
Dillon Lake 76 D2
Dills Lakes 29 B6
Dills Mills 111 A6
Dilworth 97 B4
Dimple 54 C2
Dinsmore 31 A4
Dirty Creek 44 C3
Dishpan Lake 25 C5
Dishrown Creek 18 D2
Dishwater Branch 36 C1
Dismal Creek 31 D5
Dismal Swamp 105 A5
Dismukes Branch 120 B2
Distress Creek 53 B4;C4
Ditch Bayou 126 A2
Divide Hill 24 D1
Divide Mountain 46 B2
Dixie Bayou 94 C3
Dixie 27 C4
Dixie 39 C6
Dixie 67 C4
Dixie 69 B6
Dixie 78 B3
Dixon Bayou 105 C5
Dixon Bend 119 B5
Dixon Lake Slough 113 A4
Dobbs Spring 57 D4
Dobell 53 A6
Dobson Station 110 C3
Dobyville 99 B6
Dockeys Gap 43 A5
Doctors Creek 43 D5; 57 A5
Doctors Fork 57 A5
Dodd Branch 50 B2
Dodd City 20 C1
Dodd Mountain 35 C4; 48 A1
Dodd Ridge 34 D2
Doddridge 118 C3
Dodge City 121 D5
Dodson Creek 89 A5,6; 98 B1; 120 B3
Dodson Mountain 31 A5
Dodson 120 A2
Dodsons Corner 68 D3
Dog Branch 18 D2; 31 C6; 39 B4
Dog Creek 77 C4,5
Dog Lick Branch 50 B3
Dog Mountain 85 B4
Dog Pond 69 B5
Dogtown 96 B2
Dogwood Branch 37 A5
Dogwood Creek 66 C2; 113 B5
Dogwood Flats 73 A4
Dogwood Park 21 B5
Dogwood 41 C5
Dogwood 66 C2
Dogwood 89 C6
Doins Point 33 C4
Dollar Junction 123 C6
Dollar Knob 46 C1
Dolph 22 D1
Don Lake 83 A4
Donahue Lake 69 D5
Donahue Mountain 56 A3
Donaldson 88 C3
Donaldsonville 91 C4
Donbey 125 A6
Dongola 33 C4
Doniphan Lake 66 A2
Doniphan 66 A2
Donnell Ridge 61 C6
Dooley Bend 79 C4
Dooley Branch 59 B5
Dooley Creek 119 B6;C6
Dooley 110 C1
Dora 42 C2
Doris Creek 113 C4
Dorothy 38 C3
Dort Creek 26 C3
Dortch Bend 79 C4
Dota Creek 36 C3; 37 D4; 51 A4
Dota Old River 51 A4
Dota 37 D4
Dotson 98 C3
Dotted Lake 89 A6
Dotty Lake 90 A1
Double Branch 50 A2
Double Cabin Lake 106 B1
Double Creek 103 C4
Double Wells 90 D3
Doublehead Bluff 69 C4
Dougherty Mountain 48 B2
Douglas Branch 114 A2
Douglas Corner 78 C1
Douglas Mountain 44 B1
Douglas Old River Lake 104 A2
Douglas 104 A3
Dover 46 D1
Dow Hol 45 A4
Dowdy 37 C5
Dowell Branch 18 D3; 19 D4
DowPoint 45 A5
Doyle Flat 47 C4
Doyle 98 B2
Doylestown 90 C3
Drainage Canal 69 C6
Drainie Lake 93 D6
Drakes Creek 30 B1
Drakes Creek 30 B1
Drasco 49 B5
Driftwood Shores 49 C4
Driftwood 37 B5
Driggs 58 A2
Drip Creek 49 B4
Dripoff Hollow 29 D4
Dripping Spring 42 C2; 49 B4; 86 C3
Dripping Springs Gap 86 C3
Dripping Springs 42 B2
Driver Bar 55 A5
Driver Creek Lake 47 C4
Driver Cutoff 55 A5
Driver 55 B4
Drivers Creek 47 C4
Drowning Slough 88 C3
Drummond Lake 51 B5
Dry Bayou 69 C6; 70 B1; 79 C4; 103 B6; 116 B3; 125 A6;C6; 126 A1
Dry Branch 32 B1;C2; 33 B4; 34 A1; 36 A1;B2; 59 C5; 63 C6; 66 C1; 77 C5; 98 B3; 99 B5; 100 B2; 113 D6; 118 C3
Dry Cave 19 C6
Dry Creek Mountain 58 C2
Dry Creek 18 B2;C2; 21 C4;C5; 23 B6; 24 B3; 29 A6; 31 A4,6;C5; 32 C1,3; 33 B4; 35 C4,5; 36 C2; 37 B5; 44 A3; 45 B5; 46 B1,3;C1; 47 B4; 58 C1;D2; 59 A5; 72 B3; 77 C6; 78 D1; 84 A2; 85 A6; 90 A1; 97 B4; 101 B5; 102 D2; 109 D6; 119 A4; 121 A6;B4; 122 A3;B1; B4
Dry Fork Creek 17 D6; 18 D1; 103 B6
Dry Fork Mountain 75 A6
Dry Fork 18 C3; 30 C2; 31 A4; 34 D3; 36 C3;D3; 48 B1; 49 B6; 58 A1; 74 C3; 75 A6;B6; 86 A1; 111 B6; 112 D2; 119 C4
Dry Hollow 22 D2; 45 A4
Dry Jordan Creek 19 D4
Dry Lake 83 A4; 105 A6; 117 C6
Dry Lost Creek 89 A6; 90 A1
Dry Mazarn Creek 87 A4
Dry Music Creek 20 B2
Dry Prong 103 D6
Dry Run Creek 36 D1; 76 B1
Dry Spadra Creek 45 B4
Dryden 38 D2
Dryfork 18 D1
Dub 54 C1
Dublin 45 D4
Duce 105 D5
Duck Creek 63 D6; 90 A2
Duck Lake 117 C5
Duck Pond 110 B1
Duckett 85 C4
Dudley Lake 91 A6
Duff 33 B4
Dug Hill 49 B5
Dug Hollow 31 C4
Dugger Spring 32 A3; 35 C5
Dugger 32 A3
Dugout Mountain 63 B5
Duke Creek 48 C1
Dukes Branch 90 A3
Dumas City 122 A1
Dumas 104 C3
Dump Mountain 49 A6
Dun Hill 62 B2
Dunahay Brake 51 A5
Dunaway Hollow 30 C2
Duncan Branch 44 B1
Duncan Gap 62 C3
Duncan Ridge 62 A1
Duncan 81 D5
Dunkeffie Lake 103 B4
Dunlap 99 C4
Dunn Creek 66 D1; 113 B6; 114 C2
Dunn Lake 108 B3
Dunn 24 C3
Dunnington 51 B4
Dunns Shanty Point 81 B4
Durham 29 B6
Dustin Pond 95 C4
Dutch Bend 123 A4
Dutch Creek Mountain 58 D2; 59 D4; 73 A6; 74 A1
Dutch Creek 58 D2,3; 59 D4; 73 A6; 74 A1
Dutch Mills 28 C1
Dutchman Hollow 44 B1
Dutherage Spring 88 D3
Dutton Mountain 47 D5
Dutton 30 D2
Duvall 69 B5
Dye Branch 23 A5
Dye Creek 29 B4
Dyer 43 C4
Dyess 54 B2
Dyson Creek 91 D4; 103 A4

E

Eagle Branch 79 C6
Eagle Corner 15 C5
Eagle Gap 72 C3
Eagle Lake Bend 37 D5
Eagle Lake 37 D5; 51 B5; 123 A6
Eagle Mills 113 A5
Eagle Mountain 36 D2; 85 A4
Eagle Nest Lake 93 D6; 94 B1
Eagletie 101 C6
Eagleton 72 C3
Earl Branch 59 D6
Earle 69 A6
Earnheart Island 36 D1
Earnheart 36 D1
Easely Mountain 88 B3
Easley Branch 100 C2
Easley Creek 88 D3
Eassis Creek 24 B3
East Bayou 81 C5
East Black Oak 54 D1
East Boggy Bayou 117 D4
East Branch Cedar Creek 88 A2
East Branch Flat Creek 90 D1
East Branch Gulpha Creek 88 A3
East Branch 66 C3
East Camden 113 B4
East Cedar Creek 42 B3; 59 B4
East Cooper Creek 24 D2; 37 A5
East Elis Branch 28 D3
East End 78 D2
East Flat Creek 96 D3; 108 A3
East Flat Fork Creek 68 D1
East Fleming Creek 30 D2
East Flint Creek 15 C5
East Fork Cadron Creek 49 D4; 62 A3;B1,2; 63 A4
East Fork Cane Creek 58 A3
East Fork Cave Creek 32 C2
East Fork Clear Creek 32 A3
East Fork Crooked Creek 32 A2
East Fork Gar Creek 44 C1
East Fork Illinois Bayou 46 B3; 47 A4
East Fork Kelly Bayou 118 C3; 119 C4
East Fork Little Buffalo River 31 C5,6
East Fork of Horsehead Creek 44 C3; 45 B4
East Fork Point Remove Creek 47 D5; 61 A5;B4
East Fork Poteau River 73 A5,6
East Fork Powell Creek 72 D3
East Fork Prairie Creek 86 D3; 98 A2
East Fork Tulip Creek 101 A5;C5
East Fork West Creek 124 C3
East Gafford Creek 74 A3
East Greasy Creek 30 C1
East Hanna Mountain 85 B5
East Hegwood Creek 58 A2
East Lacey Creek 58 B2
East Lafferty Creek 35 C6; 36 B1
East Lake 81 D5
East Moon Lake 105 A6
East Mountain 48 C2
East Pigeon Creek 21 A5
East Pocahontas 25 C5
East Point Mountain 45 D6
East Poteau Mountain 57 D4
East Prong Baron Creek 44 B2
East Prong Minnow Creek 45 B5
East Prong of Town Branch 20 D2
East Rocky Bayou 35 B6
East Saline Creek 85 B6
East Shadley Creek 72 A2
East Slough 26 C3
East Snake Knob 58 B3
East Spiller Creek 74 A2
East Sugarfoot Creek 20 B1
East Sugarloaf Creek 19 A6;B6; 20 B1
East Twin Creek 35 B4
East Wells Creek 24 C3
Easter Creek 44 A3
Easterwood Mountain 61 D6
Eastgate Place 42 C3
Eastman Brake 104 D3
Eastport 96 D2
Eastview 54 A3
Eastwood Addition 36 D2
Eastwood Bayou 91 B4
Eastwood 91 B4
Eaton 37 A5
Ebb 90 C2
Ebenezer Branch 121 A5
Ebenezer 39 B4
Ebenezer 89 C4
Ebenezer 102 D1
Ebenezer 121 A5
Ebling 83 A5
Ebony 70 B2
Echo 57 C5
Echubby Lake 105 B4
Eckel Cave 24 C1
Economy 60 A3
Ecore Fabre Bayou 112 A2,3
Eddy Lake 80 A3
Eden Bluff 16 C2
Eden Isle 49 C4
Eden 81 A5
Edgeman Creek 31 B4;C4
Edgemont 48 B3
Edgewood 77 D6
Edgewood 82 C3
Edison Spring 28 A1
Edmondson Creek 22 D3
Edmondson 70 C1
Edmonson 35 C6
Edna 44 B3
Edwards Junction 31 C5
Edwards Lake 31 A6
Edwards 66 D1
Egard Hill 35 B6
Egg Bar Bend 83 C5
Egger Mountain 47 C5
Eglantine 48 B2
Egner Hill 50 A2
Egypt 38 C2
Eight Mile Creek 39 A5; 51 C6
El Dorado 122 B2
El Paso 63 C4
Elaine 94 C3
Elba 34 D1
Elberta 33 C6
Elberta 60 B1
Elbow Creek 50 B1;C1
Elbow Slough 66 B3
Elcana 68 D3
Elder Branch 56 B3
Elder Creek 35 D6
Eldridge Corner 92 C3
Eldridge Hollow 30 D3
Electric Springs 16 B2
Elephant Spring 20 B2
Eleven Point River 24 A3;B3; 25 D4
Elevenpoint 24 B3
Elgin 37 D5
Eli Branch 58 D2
Elixir Springs 19 B6
Elizabeth 22 C1
Elk Ranch 17 A5
Elkhorn Branch 22 A3
Elkhorn Mountain 16 A2
Elkhorn Springs 28 A3
Elkhorn Tavern 16 A3
Elkins Park 25 B5
Elkins 29 B6
Elliott 113 C4
Ellis Branch 24 B1
Ellis Chapel 68 B2
Ellis Mountain 78 C1
Ellis Ridge 24 B1
Ellis Spring 23 A6
Ellison Hill 24 B2
Ellison Lake 83 B4
Ellison 91 B6
Ellisville 114 A2
Elm Branch 19 D5; 93 B4
Elm Cave 33 A5
Elm Grove 53 A6
Elm Hollow 33 B5
Elm Park 57 D5
Elm Prong Mill Bayou 92 A3;B3
Elm Root Slough 59 C5
Elm Slough 81 D4
Elm Spring Branch 23 A4
Elm Springs 16 D1
Elm Springs 16 D1
Elm Store 24 A3
Elmo Creek 42 A3
Elmo Flats 88 C3
Elmo 51 B4
Elmwood 117 C5
Elmwood 19 D4
Elmwood 92 D1
Elnora 25 D5
Emerson Branch 114 B1
Emerson Ditch 38 D2
Emerson 121 C4
Emert Creek 56 C2
Eminence Bayou 126 A3
Eminence 126 B3
Emmet 111 A4
Emmons 81 B6
Emon 111 D6
Emory Branch 90 A1
Emory Mill Mountain 87 B6
Empire 126 C1
Enders 62 A3
Engelberg 25 B5
Engineer Lake 57 A5
England Creek 52 C3; 53 B4
England 79 D5
English Branch 59 D6
English Creek 23 A5
English Lake 92 D2
English Place 90 B3
English 92 D2
Ennis Cave 35 C6
Ennis Creek 75 A5
Enola 62 B3
Enon 116 B1
Enright 66 B3
Enterprise 56 A2
Enyart Lake 119 C5
Erbie 31 A6
Ermentraudt Mountain 78 C2
Eros 19 D6
Erving Ridge 63 D4
Erwin 51 B5
Erwin 67 D4
Escronges Lake 94 D1
Essex Bayou 93 C6;D6; 94 C1
Essex 63 C6
Estes 79 D4
Estico 51 B6
Ethel 93 C6
Etna 44 D1
Etowah 54 A2
Eubanks Mountain 30 B1
Euclid 85 D5
Eudora 126 C2
Eugene Bayou 104 C3
Eula 32 C3
Eunice Chute 117 C6
Eunice 103 A5
Eureka Springs 17 B5
Evadale 54 B3
Evans Cave 24 B2
Evans Hollow 24 B2; 31 C4
Evans Mountain 45 C6; 46 C3
Evansville Creek 28 D2
Evansville 28 D1
Evening Shade 36 A2
Evening Shade 57 D4
Evening Shade 110 B3
Evening Star 26 D1
Evening Star 33 B6
Everett Ridge 49 A4
Everton 19 D6
Ewal 94 B3
Excelsior 56 B3
Experiment 120 B1

F

Faber 88 D3
Fair Field 68 A3
Fair Oaks 68 A1
Fairbanks 48 C2
Fairfield Bay 48 B2
Fairfield 91 D6
Fairland 119 B4
Fairmount 15 D5
Fairmount 80 D3
Fairview Creek 62 A3
Fairview Ridge 62 A3
Fairview 20 C3
Fairview 22 C3
Fairview 34 B1
Fairview 39 A5
Fairview 78 C2
Fairview 79 A6
Fairview 84 D3
Fairview 100 B3
Fairview 113 B4
Fairview 126 A2
Faith 103 A4
Falcon 111 C5
Fall Branch 63 A5
Fall Creek 21 C5; 28 D3; 37 A6
Fall Hill 36 C2
Fall Mountain 77 A5
Fallen Ash Creek 20 C2,3
Fallen Creek 86 D1; 98 A1
Falling Springs 15 B4
Falling Water Creek 32 D3; 46 A3
Falling Water Falls 46 A3
Fallis 39 D4
Falloff Creek 60 C3
Falls Branch 32 D2
Falls Chapel 97 C4
Falls Hollow 29 D4
Fallsville 31 D4
Fancy Hill Mountain 86 B1
Fancy Hill 86 B2
Fane Creek 44 A1
Fannie 75 C4
Faras Run Creek 80 A1
Faras Run 80 A1
Farelly Lake 104 A3
Farewell 18 B2
Fargo 67 D6
Farindale 102 A1
Farmer Cove 32 C1
Farmington Branch 29 A4
Farmington 29 A4
Farmville 114 C3
Farris Creek 21 D5
Farris Spring 21 D5
Farris Springs 45 A4
Farris Springs 45 A4
Farrville 39 C5
Faulkner Gap 62 D3
Faulkner Lake 79 B4
Faulkner Mountain 30 B1
Faulkner Springs 85 B5
Faulknerville 39 A4
Fawn Park 21 B5
Fayette Junction 29 A4
Fayetteville 29 A4
Fears Lake 78 A3
Feenyville 103 B6
Felco 70 B1
Felkins Creek 31 B4
Felkins Point 46 B1
Felsenthal 123 C6
Felton 82 B3
Fender 25 D5
Fendley 87 D5
Fenter 89 B5
Ferda 91 A5
Ferguson Creek 24 C2
Ferguson Lake 78 D2
Ferguson Valley 57 B6
Ferguson 109 D6
Ferguson 94 D1
Fern Mountain 43 A6
Fern Spring 43 B5
Fern 43 A5
Ferndale Creek 77 B6
Ferndale 77 B6
Ferrel Creek 30 B2
Ferry Bayou 117 D5
Few Branch 59 C4
Fiddlers Creek 74 B2;C2
Field Bayou 110 D2,3; 119 A6
Field Creek 23 A6
Field Lake 26 A1
Field Mountain 24 D1
Fife Hill 34 D3
Fifteenmile Bayou 69 D5,6; 70 A2;B2;C1;D1
Fifty-six 34 B3
Fifty-Six 38 B3
Figure Five 42 C3
Filligrum Bend 69 B4
Finch Mountain 34 D3
Finch 39 B4
Fincher Cave 29 B5
Fincher Lake 111 C6
Finley Bar 71 d5
Finley Branch 22 A2
Finley Creek 36 A1; 102 C2
Finn Bayou 110 C1
Finnswitch 112 C3
Fire Slough 50 B3
First Creek Canal 52 D1; 68 A1,2
First Creek 68 C2
First Lake 109 B5
First Old River Lake 110 C1
First Old River 81 C5
Fish Bayou 70 D1; 126 B3
Fish Creek 78 C3;D3
Fish Lake Slough 81 B5
Fish Lake 61 B4; 67 B4; 81 B5; 110 B2
Fish Slough 92 A2
Fish Trap Slough 27 A4
Fisher Creek 75 C6
Fisher Gap 30 D1
Fisher Mountain 43 C6
Fisher Point 31 A5
Fisher 38 D2
Fisher 52 C1
Fishers Lake 113 B4
Fishing Lake 69 C4
Fishtrap Creek 33 A6
Fishtrap Slough 79 B6;C6
Fitzgerald Crossing 68 B3
Fitzgerald Mountain 16 D2
Fitzgerald 51 A5
Fitzhugh 51 D4
Five Branch 49 A6
Five Finger Cove 20 A1
Five Forks Bayou 91 C6; 92 C1
Fivemile Creek 49 A5; 86 B3
Fivemile Spring 25 C4
Fivemile 49 A5
Flag Lake Crossing 69 B4
Flag Lake 105 A4
Flag Pond 78 B3
Flag 34 D1
Flagg Lake 60 B1
Flat Bayou 91 B6
Flat Bois D'Arc Creek 110 B3;C3
Flat Branch 23 C5; 99 C4; 115 B5
Flat Creek 23 C6; 36 A3; 37 A6; 66 A2; 84 B3; 90 D1; 96 D3; 100 A1; 103 B5,6; 104 C1,2; 110 A2; 115 D5,6; 116 D1; 122 A2;C2
Flat Cypress Creek 61 C4
Flat Denton Creek 37 A5,6
Flat Fork Creek 67 D6; 68 D1; 81 A6; A1
Flat Hollow Branch 20 B1
Flat Lake Creek 25 B5
Flat Lake 26 C1; 94 C1; 105 A6
Flat Mountain 77 B5
Flat Rock Creek 17 A6; 42 C3;D3; 45 D6; 48 C3; 57 A4
Flat Rock Hollow 30 B3
Flat Rock Mountain 78 A3
Flat Rock 45 D6
Flat Top Mountain 50 C2
Flat 32 B2
Flatiron Bluff 32 A1
Flatrock Creek 32 A1
Flatside Pinnacle 76 A3
Flattop Mountain 58 B3
Flatwoods 32 B1
Fleming Gap 63 C4
Fleschmans Bayou 125 C6
Fletcher Bayou 70 C2
Fletcher Brake 104 C2
Fletcher Branch 50 B1; 57 C6
Fletcher Creek 57 C6; 77 B6
Fletcher Lake 58 B1; 70 C2
Fletcher Mountain 21 D4
Fletcher Slough 89 B5
Fletcher Towhead 41 D5
Fletchers Branch 93 D5
Flint Creek Lake 15 C4
Flint Creek 15 C5
Flint Knob 21 C6
Flint Spring 22 B2
Flint Store 45 A5
Flippin 20 C3
Float Road Slough 38 A3
Flood Mountain 58 C2
Floodway 40 D2
Floral 50 B1
Florence 104 D2
Floss 28 D3
Flowers Spring Creek 85 D5
Floyd Branch 22 D3
Floyd 63 B5
Fly Creek 28 C2
Fly Gap Mountain 30 D1
Flynn Branch 23 B4
Flynn Slough Cutoff 92 A2
Flynn Slough 92 A1
Flynn 104 B2
Fodderstack Mountain 32 A1; 85 A4; 85 B6; 86 B2

Snipe 121 A5
Snow Brake 79 C4
Snow Creek 46 B2; 73 B6
Snow Gap 63 C4
Snow Hill 113 D5
Snow Hill 63 C4
Snow Lake 106 A1
Snow Lake 103 D6
Snow 20 C1
Snowball Branch 19 D6; 32 A2
Snowball 33 C4
Snowrick Mountain 47 B4
Snyder Mountain 29 B5
Snyder 125 A5
Soapstone Hill 50 C3
Social Hill 88 C3
Soda Creek 62 A2
Soda Hollow 44 A1
Soda Mountain 62 A2
Soda Valley 62 A2
Solgohachia 61 A5
Sollars Reservoir 92 D3
Sollys Knob 46 A1
Solo 46 B2
Sonora 16 D2
Sook Creek 21 D4
Sore Eye Point 25 C6
Sorrells 91 D4
Sorrells Creek 88 B1
Soudan 79 A4
Soso Bayou 126 A3
South Alligator Bayou 83 B5,6
South Alum Creek 76 B2
South Bayou 112 B2,3
South Bend 79 A4
South Big Creek 36 B2,3; 37 B4
South Bluff 80 C2
South Bratton Creek 33 B6
South Brushy Creek 22 C1;C2
South Central 100 A1
South Clear Creek 115 C6
South Creek 121 A6
South Cypress Creek 121 C4
South Fork Bee Bayou 94 D1
South Fork Big Creek 27 B4
South Fork Brown Creek 76 A3
South Fork Dry Creek 18 C2
South Fork Frank La Pere Creek 123 D6
South Fork Little Red River 60 D2
South Fourche La Fave River 56 A2
South Fourche la Fave River 75 A4,6
South Fourche La Fave River 76 A1,2
South Lapile Creek 123 C4
South Lead Hill 19 B6
South Mountain 29 B4; 33 C5; 78 C2
South Ozark 44 C1
South Panther Skin Creek 49 A4
South Plains 82 A1
South Pond 113 A6
South Prong Big Creek 49 B5
South Prong Middle Creek 34 A3
South Prong Roasting Ear Creek 34 C3,5
South Prong Spavinaw Creek 15 D6
South Shore Park 47 C4
South Stuttgart 92 A3
South Sylamore Creek 34 C3; 35 C4
South Twinkle Creek 88 A3
South Wicked Creek 58 D7
Southern Creek 73 D5
Southern Hill 35 C1
Southern Lake 93 B6
Southland 39 D6
Southland 83 D4
Southside 50 A2
Spadra Creek 45 B4;C4
Spadra 45 B4
Spainhour Falls 45 B4
Spanker Creek 16 A1
Sparkman Lake 21 C6
Sparkman 101 C4
SparkSpring 22 A1
Spavinaw Creek 15 B4,5
Speak Point 35 D6
Spear Lake 54 B1
Spence Jucntion 32 C1
Spencer Bay 88 A2
Spencer Bayou 91 C4
Spencer Creek 22 A5; 103 B6
Spencer Lake 61 C6
Spencer Ridge 34 A1
Spicewood Creek 20 B1
Spider Creek 17 A4;
32 B1; 33 C4
Spiller Creek 74 A2
Spirit Lake 110 D2
Spirits Creek 43 A4
Spivey Lake 67 C6
Spoke Plant 30 D3
Spoon Lake 113 C5
Spooner Branch 122 C1
Spotville 19 B6
Spout Spring 35 D6
Spriggs Mill 51 C5
Spring Creek 36 D1
Spring Bank 119 C4
Spring Branch 15 B4; 22 A3;
63 A5; 73 C6; 77 D4;
103 C6; 112 D1; 119 C4;
118 A3; 120 B3
Spring Creek 16 C1;D1;
18 A2; 22 D1; 25 A5;
33 A5;B6; 34 A1; 36 C1;D1;
46 A1; 59 B4;C6; 62 A2;
78 A2; 82 B2;C2; 98 A3
Spring Creek 16 D1
Spring Creek 52 C5
Spring Hill 110 B3
Spring Hill 112 C2
Spring Lake Estates 21 B4
Spring Lake 59 D6; 62 D3;
78 B1;D2
Spring Mountain 59 B6;
75 B5
Spring River 23 A6;B6;C6;
24 C1;D2,3; 34 A2;3
Spring Valley 16 B1
Spring Valley 117 C2
Springdale 16 C2
Springfellor Hill 62 B1
Springfield 61 B4

Springhill Creek 114 C3
Springhill 62 B1
Springhill 77 D6
Springtown 15 C5
Sprudel 110 B2
Spur Four 54 B3
Spurlock Hollow 23 D6
Spy Branch 102 A1
Spy Rock 44 A2
Spybuck Drainage Canal 68 C2
Square Rock Creek 57 D5; 73 A4
Square Rock Lake 57 D5
Square Rock Ridge 57 D5
St Francis Bay Straight Slough 53 D4
St Francis Old River 69 D4
St Francis River 27 B6;D5;
39 C6;D6; 40 A1;B1;D1;
53 A6;B6;D5,6; 83 B5
Stack Rock 32 C3; 35 D4
Stacy Creek 24 C3; 37 C4
Stacy Springs 49 C4
Stacy 53 A5
Stacy 54 D2
Stafford 59 B4
Stair Knob 21 D4
Stalcup Bend 51 B4
Stalling Bend 37 B6
Stamps 111 D4
Standard Umpstead 113 D5
Standing Rock 20 D1
Standing Rocks Hill 33 B6
Standing Mountain 30 C1
Stanford 39 A4
Stanley Gap 62 B3
Stanley Mountain 48 B2
Stanley Spring 50 C3
Staple 104 A3
Star City 93 B6
Star Gap 35 C4
Star Lake 94 C1
Star Mountain 33 D5
Stark City 97 C6
Stark Ridge 41 B4
Stark Spring 15 D4
Starkey Creek 85 A4
Starkey Hill 63 C4
Starkey Mountain 61 A4
StarkPoint 49 C4
Starks 28 B3
Starling Creek 24 D2
Starnes Spring 50 A1
State Creek 72 D2
State Line 120 C1
State Line 22 A1
Statehouse Mountain 86 B1
Stave Island 46 B4
Stave Lake 54 C2
Staves 102 D3
Stayeyard Bend 124 B1
Steamboat Bend 101 D6
Steeds 60 D4
Steel Creek 31 B5;D6;
99 D4,5; 110 D3; 119 A6
Steele Bend 79 C4
Steele Hill 97 C5
Steele 16 D2
Steenberger Lake 51 C4
Steep Bank Creek 37 B5
Steep Creek 49 D2
Steep Gut Bayou 33 C5
Steep Hollow Creek 73 C3
Steepbank L'Aigle Creek 114 B3
Stegall 54 B1
Stella 35 B3
Stelltown 99 A4
Stennitt Creek 24 D3; 37 A6
Stephens Creek 116 C1
Stephens 112 B2
Stephenson Mountain 33 C6
Stepp Creek 31 C6
Steprock 50 D1
Sterling Branch 108 A2
Sterling Spring 39 C4
Steve 75 A5
Stevens Creek 50 D2; 73 B5
Stevenson Mountain 28 B3; 74 C2
Stewart Branch 57 D4
Stewart Creek 21 D4
Stewart Fork 34 A2
Stewart Hill 36 C1
Stewart 53 C5
Stick Bend 123 A4
Stier 54 A1
Still Branch 75 B4; 76 C2
Stillhouse Branch 48 D2
Stillhouse Creek 76 B3
Stillhouse Spring 24 A2
Stillions 124 A1
Stillwater Bayou 92 C1
Stillwater 75 B3
Stilwell Mountain 45 C4
Stimson 106 B1
Stinking Bay 93 B6
Stinking Bay 93 B6
Stinnett Creek 59 A5
Stob Gap 43 A6
Stockton Bottom 111 C6
Stoebuck Mountain 47 C4
Stokes Branch 101 B5
Stokes Creek 48 D1
Stokes 25 B3
Stone Creek 44 D1
Stone Dam Creek 62 C1
Stone Hill 24 B3
Stone Quarry Creek 89 B4
Stone Ridge 31 D6
Stonewall 26 C2
Stoney Point 25 C4
Stony Creek 86 D1; 98 A1;B3
Stony Point Branch 17 A6
Stony Point 63 C5
Storm Creek Lake 83 A4
Storm Creek 83 B4
Stormhole Bend 123 B6
Story Branch 74 C5; 96 A3
Story Mountain 48 B2
Story 75 C4
Stout Spur 40 A1
Stouts Point 61 C4
Stoverville 31 B5
Stowe Creek 59 D4
Straight Creek 25 D4
Straight Creek 85 B6
Straight Lake 25 D4; 66 D3;
82 B4; 81 A4;B4; 123 B6
Straight Rock Creek 75 A4
Strain Branch 49 D4
Strain 29 A5
Strand Knob 34 C2
Strangers Home 37 C6
Stratton Creek 61 A6
Strawberry Branch 20 B2
Strawberry Ferry 37 C5
Strawberry River 22 C2;D3;
D4; 36 A2,3; 37 A4;B5
Strawberry 45 B5
Strawberry 35 A4
Strickler 28 C3
Stricklin Creek 85 D4
Stringers Mill 51 C6
Strington Creek 96 B3
Stringtown 99 B4
Strong 123 C5
Strother Mountain 50 A2
Stroud Creek 87 D6; 99 A6
Stuart Island 117 D5
Stuart 29 D3
StubsPoint 49 A4
Stump Mountain 33 C4
Stumptoe 47 C4
StumpyPoint 81 A4
Sturgis Pond 77 B6
Sturkie 22 A3
Stuttgart 92 A2
Styles Mountain 34 D1

Subiaco Reservoir 58 A3
Subiaco 58 A3
Success 26 A1
Suck Creek 99 A4
Suck Mountain 74 C3; 77 A4
Spurlock Hollow 47 D5
Suckles Lake 99 C5
Sugar Camp Creek 49 A4
Sugar Creek 24 C1; 27 B5;
45 A6; 50 B2;D3; 53 D4;
57 D6; 58 C1; 122 D1;
83 C4; 85 B6; 122 D1
Sugar Gap 32 D2
Sugar Grove 58 C1
Sugar Hill 28 C2; 34 D3
Sugar Loaf Creek 56 D2
Sugar Loaf Mountain 19 B6;
39 C6;D6; 40 A2;B1;
43 A6; 49 C5
Sugar Loaf Mountains 56 D2
Sugar Orchard Creek 19 C5;C6
Sugar Tree Knob 32 D2
Sugar Tree Mountain 30 D2
Sugarloaf Creek 36 B6;
34 A3; 87 B5;C5
Sugarloaf Knob 19 B6; 87 C4
Sugarloaf Lake 56 C2
Sugarloaf Mountain 34 A3; 88 A1
Sugartree Gap 85 A5
Sugartree Mountain 28 B1;
85 A4;B6
Suggs Mountain 34 A1
Sulfur Springs 19 B6
Sulfur Creek 31 D4
Sullivan Creek 36 D2
Sulpher Creek 45 D6; 85 A5
Sulphia Springs Creek 43 D5
Sulphur City 29 B5
Sulphur Creek 31 A2; 44 C2;
45 B6; 46 A2; 49 C4; 86 A1
Sulphur Fork 28 C3
Sulphur Mountain 32 A2;
45 D6
Sulphur River 118 A3; 119 C4
Sulphur Rock 36 D3
Sulphur Slough 97 B5
Sulphur Spring Branch 33 D4; 49 C5
Sulphur Spring 35 C4; 49 B4
Sulphur Springs 15 A5
Sulphur Springs 44 C3
Sulphur Springs 48 C2
Sulphur Springs 91 D4
Sulphur Springs 124 C2
Sumac Creek 48 D6
Sumac Lake 25 B6
Summers 27 B6
Summerville 114 C2
Summit 20 C2
Summit 44 A1
Sumpter 17 B6
Sun Valley Addition 36 D2
Sunflower Bend 94 D3
Sunny Hill 46 C1
Sunny Land 34 C1
Sunnydale 50 C1
Sunnyside Creek 47 D6
Sunnyside 47 D5
Sunrise Point 59 B6
Sunset Creek 59 B6
Sunset Point 59 B6
Sunset Ridge 20 B2
Sunset 70 B2
Sunshine 87 A6
Sunshine 74 C3
Supply 25 A6
Surge Pond 78 D1
Surrat Slough 59 C4
Surrounded Hill 51 A4; B4
Surrounded Ridges 59 C5
Sutherland Crossroads 44 B2
Suttle 50 D1
Sutton Bayou 105 C6
Sutton Creek 63 A5
Sutton Knob 32 D2
Sutton 111 A5
Swaggerty Branch 71 A5
Swaim Branch 74 A3
Swain 35 C1
Swan Deer Brake 105 C6
Swan Lake 69 A5; 70 C2;
79 A6; 92 D1; 94 C3;
105 B6 ; 106 A1,2; 119 A5
Swan Lake 92 D1
Swan Pond Lateral 26 D1
Swan Pond Lake 99 B5
Swan Ponds 66 B1
Swearngin Cave 35 D6
Sweat Hollow 22 B3
Sweden Creek 31 B4
Sweden 92 D1
Sweeden Island 60 B2
Sweet Home 61 D4
Sweet Home 92 B2
Sweethome 74 D3
Sweetwater Creek 74 C1;
86 C3
Swift Creek 117 D5
Swift Slough 117 D5
Swifton 37 D6
Swindle Creek 86 A3
Sycamore Bend 25 C5
Sycamore Creek 23 A5;
43 B5; 84 D3; 97 B4
Sycamore Heights 21 C5
20 C1
Sycamore Spring 21 C6
Sycamore 100 C1
Sycamore 19 A5
SycamorePoint 81 C4
Sylamore 34 C3
Sylvania 63 D5
Sylverino 18 A3
Sylvester Branch 121 A5

T Lake 93 B6
T Lateral Creek 52 B3
Tackett Creek 47 C4
Tackey Hill 45 B6
Tafton 78 D3
Tag 46 C2
Tall Peak 85 B5
Talley 121 B5
Tamo 104 A1
Tan Yard Branch 18 D1
Tan Trough Creek 21 D6;
34 A3
Tan-a-Hill Creek 73 C5
Tanglewood 16 C3
Tanner Creek 24 D5
Tanyard Branch 60 B1
Tanyard Creek 18 B6; 102 B2
Tanyard Spring 18 C2
Tar Camp Creek 91 A4
Tar Kiln Branch 19 C6
Tar Kiln Creek 19 C6
Tar Kiln Mountain 47 C4
Taral 46 D1
Tarleton Creek 78 B3-D6
Tarlton Flats 32 D2
Tarncville 80 A2
Tarry 103 A6
Tarsus 69 C6
Tarwate rSpring 35 D4
Tassel Spring 34 A2
Tate Spring 36 C1
Tate 57 D6
Tater Hill 24 D1; 34 A1;
35 C5; 35 D4; 48 D1;
62 B1,2; 59 A4;B6;
62 B1,2; 85 D5
Tater Knob 28 D1; 46 C1
Tates Bluff 100 D3
Tates Mill 62 D3

Tatter Knob 15 A6
Tattle Creek 25 B6
Tatum Branch 111 D4; 123 B5
Tatum Spring 25 C6
Taw Branch 47 D4
Taylor Branch 36 D2; 101 C5
Taylor Creek 44 A6; 61 D6;
68 B3;C3; 77 D6; 112 C1;
114 B1
Taylor Lake 69 D6
Taylor Mountain 31 C6
Taylor Old River Lake 104 A3
Taylor Point 66 C3
Taylor Pond 15 D4
Taylor Ridge 34 D3
Taylor 120 C1
Taylors Ditch 39 D6
Taylors Store 97 D4
Tea Table Knob 32 D2
Teague Creek 51 D4
Teague 51 D4
TealPoint 21 B6
Tellier Island 115 D4
Temperanceville Creek 97 B6
Temperanceville 98 B1
Temple Hill 18 B1
Temple 109 B6
Tenmile Creek 50 B-D2; 76
D3; 77 D4; 88 C3;
89 A4,5;B5;C4; 101 A6;
102 A1; 103 C6;D5; 115 B5,6
Tennessee Branch 109 D6
Tennessee Creek 85 B4
Tennessee 15 B6
Tenny Branch 47 D5
Terrapin Creek 18 C3;D3;
21 D5; 72 B3
Terre Noir Creek 87 D5;
99 A6
Terre Rouge Creek 98 D3;
B6; 111 A4,5
Terrapin Branch 31 C5
Terry 103 A6
Terrytown 78 C1
Texarkana 109 D5
Thatch Creek 25 B4
The Backbone 36 A2; 59 D4
The Bar 117 A6
The Basin 32 A1
The Basin 33 B5
The Cliffs 66 A2
The Gourd 34 C2
The Island 59 C4
The Mounds 110 D2
The Narrows 43 A5; 45 B5;
46 B1; 62 A2
The Narrows 47 D5
The Old Sag 109 B4
The Pines 27 B6
The Quarry 36 D1
The Rock House 20 C2
Thebes 125 A5
Thida 50 C1
Thiel 89 C6
Thola 34 C1
Thomas Allen Point 80 B3
Thomas Branch 111 C4
Thomas Creek 31 C5;B4
Thomas Lake 78 A3
Thomas Mountain 67 C2;
93 C4
Thomasville 82 B2
Thompson Brake 125 D5
Thompson Branch 59 A4;
90 A2
Thompson Creek 25 C4;
48 B2; 102 D3; 124 B3
Thompson Knob 45 A5
Thompson Mountain 35 B5; 45 C5
Thompson Point 33 D5
Thompson 29 C6
Thorn Hill 122 C1
Thornburg 61 D4
Thorney Creek 29 B6
Thorney 29 B6
Thornton 101 B6
Thornton 102 D1
Thorpe Mountain 74 C3
Three Brothers Peak 24 A4
Three Creeks 121 B6;C6
Three Forks 121 C6
Three Knob Mountain 46 C1
Three Knobs 59 B5
Three Mile Creek 52 C1
Three Mile Slough 53 B6;C5
Three Oak Gap 85 A5
Three Way 38 C4
Three Way 34 C2
Threemile Branch 114 D2
Threemile Creek 58 A1
Throckmorton Hill 50 C3
Thunder Branch 85 C3
Thurman 66 D1
Tichnor 93 C5
Tick Creek 34 C1;D1
Tick Hill 14 D3
Tide Water 121 B4
Tidwell Branch 111 B6
Tie Chute Bluff 20 B2
Tiger Ditch 37 D6
Tiger Creek 88 A3; 89 A4
Tillar Brake 116 A3
Tillar 116 A3
Tilly 47 A4
Tilton 68 A1
Timber Lake Manor 21 C6
Timber Lake 77 D6; 106 C1
Timbo Creek 34 C2
Timbo 34 C2
Timon 16 B2
Tin Spring 15 D6
Tiny Creek 32 D1
Tipp 67 B2
Tipperary 26 C3
Tipsey Branch 93 D6
Tipton 102 D2
TJ House Reservoir 43 B5
Toad Creek 102 B1
Toad Suck 61 B6
Tobe Lake 110 B1
Toder Cave 23 A6
Togo 23 A5
Tokalon 15 D4
Tokio 102 C3
Tolar Lake 89 C6
Tollette 102 C3
Tollman Branch 90 B2
Tollville 80 C3
Toltec Mounds 79 C4
Toltec 79 C4
Toluca 43 D1
Tom Cook Brake 113 C6
Tom Creek 122 A3
Tom Moore Branch 36 A1
Tom Thumb Spring 15 A6
Tom Young Spring 18 C2
Tomahawk Creek 33 A4;B5;
34 D3; 35 D4
Tomahawk 33 A5
Tomato 41 C6
Tomberlin 91 A6
Toms Branch 45 B6
Toms Fountain 61 C5
Toney Bend 33 A6
Toney Old River 112 A3
Toney 41 C5
Tongin 33 A1
Tontitown 16 C1
Topaz 70 C1

Tosh Hill 35 C6
Touchstone Prairie 104 D1
Tow Point 31 D5
Tower Mountain 85 A4
Towhead Island 51 B5
Town Creek 20 C2; 23 D4;
29 A4; 30 A2; 36 A2;
48 B1; 115 B4
Town Lateral 26 A1
Townsend Lateral 26 A1
Trace Creek 43 C5; 66 B1; 77 B4;
89 A5,6
Trace Ridge 47 A5
Trace 100 C3
Trafalgar 116 D2
Trailer Creek 99 A6
Trailer Bridge 104 D3
Trammel Creek 41 B5
Trammel Mountain 29 A6
Trap Mountain 87 B5; 88 B1
Traskwood 89 A5
Treat 46 B1
Tremble Creek 47 A4
Trent Creek 97 C5
Tribble Creek 99 C4
Tri-County Lake 102 D2
Trident 28 A1
Trimble Creek 20 B1
Trimble Island 81 A4
Trimble Mountain 31 C5
Trinnon 27 B6
Triplett's Bluff 91 B4
Trotter Branch 19 A5
Trotters Brake 19 A5
Trout Branch 35 D6
Troy 72 C1
Truett Creek 59 B4;C4
Trull 122 B1
Truman 53 A6
Trumann 53 A6
Tubal 101 B3
Tubbs Creek 66 D3
Tucker Bay 37 B6
Tucker Bluff 63 B4
Tucker Creek 59 B5
Tucker Creek 43 C6; 116 B2
Tucker Mountain 46 D1
Tucker 91 A5
Tuckerman 51 A6
Tuckertown 41 D5
Tulip Creek 100 B1
Tulip 101 A5
Tull 89 A6
Tulley Lake 91 B4
Tulley Slough 53 C4
Tumbling Shoals 49 B5
Tuni Creek 69 D4
Tunica Lake 83 C6
Tunis 79 B5
Tunnel Branch 112 A1
Tupelo Bayou 61 D6;
62 D1; 92 C1
Tupelo Brake 69 A6
Tupelo Creek 100 A2
Tupelo Hole 91 D5
Tupelo Lake 94 D1
Tupelo 51 D5
Turbin Creek 73 D6
Turkey Creek 33 C6;
34 C1;D3; 35 D4; 38 B1;
67 C5;D5; 68 A3; 73 B6;
77 B5; 90 A3; 109 C6;
110 A1; 118 B3; 122 C1
Turkey Creek 34 D3
Turkey Hill 31 C4; 37 A5;
45 B6
Turkey Island Slough 54 A1
Turkey Knob 21 B6; 22 B3;
A2; 35 A4; 49 A4; 58 B2
Turkey Mountain 21 A4;
45 B4
Turkey Pen Creek 34 C5
Turkey Pen Mountain 74 C1
Turkey Scratch 82 C2
Turkey Slough 51 C6
Turkey Swamp 61 D5
Turkey 20 C1
Turner Creek 25 A4; 36 C1;
73 C6; 75 A5
Turner Knob Creek 31 C4
Turner 40 C3
TurnerLake 112 B3
Turner 94 A1
Turners Bend 44 A1
Turners Creek 102 D1
Turpin Hill 63 B5
Turrell 54 D2
Turtle Creek 81 C6; 103 B5,6
Tuttle Branch 29 A4
Tuttle Ridge 35 D5
Tuttle 29 A4
Tuttleton 80 A4
Tweedie Mountain 86 B2
Twen Cen 78 D1
Twentythree 50 D3
Twin Bridges 114 D2
Twin Bridges 87 D4
Twin Creek 35 B4
Twin Groves 62 A1
Twin Knobs 48 A3
Twin Lakes 66 D3; 93 D6
Twin Mountain 108 D3
Twin Mountain 35 A4
Twin Slough 93 A6; 104 C2
Twin Oaks 26 B1
Twin Oaks 39 A4
Twin Springs 84 B2
Twin Springs 27 B6
Twist 54 C2
Two Bayou 112 B3;
113 A6;B4
Two Springs 78 B3
Twomile Branch 90 B2
Twomile Creek 36 D6;
52 D2; 72 A3; 75 A4;
84 A2,3; 85 A4; 116 A3
Tyler Slough 109 A4
Tyner Hill 24 D1
Tyro 50 B3
Tyronza Bayou 38 B3; 55 B4
Tyronza Junction 54 C1
Tyronza River Cutoff 53 D6
Tyronza River 53 D6;
54 B2;C1; 69 A5;6
Tyronza Sunk Lands 54 A3
Tyronza 54 C1

Uhiren Reservoir 80 C1
Ulm 80 A3
Umphers Knob 46 A1
Umpire 85 C5
Uncle Bud Creek 74 B1
Uncle Joe Warren Mountain 19 B6
Unco 114 C1
Underwood Branch 23 D5
Union Branch 111 B5
Union City 45 C4
Union Hill 51 A5
Union Hill 74 A2
Union Hill 44 A1
Union Ridge 57 C4
Union Valley 79 B5
Union 22 C2
Union 54 C1
Union 67 A5
Union 96 A2
Union 116 D1
Uniontown 28 B2
Unity Bayou 80 A3;C4
Unity 91 A4
Unity 98 C1
Uno 52 A1

Upland 122 C2
Upper Crooked Lake 81 D3
Upper Cut-Off Creek 1
03 D6; 104 D1; 116 A2
Upper Eagle Nest Lake 93 A5
Upper Forked Lake 93 A6
Upper Hooked Lake 93 A6
Upper Moore Lake 109 C6
Upper Old River 81 C4
Upper Panther Island 46 A2
Upper Poplar Ridge 39 C6
Upper Seibert Lake 67 C6
Upper Swan Lake 93 B5
Upper Taylor Lake 94 D1
Upshaw Creek 24 B3
Upton Creek 24 D2
Urbana 123 B4
Ursula 51 A5
Utley Lake 100 D3

Vaby 80 C3
Vache Grasse Creek 43 D4;
56 A3; 57 A4;B4
Vaden 40 D1
Vagabond Lake 24 C1
Vail 40 D1
Valentine 78 B3
Valley Brake 104 D3
Valley Branch 90 A3
Valley Creek 53 D4; 87 C6
Valley Gin 119 B4
Valley Junction 116 C1
Valley Springs 19 B6
Valley Stone 24 D3
Valley 115 C5
ValleyView 39 D4
Vallier 92 C2
Van Buren 44 A1
Van Wagoner Ridge 24 D1
Van 93 C5
Vance Branch 36 A3
Vance Lake 51 B5
Vance 37 C5
Vandergriff Creek 25 B4
Vandervoort 84 B3
Vandeventer Mountain 30 C1
Vanduzer 16 C3
Vandale 68 A1
Vanness Crossing 83 A4
Varnell Creek 102 C3
Varner 104 A2
Vass Reservoir 49 A6
Vaucluse Bar 126 A3
Vaucluse 117 D6
Vaughan Mountain 29 B4
Vaughn Creek 98 B3
Vaughn 15 C6
Vaughts Reservoir 80 B2
Velie 113 A4
Velvet Ridge 50 D2
Vendor 32 B2
Venice 123 C1
Venus Mountain 30 C3
Venus 30 C3
Verner Ridge 35 A5
Verona 39 A4
Vesta 43 D5
Vick 124 A1
Vickers Creek 49 B4
Vickory Creek 21 C5
Victoria Bluffs 38 C6;
34 C1;D3; 35 D4; 38 B1;
67 C5;D5; 68 A3; 73 B6
Victoria 40 C1;
Victoria 123 C5
Victory Lake 26 B2
Vidette 22 B1
Villages Creek 38 C6; 38 C1;
39 B5; 50 B5; 51 A4;6;B5;
69 B4; 104 C1; 121 A5
Village Junction 121 A5
Village 45 A6
Village 36 B2
Vilonia Creek 62 C3
Vilonia 62 C3
Vince Bluff 103 D6
Vincent 91 A4
Vine Prairie Creek 43 C5
Vinegar Hill 108 A3
Vineyard Brake 56 B3
Vineyard Branch 16 D2
Vineyard Creek 56 B3
Vineyard 62 C2
Vinity Corner 66 C1
Viola 22 B3
Violet Hill 22 D3
Vision Branch 78 C2
Vista Shores 16 B3
Voss Lake 91 A4

Wabash 94 B3
Wabbaseka Bayou 91 A5;B6;
92 B1
Wabbaseka Bayou 92 B1
Wabbel 79 D5
Wade Hill 35 D4
Wade 96 B2
Wades Chapel 108 A3
Wadleigh Branch 112 B3
Wadley Lake 109 C6
Wafers Crossing 110 B2
Waggie Creek 100 B3
Wagley Hollow 44 A3
Wagner Creek 66 B1
Wagnon 114 A2
Wagon Bayou 104 A1;B2
Wagon Branch 48 B3
Wagon Wheel Creek 49 B6; 50 B1
Wahl Branch 14 C2
Waits Hill 36 C3
Wake Creek 87 A4
Wakefield Mountain 29 D5
Walcott 38 A4
Waldenburg 52 B2
Waldo Mountain 45 B6;
46 B1
Waldo 111 D6
Waldon Mountain 35 B4
Waldrop Creek 111 C6
Waldron Ridge 73 A6
Waldron 73 A5
Walker Bayou 55 A4
Walker Branch 55 A6
Walker Mountain 46 A3;
72 A3
Walker 120 C1
Walker Creek 31 B4;C5;
115 A4; 120 B1; 122 C2
Walker Cypress Creek 81 D5
Walkers Corner 79 C4
Walkers Slough 125 C5
Walkerville 120 C2
Wall Creek 36 D3; 93 D6
Wall Lake 51 A4
Wall Rock 87 D4
Wall Branch 76 A2
Wallace Creek 35 D6; 60 D1
Wallace Knob 21 B5; 22 B3
Wallace 108 A3
Wallace 125 A4
Wallaceburg 97 C4
Waller Creek 36 A3
Waller Gap 62 C3
Walls Hollow 29 D6
Walnut Bayou 108 A1,3;B3
Walnut Branch 100 B3
Walnut Corner 38 A3
Walnut Corner 38 A3
Walnut Creek 31 D5;
63 A4; 87 A5

Walnut Grove Branch 37 C4
Walnut Grove Corner 53 B4
Walnut Grove Creek 74 C1
Walnut Grove 36 B3
Walnut Grove 37 C4
Walnut Grove 47 B6
Walnut Grove 120 C2
Walnut Hill 119 C5
Walnut Hollow 47 B6
Walnut Knob 47 A6
Walnut Lake 104 C3
Walnut Ridge 38 A1
Walnut Ridge 46 A1; 49 D6
Walnut Ridge 90 B3
Walnut Springs Creek 96 C3
Walnut Springs 96 B3
Walnut 31 D5
Walters Bluff 91 C6
Walters 40 C1
Walton Lake 78 D3
Waltreak 58 A3
Walworth Reservoir 49 A4
Wamac Point 101 C6
Wampoo 79 D4
Wapanocca Bayou 70 A2
Wapanocca Lake 54 D2
War Eagle Creek 16 D3
War Eagle Creek 16 C3;D3;
17 D4;D5; 30 A-C2
War Eagle 16 D3
Warbritton 90 A3
Ward 63 D5
Ward 78 C2
Ward Creek 45 A4;B6;
60 D1; 73 D4; 122 B3
Wardell 54 A2
Warden Branch 18 B1
Wards Bayou 116 D3
Wards Creek 96 D3
Ware Creek 121 D4,5
Ware 117 D5
Warehouse Bayou 91 B4
Warm Springs 23 A4
Warm Springs 25 A4
Warner Creek 39 C4
Warner Mountain 42 A2
Warner 113 A4
Warnock Springs 121 A4
Warner Branch 51 B4
Warren Creek 62 C2
Warren Mountain 49 B6
Warren 101 B5
Warrior Bottom 82 C1
Warrior Creek 20 D3
Warsaw 62 D3
Wasburn Mountain 29 B4
Wash Lake 92 D1
Washburn Creek 57 B5
Washburn Mountain 57 B5;
Washburn 57 B5
Washington Creek 81 C4
Washington Mountain 29 A4
Washington 29 B5
Washington 98 D2
Washita Creek 44 A3
Washita 75 C4
Watalula 44 B4
Water Can Crossing 85 D6
Waterfall Hollow 34 D3; 114 A2
Water Fork Branch 23 A5
Watered Fork Creek 23 B6; 24 B1
Waterfall Branch 49 D4
Waterfall Hollow 49 C5
Waterfield Creek 87 B4
Waterloo Bayou 91 B4
Waterloo 11 B6
Waterproof 80 A1
Waters Bayou 93 B6; 94 B1
Waters Creek 49 D5
Waters Spring 34 D2
Watkins Corner 94 A2
Watkins Pond 78 B3
Watson Bluff 67 D6
Watson Chapel 91 B4
Watson 105 C5
Watson Lake 51 B5; 58 A1
Watson Spring 30 C2
Watson 105 C5
Waugh Mountain 36 C1
Wautauga Spring 24 D2
Wave 101 B5
Waveland 58 C3
Waverly 70 C1
Wayland Creek 24 D3
Wayland Spring 24 D3
Wayton 31 C5
Weathers 31 B4
Weaver Bayou 126 A3;B2
Weaver Creek 114 A1;B2;
74 A2; 90 A3
Weaver Hill 28 A3
Webb Branch 31 A6; 63 B5
Webb City 44 C1
Webb Lake 80 B3; 113 B4
Webber Creek 42 B2
Webber Mountain 16 D2
Weber 93 D6
Webfoot Lake 105 B6
Weddington Creek 28 A3
Weddington 28 A2
Wedington Woods 28 A3
Wedington 28 A2
Weed 53 B6
Weehunt Mountain 72 C2
Wehunt Creek 86 A3
Weeks 72 A2
Wegert Reservoir 58 A3
Wehunt Creek 86 A3
Weiner 52 B2
Welch 87 D2
Welcome Home 33 D4
Welcome 100 D1
Welcome 46 C3
Weldon 51 C5
Wellford 126 C1
Wells Bottom 50 D1
Wells Creek 21 C6; 32 A2;
56 A2
Wells Point 105 B6
Welsh 87 D2
Weona Junction 53 C5
Weona 53 B4
Wesson 28 B2
Wesley Chapel 61 A4
West Aplin 60 D2
West Bayou 93 D6
West Boggy Bayou 117 C4;D4
West Branch Flat Creek 90 D1
West Branch 76 A2
West Cache River Slough 38 B2
West Cedar Creek 42 B3
West Cobb 37 A5
West Cove 56 C2;D2;
84 C2; 124 C3
West Crossett 124 B2
West Dry Creek 58 A3
West End 91 B4
West Fiddlers Creek 74 C2
West Flat Creek 67 D6; 68 D1

West Fleming Creek 30 D1
West Fork Beech Creek 100 C1
West Fork Big Cedar Creek 74 C1
West Fork Big Piney Creek 31 D3
West Fork Cane Creek 58 A3
West Fork Creek 86 C1;
98 D3
West Fork of Lisle Creek 88 C2
West Fork Knob 47 A6
West Fork Mill Creek 59 A5
West Fork Point Remove Creek 47 C5;D6; 60 A3
West Fork Powell Creek 72 C3
West Fork Prairie Creek 86 D2
West Fork Shop Creek 31 C6
West Fork Spring River 22 A3
West Fork Tulip Creek 101 A5;B6;A4
West Fork White River 29 A5;B4;C5
West Fork 29 C4
West Gafford Creek 74 A3;B3
West Greasy Creek 30 C1
West Hanna Mountain 85 B4
West Hartford 56 D2
West Helena 83 D4
West Kennett 27 C6
West Lacey Creek 58 B2
West Lafferty Creek 35 B6;C6
West Leatherwood Creek 17 B5
West Liberty 17 C5
West Line 96 B2
West Livinstone Creek 35 B4
West Marche 78 A1
West Memphis 70 B2
West Otis 16 C5
West Pangburn 49 D6
West Point 15 C4
West Point 66 B2
West Prong Baron Creek 44 A1
West Prong Horsehead Creek 44 B3
West Richwoods 34 D3
West Ridge 54 A2
West River 27 B6
West Rocky Bayou 35 B5
West Shadley Creek 74 C2
West Spiller Creek 74 A2
West Spring Creek 74 D3
West Spring 74 D3
West Sugarloaf Creek 16 A6;B5
West Three Creeks 121 B6
West Trace Creek 96 B3
West Twin Creek 35 B4
West Valley 84 A1
West Weaver Creek 74 B2
West Yocum Branch 18 B1
Western Grove 32 A2
Western 67 C2
Westor 94 D2
Westover 54 C2
Westover 95 B4
Westville 82 D2
Wet Lost Creek 90 A1
Whaley Creek 16 A3
Wharton Creek 30 A2;B3
Wharton 30 B3
Wheatley 81 A6
Wheeler Bend 114 B2
Wheeler Creek 119 C6
Wheeler Gap 29 D6
Wheeler Knob 46 A1
Wheeler Lake 93 A6
Wheeler Mountain 86 A3;B4
Watson Bluff 67 D6
Wheeler 28 A3
WhelenSprings 100 C3
Whetstone Creek 58 B3
Whetstone Mountain 100 C1
Whippie 48 D1
Whipple Ridge 34 D2
Whippoorwill Creek 66 D2
Whirl Lake 67 B4
Whiskerville 38 A3
Whiskey Chute 83 B5;
117 D5 126 A3
Whiskey Island 83 B5
Whiskey Peak 84 B2
Whiskey Spring 42 A3
Whisky Creek 76 A1
Whisp 40 C2
Whispering Springs 48 B3
Whistleville 40 D3
Whistling Lake 82 B1
Whitaker Branch 116 A2
Whitaker Creek 31 C4
Whitaker 53 B4
White Bluff 15 B5;
61 C5; 77 A5
White Hall 91 C4
White Hill 36 B2
White Lake 51 D5; 67 A6
White Oak Bayou 78 A2
White Oak Bluff 102 B2;
63 D4; 120 B3
White Oak Creek 19 C5;
43 C6; 44 C1; 60 A3 62 A3;
55 B6; C2; 85 C5,6;
86 C1; 88 B2;D1,2;
90 B2,B3;D2; 101 C4,5;
101 C4,5; 111 B4; 112 A1;B1;
114 A2; 126 A3;
124 A1,2; 125 C4
White Oak Lake 93 A6;
112 A1
White Oak Mountain 19 B5;
46 C3; 47 B4; 48 D7 D6;
62 A3; 75 D4; 84 A2
White Oak Slough 38 B1,2;
100 B2
White Oak 27 D5
White Oak 64 D4
White Pond 37 B6
White River 16 C2;D2; 17 A4;
19 A6; 20 A1;
20 A2; 20 C3; 21 D4;B5;D6;
29 A5;B6;C6; 30 D2;
34 A3; 35 B4;C5;D6;
34 A3; 35 B4;C5;D6;
50 D1;A2;A5; 63 A6;
A4;C4,D4; 64 A3; 65 A5;
80 A3; 81 B4;D4; 67 A4;A5
94 B1;D1; 105 A6;A6;
94 B1;D1; 105 A6;A6;
White Rock 43 A6
White Rock Creek 38 B2;
100 B2
White Rock Mountain 56 B3
White Rock 43 B6
White Sulphur Springs 88 A2
West Walnut Creek 27 C5
White 111 D2
Whitefield 104 A1
Whitehall 53 C4
Whitehall 83 B5
Whitehead Bluff 48 C5
Whitehill Lake 117 A6

Whitener Branch 16 D3
Whitener 17 D4
Whiteoak Mountain 79 B6;
80 B1
Whiteside Creek 111 A4
Whitetown 74 D2
Whiteville 21 C4
Whitewater Creek 102 D1;
114 A1
Whiting Mountain 30 D1
Whitlow Junction 119 C5
Whitlow 124 B2
Whitmore Mountain 62 B3
Whitmore 16 C3
Whitney Mountain 16 B3
Whitten Branch 111 A4
Whitten Spring 25 A4
Whittington 76 D3
Whittmore Mountain 30 C2
Whitton 54 C2
Whitzen Hollow Creek 42 A2
Wick Mill 68 A3
Wicked Creek 58 B2
Wickham Creek 121 A6
Wideman Creek 35 B6
Wideman Mountain 49 B6
Wideman 22 D2
Widener 69 D4
Wiederkehr Village 44 C2
Wiedower Mountain 61 A4
Wiggins Lake 69 C5
Wilbeth 54 C1
Wilborn Brake 104 D3
Wilburn Branch 39 B6;C6,6
Wilburn Hill 109 C5
Wilburn Knob 48 B3
Wildcat Spring 99 A4
Woodson 90 A3
Wildcare 104 A1
Woodyardville 78 C2
Wooldridge Creek 36 B2
Wild Cherry 22 C1
Wild Goose Branch 48 C3
Wild Goose Creek 48 A3
Wild Hog Mountain 21 D4
Wild Horse Creek 23 C5
Wild Plum Lake 23 C6
Wildcat Bayou 69 B6
Wildcat Bluff 50 C3; 88 A1
Wildcat Creek 15 D6; 20 B2;
75 A4; 90 A3
Wildcat Hill 50 C4
Wildcat Hollow 33 B6; 49 B4
Wildcat Knob 22 B3
Wildcat Mountain 42 D3;
47 D4; 77 C4
Wildcat Spring 99 A4
Wildwood 69 D6
Wiley Crossing 53 C4
Wilford Peak 77 B5
Wilkerson Branch 20 B2
Wilkins 68 B3
Wilkins 15 C5
Willbo Slough 83 A5; 69 D5
Willey's Cove 33 C6
William Hollow 31 B4
Williams Creek 68 B3; 73 B6;
74 D3; 77 D5; 86 A3;
111 B6; 123 B5
Williams Junction 77 A4
Williams Lake 57 B6; 109 C6
Williams Rocks 32 A3
Williamson 96 C3
Williamson 124 D2
Williford 24 C1
Willis Bald 19 B5
Willis Branch 19 B5
Willis Slough 54 C4
Willis 19 C4
Willow Beach Lake 79 C4
Willow Bend 61 C4
Willow Creek 38 C1
Willow Hollow 54 D2; 110 B1;
117 D6; 126 C3
Willow Point 83 C4
Willow Pond 54 A4
Willow Slough 54 B3; 105 C5
Willow Springs Branch 78 C2
Willow 89 D4
WillowBelle 79 C4
Wills Mountain 47 C4
Wilmar 115 C5
Wilmot 125 C5
Wilson Brake 125 B6
Wilson Branch 15 C4; 43 A4;
62 C5; 96 B2; 122 D1
Wilson Creek 35 C6; 45 C6;
46 C1; 47 B4; 86 A3; 96 A3;
97 C5;D6; 99 C5
Wilson Hill 62 D2,D3
Wilson Junction 40 C3
Wilson Lake 55 D4; 102 B2
Wilson Mountain 86 C3
Wilson Reservoir 96 B2
Wilson Slough 59 D4
Wilson 55 B4
Wilton 101 C6
Wilton 97 B4
Winchester 104 D3
Windy Branch 74 B1
Windy Mountain 61 A6
Winebaugh Lake 25 C5
Winesburg 28 C2
Winfield 72 A3
Winfrey 73 A4
Wing Meade Reservoir 92 A3
Wing 59 D4
Wingfield Creek 87 D6;
99 A6
Wingfield Lake 122 C2
Winham Lake 109 B5
Winifree Creek 78 B3
Winington 19 B6
Winn Mountain 43 B4
Winningham Creek 25 A6
Winnings Spring 17 B5
Winona 83 A5
Winrock 62 B3
Winset Mountain 58 A3
Winslow 29 C4
Winters Creek 97 C4
Winthrop 96 D2
Winton Spring 19 A4
Wirth 24 A1
Wiseman 22 B3
Witcherville 56 B3
Witherington 88 D2
Withrow Springs 17 D5
Witter 30 B2
Witts Springs 32 D3
Wittsburg Island 52 C1
Wittsburg Lake 69 B4
Wittsburg 69 B4
Wiville 67 B5
Wolf Bayou 49 A4
Wolf Bayou 49 A5,6; 105 A6
Wolf Creek 44 A4;
86 D3; 98 A3;
99 A4;B415 B5;C5; 19 C4;
20 A3; 23 B5;
32 B1;C1; 73 D4;
76 B3; B5; 100 C2;D2;
8 B1; 100 C2;D2;
98 C2;C3; 98 C2,3
White Oak Creek 27 C5
Whitefield 104 A1
Wolf Den Mountain 35 B5
Wolf Divide 45 B5
Wolf Island Slash 80 C2
Wolf Knob 21 C6
Wolf Lake 93 D6
Wolf Mountain 35 B4; 74
D3; 110 D3
Wolf Pen Gap 85 A5
Wolf Pen Hollow 47 C6
Wolf Pinnacle 73 C5; 76 B3

Whitener Branch 16 D3
Whitener 17 D4
Wolf Slough 53 D5;
123 C6; 124 D1
Wolf Wallow Ridge 20 B2
Wolfe Creek 52 D2
Wolfe Slough 69 A4
Wolford Addition 36 D2
Wolfpen Branch 20 B2
Wolquarry 35 C6
Wonderland Cave 16 B1
Wonderview 61 A4
Wood Spring 18 A1
Woodall Creek 86 D3
Woodard Creek 16 B3
Woodard Lake 113 B4
Woodberry 113 A5
Wooden Hills 19 B5
Woodland Hills 23 B6
Woodland 45 C4
Woodland 79 A6
Woodlawn 103 B4
Woodrow 49 A4
Woodruff Creek 78 A2
Woods Bend 53 D5
Woods Gap 43 A6
Woods Mountain 45 B5
Woodson 90 A3
Woodyardville 78 C2
Wooldridge Creek 36 B2
Wooldridge Spring 25 A4
Woolfolk Lake 54 B3
Woolsey Creek 97 C4
Woolsey 29 A4
Woolum 47 A5
Woolverton Mountain 62 B1
Wooster 62 B1
Wooten Lake 109 D6
Worden 66 A3
Worley Mountain 75 B5
Worshams Bluff 81 B4
Wortham Mountain 81 A4
Wortham Lake 109 A4
Worthen 60 A2
Worthington Creek 23 C5
Wrenton 61 B5
Wright Branch 76 A2; 121 D6
Wright Creek 27 C5
Wright Cutoff 50 A3
Wright Island 50 A3
Wright Mountain 48 C2
Wright Town 42 D3
Wright 91 B4
Wrightland 82 A3
Wrights Corner 50 D2
WrightsPoint 41 A6
Wrightsville 78 C2
Wyanoke 70 C2
Wyatt Spring 87 A4
Wye Mountain 77 A5
Wye 61 D5
Wyles Pond Slough 69 D4
Wylie Spur 70 B2
Wyman 29 A4
Wynn Creek 112 C1
Wynne 68 B3
Wyola 29 C5

Y City 73 B5
Yale 44 A3
Yancey Creek 87 C6
Yancopin 105 B5
Yancy 98 C1
Yarbo Place 105 C6
Yarborough Landing 109 A5
Yarborough Gap 44 B3
Yarbro 41 B5
Yardelle Branch 32 A2
Yardelle 32 A2
Yates Mountain 31 B4
Yeager Hollow 24 D2
Yeager Hollow 24 D2
Yellow Bank Creek 94 C3
Yellow Bank Slough 94 C3
Yellow Banks 53 C6
Yellow Bayou 117 D5
Yellow Bend 117 B5
Yellow Bluff Bend 123 A4
Yellow Bluff 91 C4
Yellow Bluffs 49 A4
Yellow Branch 49 B5; 50 A1
Yellow Creek 101 A1
Yellow Lake 99 B4
Yellville 20 D2
Yocana 17 D5
Yocum Creek 18 A2;B1,2
Yoder Creek 16 A3
Yoder 55 B4
Yoestown 43 D4
Yoncopin Lake 37 D5
York Chapel 78 B3
Yorktown 103 B6
Young Branch 24 D2
Young Creek 77 A5
Young Gravely 74 A2
Young Ridge 56 B3
Young Subdivision 63 D6
Young 112 B1
Younger Hill 36 B1
Younger Bayou 117 D5
Younger Mountain 46 B3
Younger Knob 109 B6
Youngs Creek 32 B1
Youngs Pond 80 A1
YoungsPoint 116 D1
Youngstown 116 D1
Yukon 104 D3

Zack Hollow 47 A6
Zack 33 B5
Zanone Bayou 70 D3
Zent 67 D6
Zentz Hollow 24 A1
Zinc 19 C6
Zion Hill 43 B4
Zion Hill 63 D4
Zion 36 A1

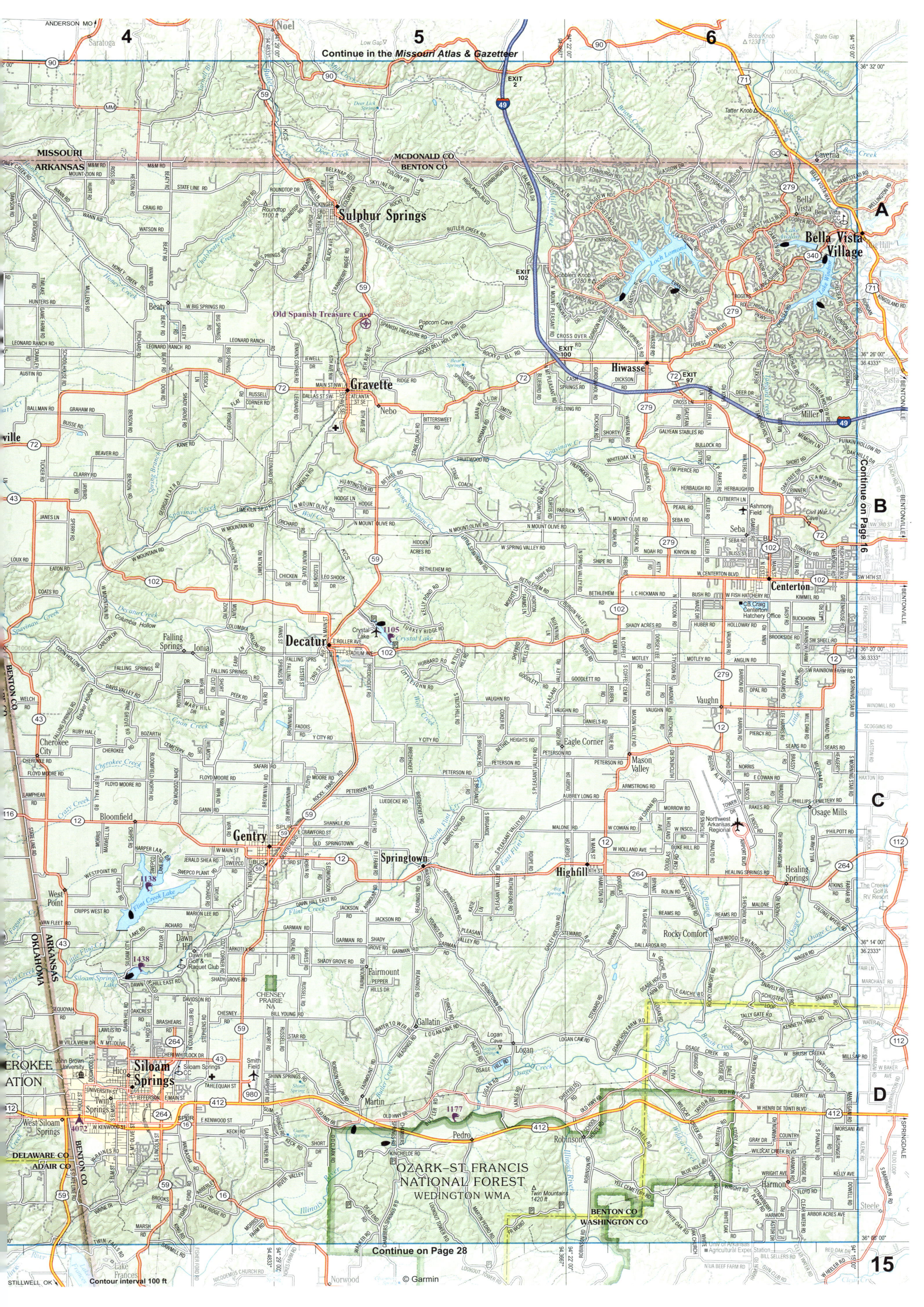

Continue in the *Missouri Atlas & Gazetteer*

A

B

C

D

Continue on Page 16

Continue on Page 28

OZARK–ST FRANCIS
NATIONAL FOREST
WEDINGTON WMA

Contour interval 100 ft

© Garmin

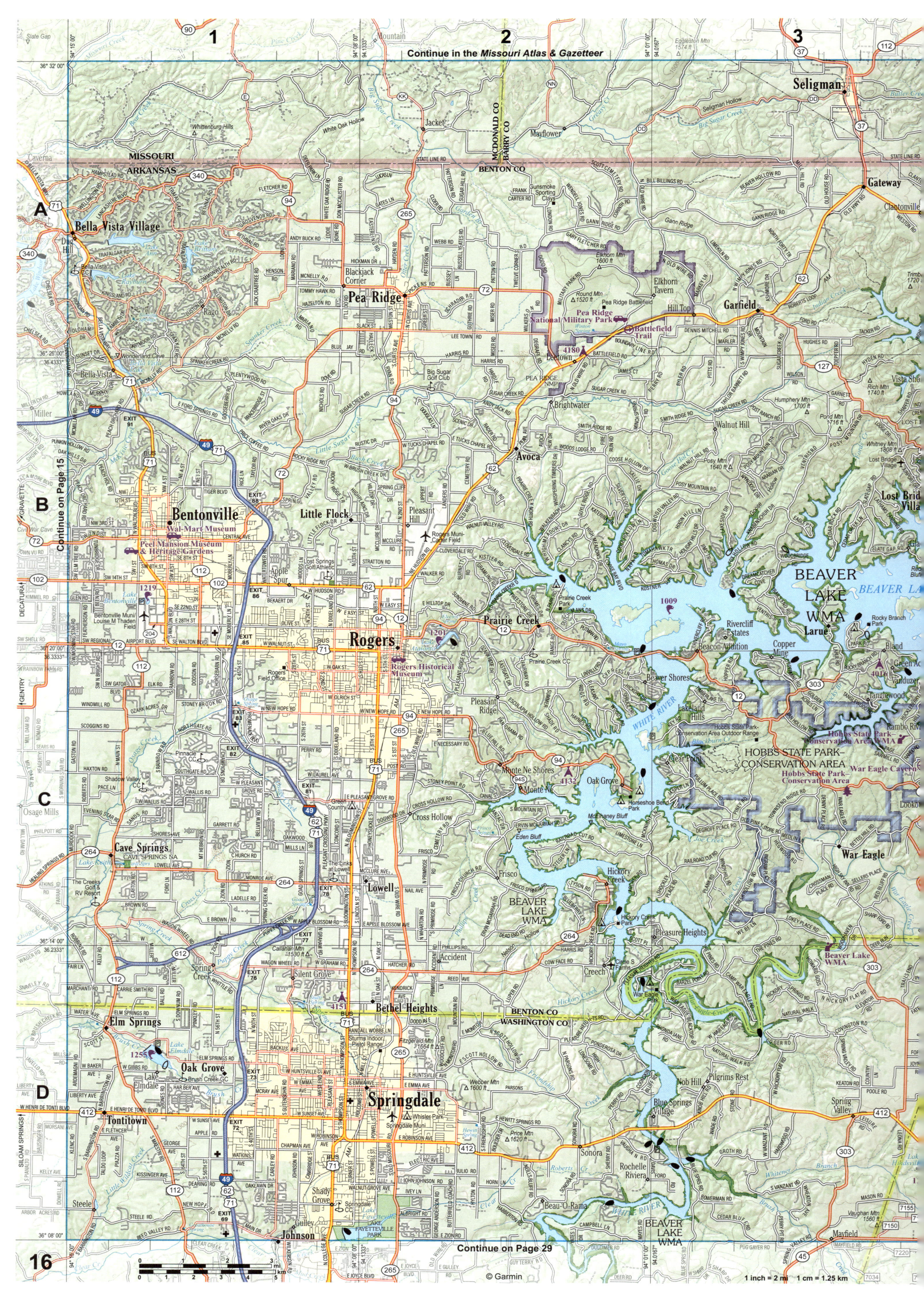

1   2   3

Seligman

Gateway

Clantonville

MISSOURI
ARKANSAS

MCDONALD CO
BARRY CO

BENTON CO

A

Bella Vista Village

Elkhorn
Tavern

Garfield

Bella Vista

Pea Ridge
National Military Park

Battlefield Trail

Pea Ridge
NMP

Vista Sub

Miller

Blackjack
Corner

Pea Ridge

Brightwater

Walnut Hill

B

Bentonville
Wal-Mart Museum

Peel Mansion Museum
& Heritage Gardens

Little Flock

Avoca

Lost Brid
Villa

Pleasant
Hill

Rogers Muni-
Carter Field

**BEAVER
LAKE
WMA**

BEAVER LA

Larue

Rivercliff
Estates

Rocky Branch
Park

Copper
Mine

Green AC
Vanduzer

Apple
Spur

Prairie Creek

Beacon Addition

Rogers

Rogers Historical
Museum

Prairie Creek CC

Tanglewood

Beaver Shores

C

Lakeland
Hills

Hobbs State Park-
Conservation Area Outdoor Range

Hobbs State Park-
Conservation Area WMA

War Eagle Cavern

Pleasant
Ridge

Monte Ne Shores

Monte Ne

Oak Grove

Clear Creek

**HOBBS STATE PARK-
CONSERVATION AREA**

Hobbs State Park-
Conservation Area

Cave Springs
Cave Springs NA

Cross Hollow

McChaney Bluff

Horseshoe Bend
Park

Eden Bluff

War Eagle

The Creeks
Golf &
RV Resort

Osage Mills

Lowell

Frisco

Hickory
Creek

Railroad Curves

Pleasure Heights

Hickory Creek
Park

Accident

**BEAVER
LAKE
WMA**

**Beaver Lake
WMA**

Silent Grove

Creech

BENTON CO
WASHINGTON CO

D

Elm Springs

Bethel Heights

Nob Hill

Pilgrims Rest

Spring
Valley

Oak Grove

Blue Springs
Village

Springdale

Whisler Park

Schnidale Muni

Sonora

Rochelle
Riviera

Tontitown

Shady
Grove

Springdale

Fayetteville
Park

Beau-U-Rama

**BEAVER
LAKE
WMA**

Johnson

Mayfield

16

© Garmin

1 inch = 2 mi   1 cm = 1.25 km

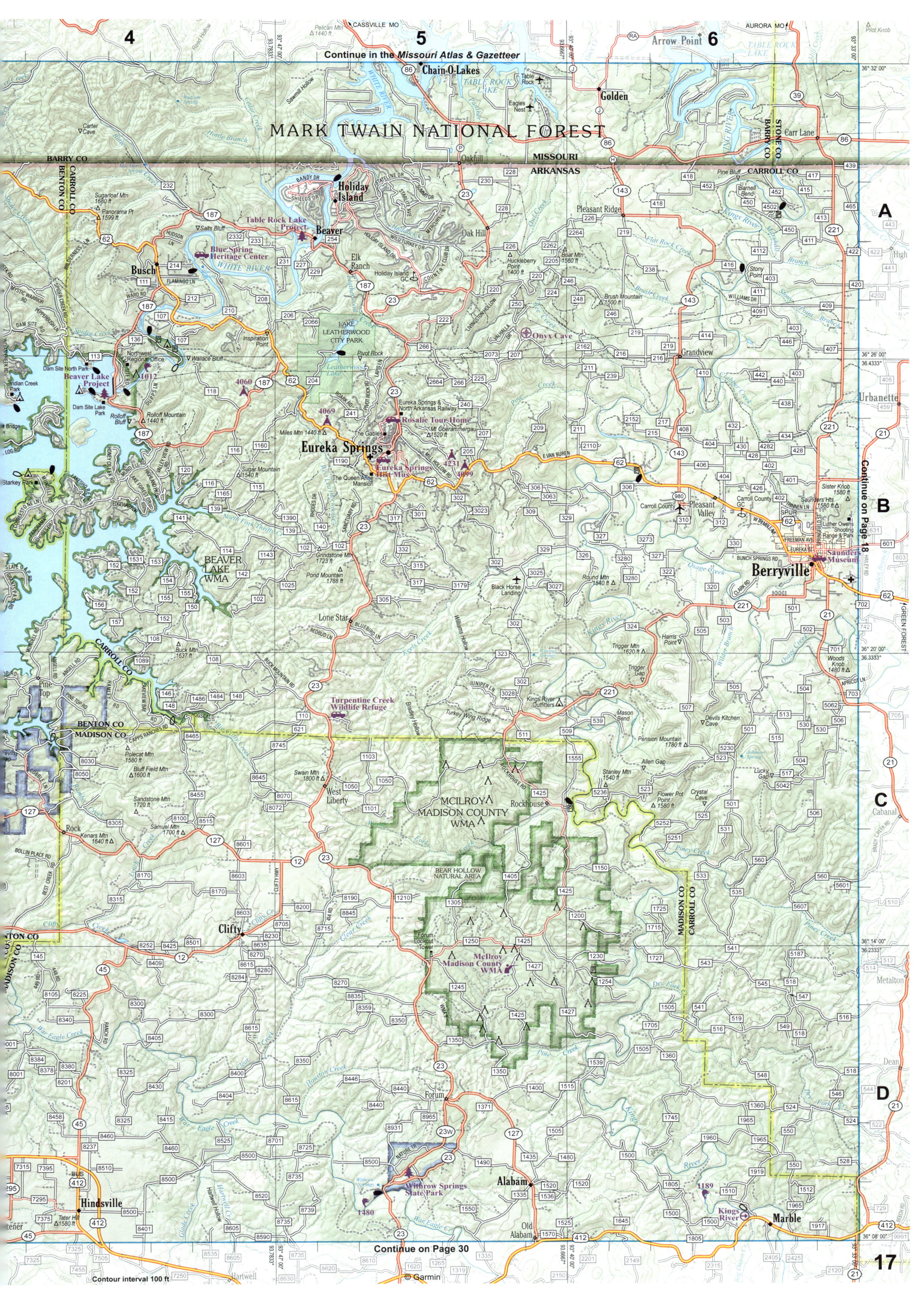

Continue in the *Missouri Atlas & Gazetteer*

MARK TWAIN NATIONAL FOREST

MISSOURI
ARKANSAS

Chain-O-Lakes

Golden

Holiday Island

Beaver

Table Rock Lake Project

Blue Spring Heritage Center

Busch

Northwest Regional Office

Beaver Lake Project

Dam Site Lake Park

LAKE LEATHERWOOD CITY PARK

Eureka Springs

Rosalie Tour Home

Eureka Springs & North Arkansas Railway

The Queen Anne Mansion

Eureka Springs Hist. Mus.

Grandview

Onyx Cave

Pleasant Ridge

Carr Lane

Pleasant Valley

Berryville

Saunder Museum

BEAVER LAKE WMA

Lone Star

Turpentine Creek Wildlife Refuge

Kings River Outfitters

Trigger Gap

Devils Kitchen Cave

Pine Top

BENTON CO
MADISON CO

West Liberty

Rockhouse

MCILROY MADISON COUNTY WMA

BEAR HOLLOW NATURAL AREA

Crystal Cave

MADISON CO
CARROLL CO

Clifty

Forum Lookout Tower

McIlroy Madison County WMA

Forum

Alabam

Withrow Springs State Park

Old Alabam

Kings River

Marble

Hindsville

Continue on Page 18

Continue on Page 30

Contour interval 100 ft

© Garmin

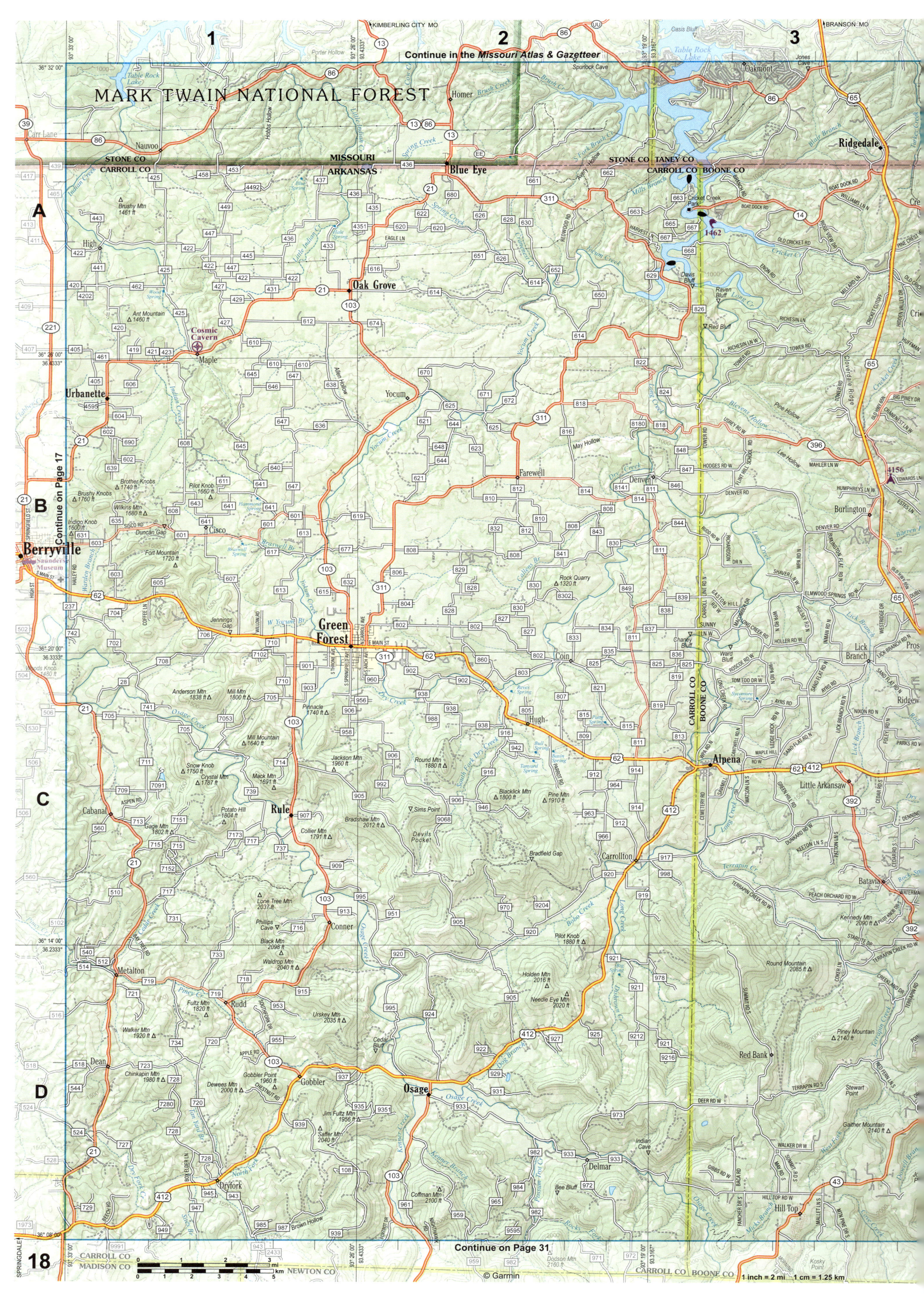

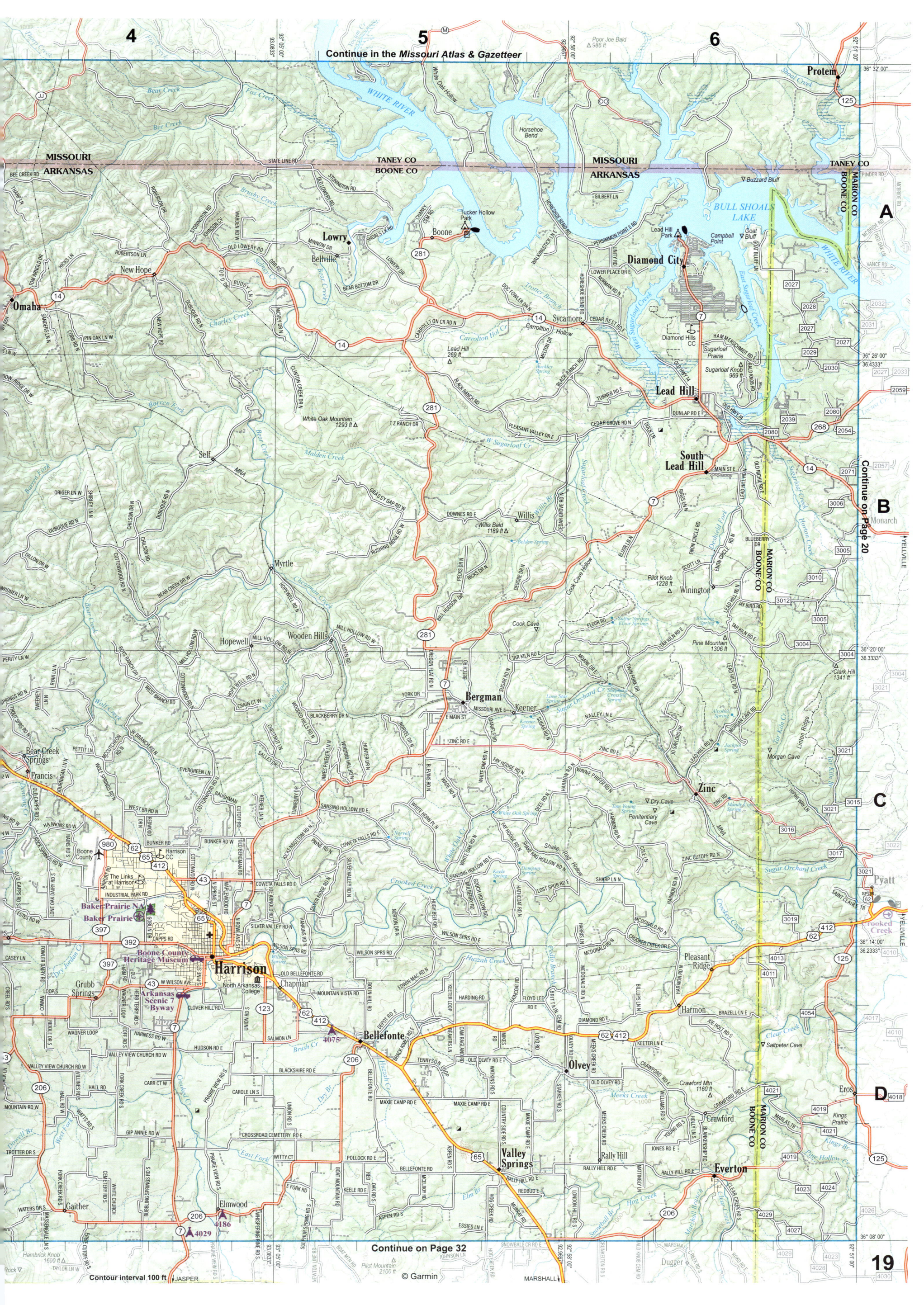

Continue in the *Missouri Atlas & Gazetteer*

A
B
C
D

Continue on Page 20

Contour interval 100 ft

© Garmin

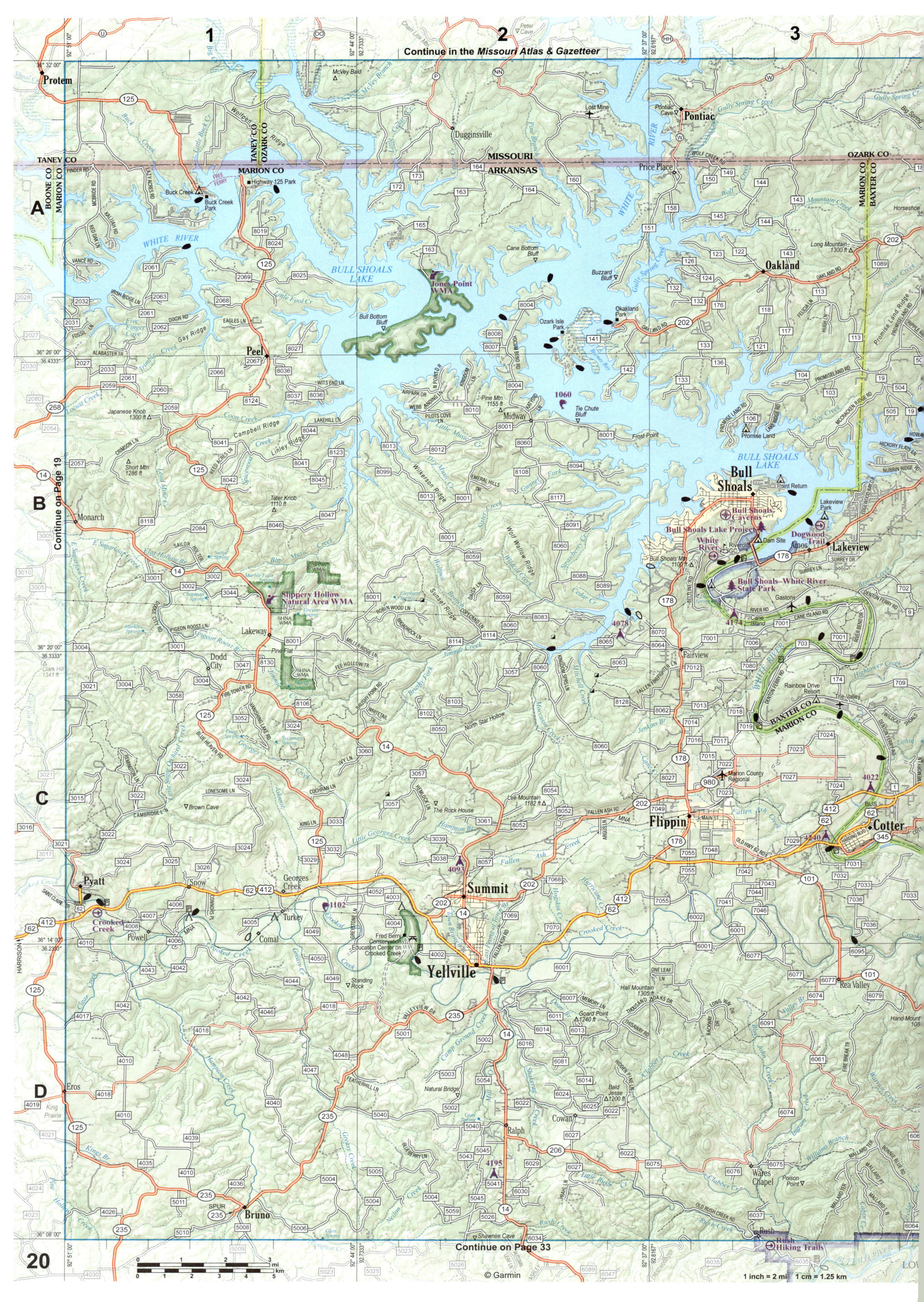

Continue on Page 19

1 inch = 2 mi   1 cm = 1.25 km

© Garmin

20

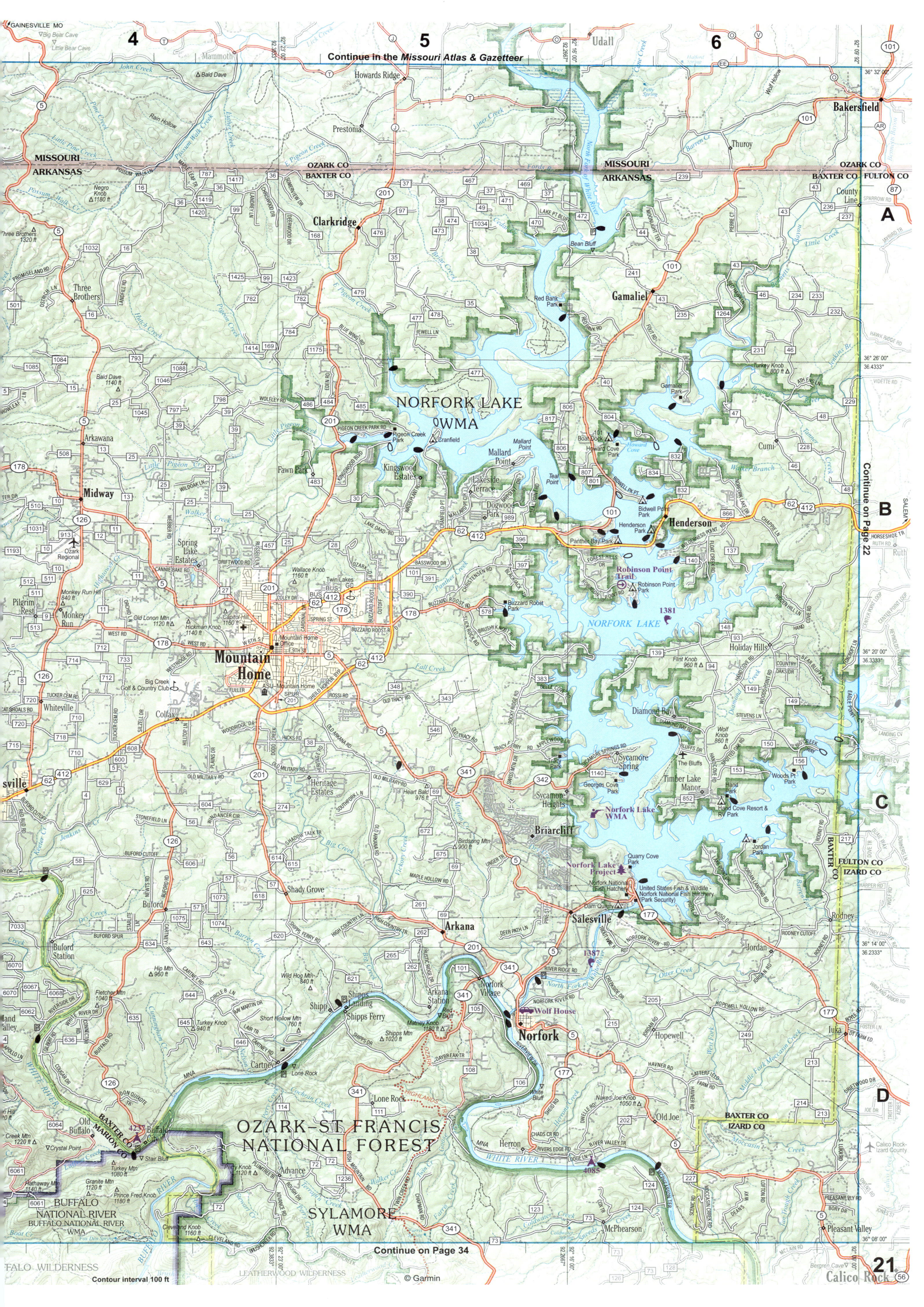

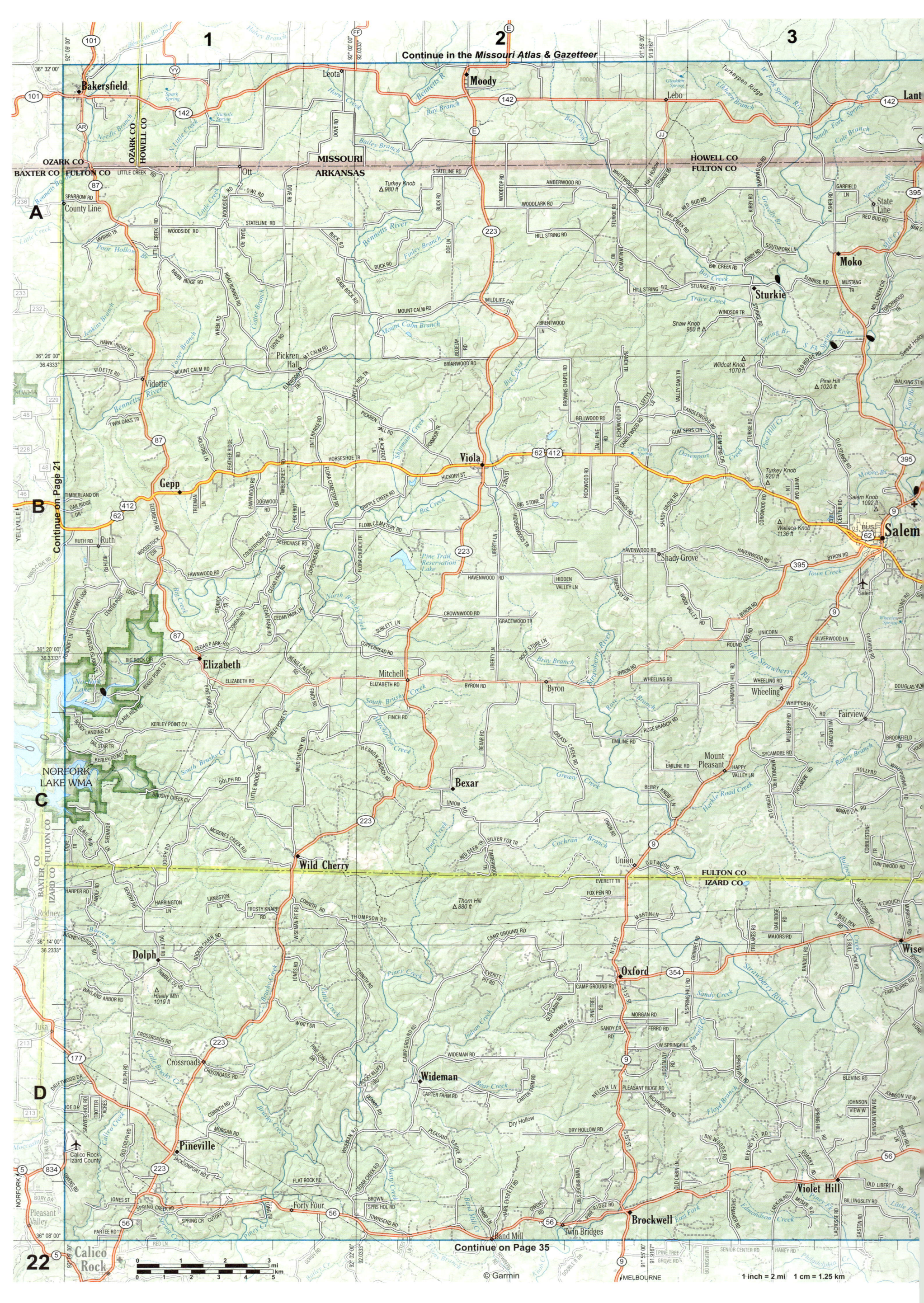

Continue in the *Missouri Atlas & Gazetteer*

Bakersfield
Leota
Moody
Lebo
Lant

101
142
142

OZARK CO
HOWELL CO
MISSOURI
ARKANSAS
HOWELL CO
FULTON CO

OZARK CO
BAXTER CO FULTON CO
Ott

State
Line

A

County Line
Moko
Sturkie

223

Pickren
Hall

Vidette
Turkey Knob
980 ft

Shaw Knob
980 ft

Wildcat Knob
1070 ft

Pine Hill
1020 ft

Gepp
Viola
62 412
Turkey Knob
920 ft
White Oak
Salem Knob
1092 ft
Salem

B

412
62
Ruth
Wallace Knob
1136 ft
62
BUS

Flora Cemetery Rd
223
Shady Grove

395

Salem

9

Elizabeth
Mitchell
Byron
Wheeling
Fairview

87

Norfolk
Lake
Starter

Unicorn

Round

NORFORK
LAKE WMA

C

Bexar

Union

Mount
Pleasant

223

Wild Cherry

FULTON CO
IZARD CO

Union

9

BAXTER CO
IZARD CO

Thom Hill
880 ft

Wise

Dolph
Oxford
354

Hively Mtn
1019 ft

D

177

Crossroads
223

Wideman

9

Pineville
Calico Rock
Izard County

223

Violet Hill
56

5
834

Forty Four
56

Brockwell
Twin Bridges

Norfork
Pleasant
Valley

56

Juka
213

Melbourne

Calico
Rock

Continue on Page 35

0 1 2 3 mi
0 1 2 3 4 5 km

© Garmin

1 inch = 2 mi   1 cm = 1.25 km

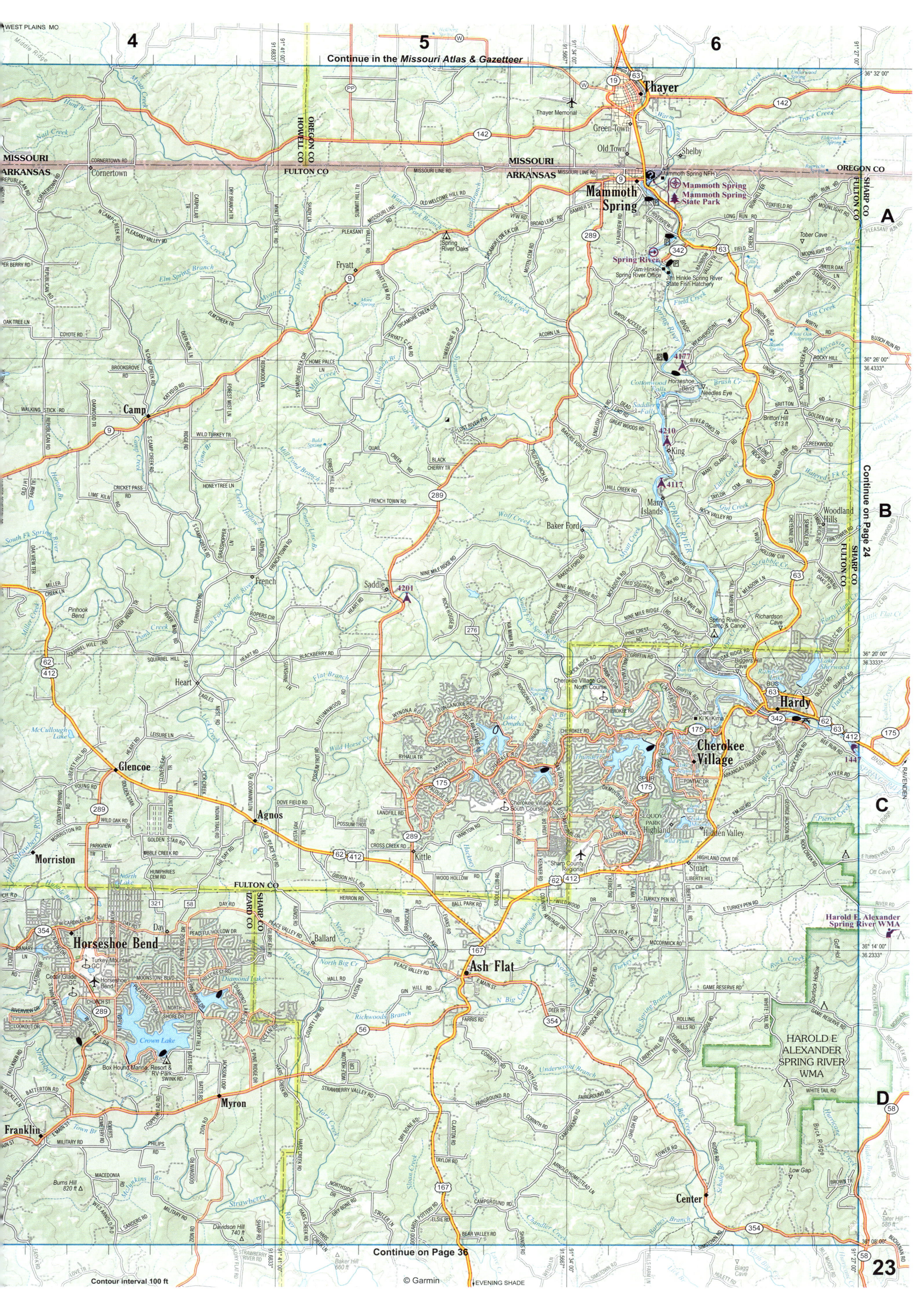

4 5 6

Continue in the *Missouri Atlas & Gazetteer*

Thayer

MISSOURI
ARKANSAS

MISSOURI
ARKANSAS

OREGON CO
HOWELL CO

OREGON CO
FULTON CO

Green-Town

Old Town

Shelby

Mammoth
Spring

Mammoth Spring NFH
Mammoth Spring
Mammoth Spring
State Park

Spring River
Jim Hinkle Spring River
Spring River Office

Jim Hinkle Spring River
State Fish Hatchery

Cornertown

Cornertown

Pryatt

Spring River Oaks

Tober Cave

A

Camp

Horseshoe
Bend

Needles Eye

King

Many Islands

Woodland
Hills

B

Baker Ford

French

Saddle

Many Islands

Spring River
Camp & Canoe

Richardson
Cave

Cave

Glencoe

Heart

Cherokee Village GC
North Course

Cherokee
Village

Hardy

C

Agnos

Morriston

Kittle

Cherokee Village GC
South Course

Sharp County
Regional

Stuart

Sequoyah
Park
Highland

Hidden Valley

Harold E. Alexander
Spring River WMA

FULTON CO
SHARP CO

FULTON CO
IZARD CO

Ballard

Ash Flat

Horseshoe Bend

Turkey Mountain
GC

Horseshoe
Bend

Diamond Lake

Crown Lake

Box Hound Marina
Resort &
RV Park

HAROLD E
ALEXANDER
SPRING RIVER
WMA

Myron

D

Franklin

Center

Continue on Page 36

Continue on Page 24

Contour interval 100 ft

© Garmin

EVENING SHADE

23

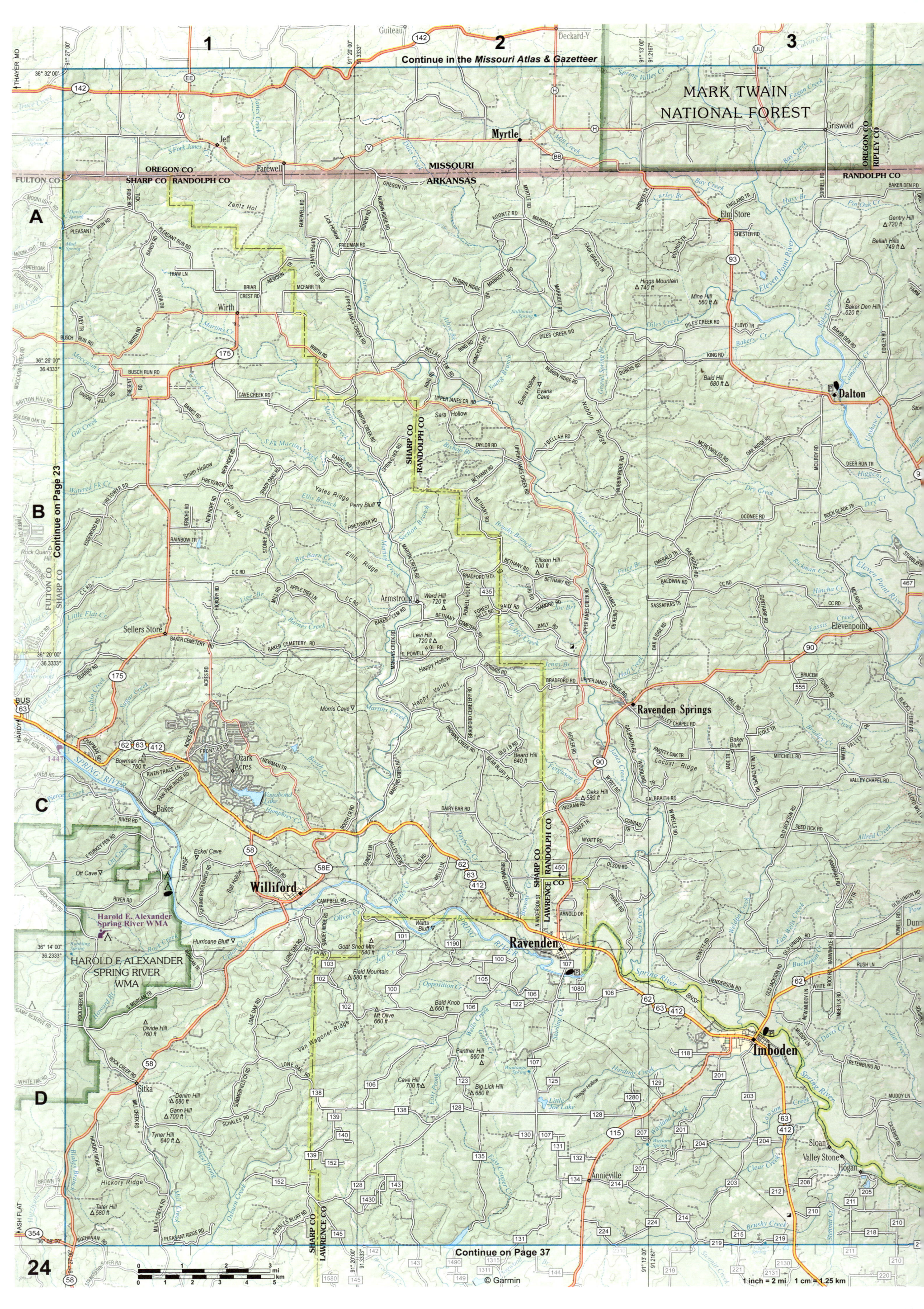

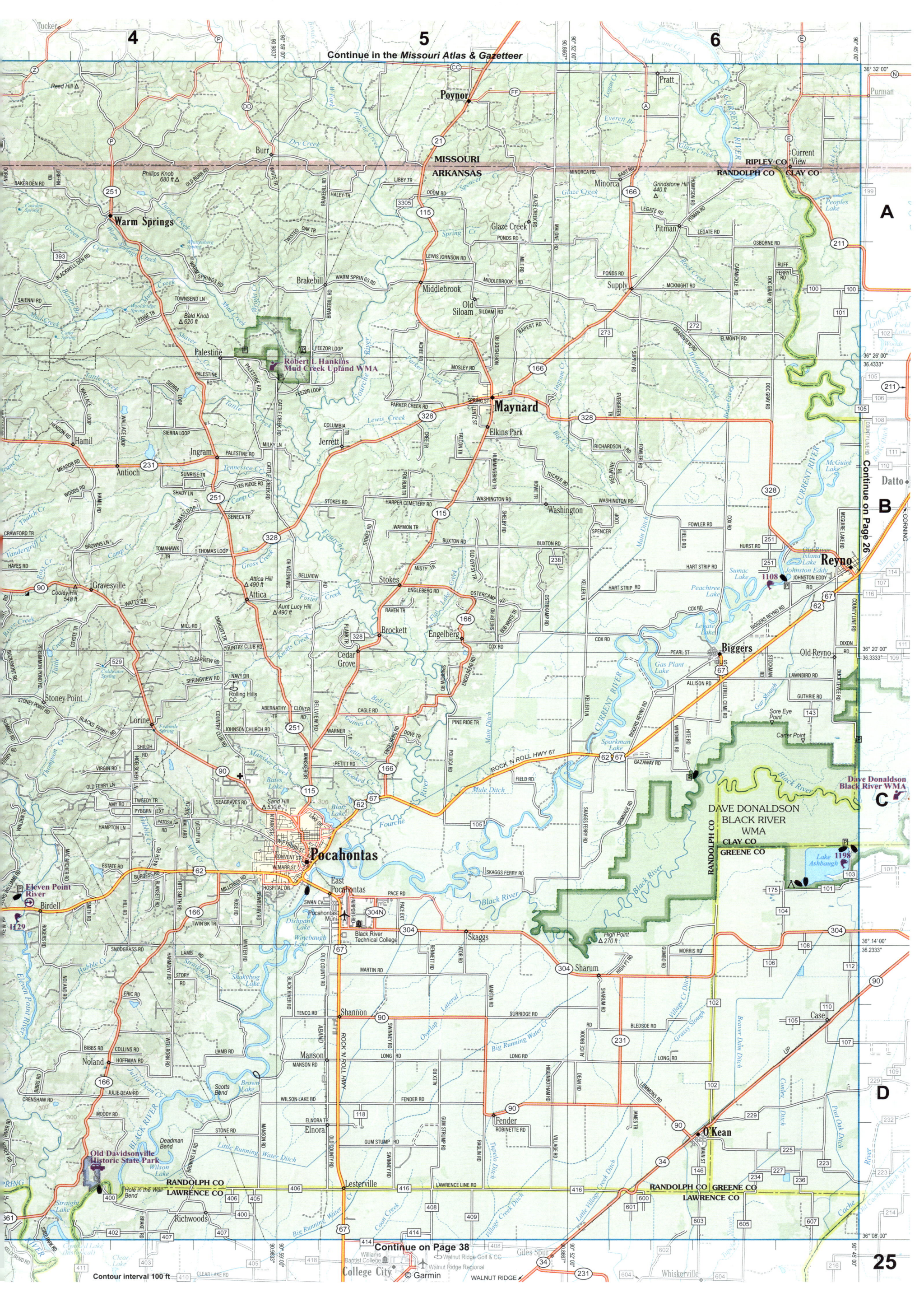

Continue in the *Missouri Atlas & Gazetteer*

Continue on Page 26

Continue on Page 38

Contour interval 100 ft

© Garmin

25

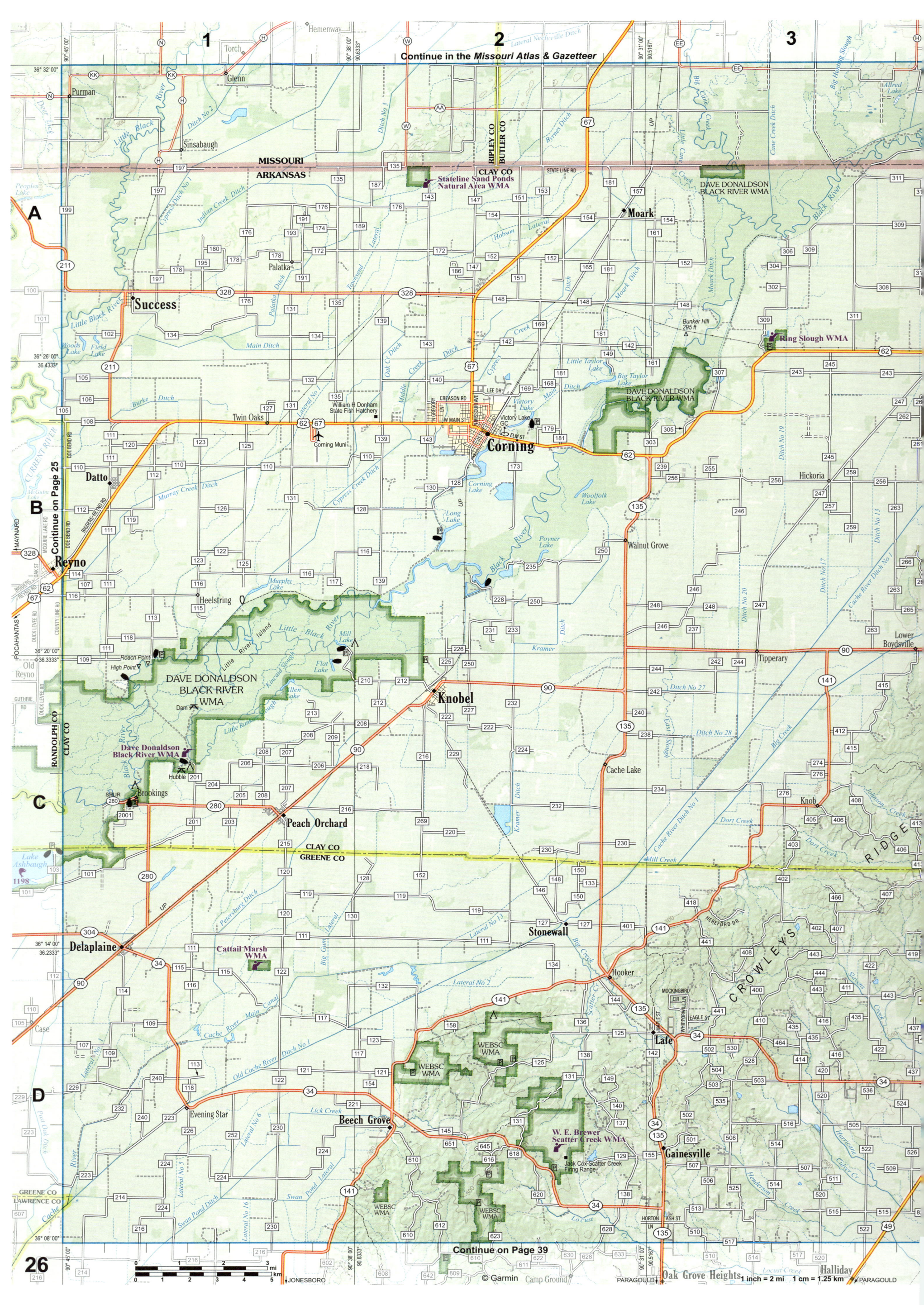

Continue on Page 25

1 inch = 2 mi   1 cm = 1.25 km

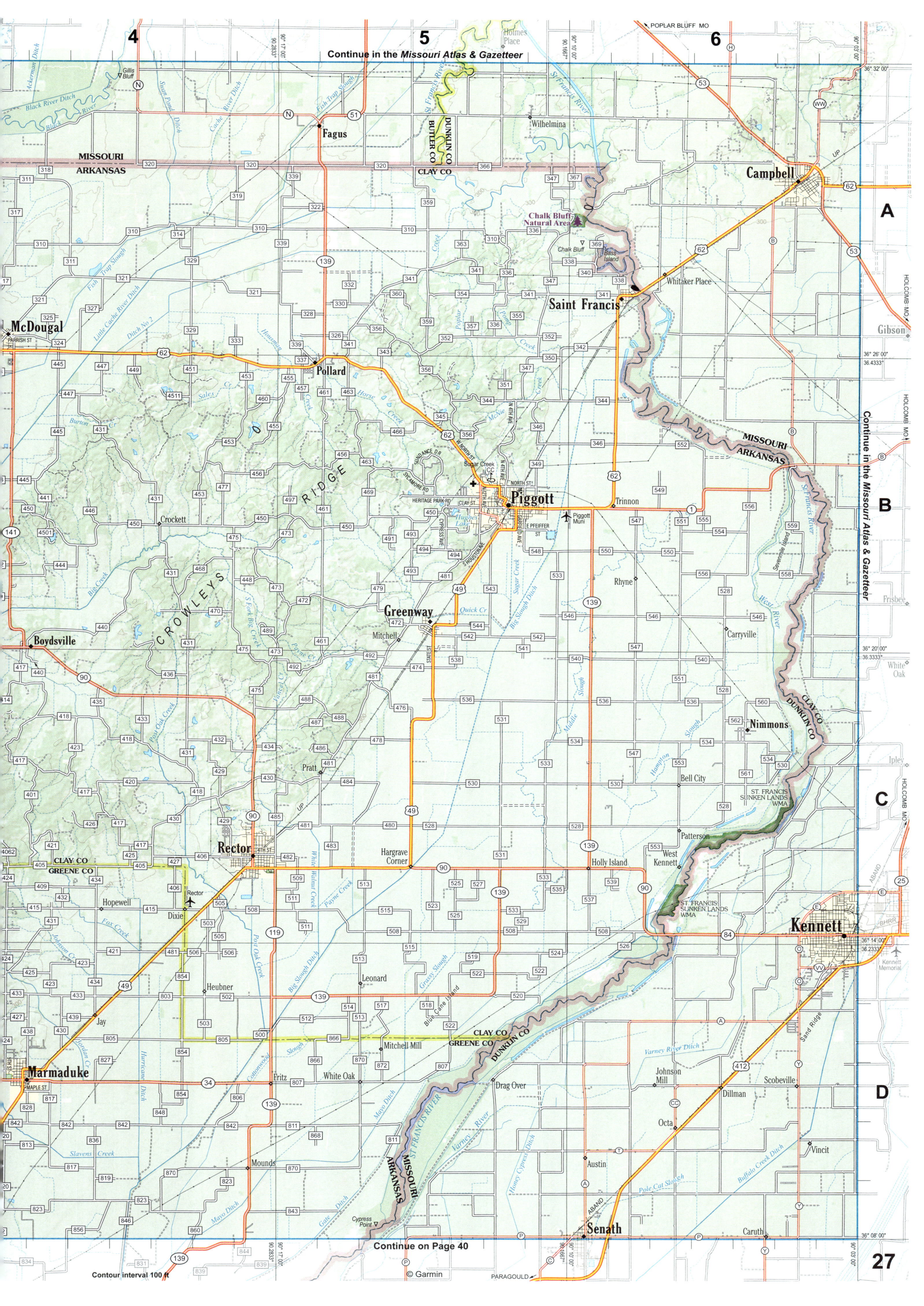

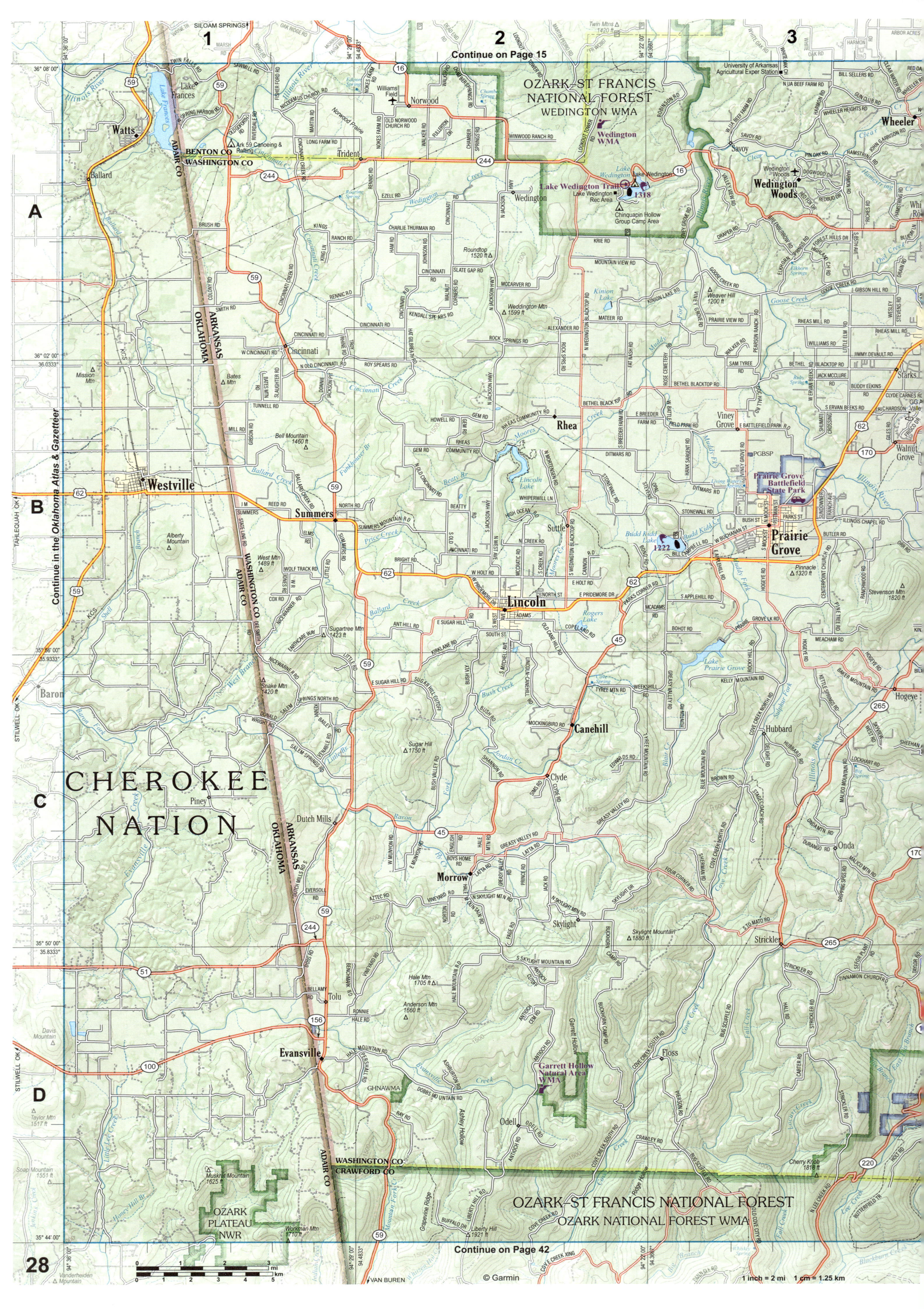

Continue on Page 15

CHEROKEE
NATION

OZARK ST FRANCIS
NATIONAL FOREST
WEDINGTON WMA

OZARK-ST FRANCIS NATIONAL FOREST
OZARK NATIONAL FOREST WMA

Continue on Page 42

28

© Garmin

1 inch = 2 mi   1 cm = 1.25 km

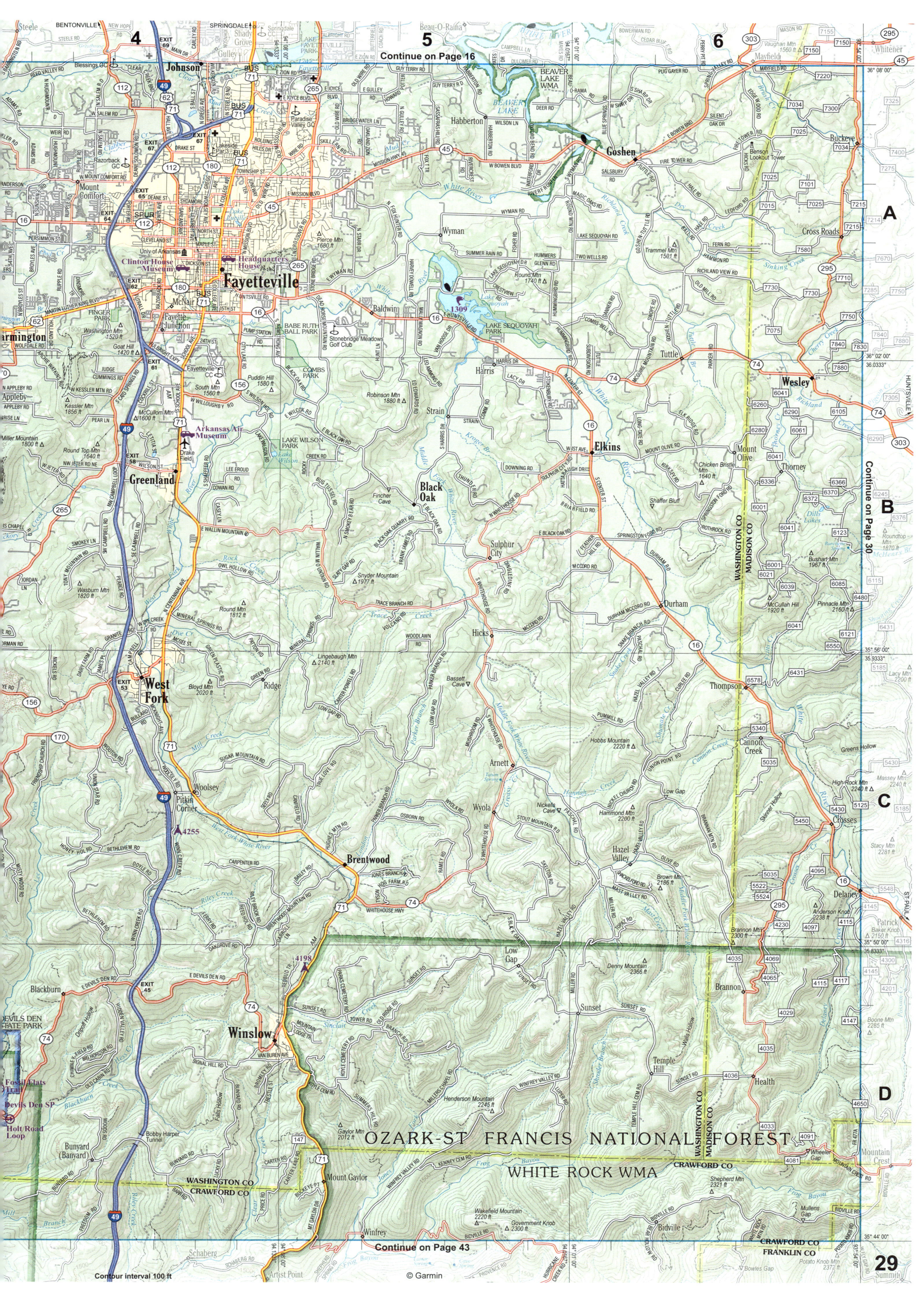

Continue on Page 16

A

B

Continue on Page 30

C

D

Johnson

Fayetteville

Greenland

West Fork

Goshen

Wyman

Baldwin

Harris

Strain

Elkins

Wesley

Cross Roads

Black Oak

Sulphur City

Hicks

Durham

Thompson

Mount Olive

Thorney

Ridge

Arnett

Wyola

Cannon Creek

Crosses

Delaney

Patrick

Brentwood

Hazel Valley

Woolsey

Pitkin Corner

Blackburn

Winslow

Bunyard (Banyard)

Brannon

Sunset

Temple Hill

Health

OZARK-ST FRANCIS NATIONAL FOREST

WHITE ROCK WMA

WASHINGTON CO
CRAWFORD CO

WASHINGTON CO
MADISON CO

CRAWFORD CO

CRAWFORD CO
FRANKLIN CO

Mount Gaylor

Winfrey

Bidville

DEVILS DEN STATE PARK

Fossil Flats Trail

Devils Den SP

Holt/Road Loop

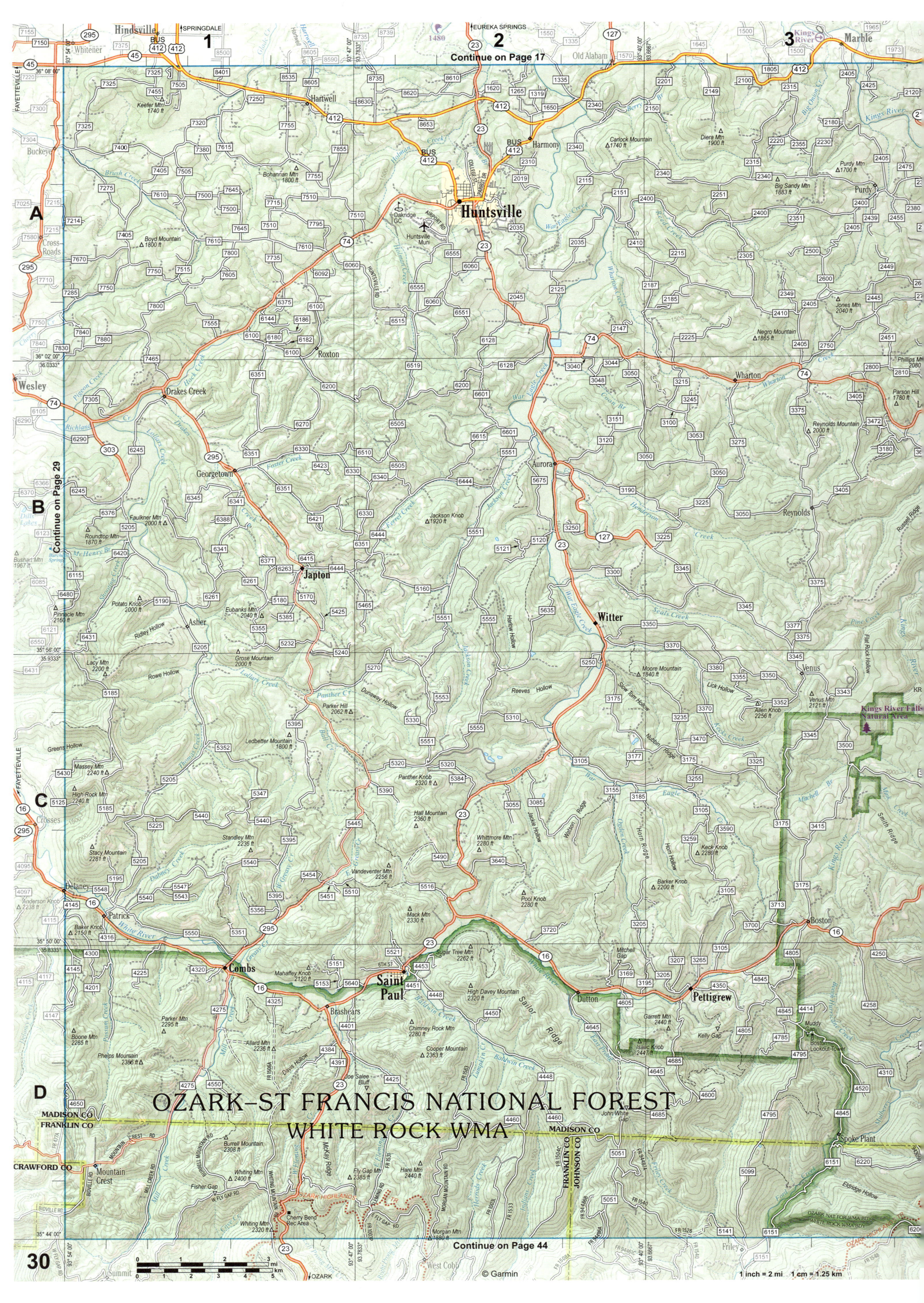

Continue on Page 17

Continue on Page 29

OZARK–ST FRANCIS NATIONAL FOREST
WHITE ROCK WMA

Continue on Page 44

30

© Garmin

1 inch = 2 mi   1 cm = 1.25 km

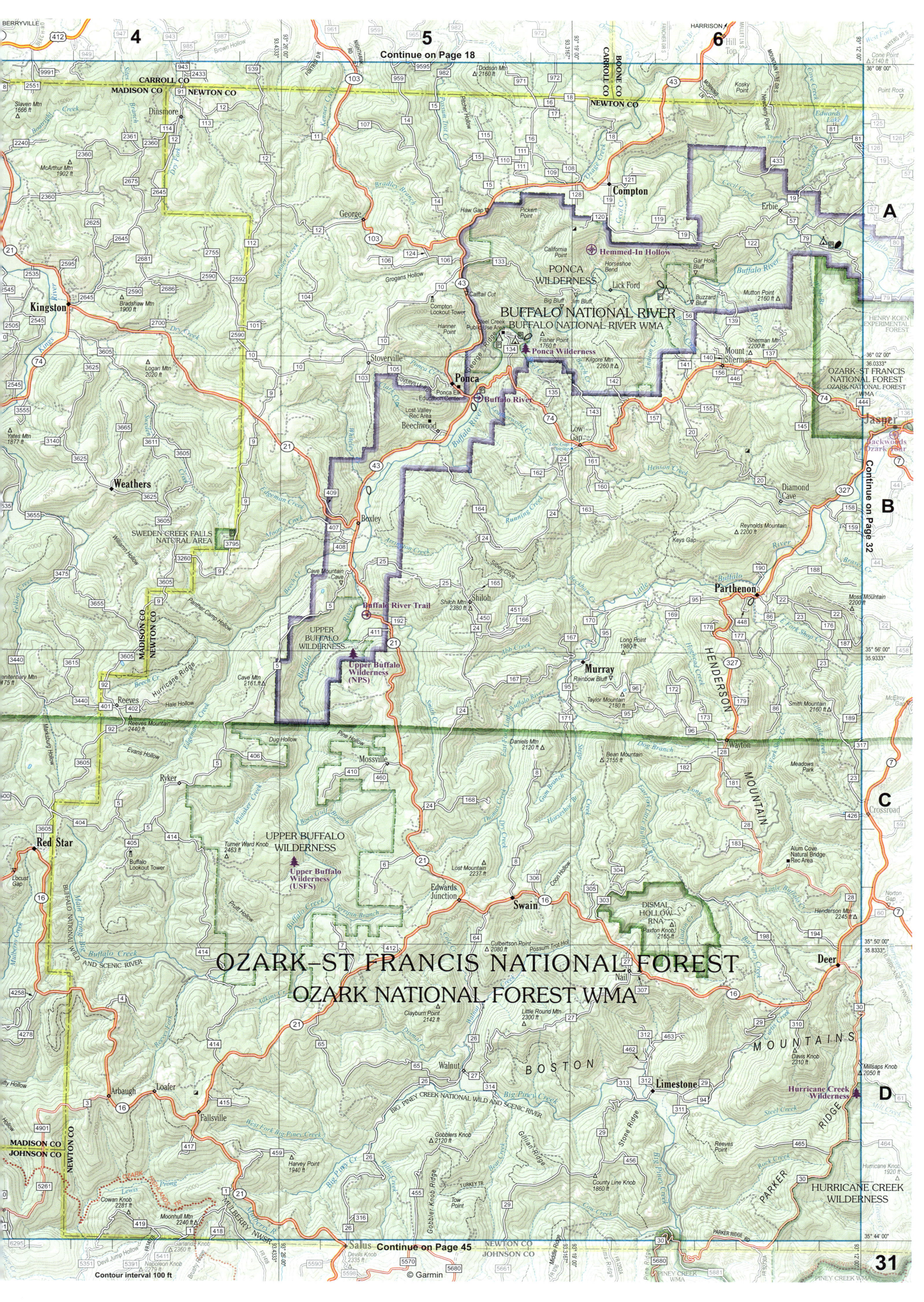

Continue on Page 18

Continue on Page 32

BUFFALO NATIONAL RIVER

PONCA WILDERNESS

BUFFALO NATIONAL RIVER WMA

Ponca Wilderness

UPPER BUFFALO WILDERNESS

Upper Buffalo Wilderness (NPS)

UPPER BUFFALO WILDERNESS

Upper Buffalo Wilderness (USFS)

OZARK–ST FRANCIS NATIONAL FOREST

OZARK NATIONAL FOREST WMA

HURRICANE CREEK WILDERNESS

BOSTON MOUNTAINS

PARKER RIDGE

Contour interval 100 ft

© Garmin

Continue on Page 45

31

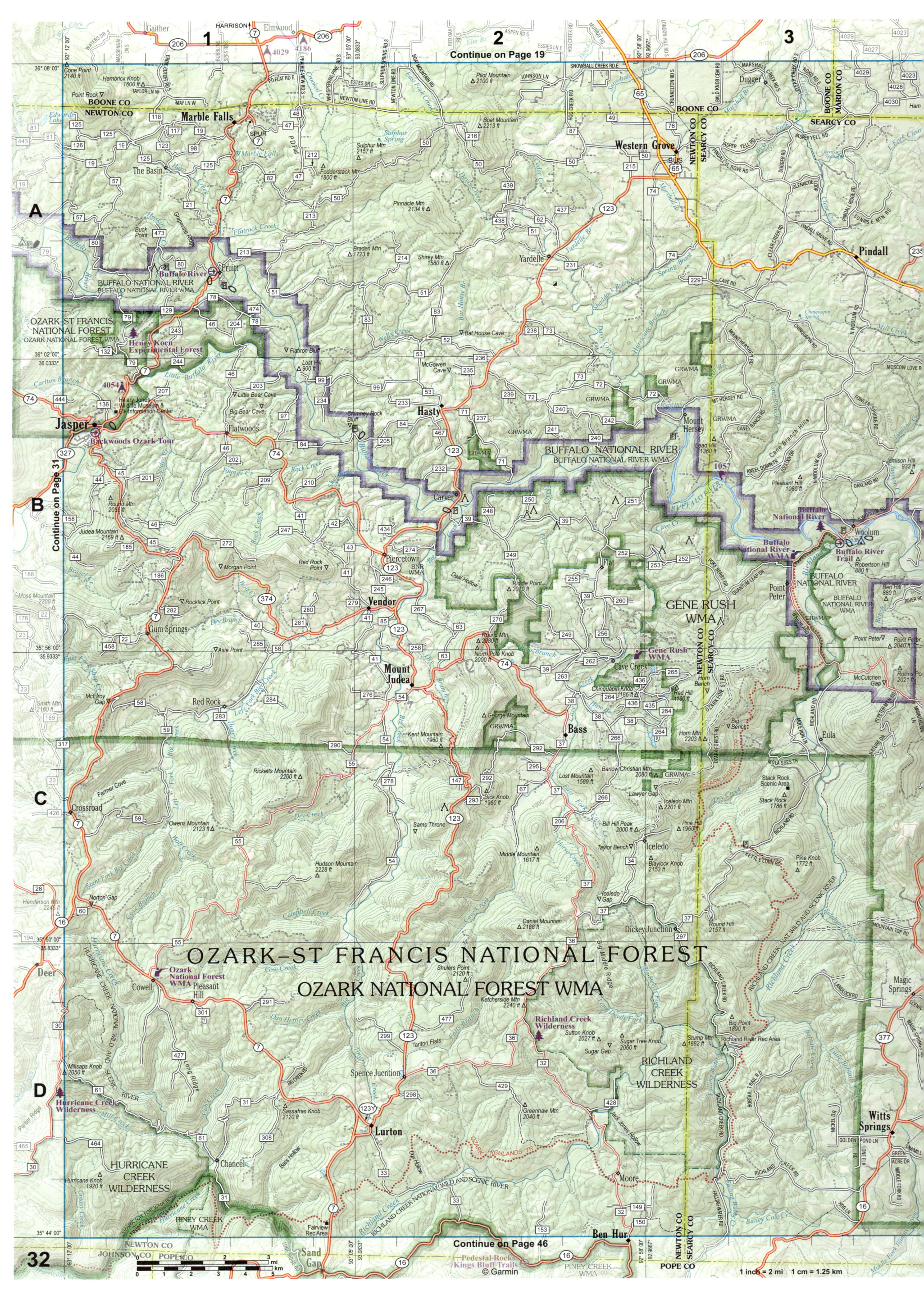

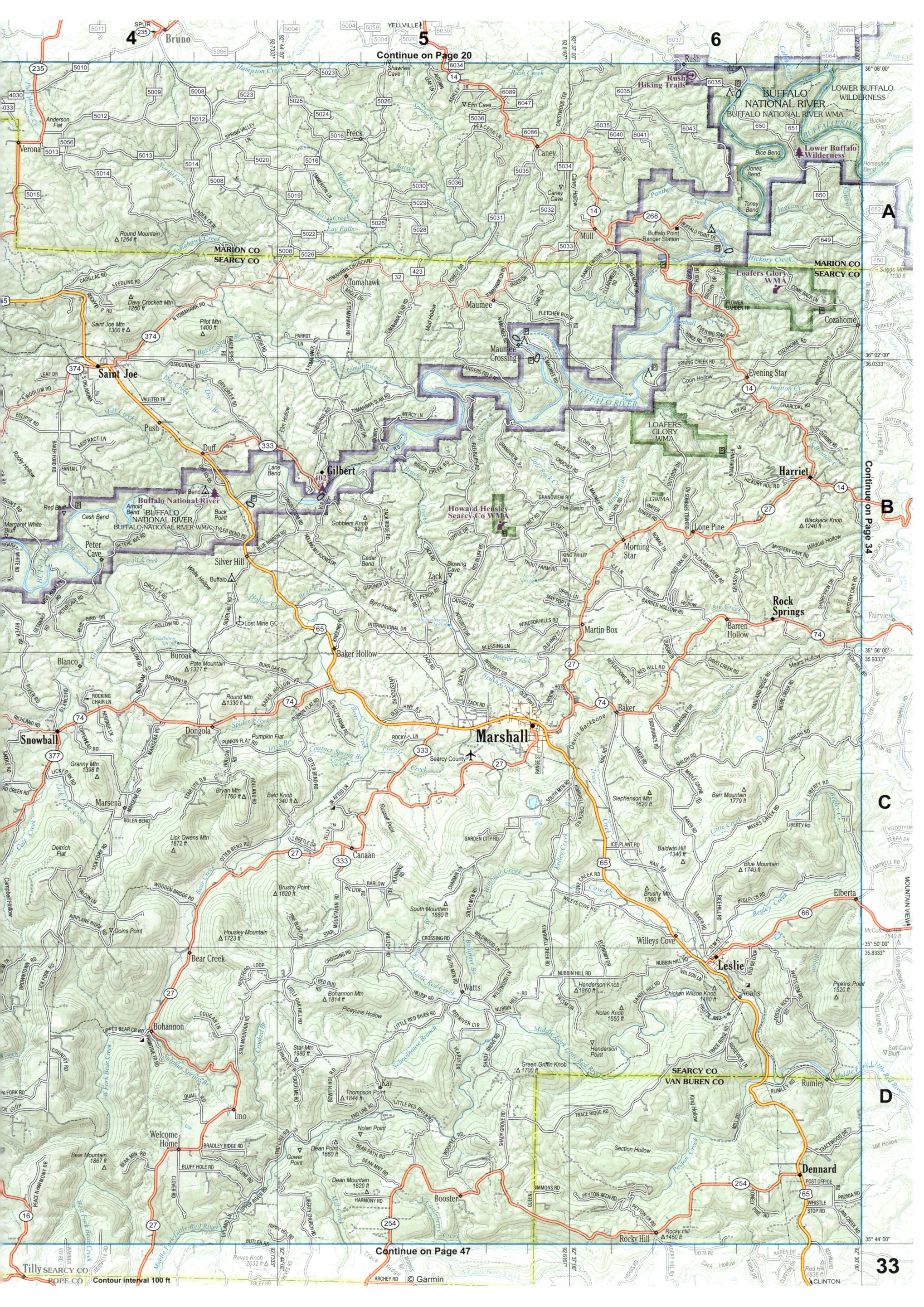

Continue on Page 20

Continue on Page 34

Continue on Page 47

Contour interval 100 ft   © Garmin

33

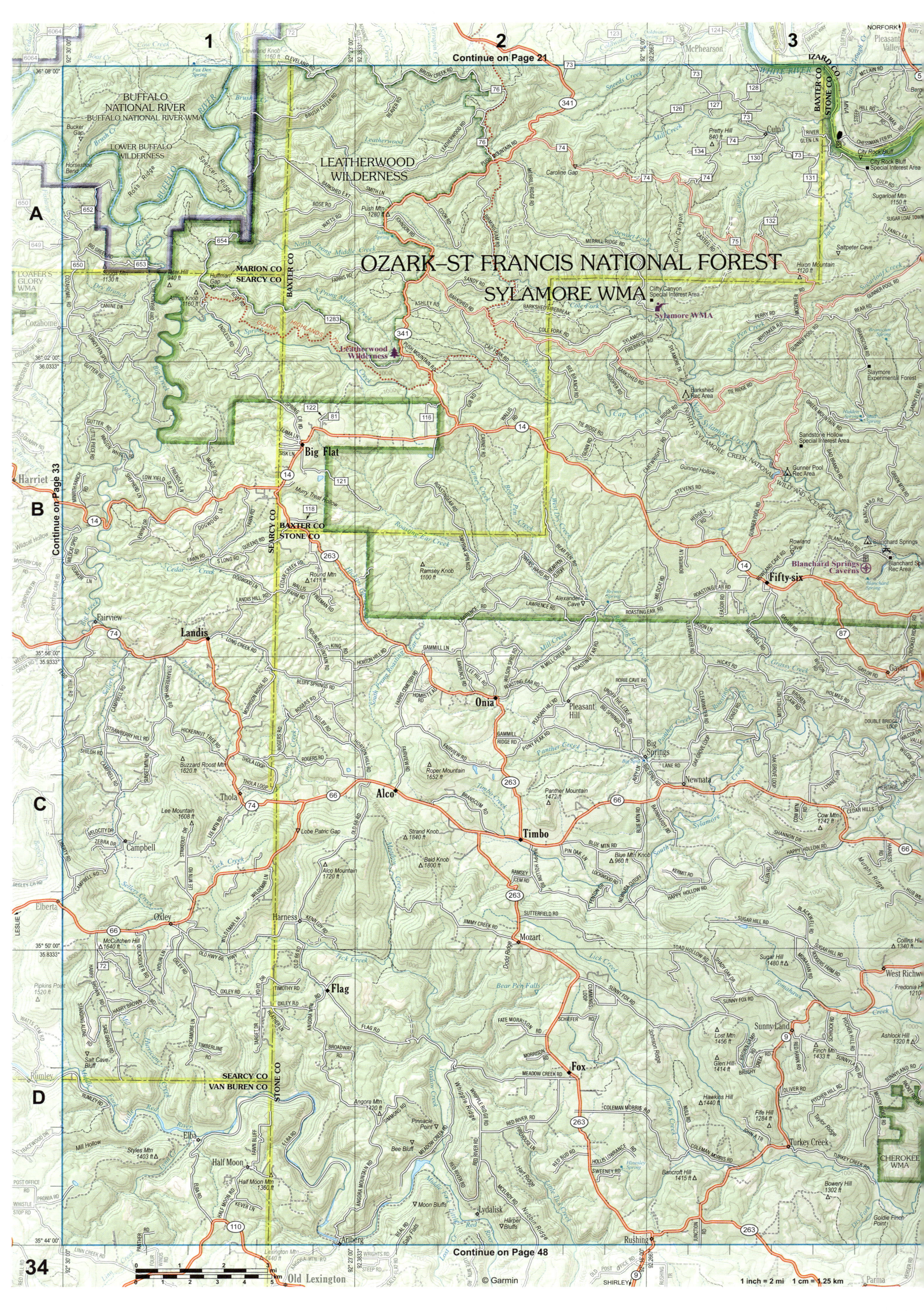

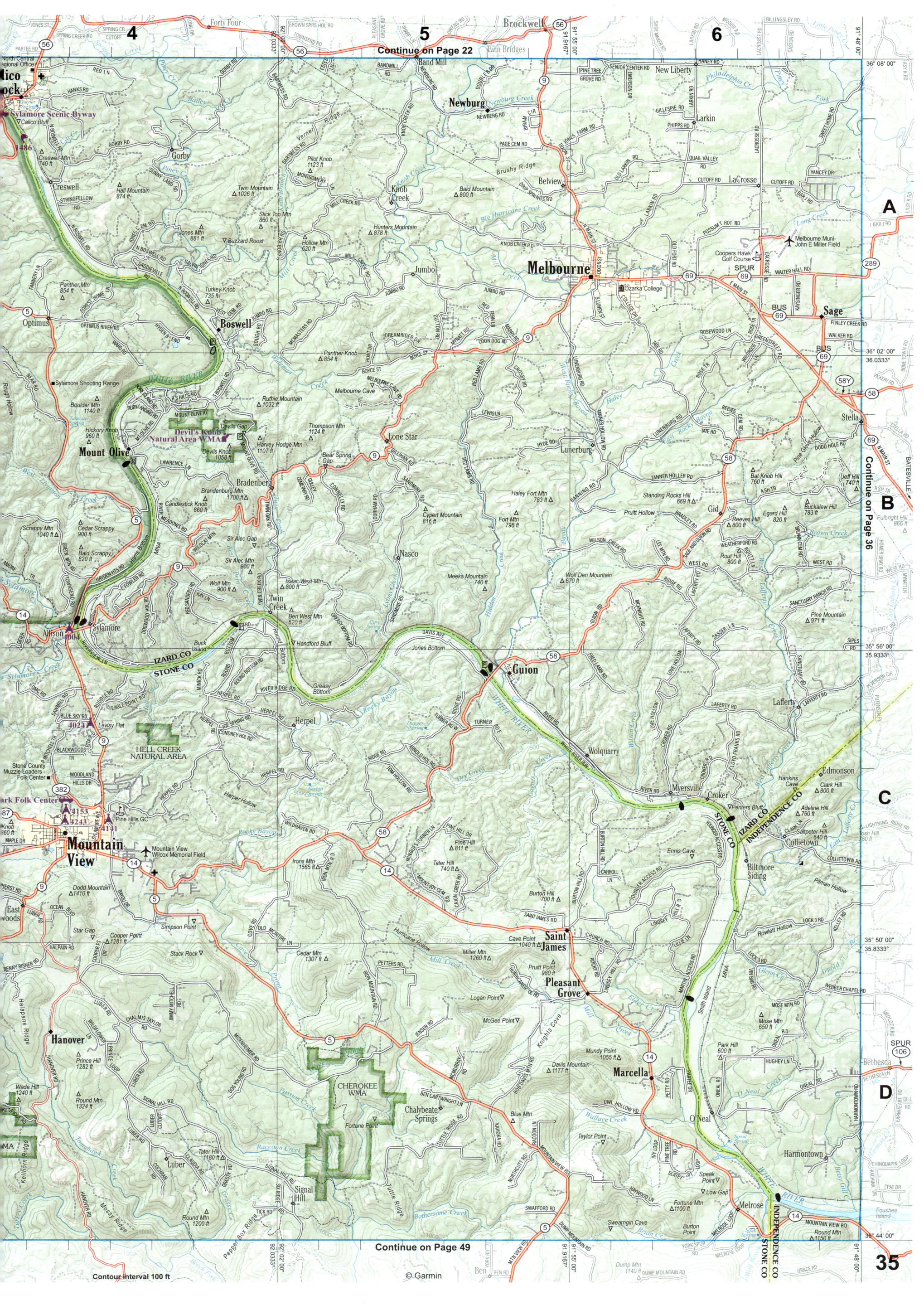

Brockwell

Forty Four

Band Mill

Newburg

New Liberty

Melbourne

A

Sage

Belview

LaCrosse

Boswell

Lone Star

Lunerburg

B

Mount Olive

Bradenberg

Nasco

Gid

Devil's Knob Natural Area WMA

Sylamore

Guion

Laffern

C

Herpel

Wolquarry

IZARD CO STONE CO

HELL CREEK NATURAL AREA

Croker
Myersville

Edmonson

Collietown

Biltmore Siding

Mountain View

Saint James

Pleasant Grove

Marcella

IZARD CO INDEPENDENCE CO

STONE CO

D

Hanover

O'Neal

CHEROKEE WMA

Chalybeate Springs

Harmontown

Signal Hill

Melrose

INDEPENDENCE CO STONE CO

© Garmin

Contour interval 100 ft

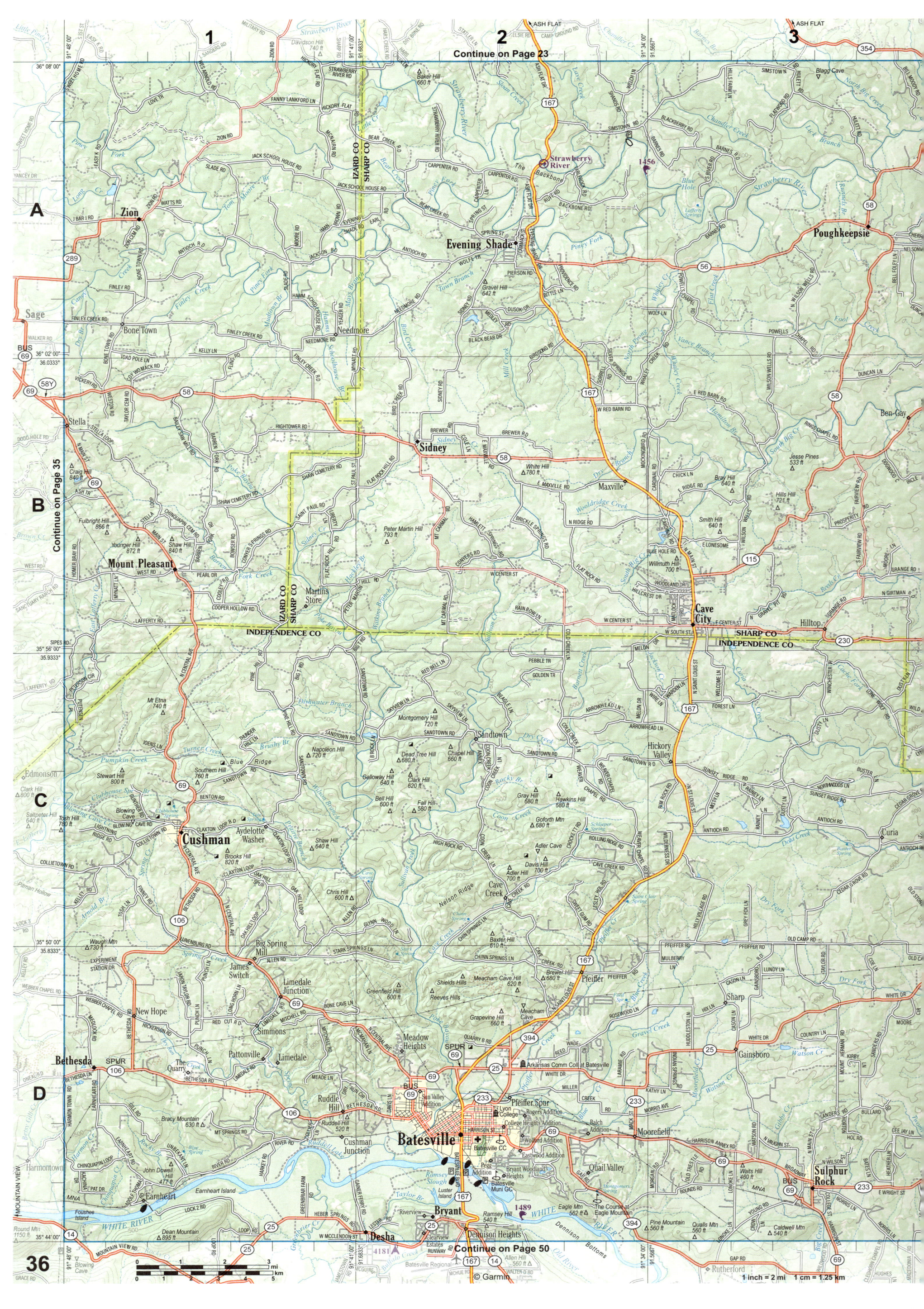

Continue on Page 23

Continue on Page 35

1 **2** **3**

A

B

C

D

36

Continue on Page 50

1 inch = 2 mi   1 cm = 1.25 km

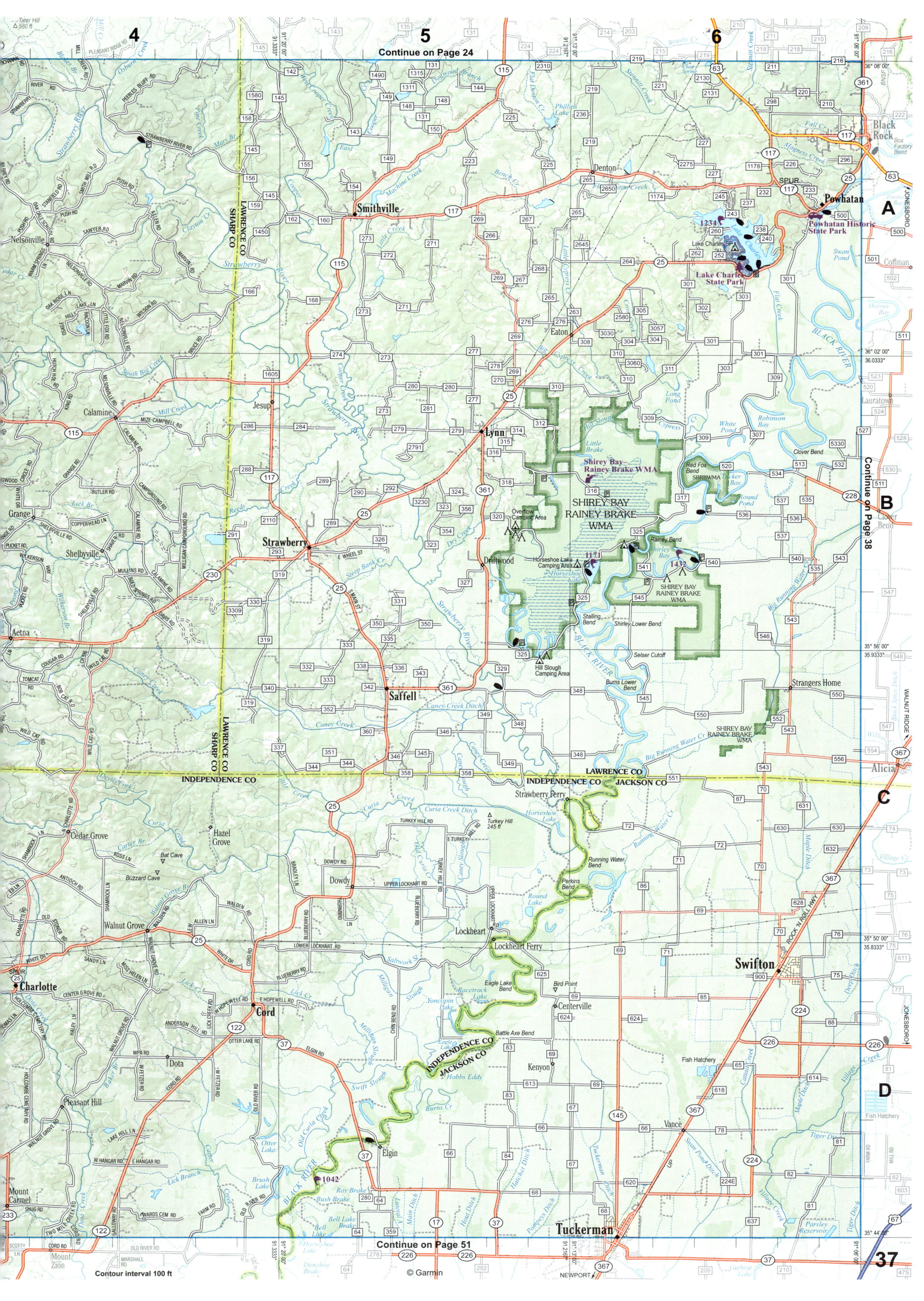

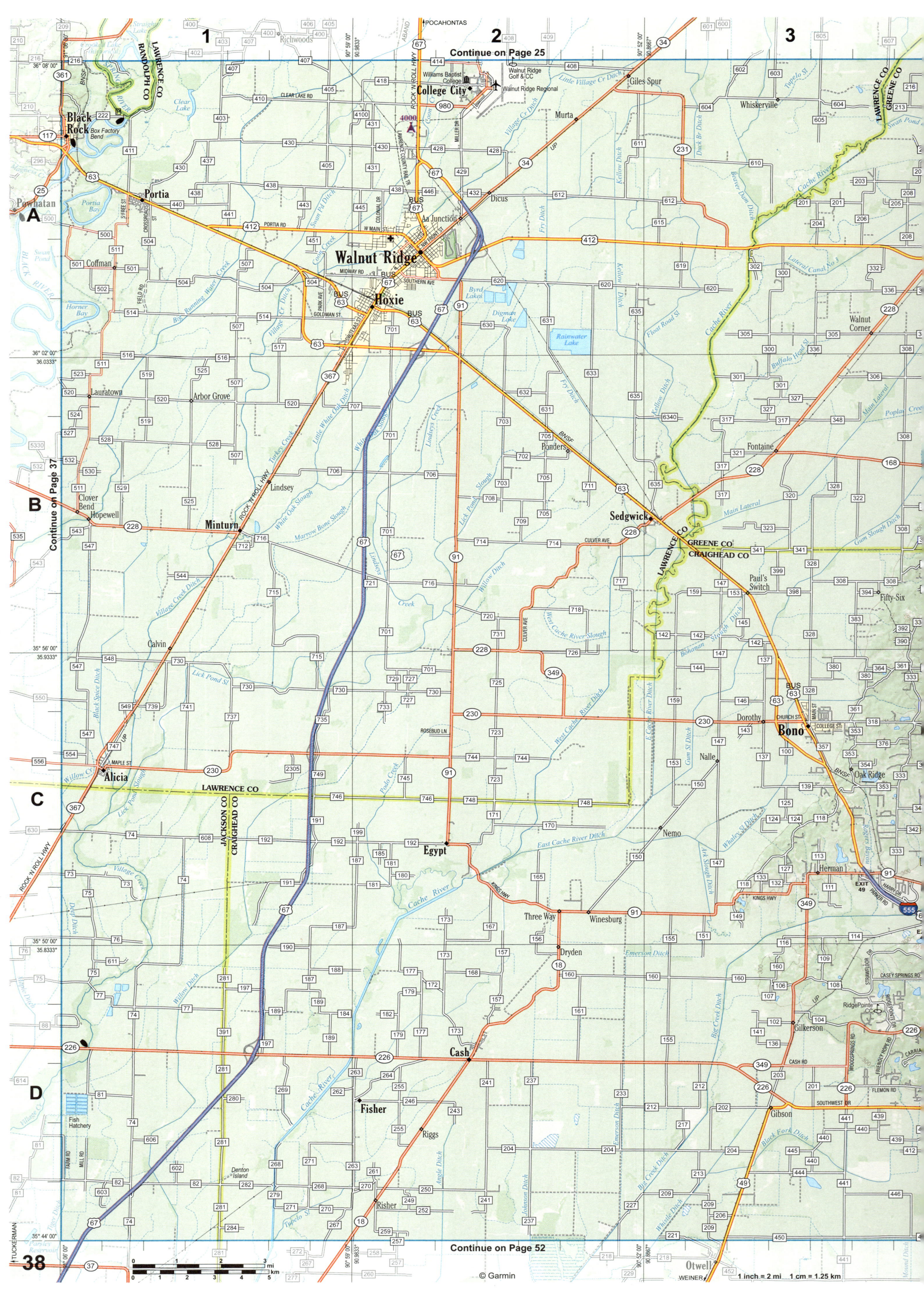

Continue on Page 25

Continue on Page 37

Continue on Page 52

38

1 inch = 2 mi   1 cm = 1.25 km

© Garmin

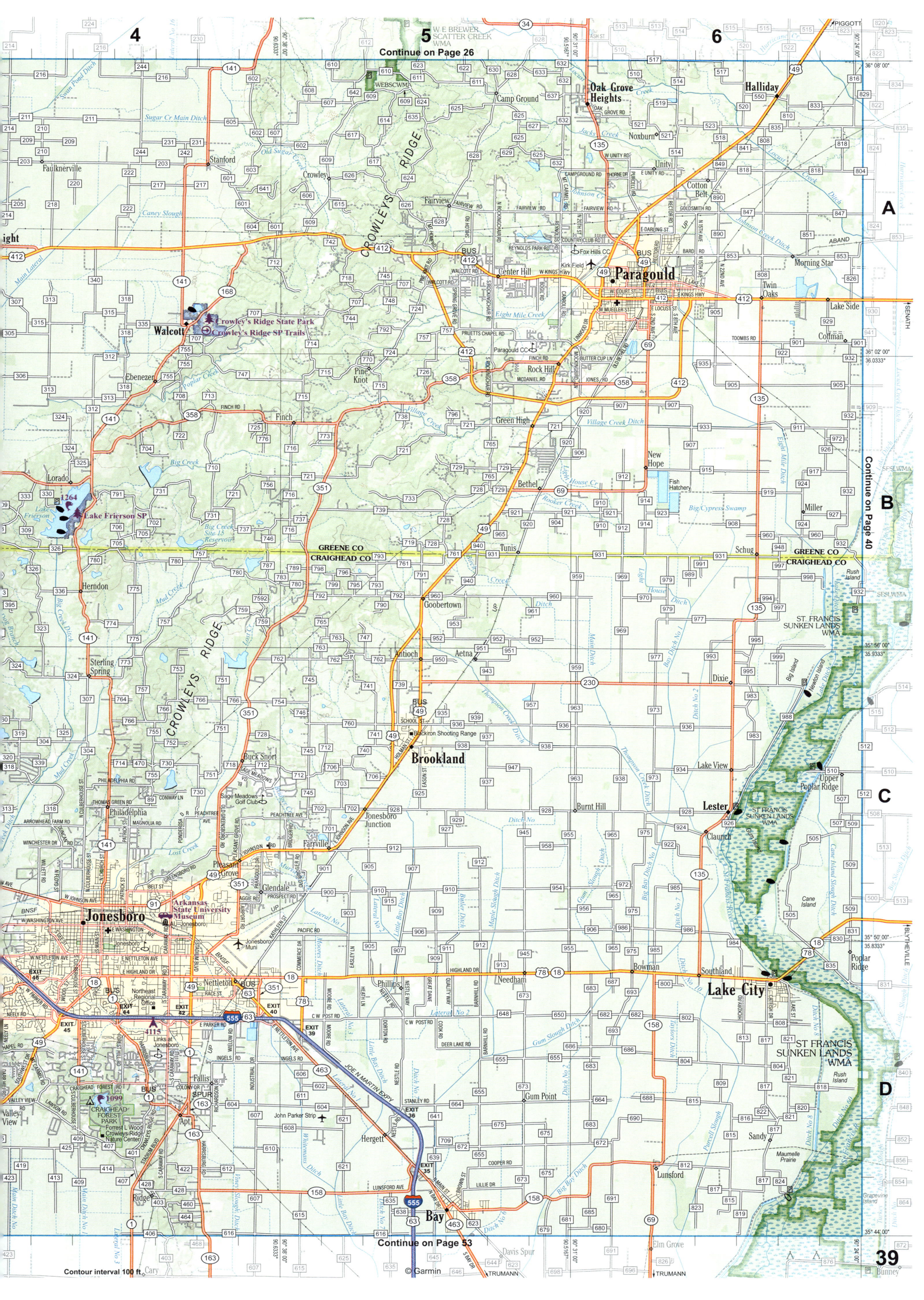

Continue on Page 26
Continue on Page 40
Continue on Page 53

W E BREWER
SCATTER CREEK
WMA

Oak Grove
Heights

Halliday

Noxburn

Cotton
Belt

Morning Star

Paragould

Twin
Oaks

Lake Side

Coffman

Camp Ground

Fairview

Center Hill

Walcott
Crowley's Ridge State Park
Crowley's Ridge SP Trails

Pine
Knot

Rock Hill

Ebenezer

Finch

Green High

New
Hope

Bethel

Fish
Hatchery

Big Cypress Swamp

Miller

Lorado

Lake Frierson SP

GREENE CO
CRAIGHEAD CO

Tunis

Schug

GREENE CO
CRAIGHEAD CO

ST. FRANCIS
SUNKEN LANDS
WMA

Herndon

Goobertown

Sterling
Spring

Antioch

Aetna

Dixie

Big Island

St Francis
Sunken Lands
WMA

Buck Snort

Brookland

Lake View

Lester

Upper
Poplar Ridge

Sage Meadows
Golf Club

Jonesboro
Junction

Farmville

Burnt Hill

Claunch

Cane Island

Poplar
Ridge

Jonesboro

Arkansas State University
Museum

Pleasant
Grove

Glendale

Bowman

Southland

Lake City

Northeast
Regional
Office

Nettleton

Phillips

Needham

St Francis
Sunken Lands
WMA

Rush
Island

Apt

John Parker Strip

Hergett

Lunsford

Sandy

Craighead
Forest Park
Forrest L Wood
Crowley's Ridge
Nature Center

Maumelle
Prairie

Valley
View

Bay

Contour interval 100 ft

© Garmin

TRUMANN

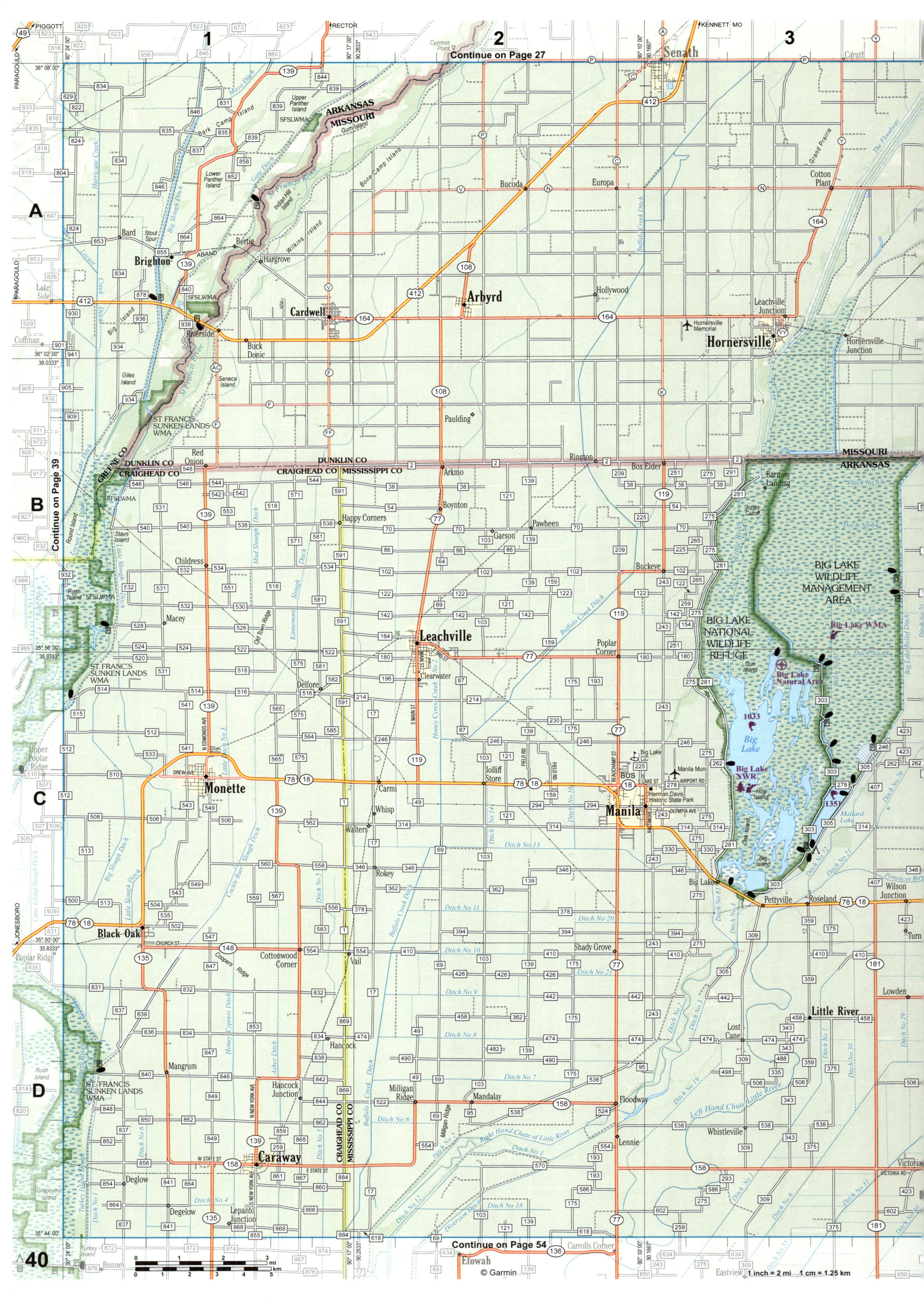

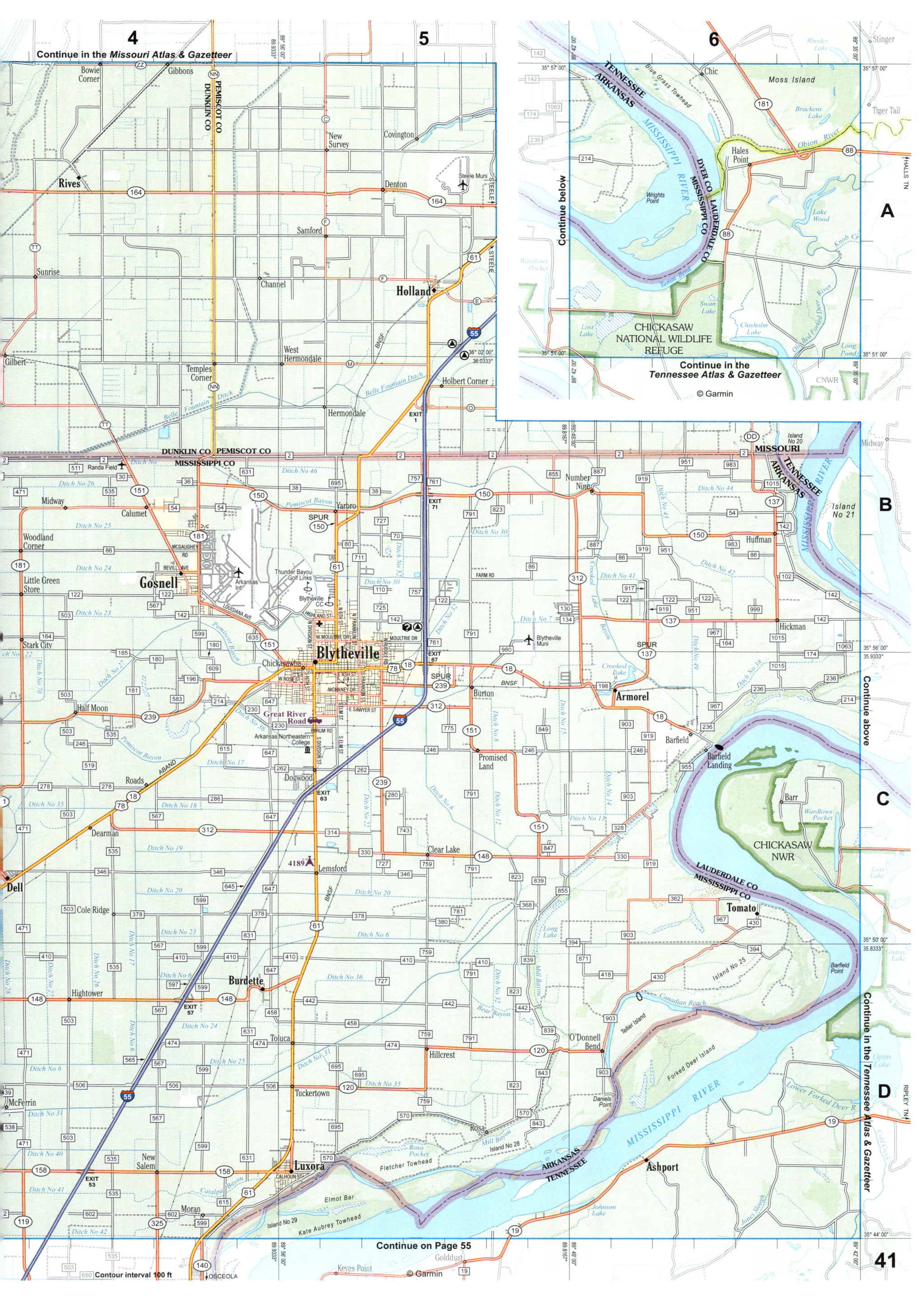

5

6

Stinger

Rhodes Lake

Chic

Moss Island

TENNESSEE
ARKANSAS

Blue Grass Towhead

Tiger Tail

Brackens Lake

Hales Point

Wrights Point

Obion River

Lake Wood

Knob Cr

A

Continue below

Tatum Bend

Wardlener Pocket

Swan Lake

Chisholm Lake

Lost Lake

Long Pond

CHICKASAW
NATIONAL WILDLIFE
REFUGE

Continue in the
Tennessee Atlas & Gazetteer

© Garmin

CNWR

Bowie Corner

Gibbons

PEMISCOT CO
DUNKLIN CO

New Survey

Covington

Denton

Steele Muni

Rives

Samford

Holland

MISSOURI

Sunrise

Channel

Island No 21

Gilbert

West Hermondale

Temples Corner

Belle Fountain Ditch

Hermondale

Holbert Corner

B

DUNKLIN CO PEMISCOT CO
MISSISSIPPI CO

Randa Field

Ditch No 26

Midway

Ditch No 25

Calumet

Pemiscot Bayou

Yarbro

SPUR 150

EXIT 71

Number Nine

MISSOURI

TENNESSEE
ARKANSAS

Island No 20

Woodland Corner

Ditch No 24

McGaughey RD
BEVILLE AVE

Thunder Bayou Golf Links

Ditch No 30

FARM RD

Ditch No 41

Ditch No 42

Huffman

Hickman

Little Green Store

Gosnell

Arkansas Intl

Blytheville CC

Ditch No 7

Crooked Lake

Ditch No 49

Stark City

LOUISIANA AVE

HIGHLAND AVE

Ditch No 12

Blytheville Muni

SPUR 137

C

Half Moon

Chickasawba

Blytheville

Burton

Armorel

Pemiscot Bayou

ABAND

Great River Road

Arkansas Northeastern College

Promised Land

BNSF

Barfield

Barfield Landing

Barr

Warllows Pocket

Roads

Ditch No 35

Dearman

Ditch No 18

Dogwood

Ditch No 22

Clear Lake

CHICKASAW NWR

Lost Lake

Dell

Lemsford

Ditch No 20

Tomato

Barfield Point

Cole Ridge

Ditch No 23

Burdette

Ditch No 36

Grass Lake

D

Hightower

EXIT 57

Toluca

Ditch No 24

Ditch No 31

Hillcrest

O'Donnell Bend

Teller Island

Canadian Reach

Forked Deer Island

Lower Forked Deer R

McFerrin

Ditch No 31

Tuckertown

Ditch No 35

Rosa

Island No 28

Daniels Point

Mill Bayou

MISSISSIPPI RIVER

Open Lake

New Salem

EXIT 53

Moran

Luxora

CALHOUN ST

Rosa Pocket

Fletcher Towhead

ARKANSAS
TENNESSEE

Ashport

Johnson Lake

Catalpa Bayou

Elmot Bar

Island No 29

Kate Aubrey Towhead

Keyes Point

OSCEOLA

Golddust

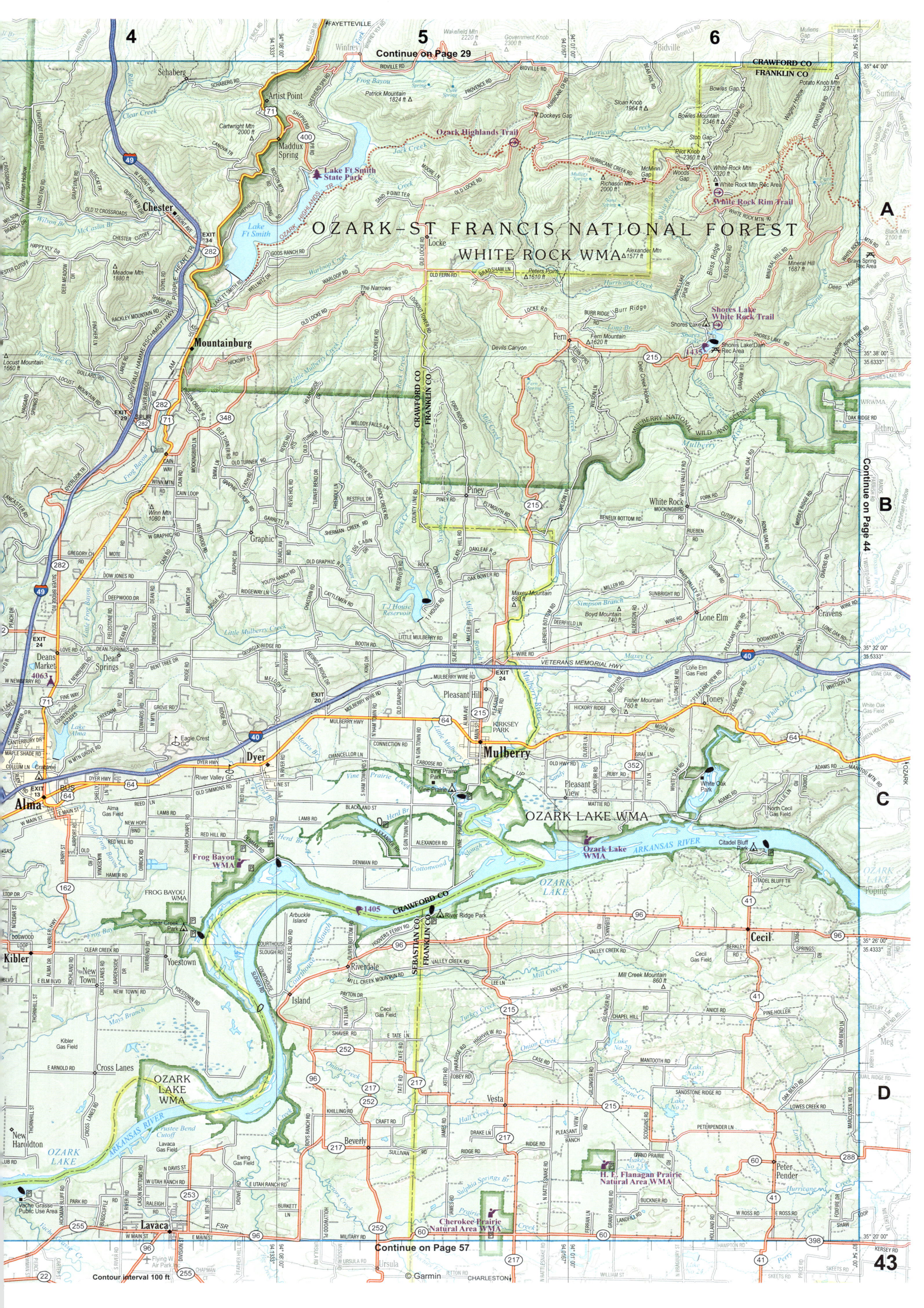

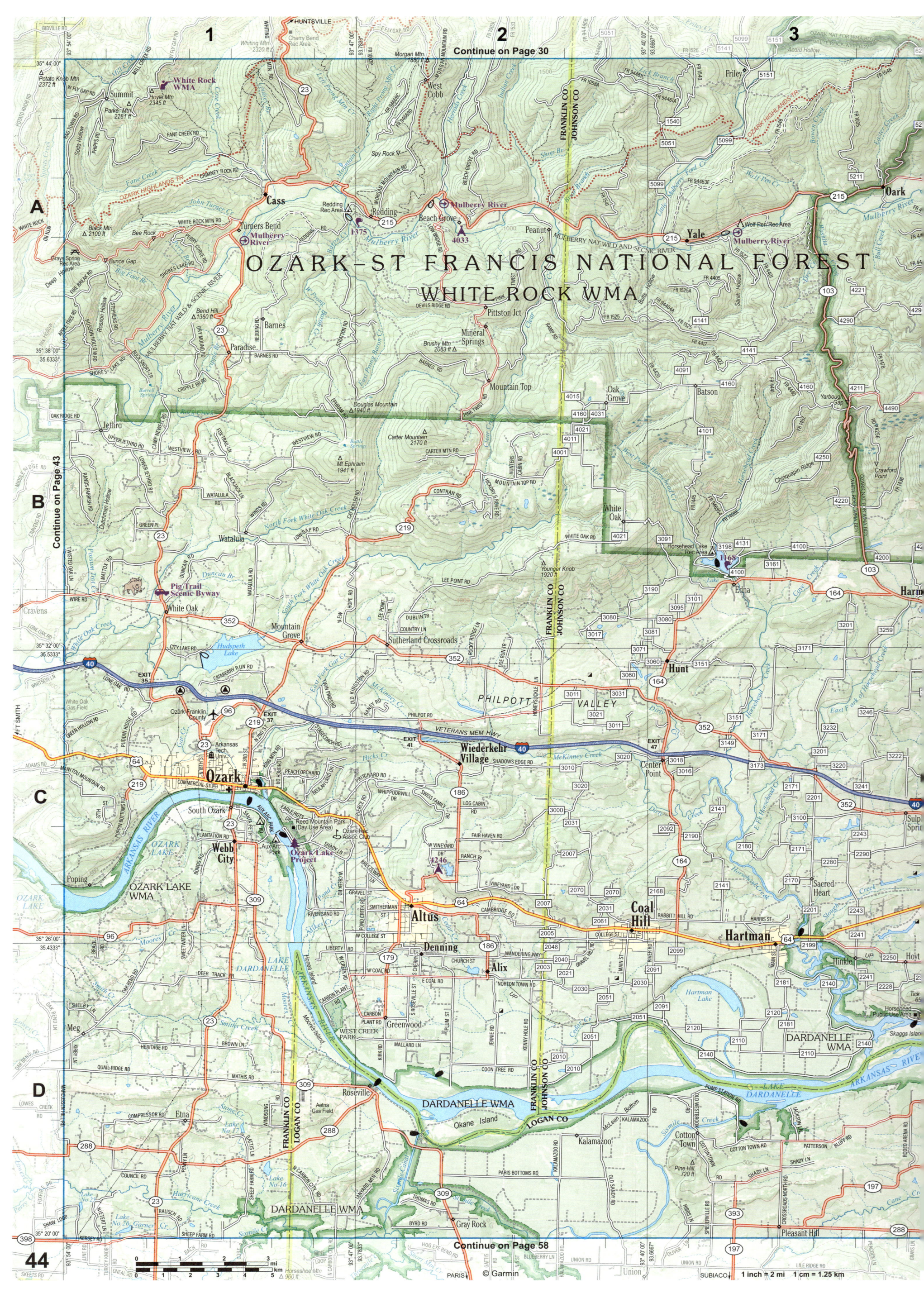

OZARK–ST FRANCIS NATIONAL FOREST

WHITE ROCK WMA

Continue on Page 43

1 inch = 2 mi   1 cm = 1.25 km

© Garmin

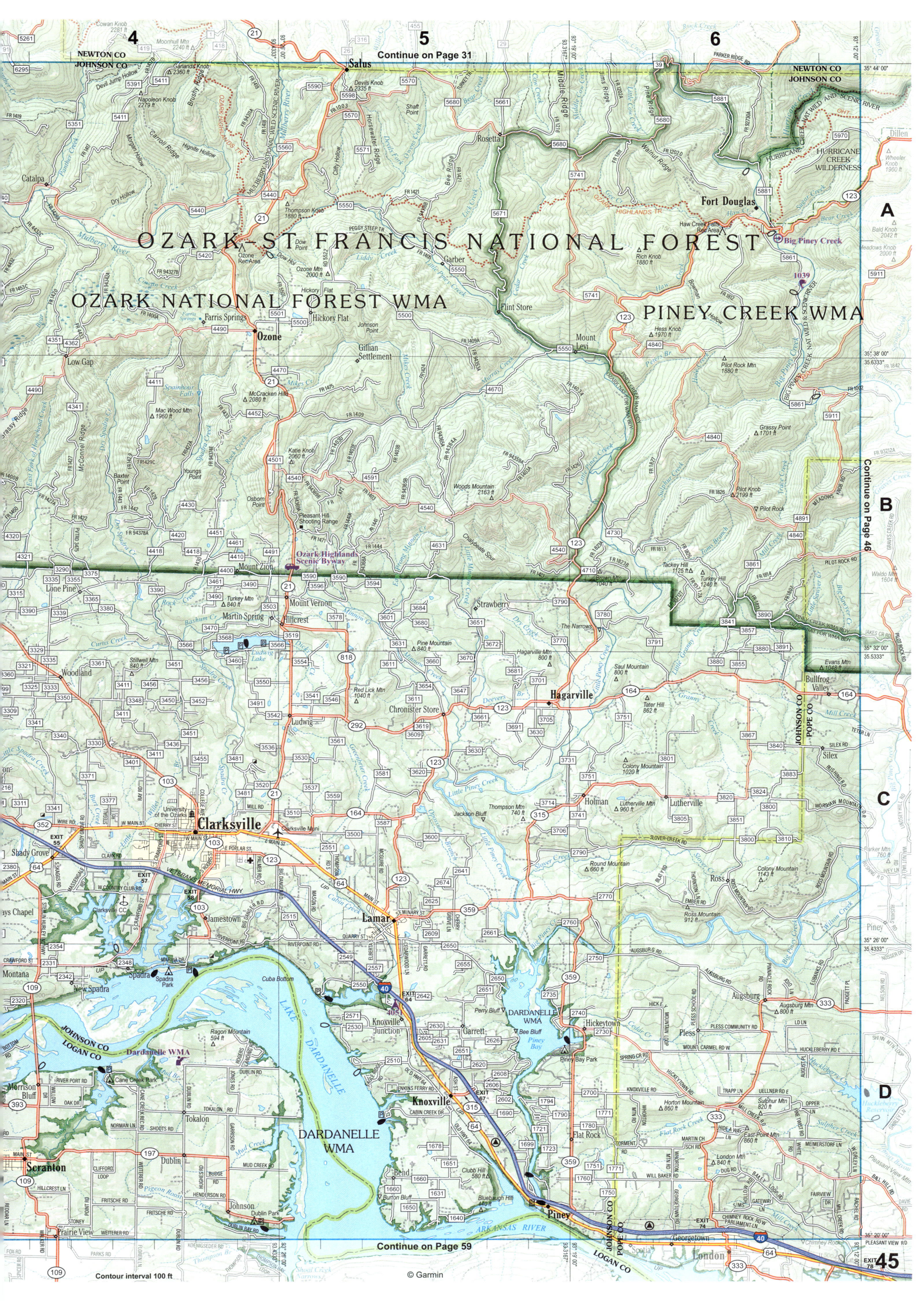

OZARK–ST FRANCIS NATIONAL FOREST

OZARK NATIONAL FOREST WMA

PINEY CREEK WMA

Continue on Page 46

45

Contour interval 100 ft

© Garmin

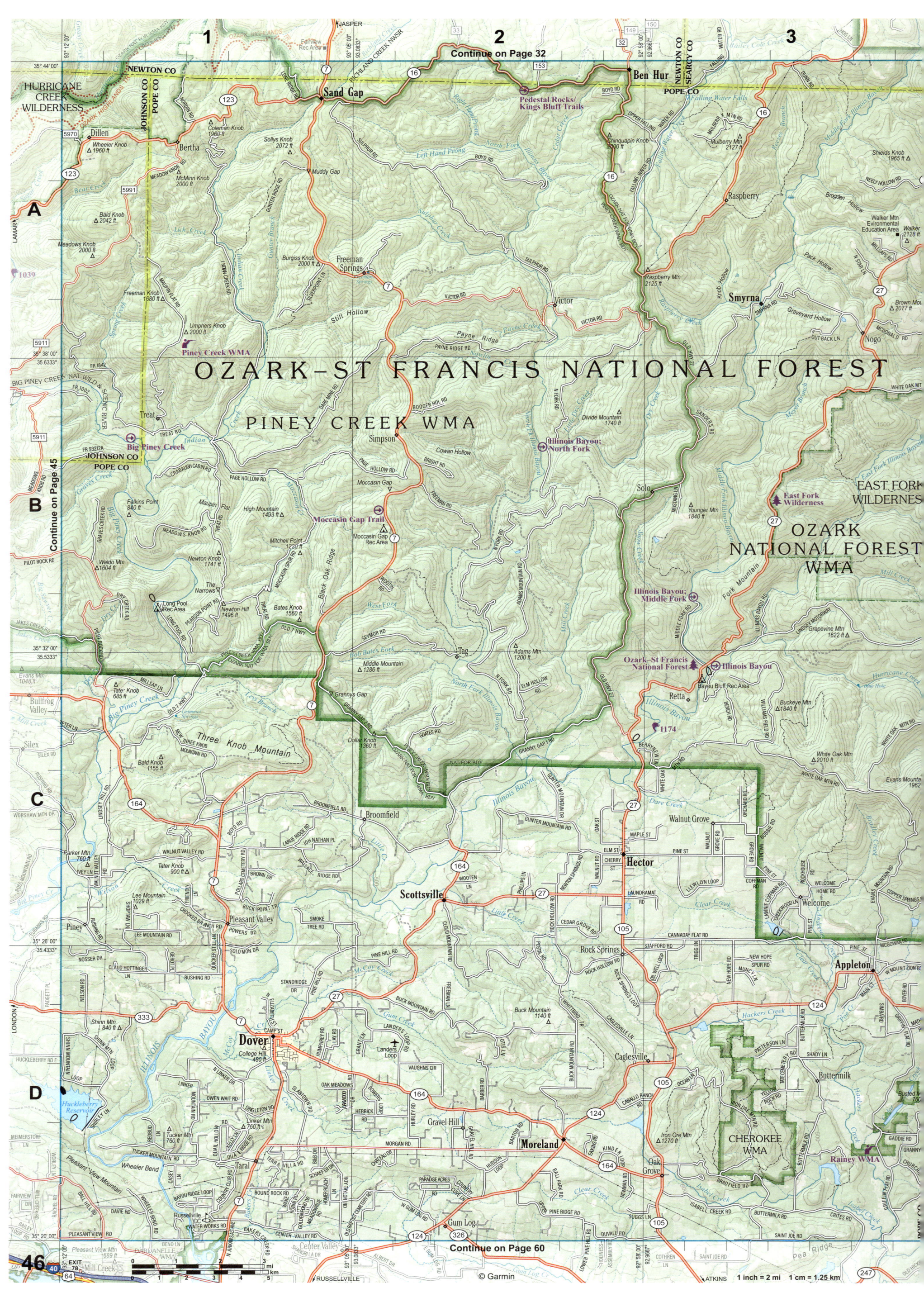

Continue on Page 32

OZARK–ST FRANCIS NATIONAL FOREST

PINEY CREEK WMA

OZARK NATIONAL FOREST WMA

EAST FORK WILDERNESS

Continue on Page 45

Continue on Page 60

46

1 inch = 2 mi   1 cm = 1.25 km

© Garmin

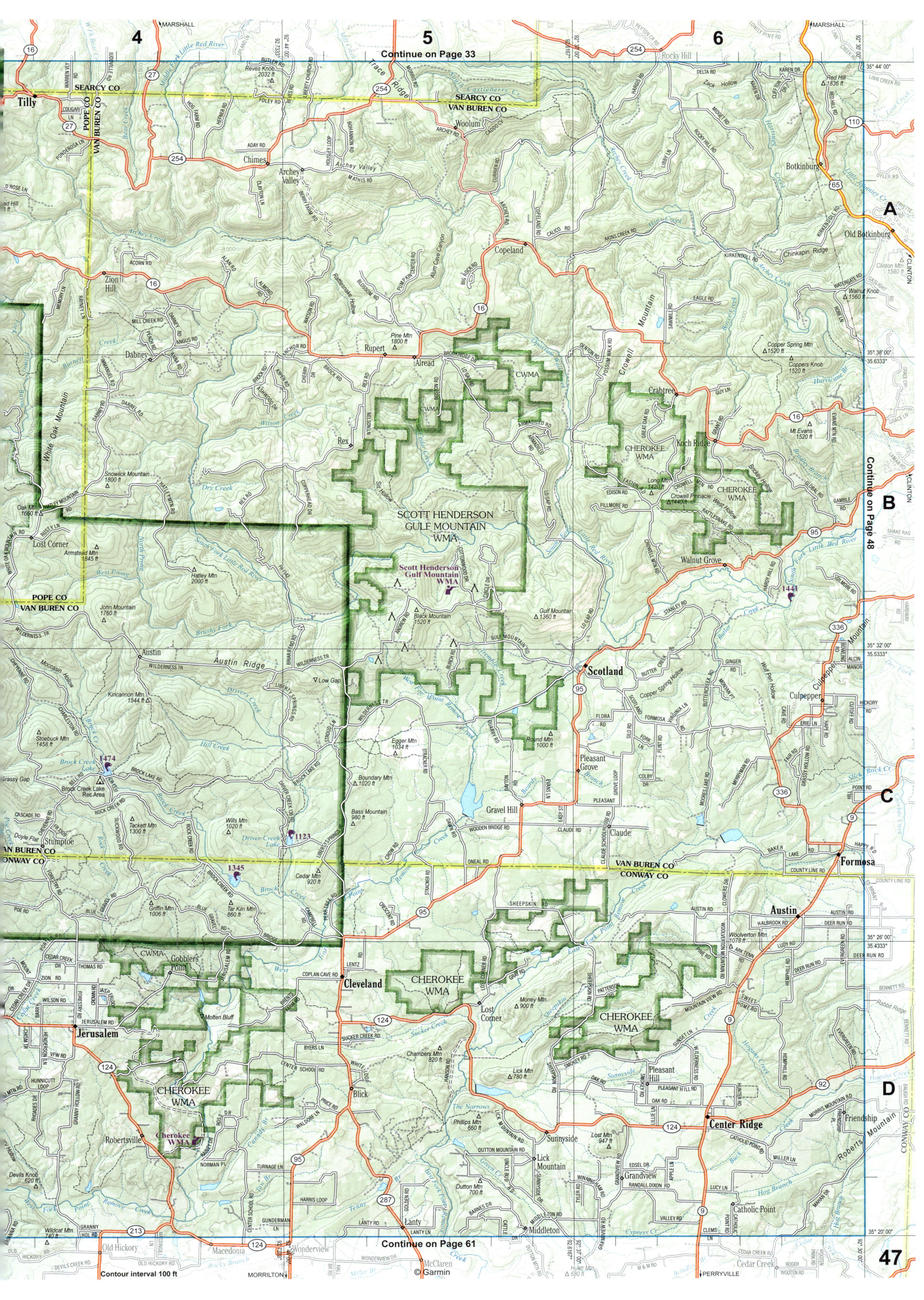

Continue on Page 48

Contour interval 100 ft

© McClaren

© Garmin

47

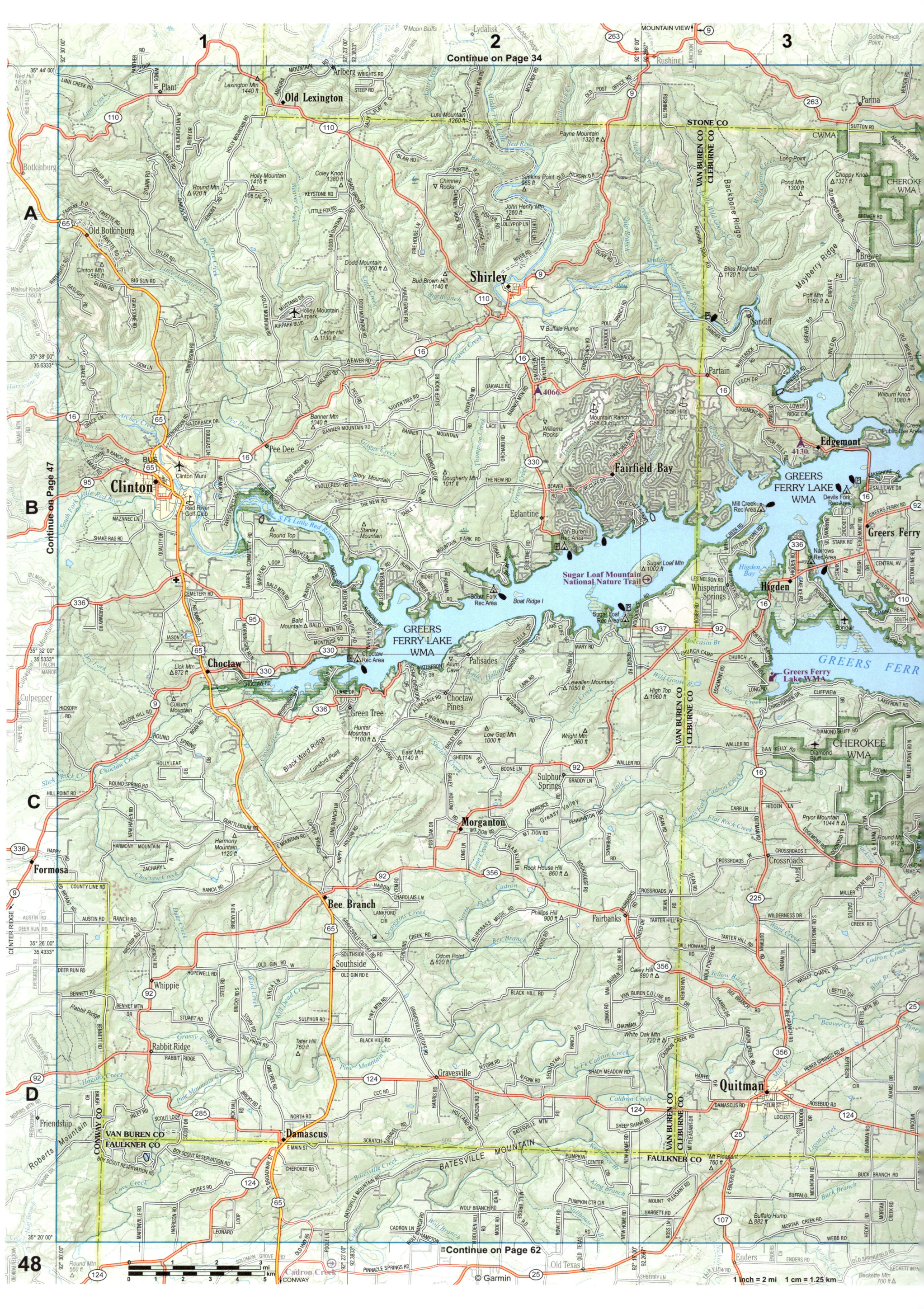

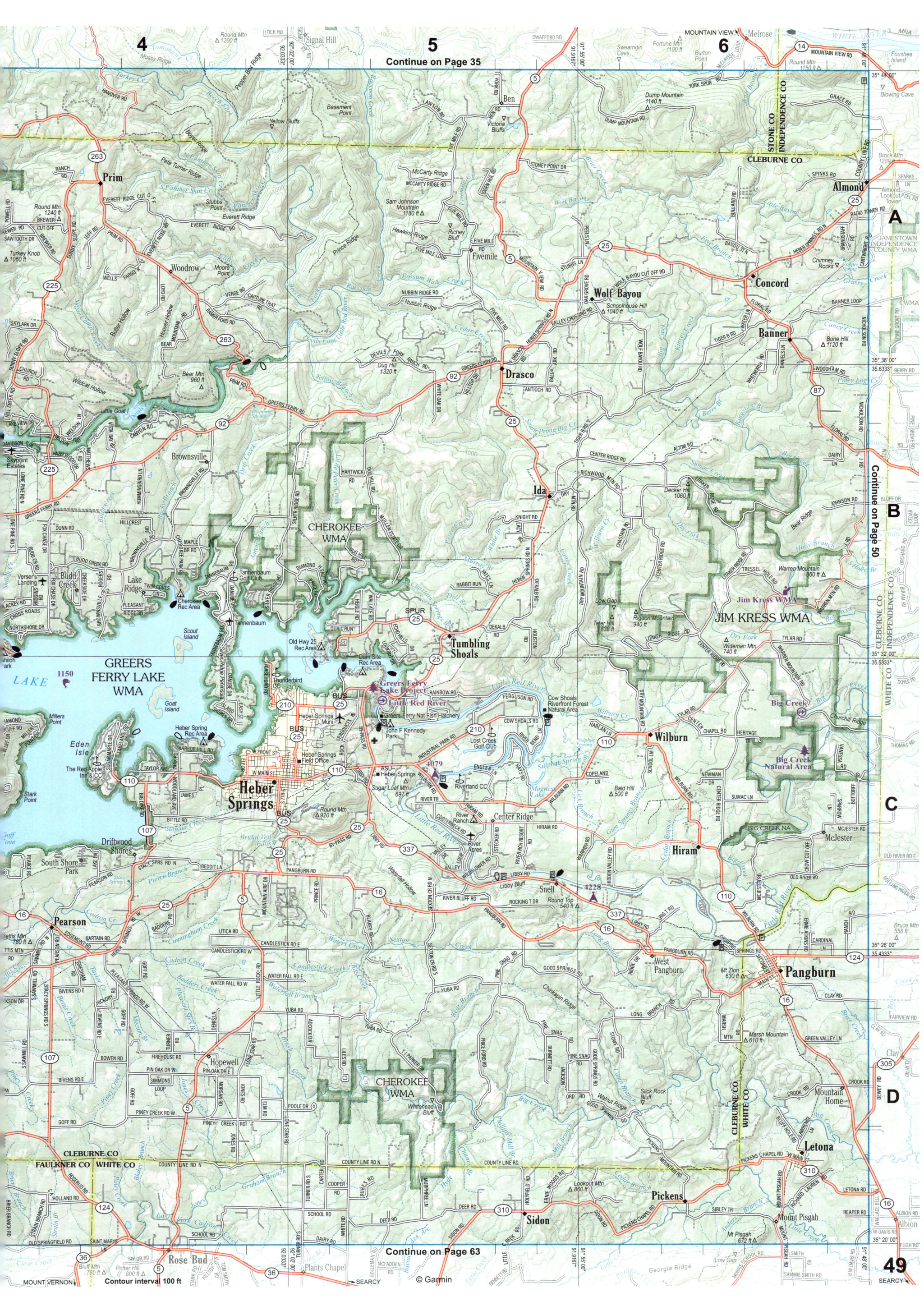

Continue on Page 50

GREERS
FERRY LAKE
WMA

CHEROKEE
WMA

JIM KRESS WMA

CHEROKEE
WMA

Heber
Springs

Prim

Woodrow

Brownsville

Pearson

Hopewell

Rose Bud

Ben

Drasco

Ida

Wolf Bayou

Concord

Almond

Banner

Tumbling
Shoals

SPUR

Wilburn

Big Creek
Natural Area

Hiram

McJester

West
Pangburn

Pangburn

Letona

Pickens

Sidon

Mount Pisgah

Snell

Contour interval 100 ft

© Garmin

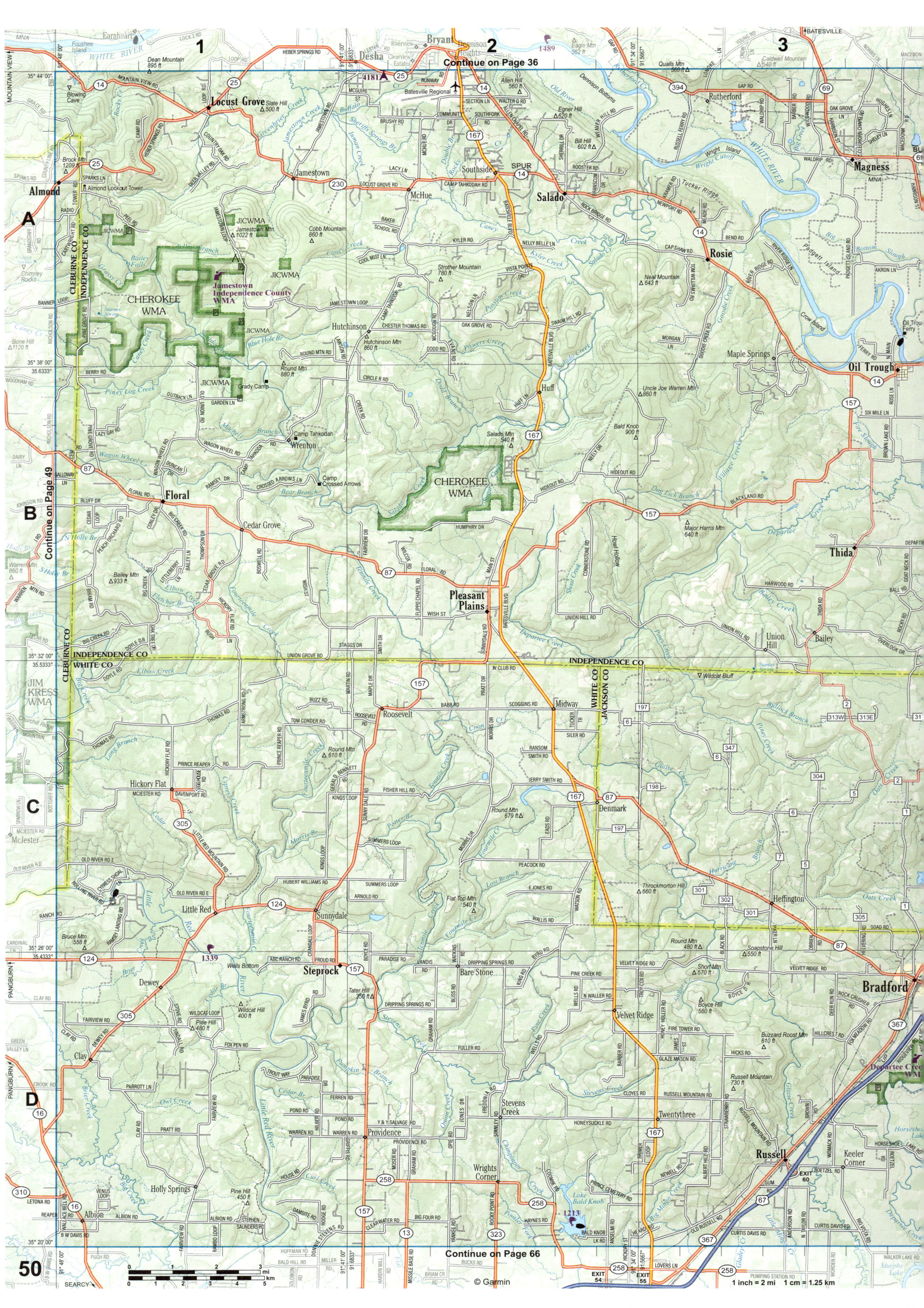

Continue on Page 49

© Garmin

1 inch = 2 mi   1 cm = 1.25 km

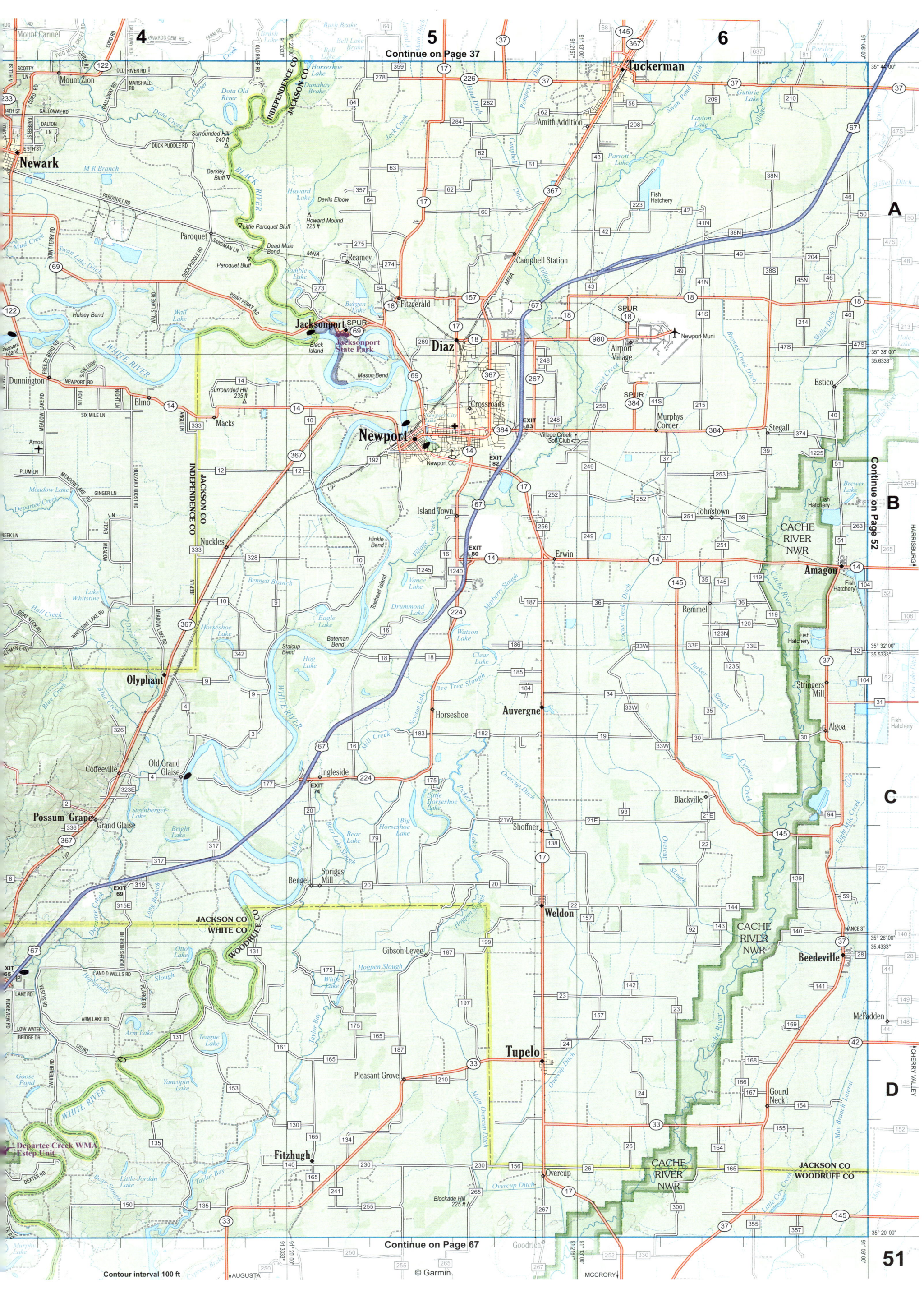

Continue on Page 52

Contour interval 100 ft

© Garmin

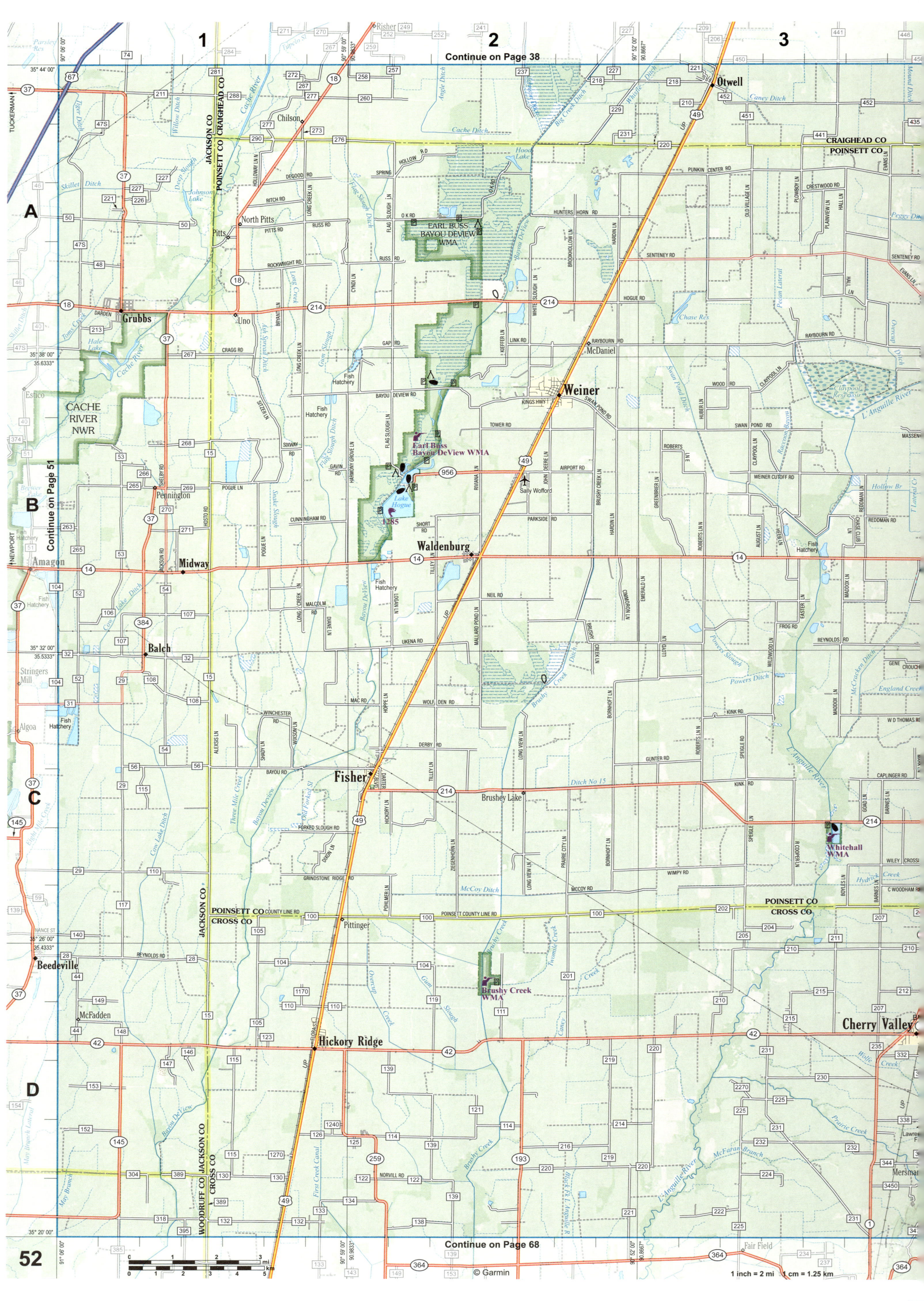

Continue on Page 38

Continue on Page 51

Continue on Page 68

52

© Garmin

1 inch = 2 mi   1 cm = 1.25 km

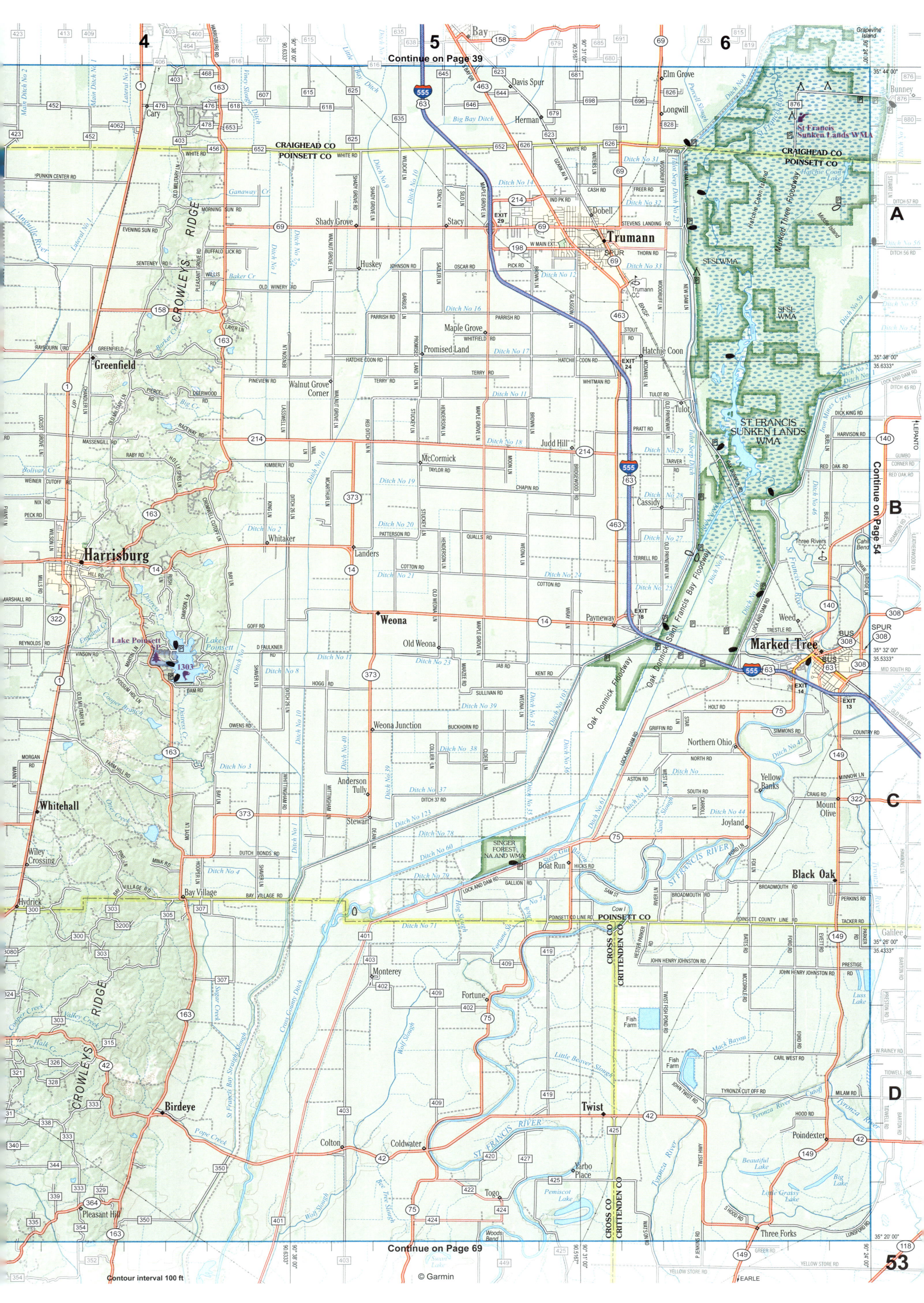

Continue on Page 39

Continue on Page 54

Continue on Page 69

© Garmin

Contour interval 100 ft

53

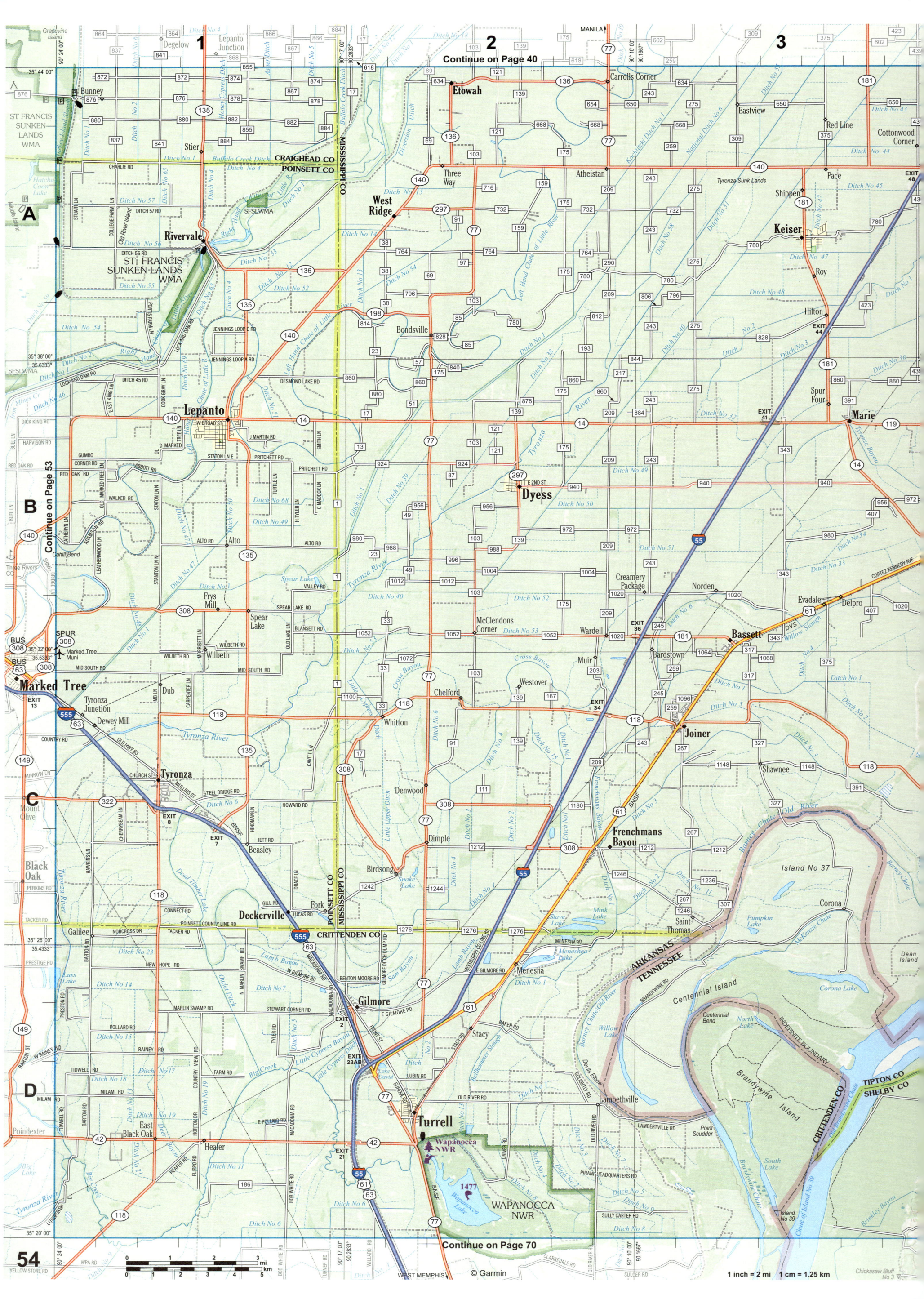

Continue on Page 40
Continue on Page 53
Continue on Page 70

54

© Garmin

1 inch = 2 mi   1 cm = 1.25 km

Continue on Page 41

A

Continue in the Tennessee Atlas & Gazetteer

B

C

D

Continue on Page 71

Contour interval 100 ft

© Garmin

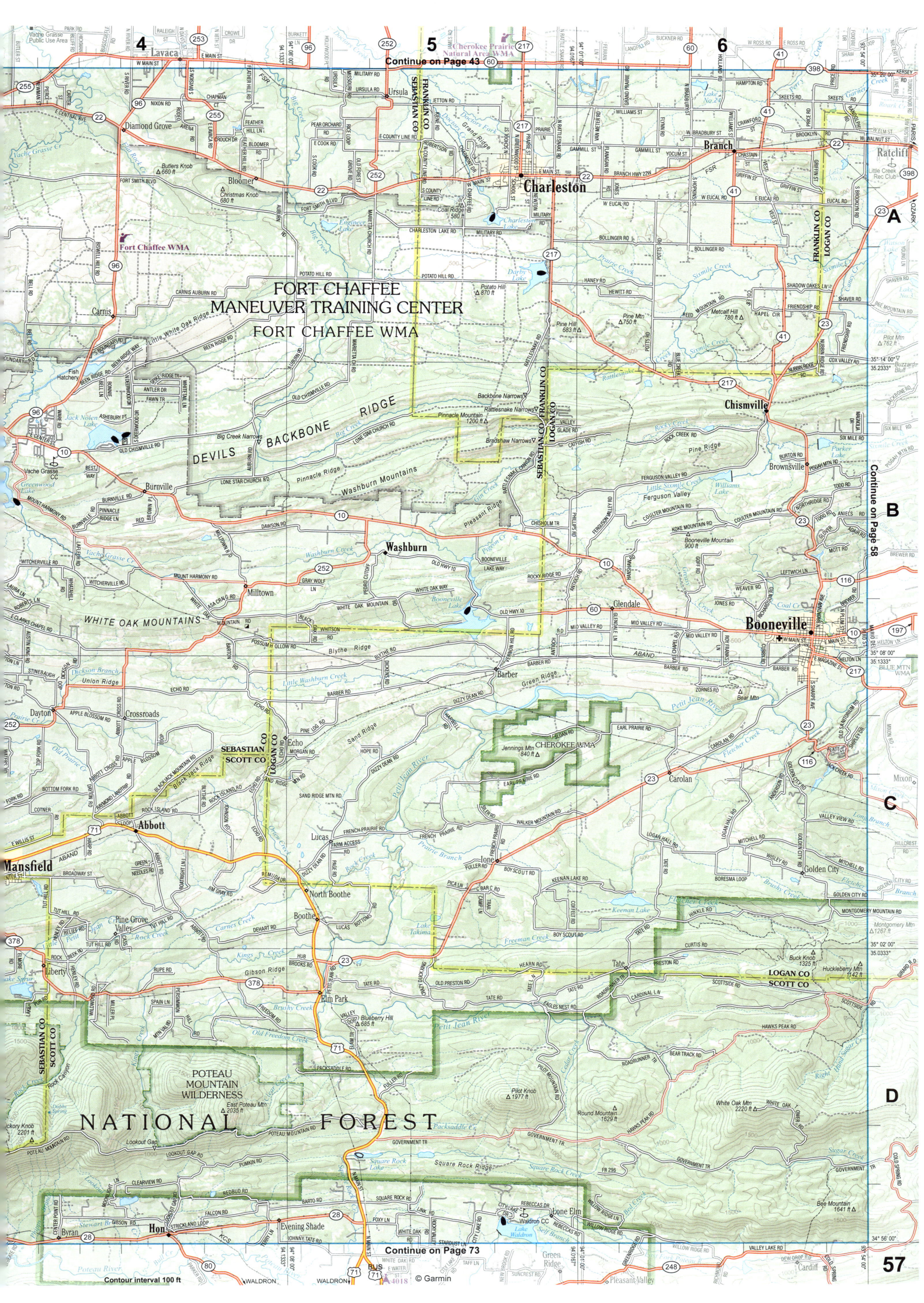

FORT CHAFFEE MANEUVER TRAINING CENTER

FORT CHAFFEE WMA

Continue on Page 43

Continue on Page 58

Continue on Page 73

DEVILS BACKBONE RIDGE

Washburn Mountains

WHITE OAK MOUNTAINS

CHEROKEE WMA

POTEAU MOUNTAIN WILDERNESS

N A T I O N A L   F O R E S T

Contour interval 100 ft

© Garmin

57

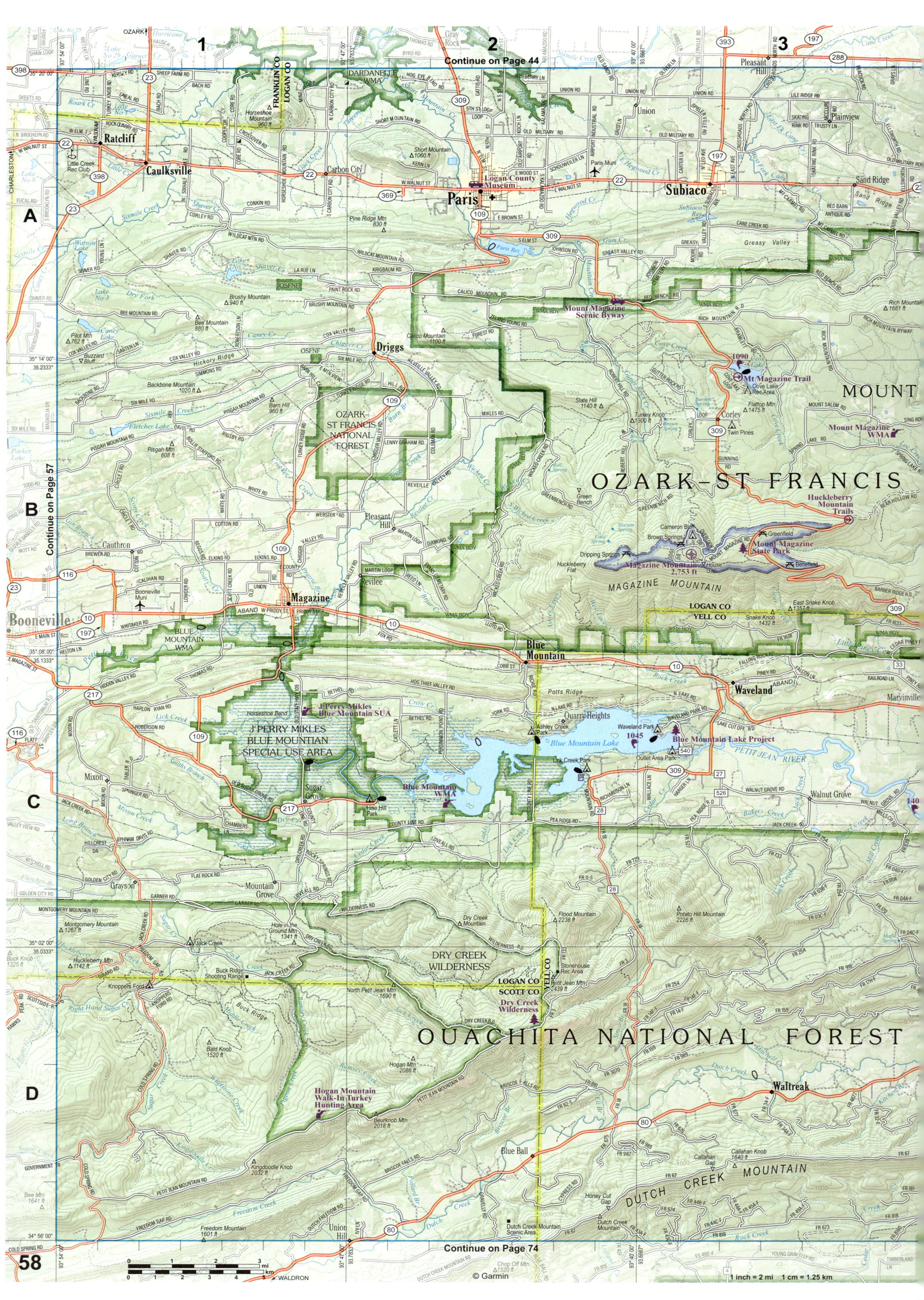

Continue on Page 57

Ozark
Ratcliff
Caulksville
Carbon City
Paris
Logan County Museum
Subiaco
Sand Ridge

A

DARDANELLE WMA
Union
Plainview

Short Mountain

OSFNF
Brushy Mountain
Bee Mountain
Pilot Mtn
Buzzard Bluff
Backbone Mountain
Hickory Ridge

Driggs
OSFNF
Calico Mountain

Mount Magazine Scenic Byway
1090
Mt Magazine Trail
Cove Lake Rec Area
Corley
Twin Pines
Mount Magazine WMA

MOUNT

OZARK-ST FRANCIS

B

OZARK-ST FRANCIS NATIONAL FOREST

Barn Hill
Pisgah Mountain
White Ridge

Pleasant Hill

Green Bench
Cameron Bluff
Brown Springs
Dripping Springs
Huckleberry Flat
Magazine Mountain 2,753 ft
Mount Magazine State Park
Greenfield

Huckleberry Mountain Trails

MAGAZINE MOUNTAIN

LOGAN CO
YELL CO

Booneville
Booneville Muni
Magazine

Blue Mountain WMA

Blue Mountain
East Snake Knob
Snake Knob 1432 ft

Waveland

Marivinville

C

J'Perry Mikles Blue Mountian SUA
Horseshoe Bend
J'PERRY MIKLES
BLUE MOUNTAIN
SPECIAL USE AREA

Sugar Grove

Blue Mountain WMA

Quarry Heights
Ashley Creek Park
Blue Mountain Lake
Waveland Park
1045
Blue Mountain Lake Project
540
Outlet Area Park

PETIT JEAN RIVER

Walnut Grove
140

Mixoll

Grayson
Mountain Grove

Flood Mountain 2238 ft
Potato Hill Mountain 2226 ft

Montgomery Mountain 1267 ft
Huckleberry Mtn 1142 ft
Buck Creek
Buck Ridge Shooting Range
Knoppels Ford

DRY CREEK
WILDERNESS

LOGAN CO
SCOTT CO
Petit Jean Mtn 2439 ft
Dry Creek Wilderness

Stonehouse Rec Area

OUACHITA NATIONAL FOREST

D

Hogan Mountain Walk-In Turkey Hunting Area
Beurknob Mtn 2018 ft

Bald Knob 1520 ft

Hogan Mtn 2086 ft

Blue Ball

Waltreak

Kingdoodle Knob 2032 ft
Freedom Mountain 1601 ft
Union Hill

Briscoe Falls Rd

Dutch Creek Mountain Scenic Area
Dutch Creek Mountain

Honey Cut Gap
Callahan Gap
Callahan Knob 1640 ft

DUTCH CREEK MOUNTAIN

WALDRON

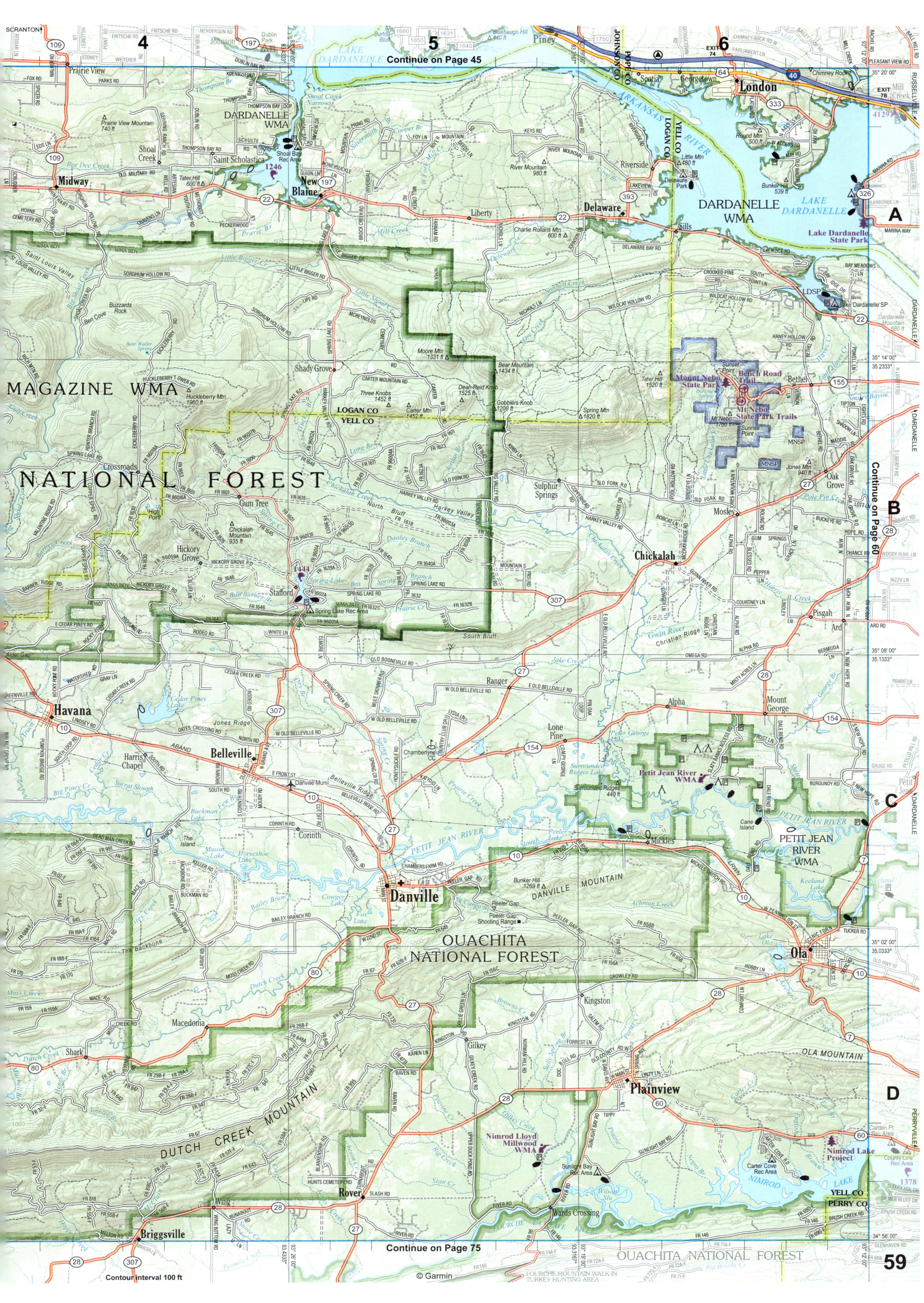

Continue on Page 45

Continue on Page 60

Continue on Page 75

MAGAZINE WMA

NATIONAL FOREST

OUACHITA
NATIONAL FOREST

OUACHITA NATIONAL FOREST

Contour interval 100 ft

© Garmin

59

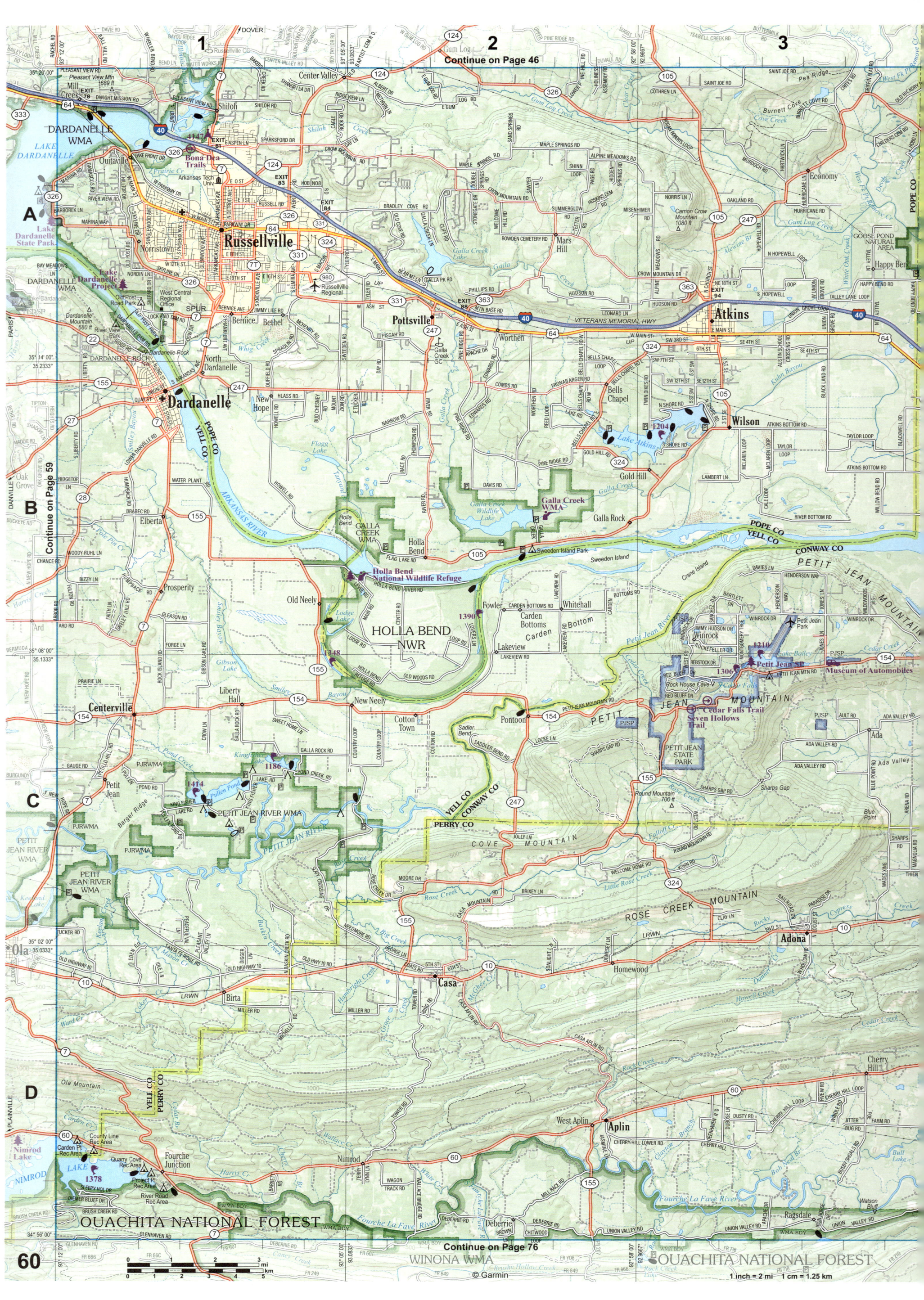

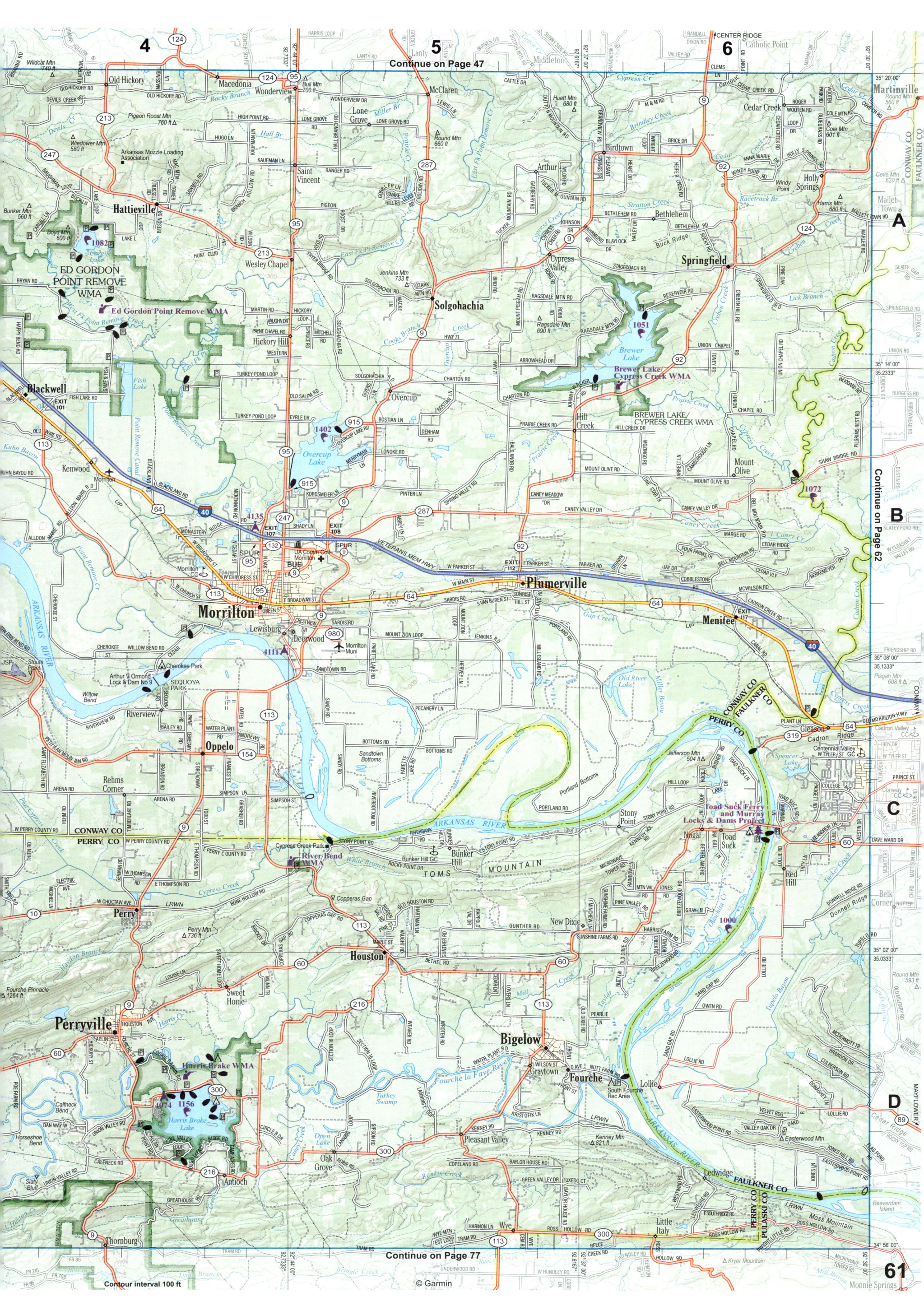

Continue on Page 47

Continue on Page 62

Continue on Page 77

Contour interval 100 ft

© Garmin

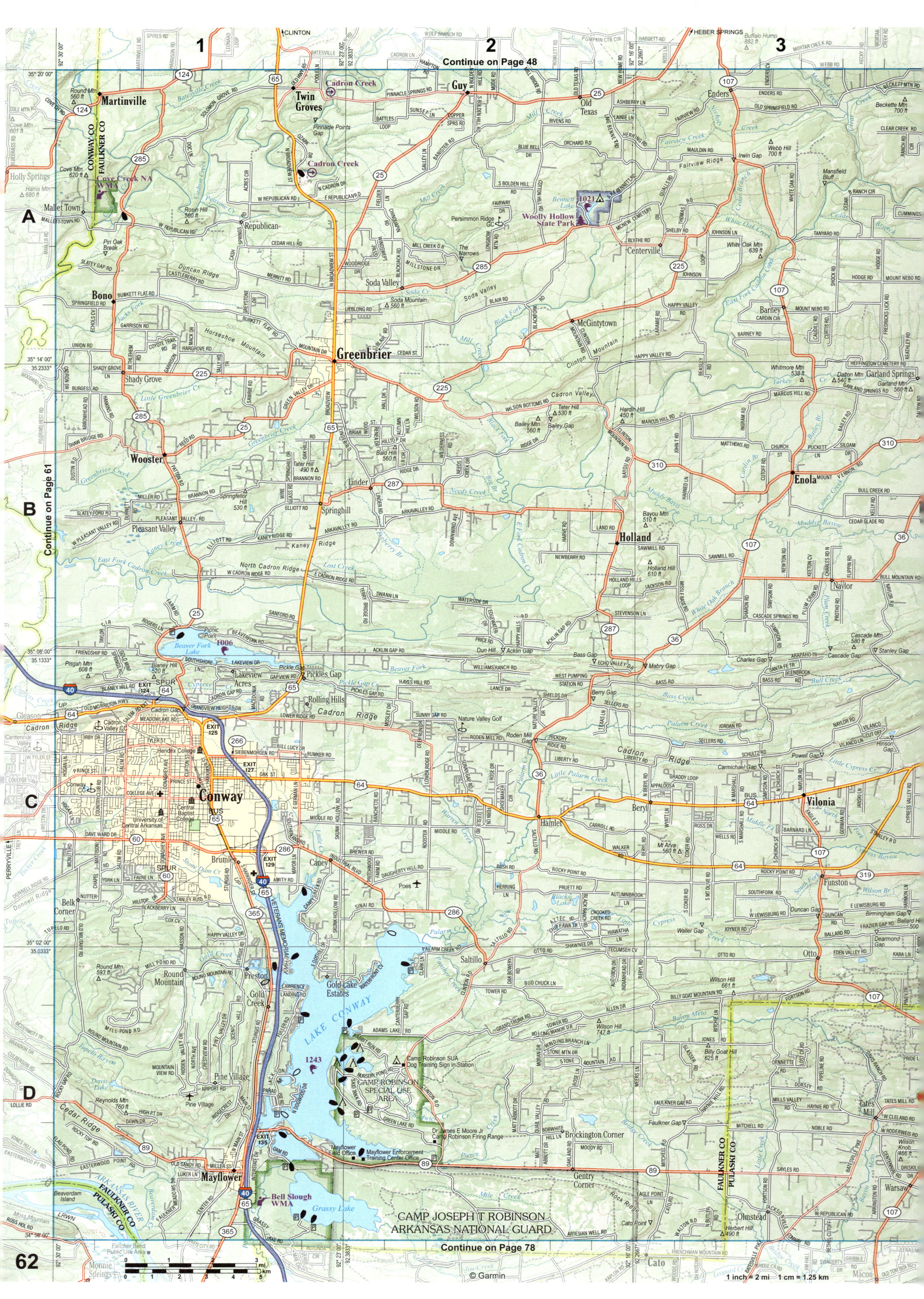

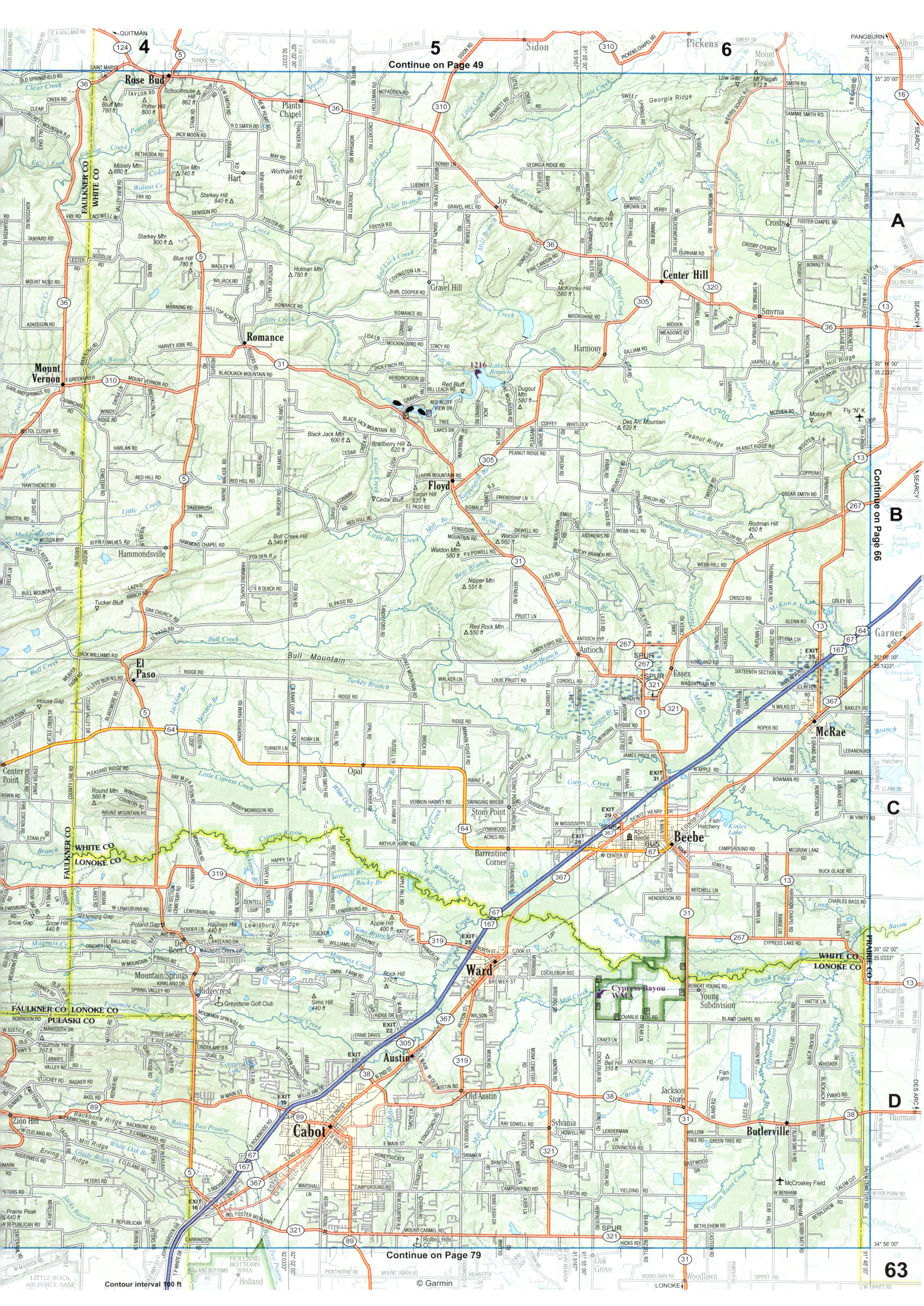

Continue on Page 49

Continue on Page 66

Continue on Page 79

Contour interval 100 ft

© Garmin

63

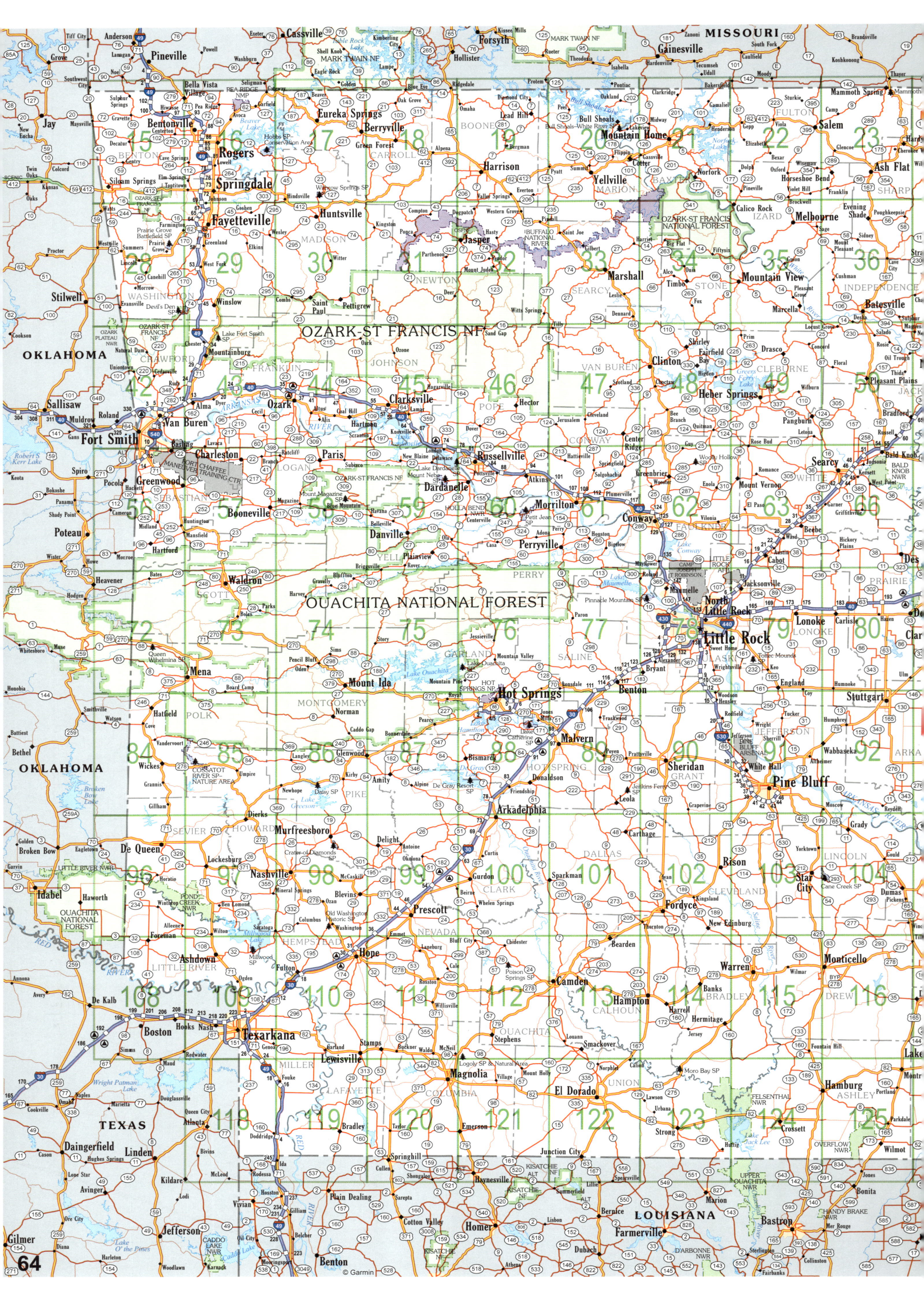

Arkansas
HIGHWAY MAP

Scale 1:1,200,000
1 inch represents 19 miles (30 km)

miles   0   10   20   30
kilometers   0   10   20   30   40   50

N W E S (compass rose)

MILEAGE CHART

	Arkadelphia	Batesville	Benton	Blytheville	Camden	Conway	El Dorado	Fayetteville	Forrest City	Ft Smith	Harrison	Helena	Hot Springs	Jonesboro	Little Rock	Magnolia	Monticello	Paragould	Pine Bluff	Russellville	Stuttgart	Texarkana
Batesville	179																					
Benton	117	45																				
Blytheville	210	127	253																			
Camden	266	87	191	51																		
Conway	129	185	55	83	98																	
El Dorado	148	32	285	108	210	83																
Fayetteville	295	162	263	306	203	214	212															
Forrest City	279	187	118	168	97	117	98	161														
Ft Smith	246	63	232	128	200	311	158	199	149													
Harrison	139	212	76	255	106	238	227	171	117	196												
Helena	252	272	43	305	191	144	172	133	143	135	176											
Hot Springs	171	159	128	146	191	117	84	85	239	31	146	36										
Jonesboro	186	108	174	260	65	253	239	132	220	53	157	74	201									
Little Rock	133	53	119	139	159	93	192	117	31	98	186	24	93	67								
Magnolia	135	257	107	209	268	210	205	273	34	166	37	303	124	228	73							
Monticello	106	91	206	118	121	228	249	141	276	71	120	68	234	95	184	119						
Paragould	227	278	152	21	205	129	178	279	86	257	260	151	241	57	176	94	220					
Pine Bluff	170	52	108	42	149	70	101	181	200	97	234	90	73	71	195	48	125	75				
Russellville	120	198	172	182	78	179	73	191	86	165	118	190	49	158	230	89	121	109				
Stuttgart	127	37	137	87	146	53	115	104	62	195	211	60	236	127	81	109	163	84	108	114		
Texarkana	188	186	152	295	150	53	143	276	112	253	272	181	236	244	87	174	82	329	121	236	78	
West Memphis	270	100	199	136	79	172	244	127	63	180	74	237	280	38	313	226	152	207	62	151	113	194

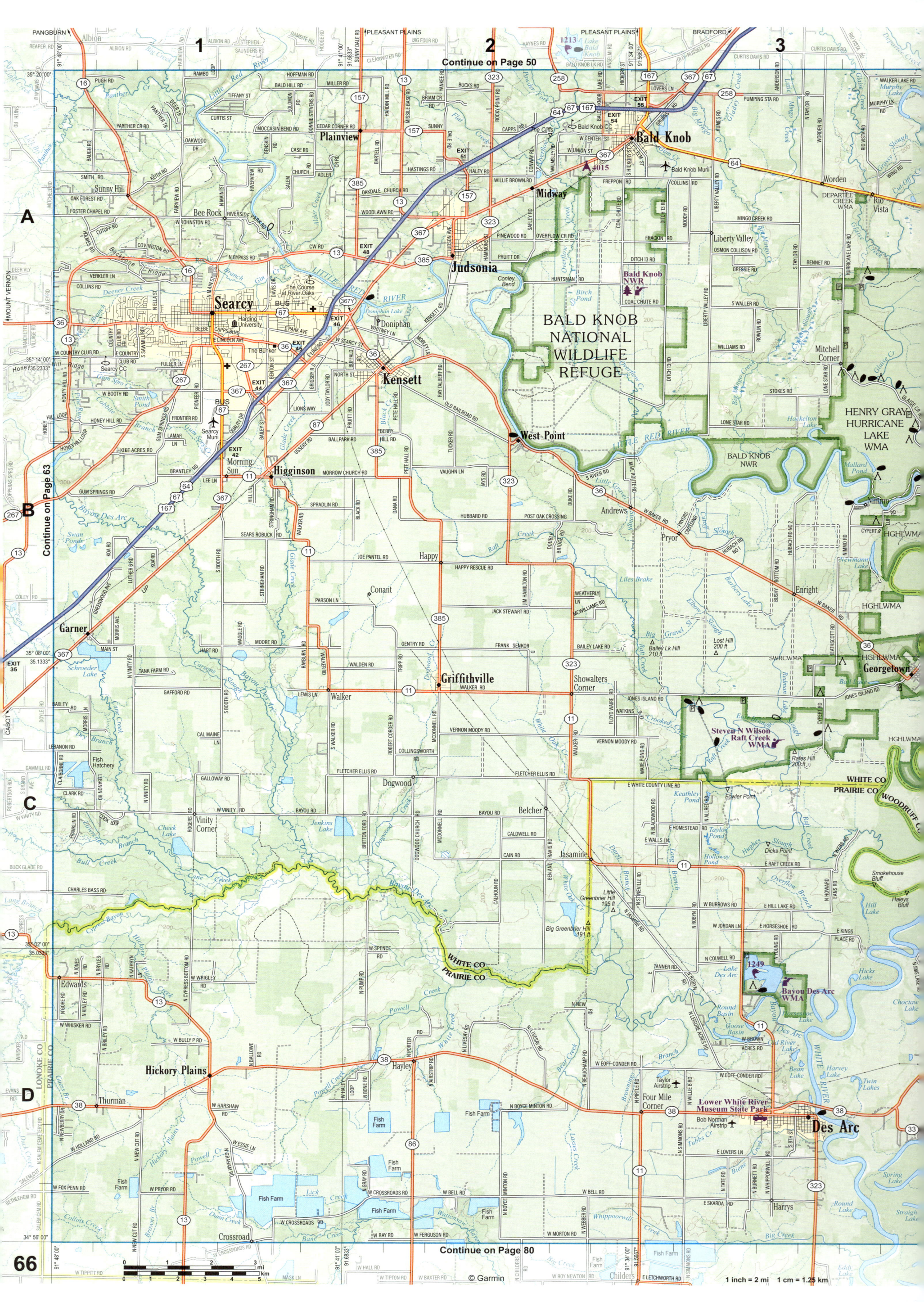

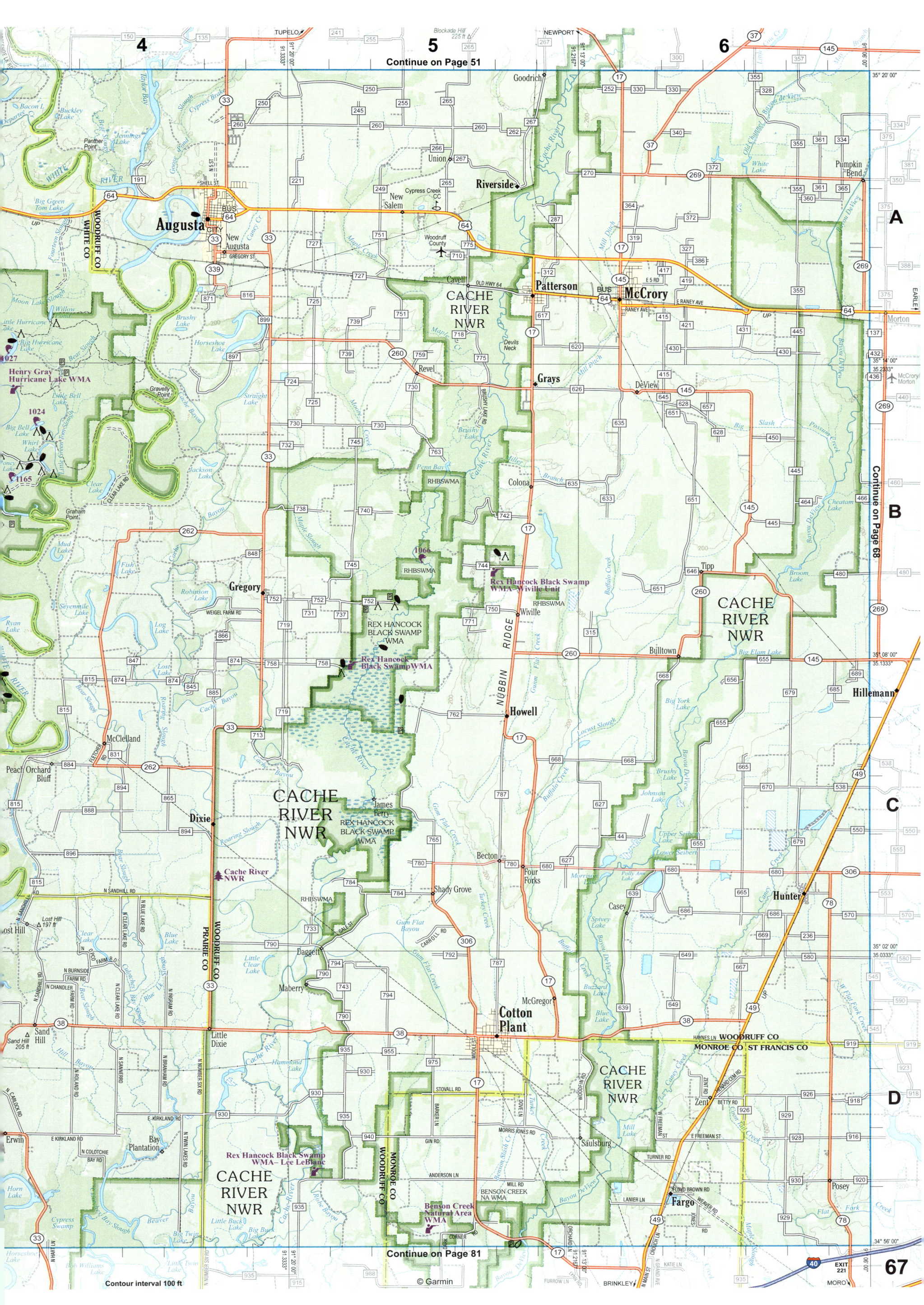

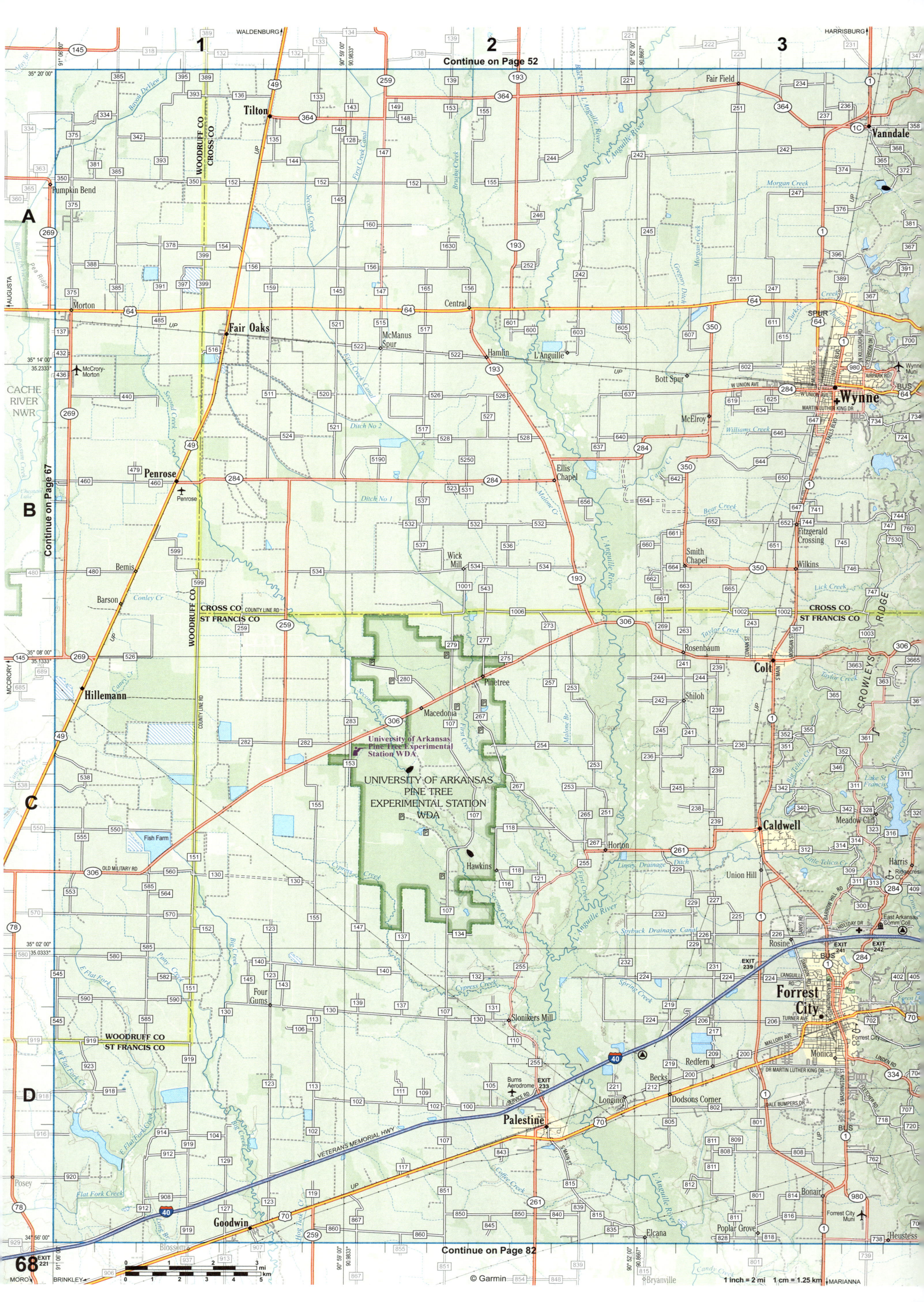

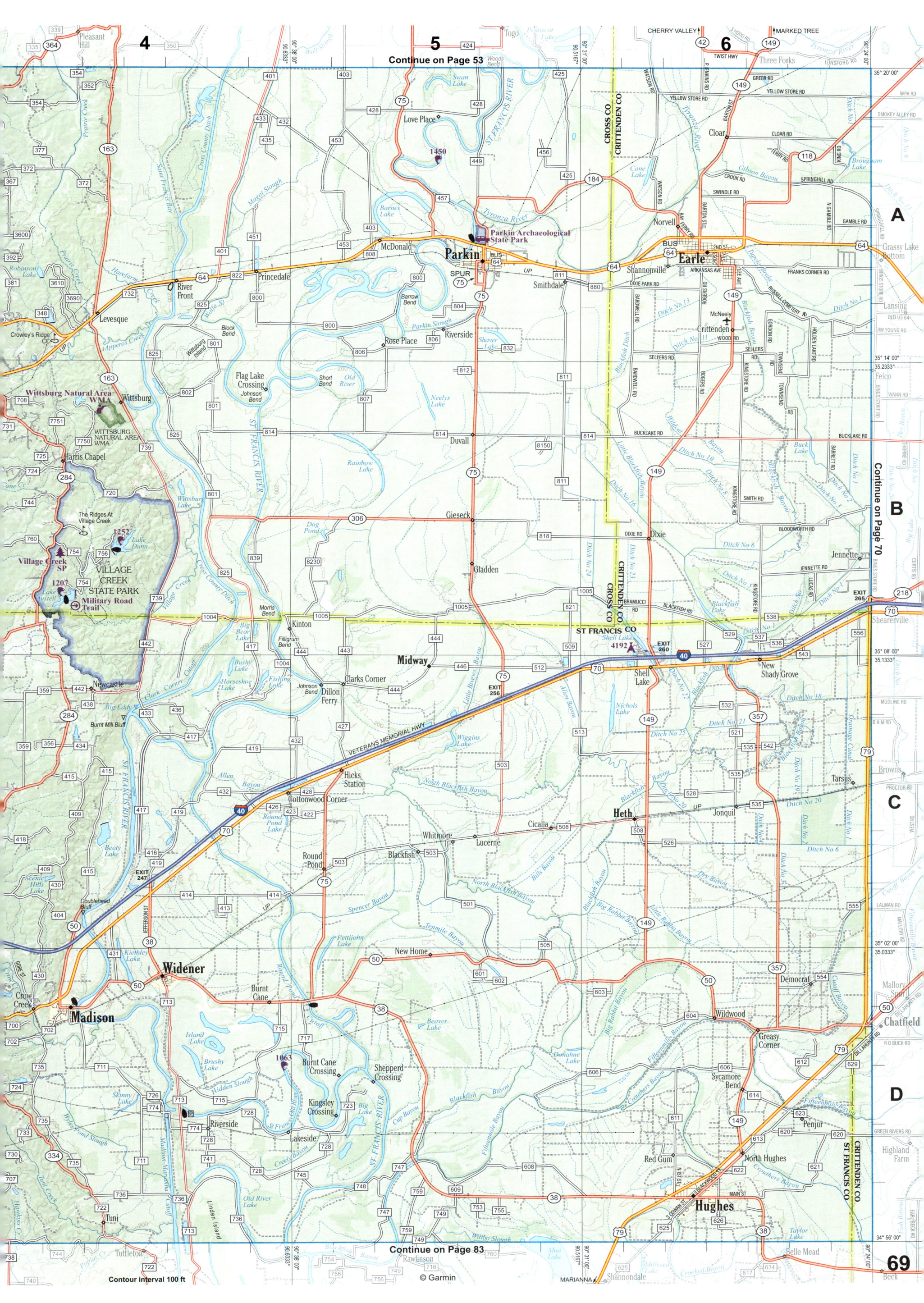

Continue on Page 55

Continue in the Tennessee Atlas & Gazetteer

Continue on page 70

Continue on page 83

Continue in the *Mississippi Atlas & Gazetteer*

Contour interval 100 ft

© Garmin

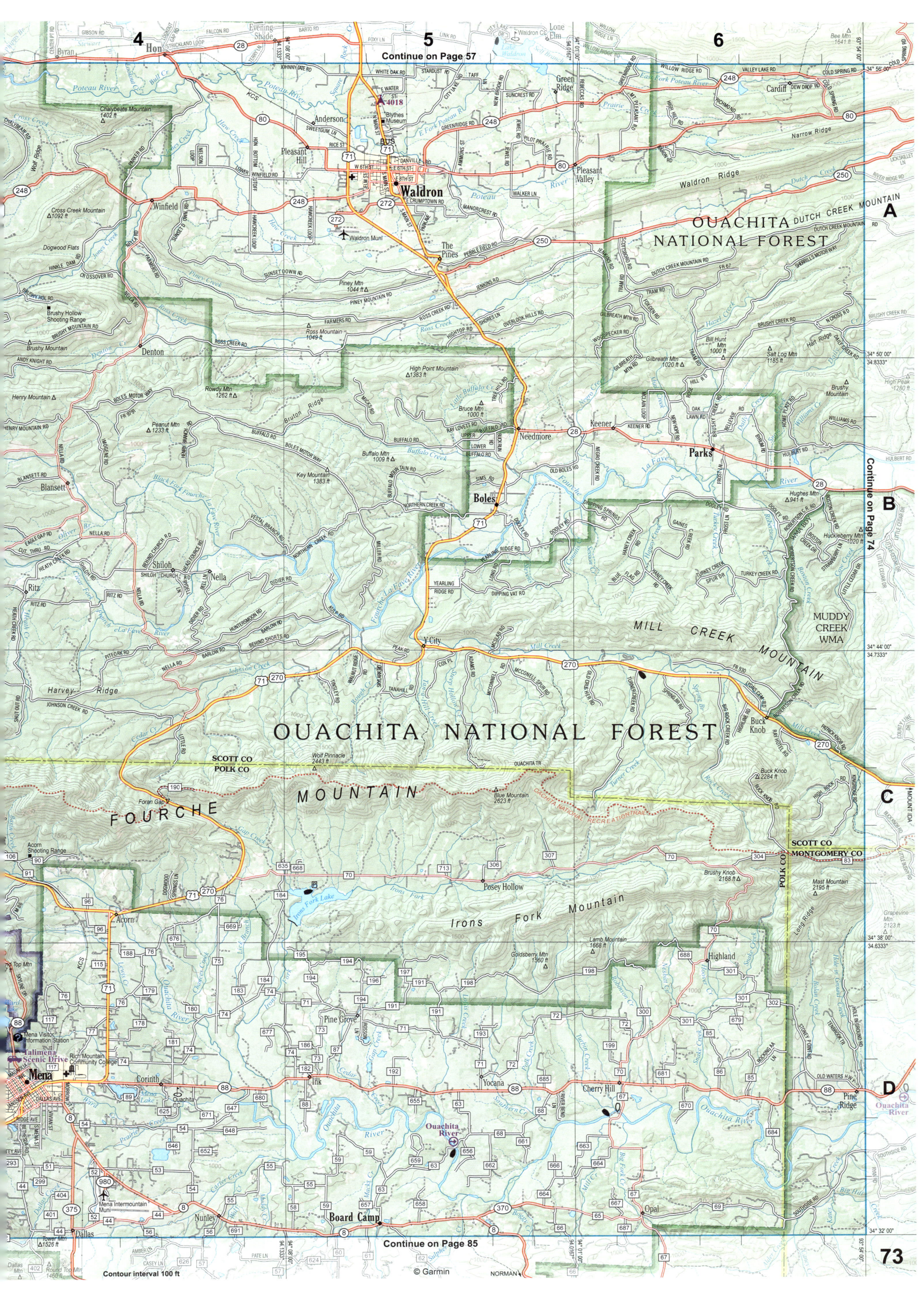

OUACHITA NATIONAL FOREST

Waldron

Needmore

Boles

Parks

Keener

OUACHITA NATIONAL FOREST

FOURCHE   MOUNTAIN

Irons Fork Mountain

MILL CREEK MOUNTAIN

MUDDY CREEK WMA

SCOTT CO
POLK CO

SCOTT CO
MONTGOMERY CO

POLK CO

Mena

Board Camp

Continue on Page 74

Contour interval 100 ft

© Garmin

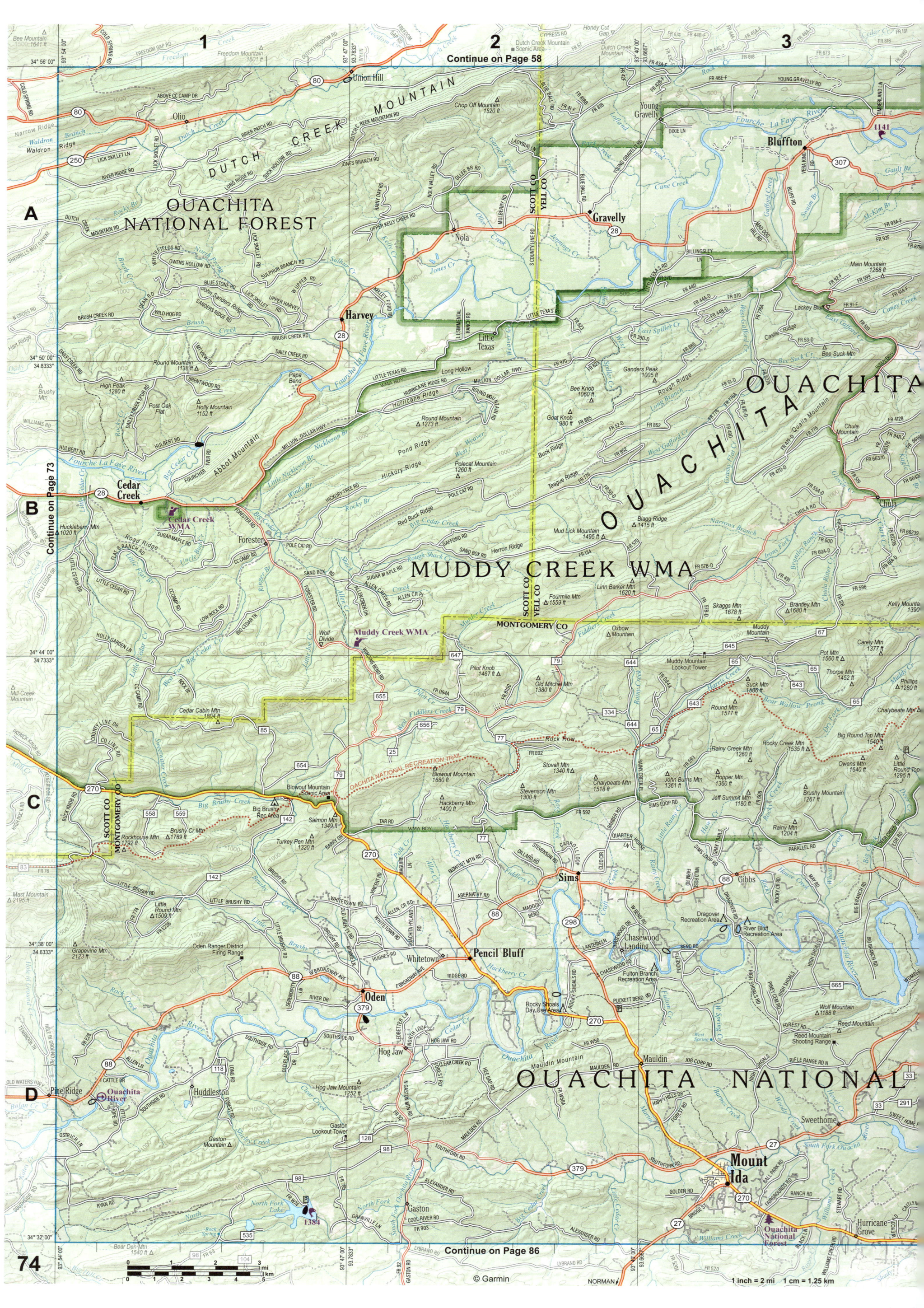

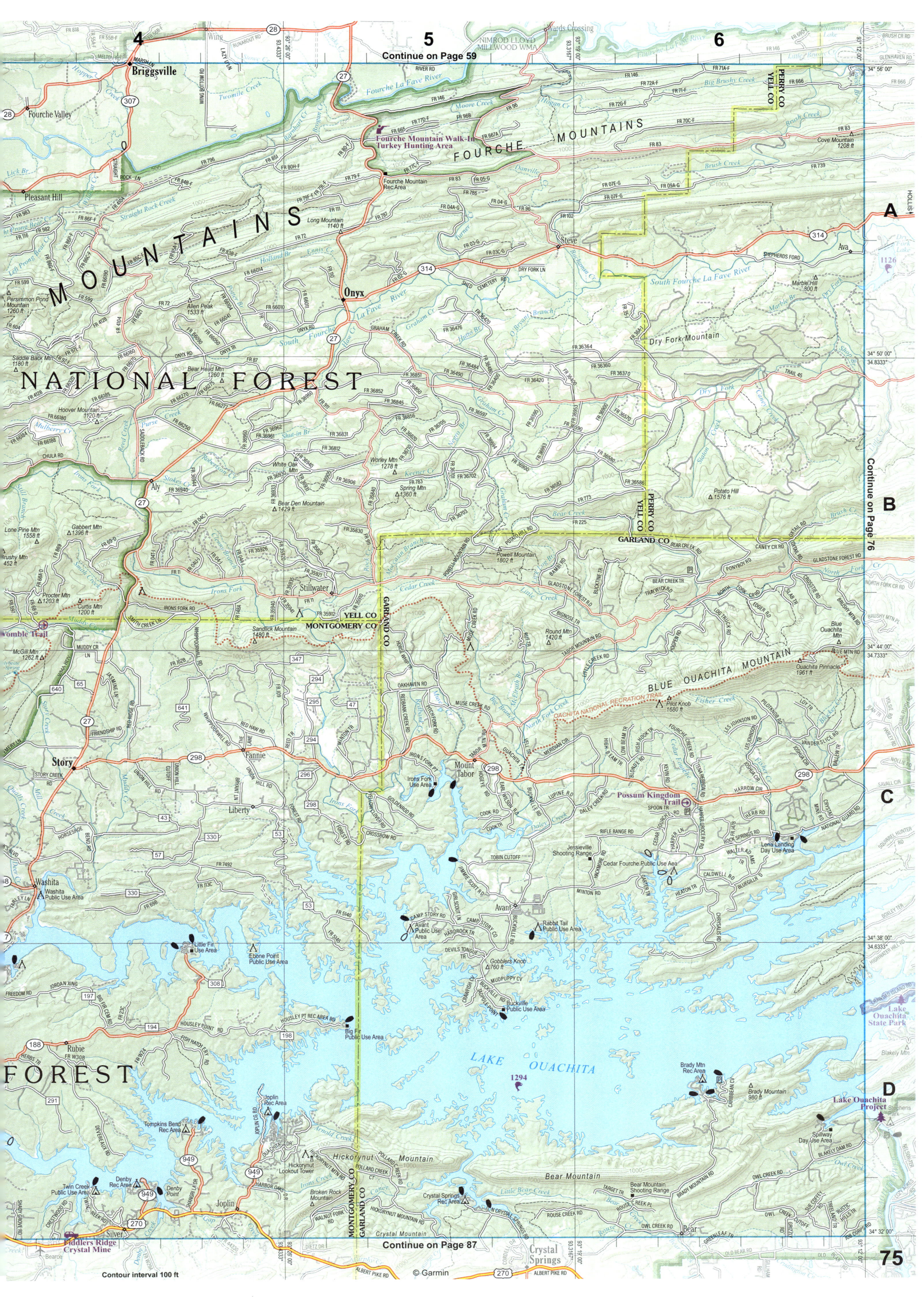

Continue on Page 59

Continue on Page 76

Continue on Page 87

4   **5**   **6**

A

B

C

D

Briggsville

Fourche Valley

Pleasant Hill

Onyx

M O U N T A I N S

FOURCHE   MOUNTAINS

Persimmon Pond Mountain 1260 ft

Saddle Back Mtn 1190 ft

N A T I O N A L   F O R E S T

Hoover Mountain 1260 ft

Bear Head Mtn 1260 ft

White Oak Mtn

Worley Mtn 1278 ft

Bear Den Mountain 1429 ft

Spring Mtn 1360 ft

Lone Pine Mtn 1558 ft

Gabbert Mtn 1396 ft

Aly

Brushy Mtn 452 ft

Womble Trail

Procter Mtn 1203 ft

Curtis Mtn 1200 ft

McGill Mtn 1262 ft

Stilwater

Sandlick Mountain 1480 ft

YELL CO
MONTGOMERY CO

GARLAND CO

Powell Mountain 1802 ft

Round Mtn 1420 ft

BLUE OUACHITA MOUNTAIN

Blue Ouachita Mtn

Ouachita Pinnacle 1961 ft

Pilot Knob 1680 ft

Potato Hill 1576 ft

Dry Fork Mountain

Marble Hill 800 ft

Cove Mountain 1208 ft

P E R R Y   C O
Y E L L   C O

GARLAND CO

Steve

Ava

OUACHITA NATIONAL RECREATION TRAIL

Possum Kingdom Trail

Story

Fannie

Liberty

Washita
Washita Public Use Area

Mount Tabor

Irons Fork Use Area

Avant

Jessieville Shooting Range

Cedar Fourche Public Use Area

Rabbit Tail Public Use Area

Lena Landing Day Use Area

L A K E   O U A C H I T A

1294

Little Fir Use Area

Ebone Point Public Use Area

Big Fir Public Use Area

Avant Public Use Area

Camp Story Rd

Devils Tower

Gobblers Knob 760 ft

Mudpuppy Cv

Buckville Public Use Area

Brady Mtn Rec Area

Brady Mountain 980 ft

Lake Ouachita State Park

Blakely Mtn

Lake Ouachita Project

Spillway Day Use Area

F O R E S T

Rubie

Joplin Rec Area

Tompkins Bend Rec Area

Twin Creek Public Use Area

Denby Rec Area

Denby Point

Joplin

Hickorynut Lookout Tower

Hickorynut Mountain

Broken Rock Mountain

Crystal Mountain

Crystal Springs Rec Area

Bear Mountain

Bear Mountain Shooting Range

Bear

Fiddlers Ridge Crystal Mine

Silver

Crystal Springs

75

Contour interval 100 ft

© Garmin

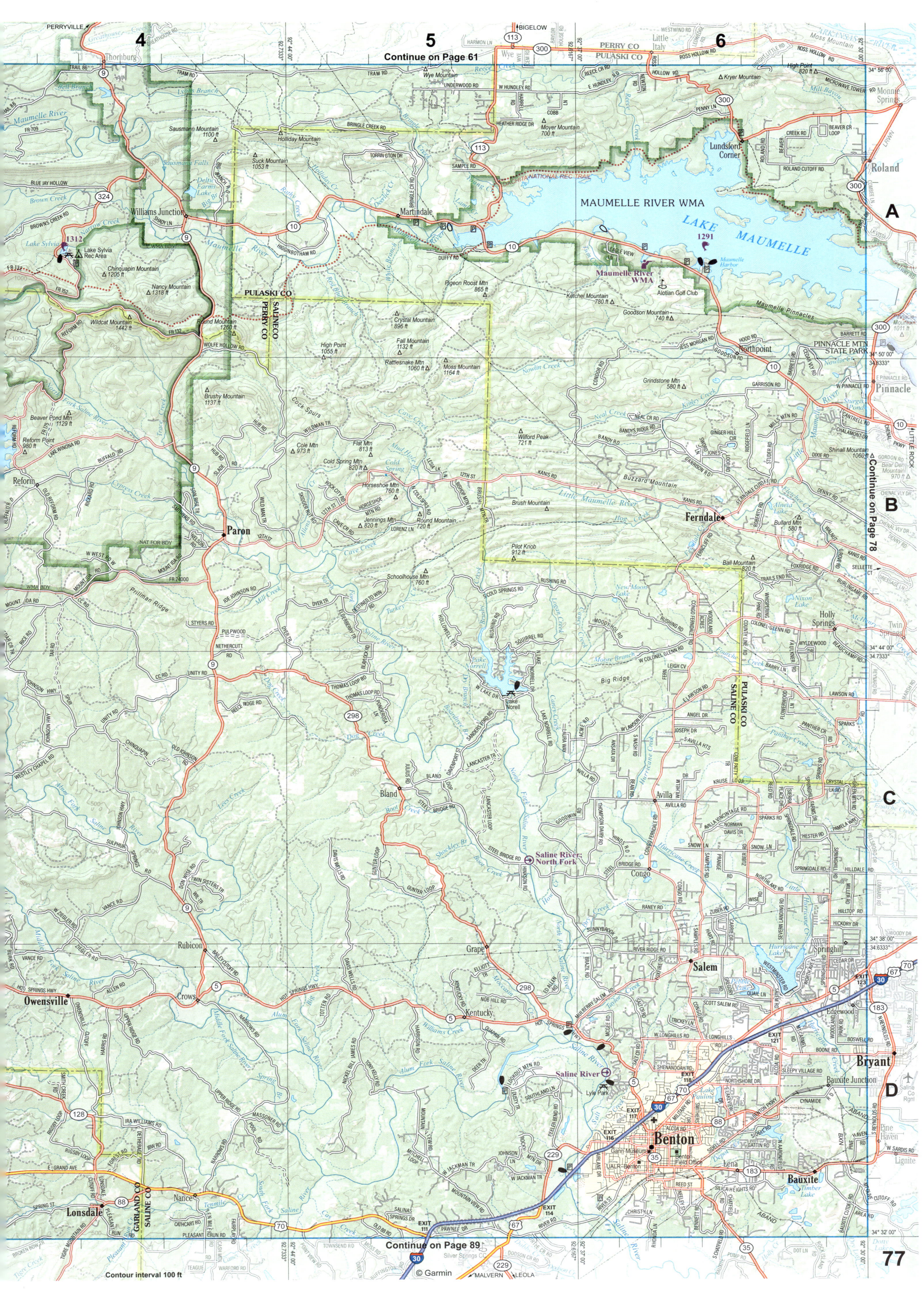

MAUMELLE RIVER WMA

LAKE MAUMELLE

PULASKI CO
PERRY CO

SALINECO
PERRY CO

Maumelle River WMA

PINNACLE MTN STATE PARK

PULASKI CO
SALINE CO

A

B

C

D

Perryville
Thornburg
Williams Junction
Lake Sylvia Rec Area
Reform
Paron
Owensville
Crows
Kentucky
Rubicon
Grape
Bland
Lonsdale
Nance
Salem
Benton
Bryant
Bauxite Junction
Bauxite
Bigelow
Martindale
Roland
Pinnacle
Ferndale
Holly Springs
Congo
Avilla
Springhill
Lundsford Corner
Northpoint

Lake Norrell
Saline River: North Fork

Contour interval 100 ft

© Garmin

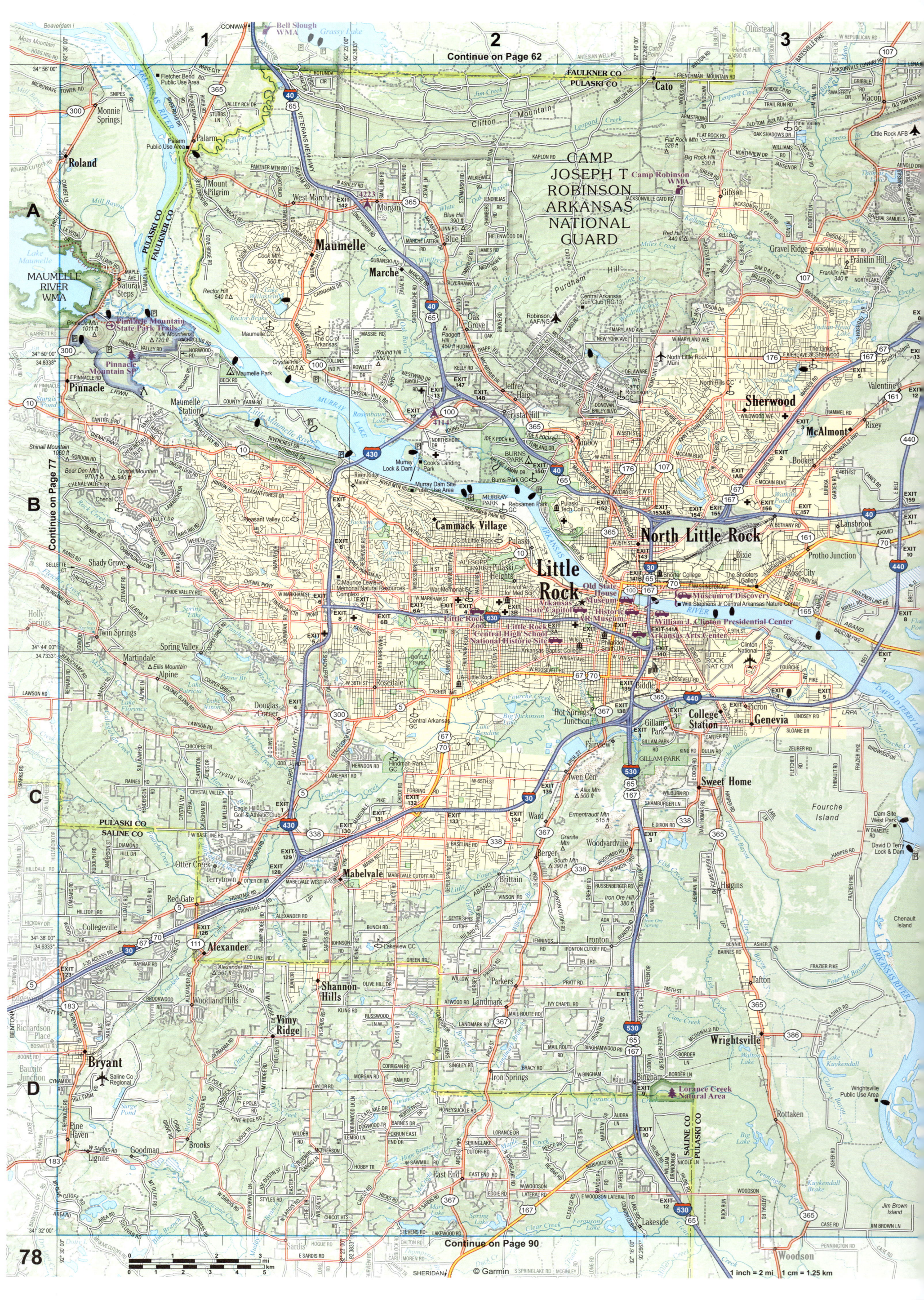

1 inch = 2 mi   1 cm = 1.25 km

© Garmin

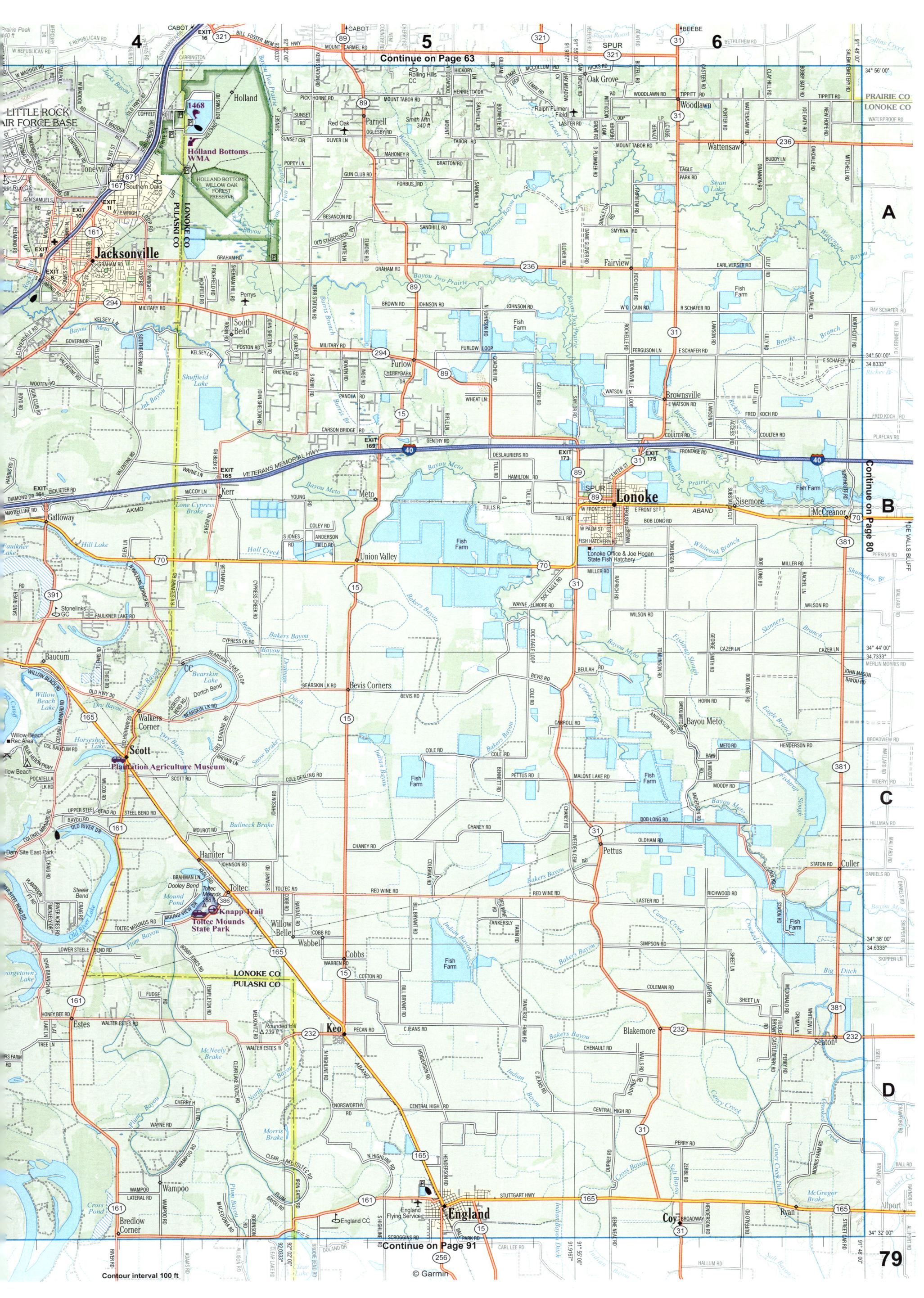

Continue on Page 63

Continue on Page 80

Continue on Page 91

Contour interval 100 ft

© Garmin

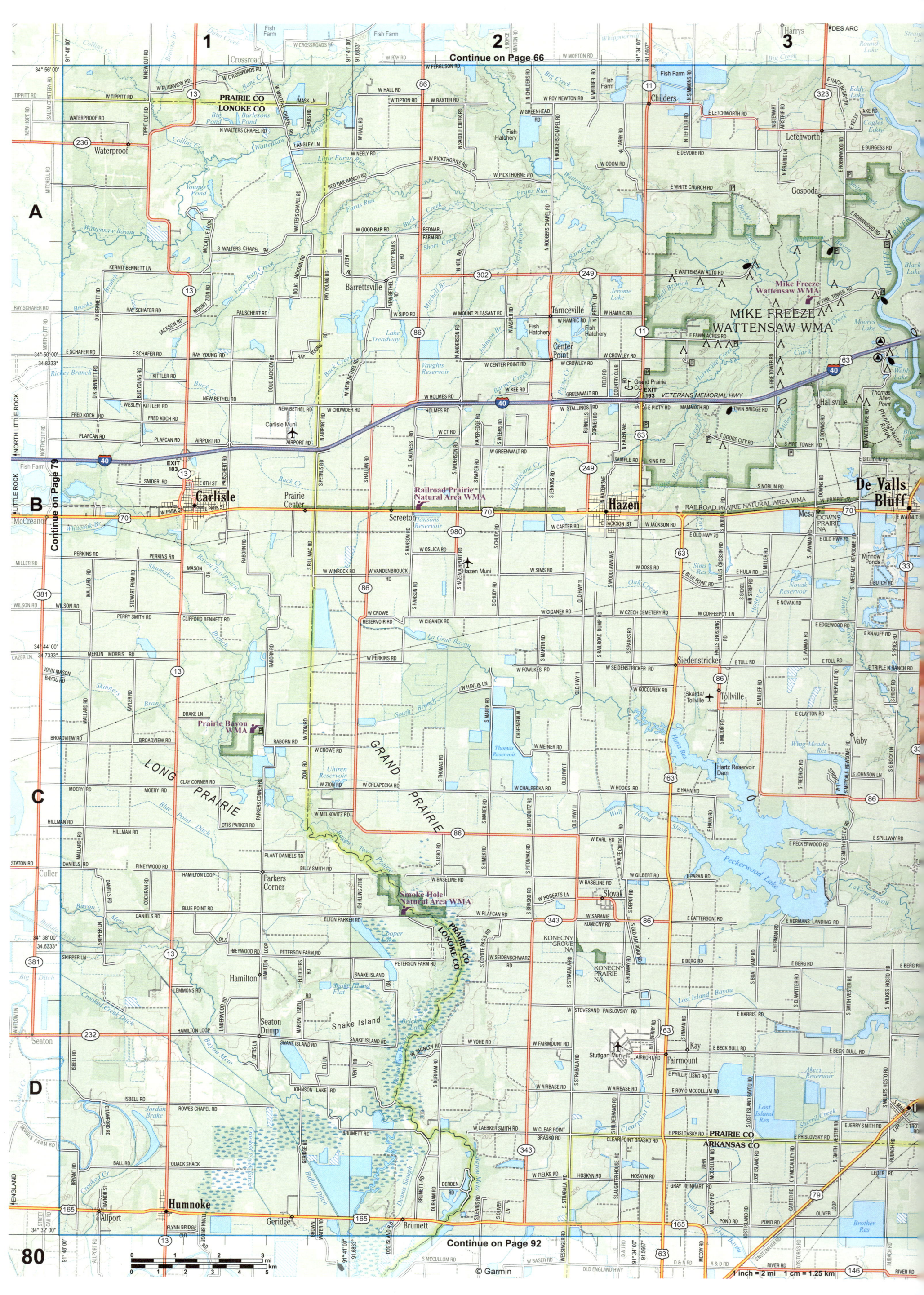

Continue on Page 66

Continue on Page 79

Continue on Page 92

80

© Garmin

1 inch = 2 mi   1 cm = 1.25 km

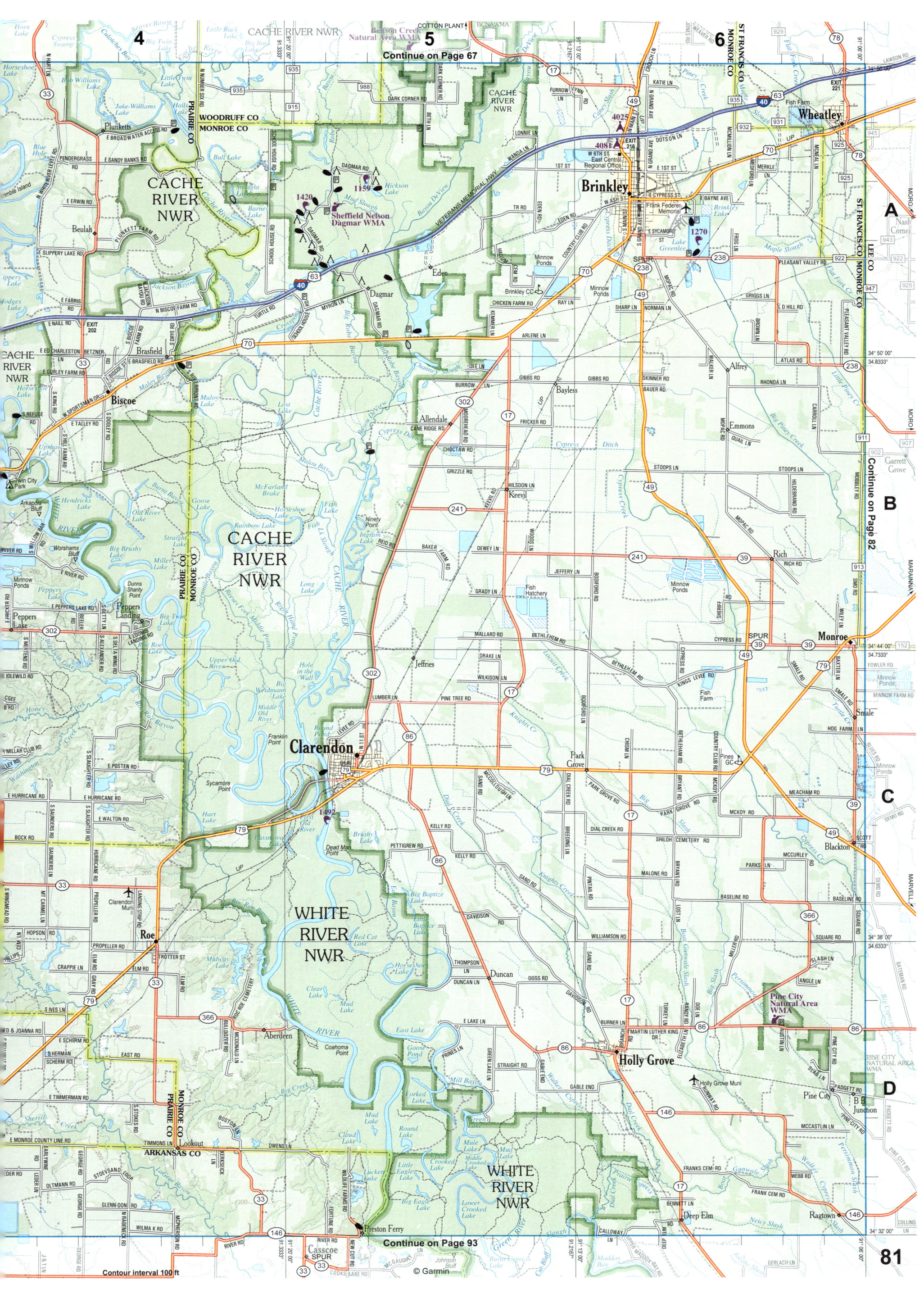

Continue on Page 67

Continue on Page 82

Continue on Page 93

Contour interval 100 ft   © Garmin

81

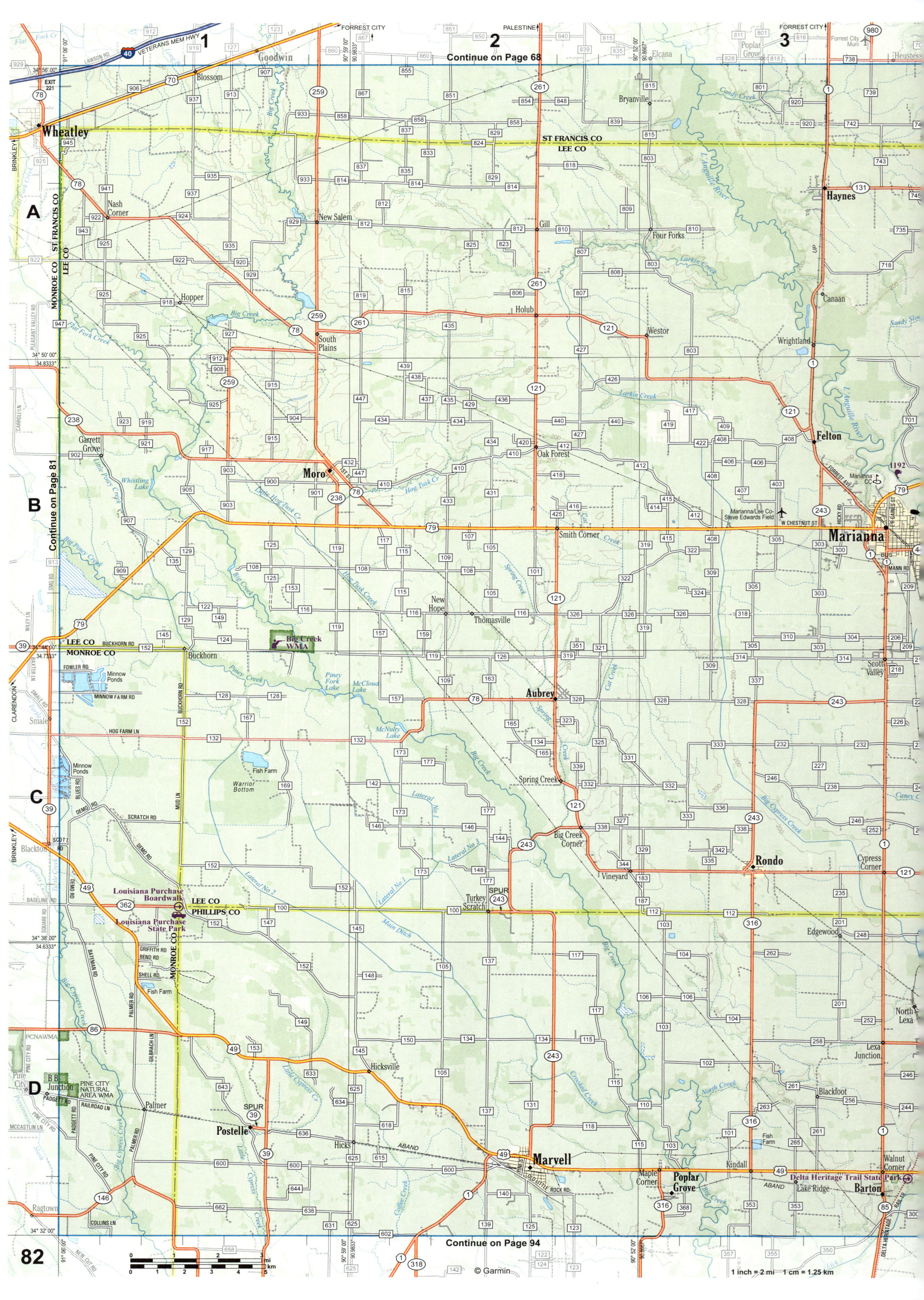

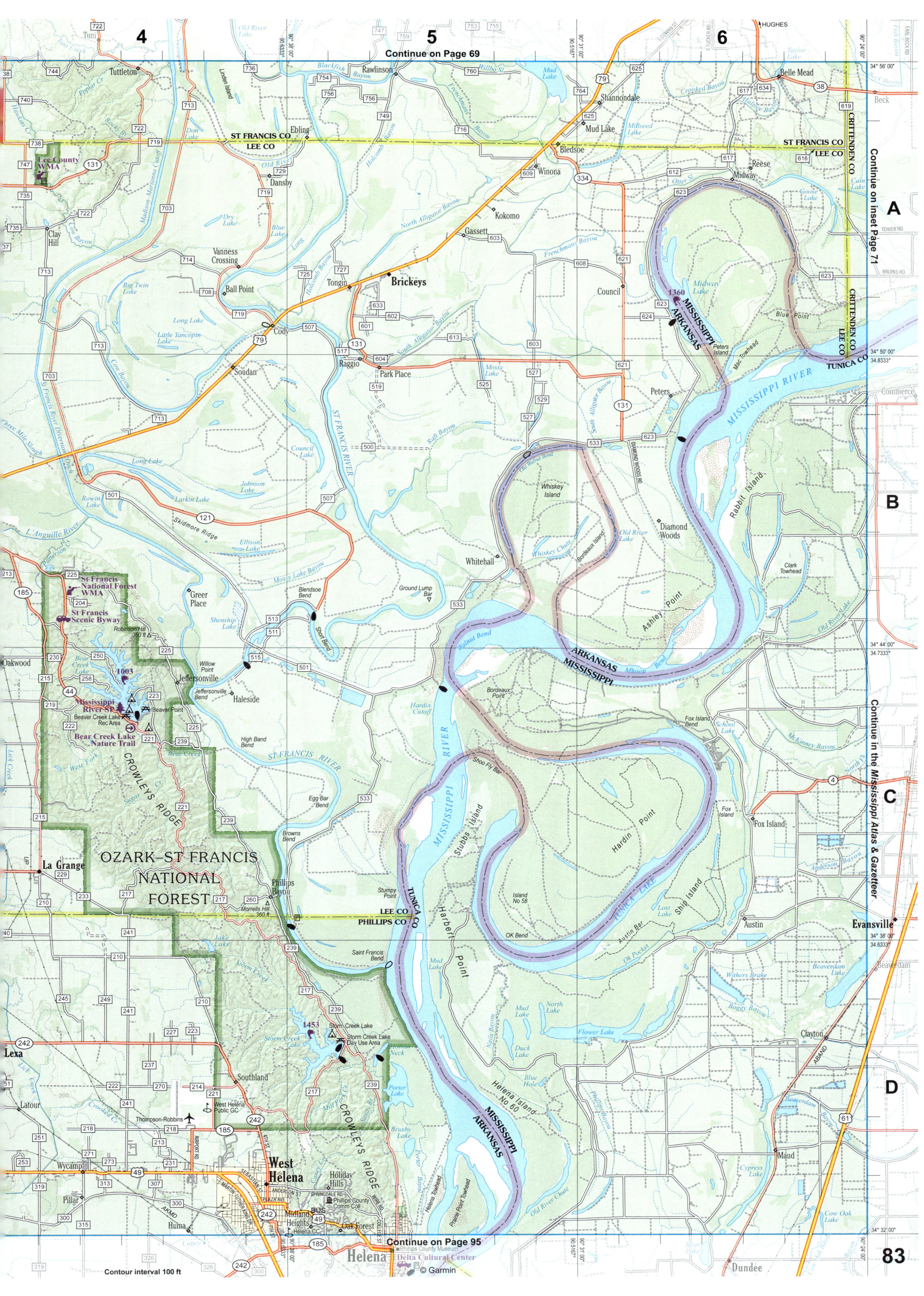

Continue on Page 69

Continue on inset Page 71

Continue in the *Mississippi Atlas & Gazetteer*

Continue on Page 95

OZARK–ST FRANCIS NATIONAL FOREST

CROWLEY'S RIDGE

Mississippi River

St Francis National Forest WMA

Lee County WMA

ST FRANCIS CO
LEE CO

ST FRANCIS CO
LEE CO

CRITTENDEN CO
TUNICA CO

LEE CO
PHILLIPS CO

Contour interval 100 ft

© Garmin

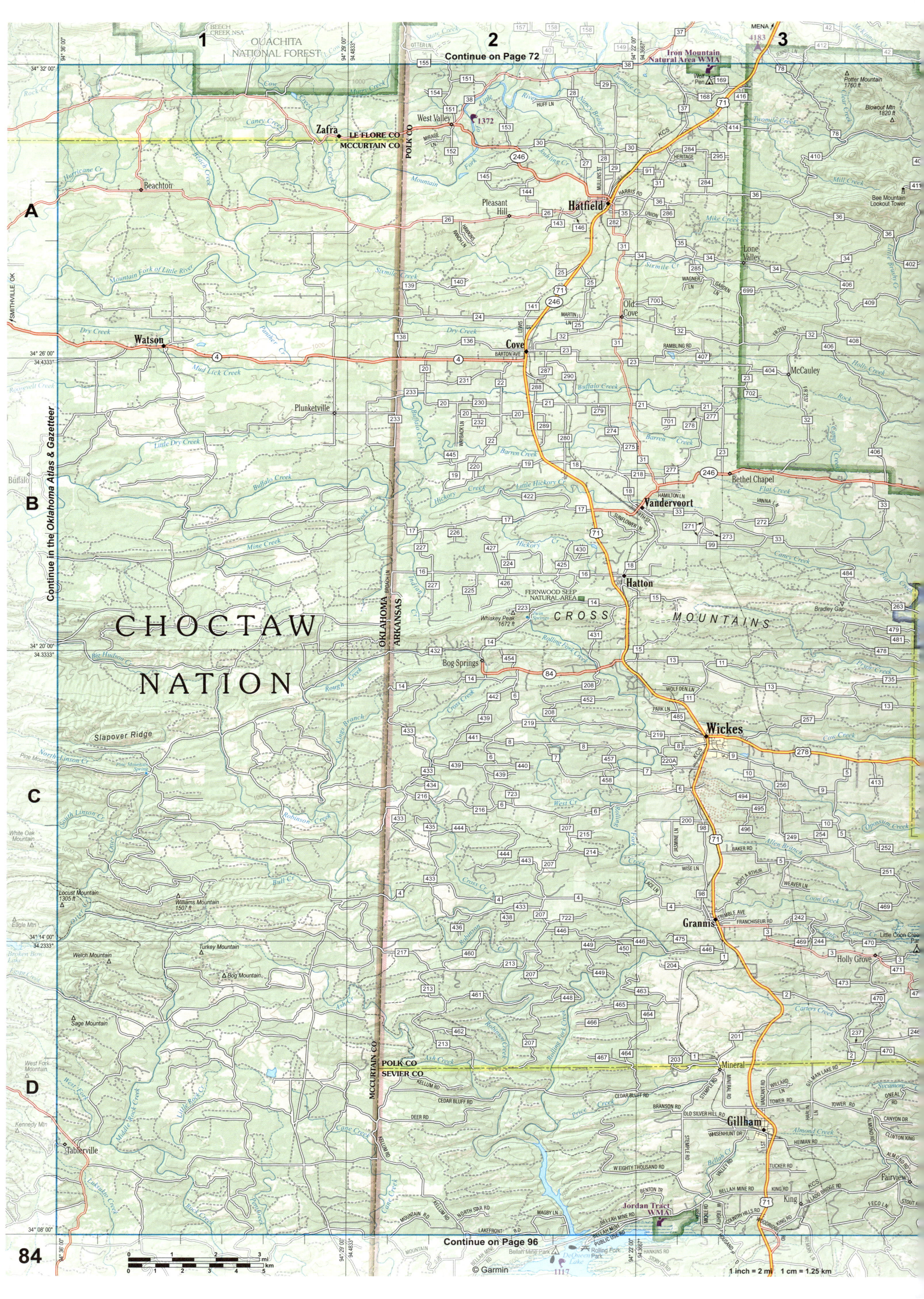

Continue on Page 72

Continue on Page 96

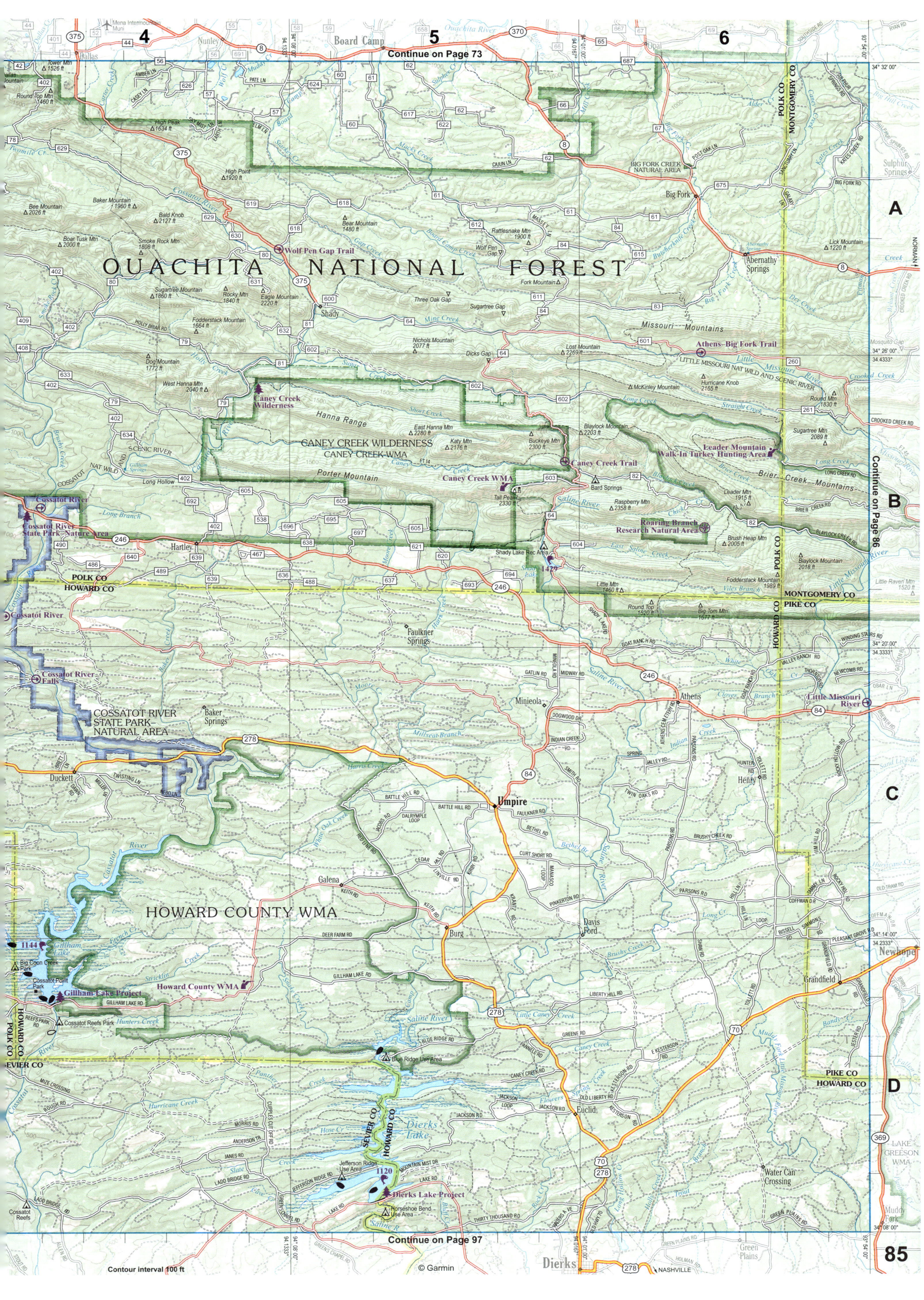

OUACHITA NATIONAL FOREST

CADDO MOUNTAINS

COSSATOT MOUNTAINS

SOUTH FORK MOUNTAINS

LAKE GREESON WMA

Black Springs

Norman

Caddo Gap

Hopper

Langley

Lodi

Salem

Kirby

Daisy

Newhope

Muddy Fork

OUACHITA NATIONAL FOREST

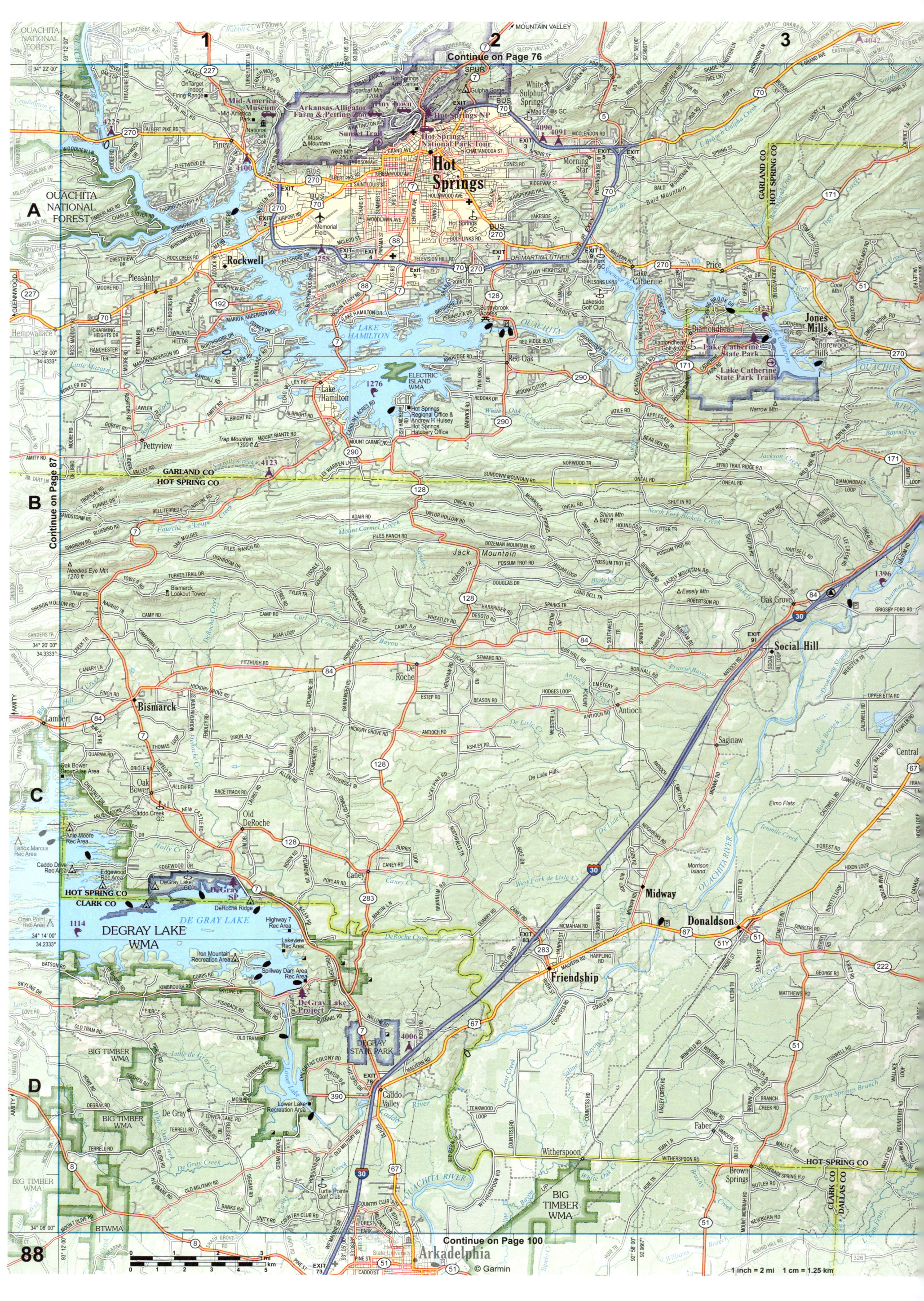

Continue on Page 87

Continue on Page 100

Arkadelphia

© Garmin

1 inch = 2 mi   1 cm = 1.25 km

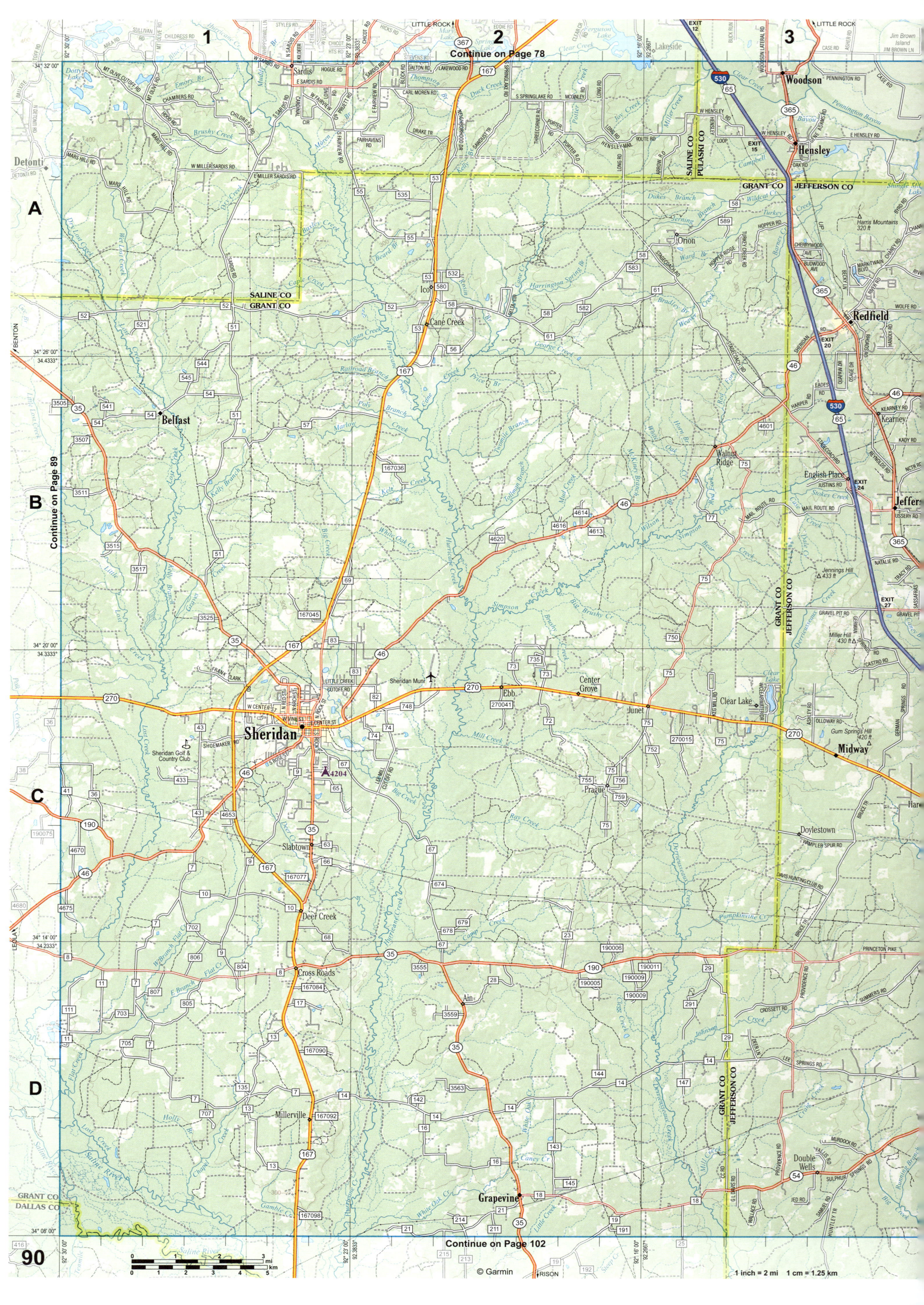

Continue on Page 78
Continue on Page 89
Continue on Page 102

90

1 inch = 2 mi   1 cm = 1.25 km

© Garmin

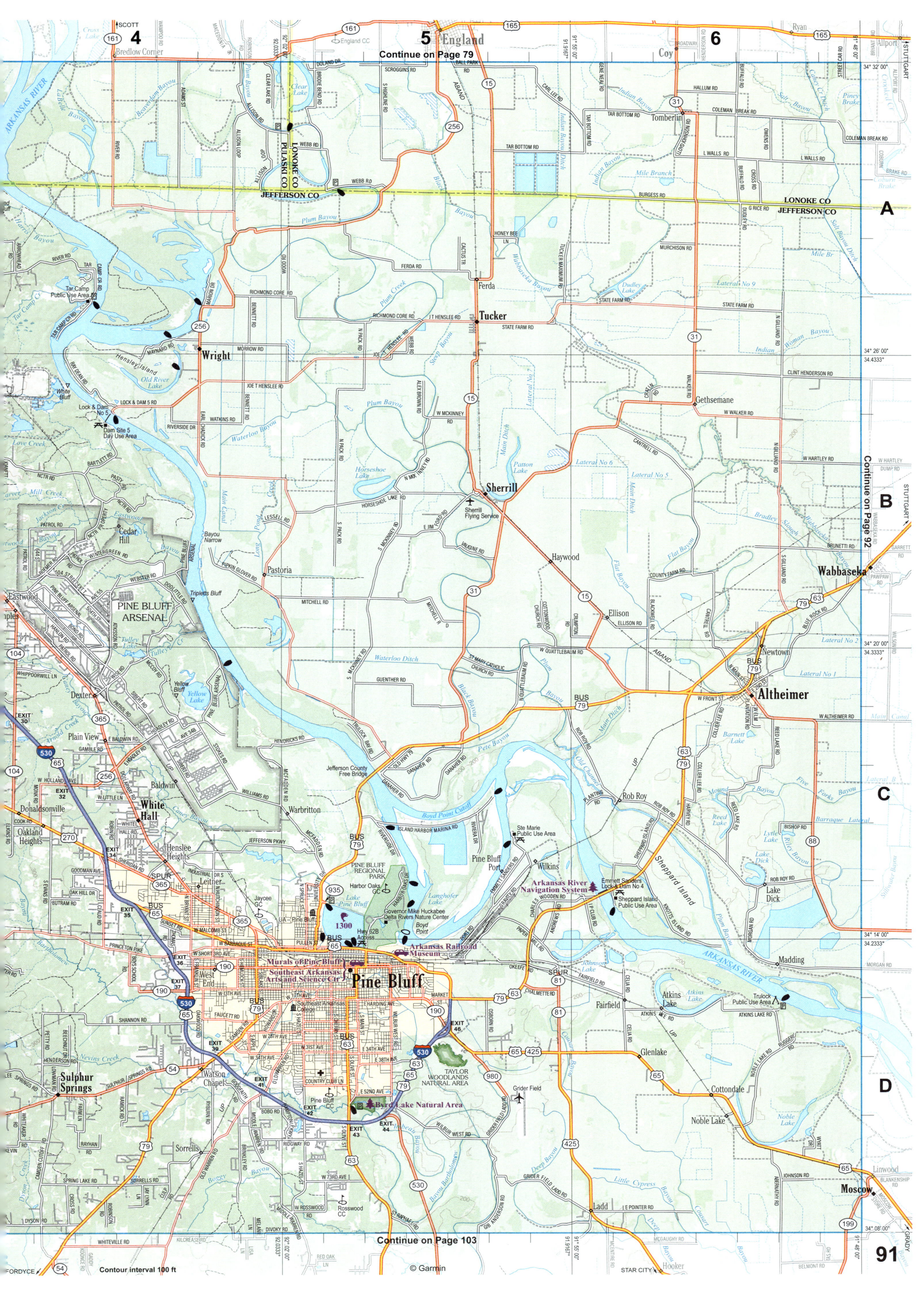

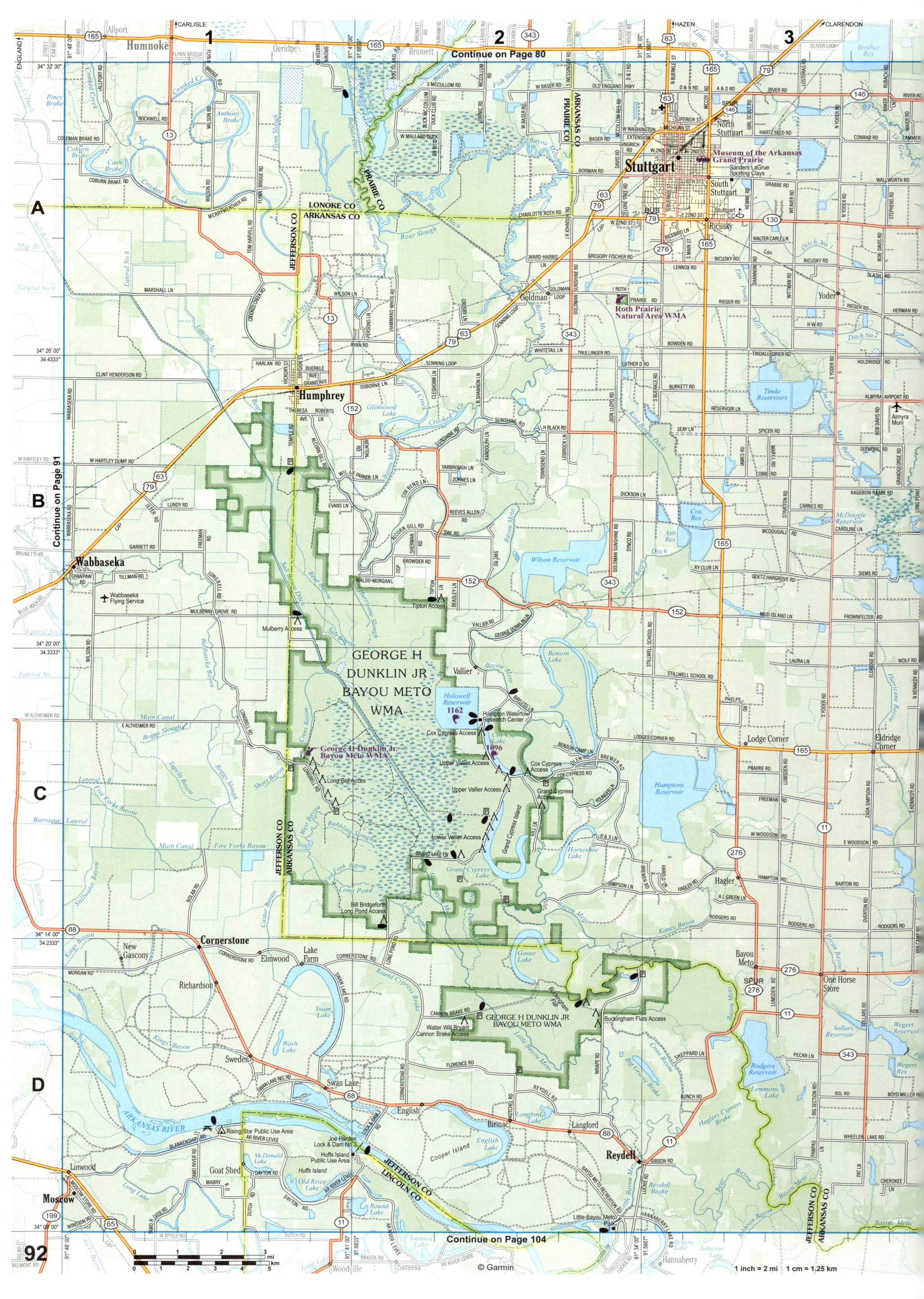

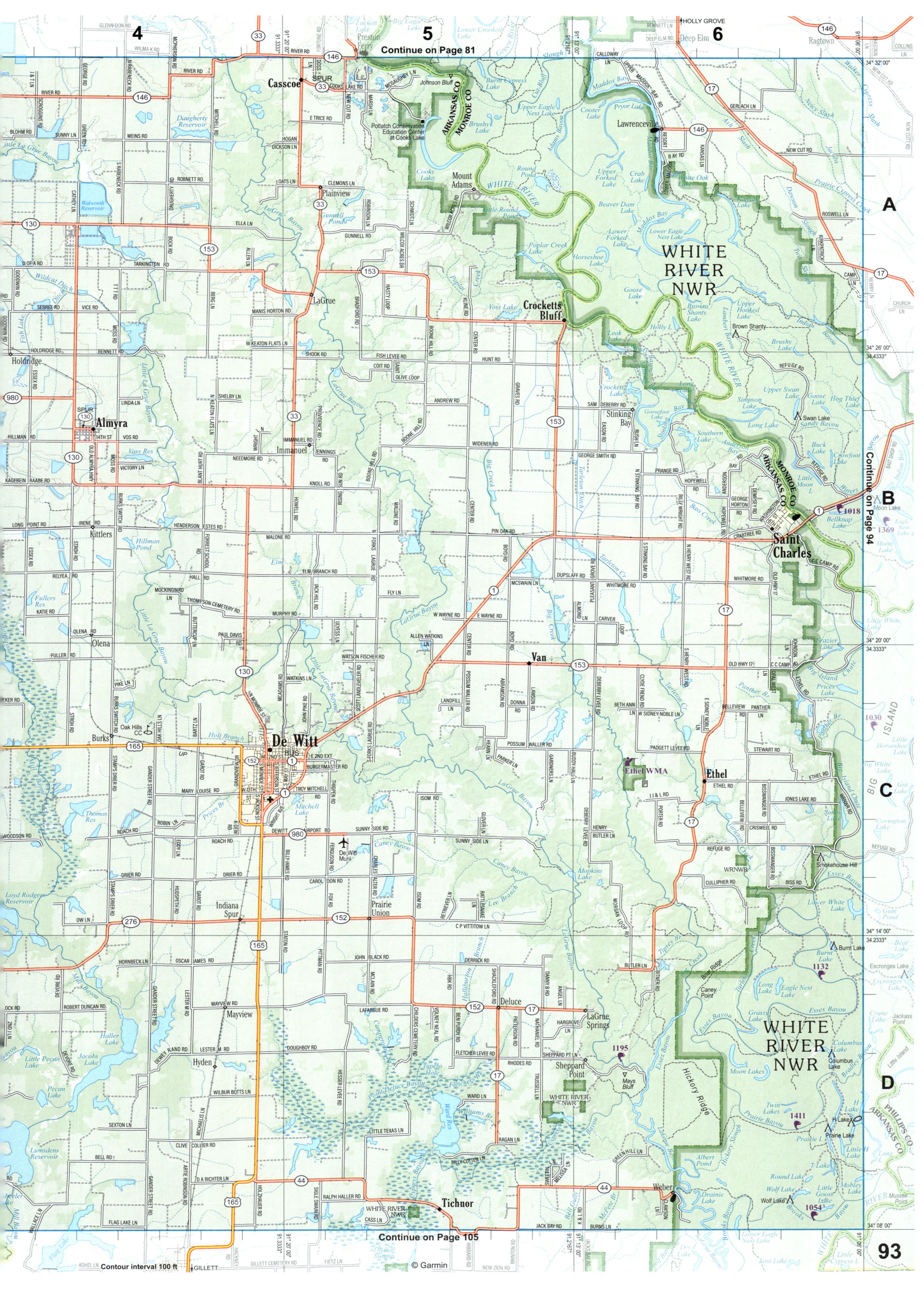

Continue on Page 81

Continue on Page 94

Continue on Page 105

Contour interval 100 ft

© Garmin

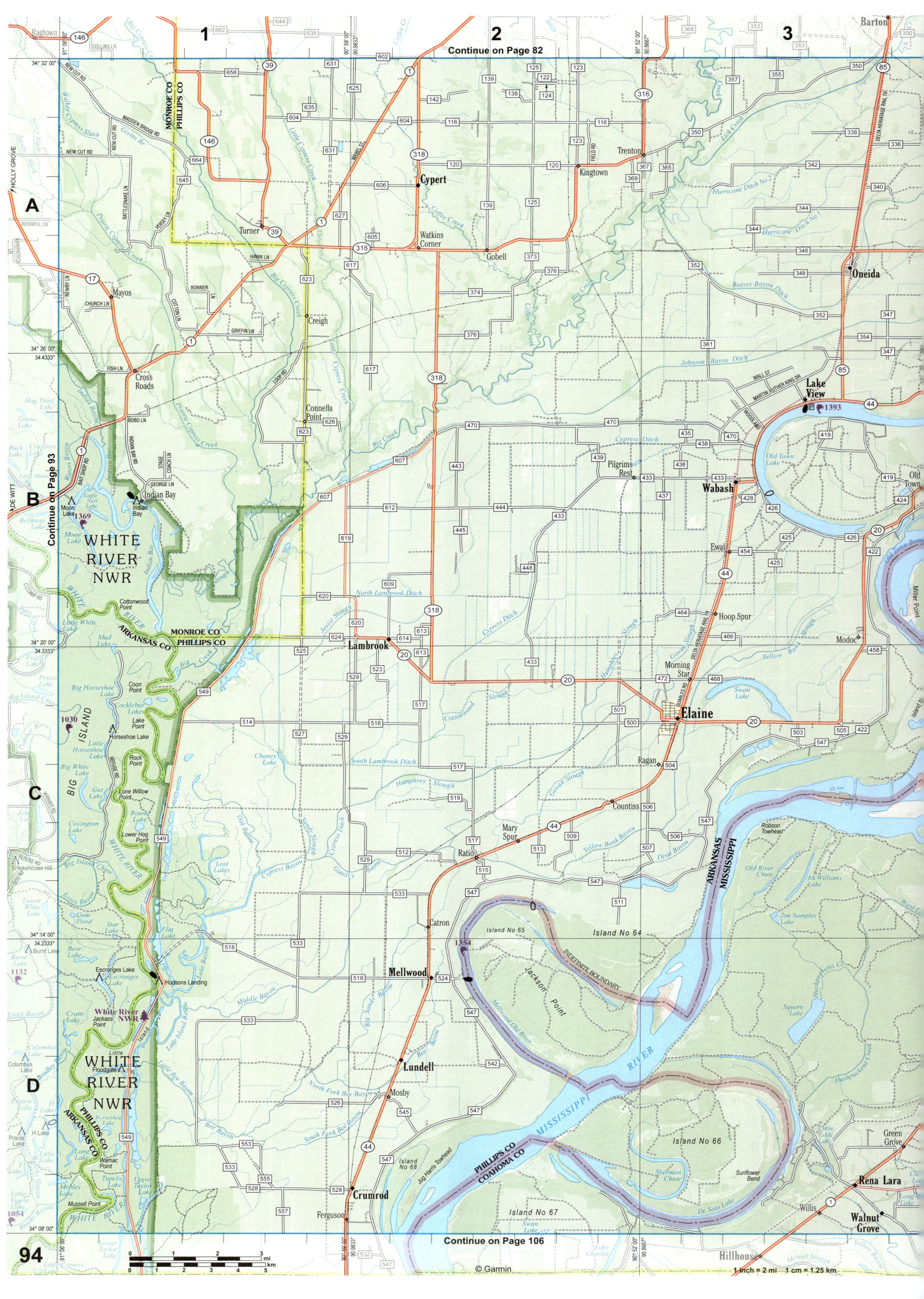

Barton

Ragtown
Collins Ln
Holly Grove
Roswell Ln

A

Turner

Mayos

Creigh

Cypert

Watkins Corner

Gobell

Kingtown

Trenton

Oneida

B

Continue on Page 93

Cross Roads

Connells Point

Indian Bay

WHITE RIVER NWR

MONROE CO
PHILLIPS CO

ARKANSAS CO
PHILLIPS CO

Lambrook

Pilgrims Rest

Wabash

Ewal

Lake View

Old Town

Hoop Spur

Modoc

C

BIG ISLAND

WHITE RIVER

Coon Point

Lake Point

Horseshoe Lake

Rock Point

Lone Willow Point

Lower Hog Point

Round Point

Elaine

Morning Star

Ragan

Countiss

Mary Spur

Ratio

Catron

Robson Towhead

Island No 65

Island No 64

ARKANSAS
MISSISSIPPI

D

WHITE RIVER NWR
Jackass Point

Hudsons Landing

Escronges Lake

WHITE RIVER NWR

ARKANSAS CO
PHILLIPS CO

Mellwood

Lundell

Mosby

Crumrod

Ferguson

Jackson Point

Mississippi River

Island No 66

Island No 67

De Soto Lake

Sherman Chute

Sunflower Bend

PHILLIPS CO
COAHOMA CO

Green Grove

Rena Lara

Willis

Walnut Grove

Hillhouse

© Garmin

1 inch = 2 mi   1 cm = 1.25 km

Continue on Page 83

West Helena

Helena

Delta Cultural Center

Helena Crossing

Preston Place

SPUR 20

Westover
Kangaroo Point

Friars Point

Armistead

Sessions

Glen Aubin

Dickerson

Stovall

King and Anderson

Farrell

Sherard

Clarksdale

Riverton

Beverly

Pullen

Bobo

Dundee

Hamlin

Jeffries

Powell

Danforth

Lula

Carter

Barbee

Moon

Rich

Roseacres

Delta

Long Lake

Coahoma

Rudyard

Matagorda

Jonestown

Clover Hill

Fletcher Field

Eagles Nest

Lyon

Myrtle Hall

Hopson

Durham

Lurand

Walnut

Sabino

Barksdale

MISSISSIPPI RIVER

ARKANSAS
MISSISSIPPI

PHILLIPS CO
COAHOMA CO

TUNICA CO
COAHOMA CO

QUITMAN CO
COAHOMA CO

Contour interval 100 ft

© Garmin

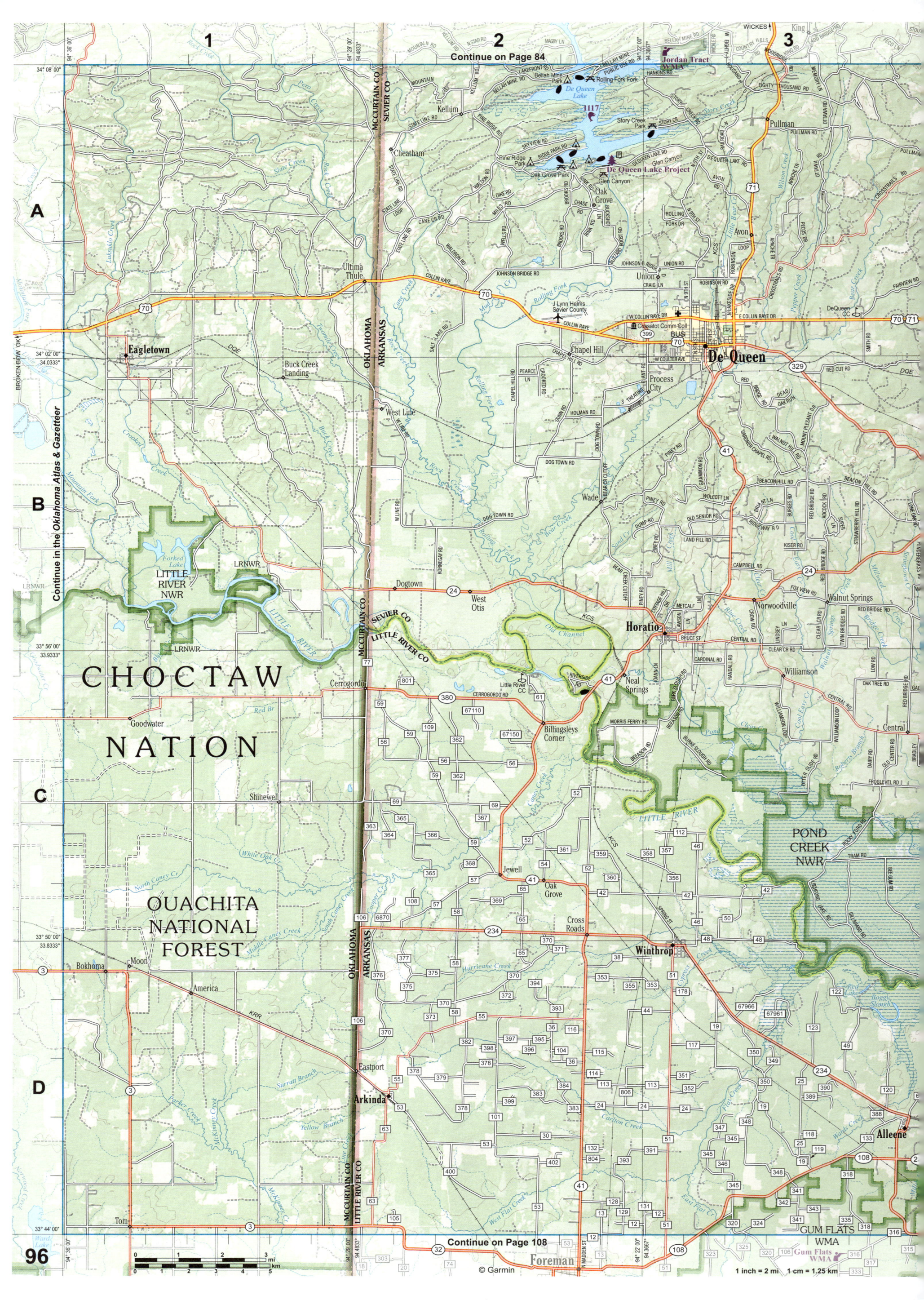

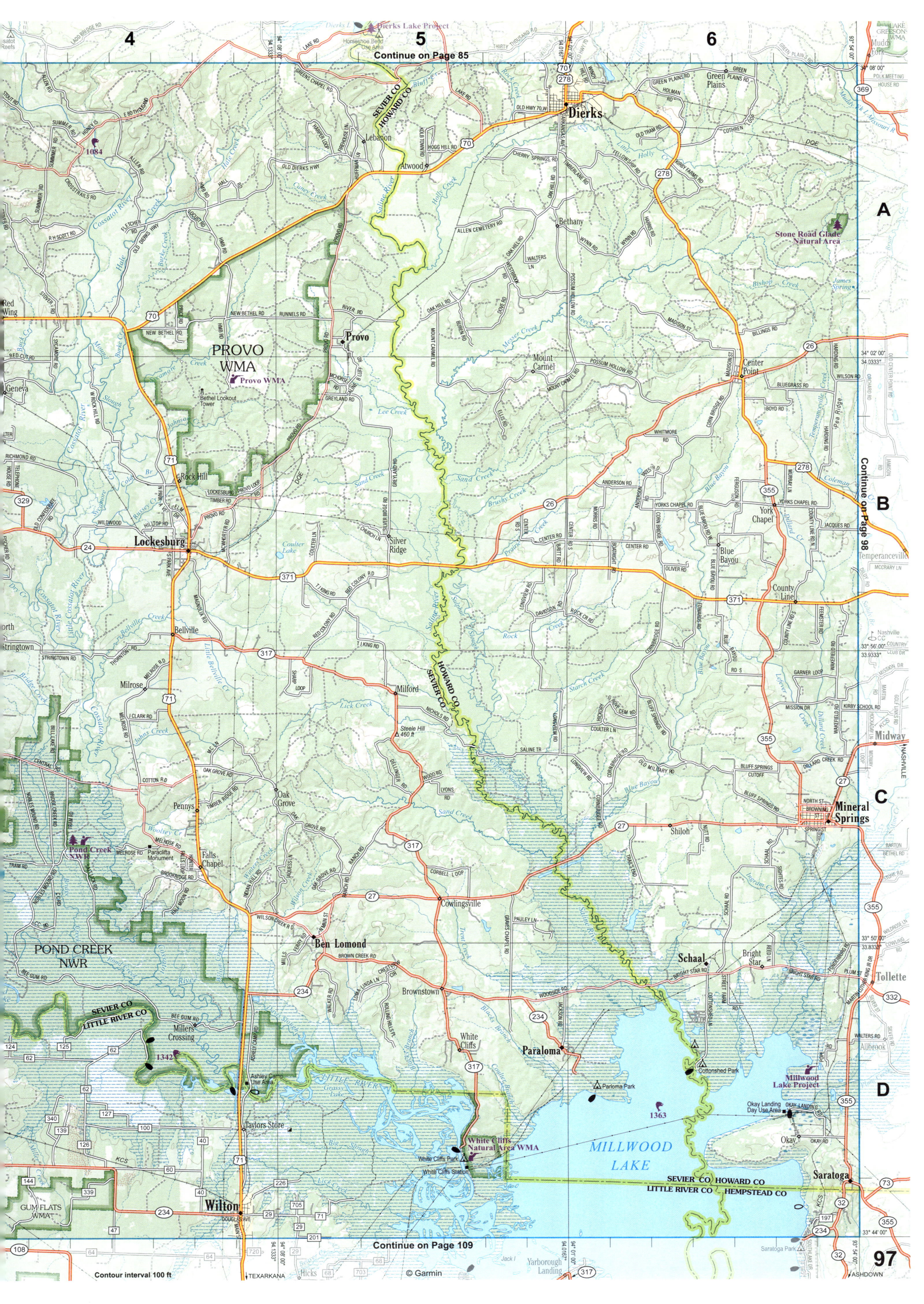

Continue on Page 85

A

B

C

D

Continue on Page 98

Dierks

Green Plains

Stone Road Glade Natural Area

Center Point

PROVO WMA

Provo WMA

Mount Carmel

York Chapel

Blue Bayou

County Line

Lockesburg

Silver Ridge

Bellville

Milrose

Milford

Steele Hill △ 460 ft

Mineral Springs

Shiloh

Midway

Tollette

POND CREEK NWR

Pennys

Oak Grove

Falls Chapel

Ben Lomond

Cowlingsville

Schaal

Bright Star

SEVIER CO LITTLE RIVER CO

Millers Crossing

Paraclifta Monument

Brownstown

White Cliffs

Paraloma

Paraloma Park

Cottonshed Park

Millwood Lake Project

GUM FLATS WMA

Taylors Store

White Cliffs Natural Area WMA

White Cliffs Park

White Cliffs Station

MILLWOOD LAKE

Okay Landing Day Use Area

Okay Landing

Okay

Saratoga

Wilton

SEVIER CO HOWARD CO LITTLE RIVER CO HEMPSTEAD CO

Continue on Page 109

Contour interval 100 ft

© Garmin

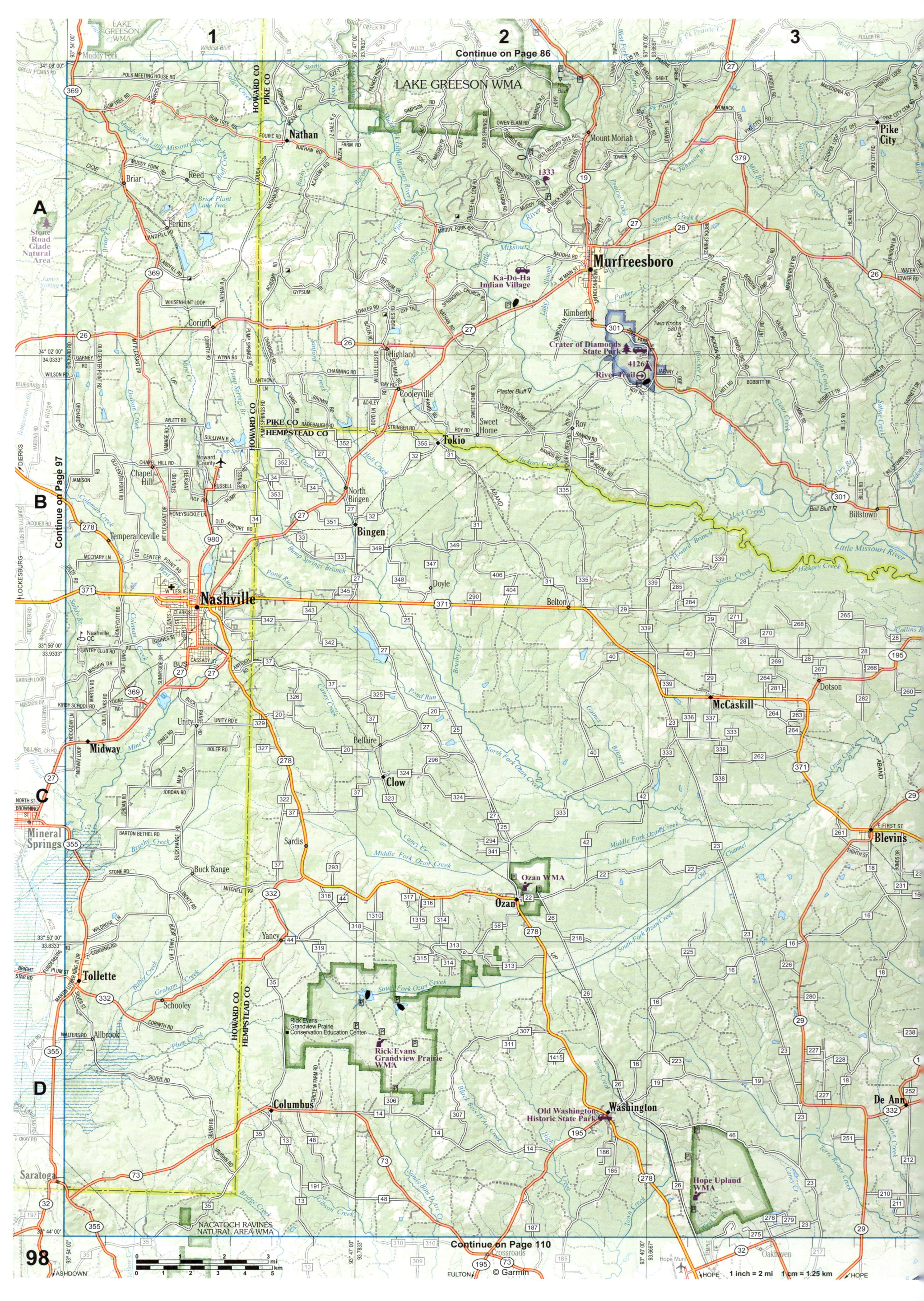

Continue on Page 86

LAKE GREESON WMA

Nathan

Briar
Reed

Perkins

Stone
Road Glade
Natural
Area

Corinth

Highland

Chapel
Hill

North
Bingen

Bingen

Temperanceville

Nashville

Midway

Unity

Bellaire

Clow

Doyle

Belton

Sardis

Mineral
Springs

Buck Range

Yancy

Tollette

Schooley

Allbrook

Columbus

Saratoga

Ka-Do-Ha
Indian Village

Murfreesboro

Kimberly

Crater of Diamonds
State Park
River Trail

Tokio

Sweet
Home

Roy

Mount Moriah

Pike City

Billstown

McCaskill

Dotson

Blevins

Ozan WMA

Ozan

Rick Evans
Grandview Prairie
Conservation Education Center

Rick Evans
Grandview Prairie
WMA

Old Washington
Historic State Park

Washington

De Ann

Hope Upland
WMA

NACATOCH RAVINES
NATURAL AREA WMA

1 inch = 2 mi   1 cm = 1.25 km

© Garmin

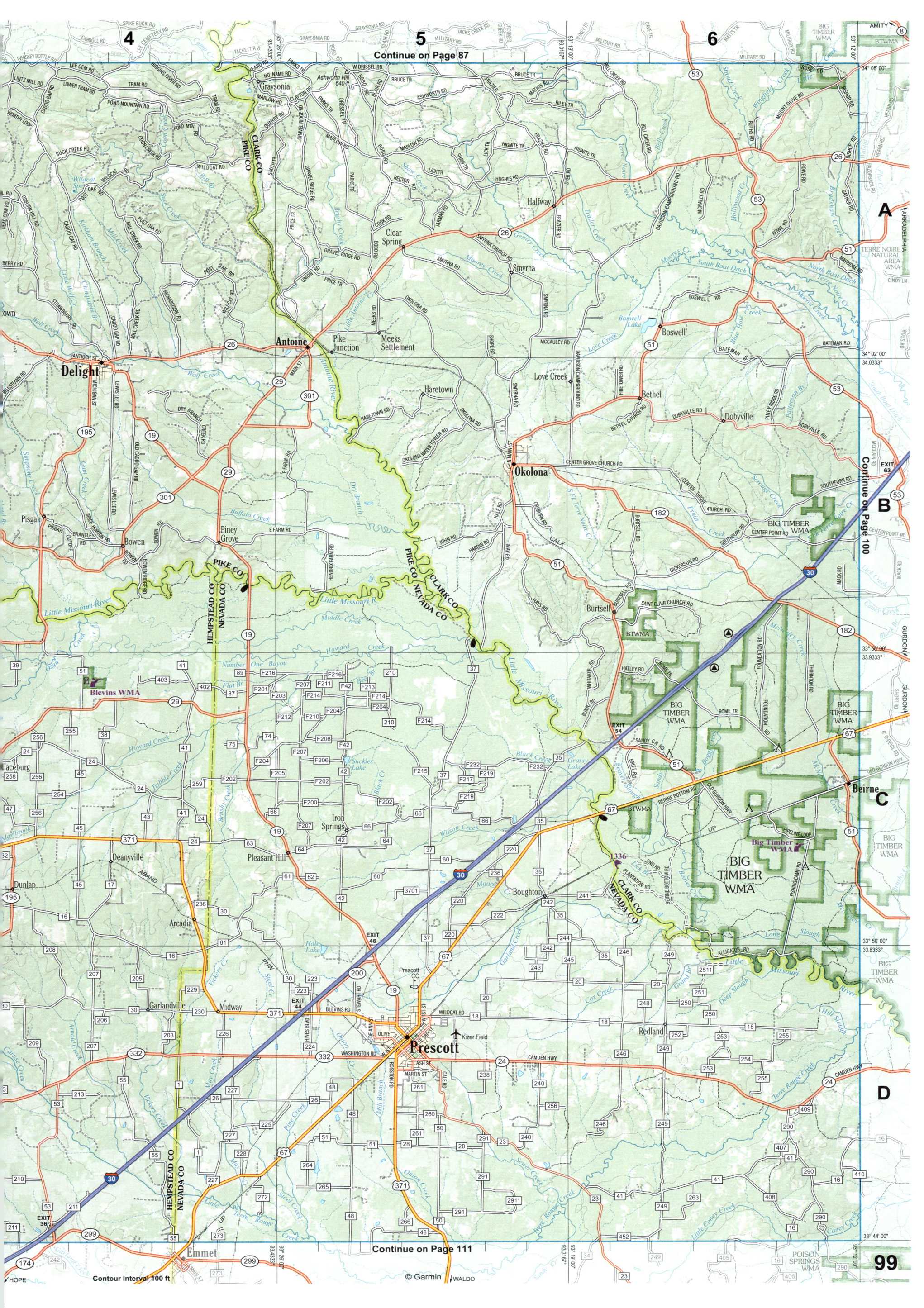

A

B

C

D

Continue on Page 100

Contour interval 100 ft

© Garmin

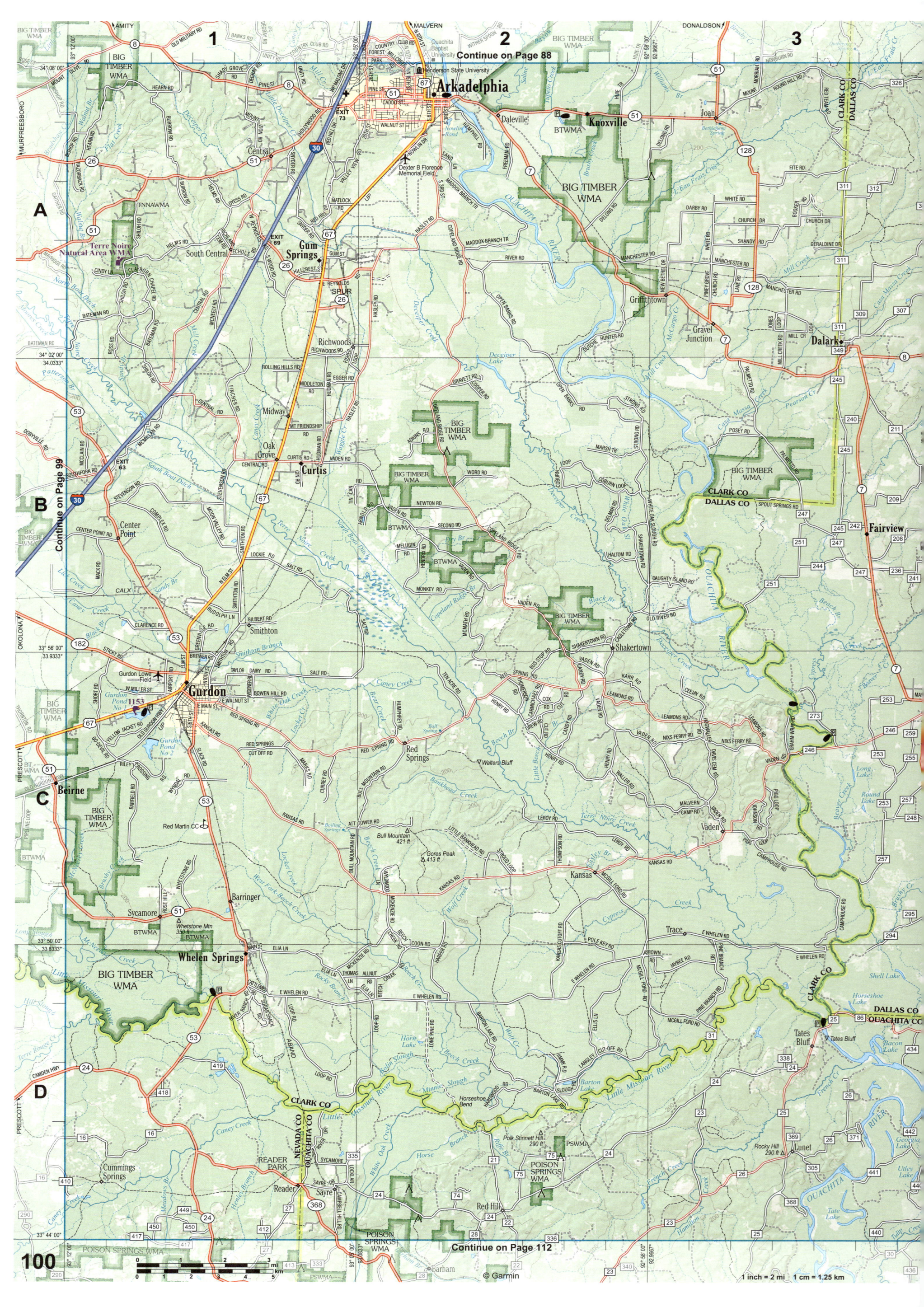

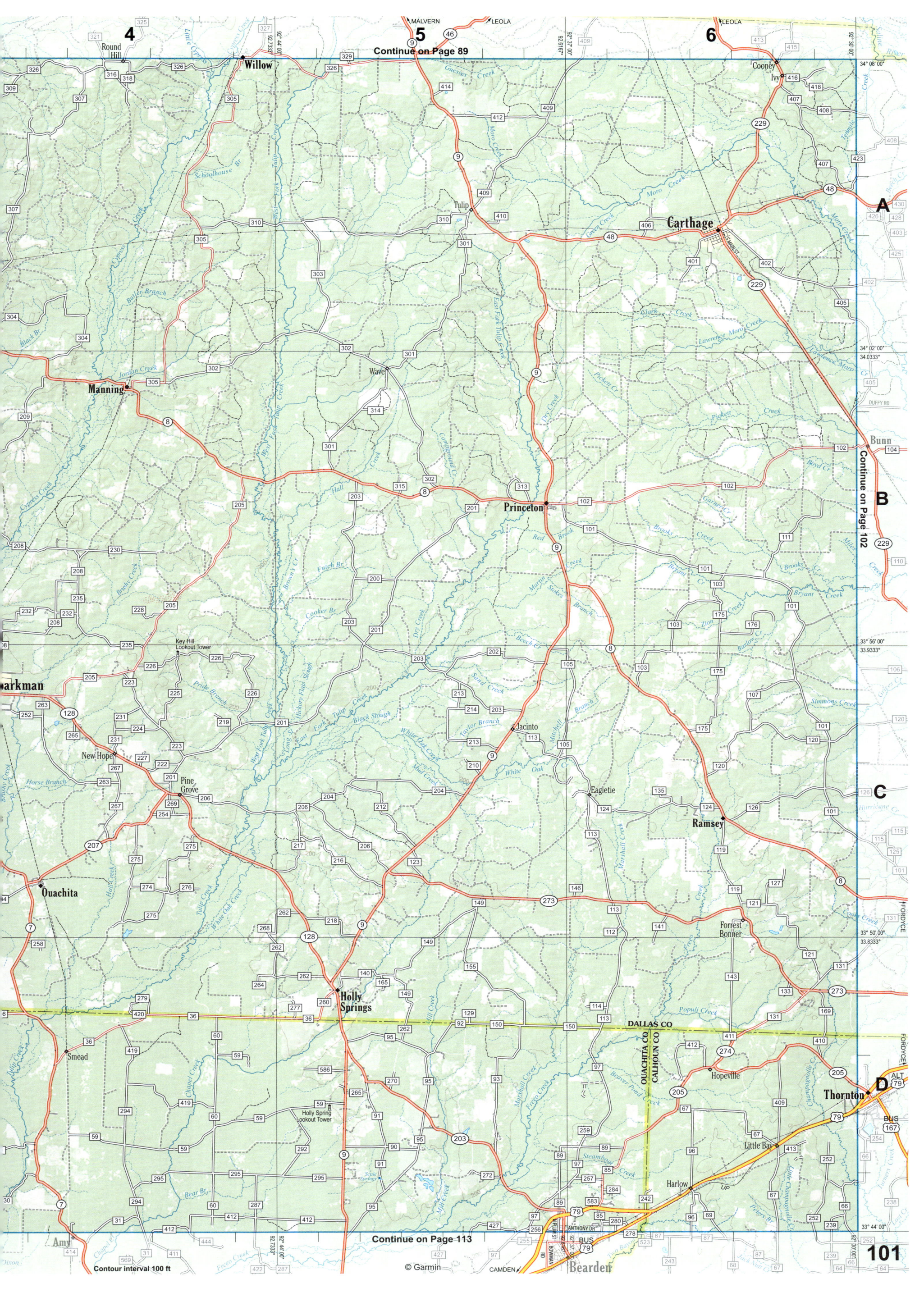

Continue on Page 89

Continue on Page 102

Continue on Page 113

Contour interval 100 ft

© Garmin

101

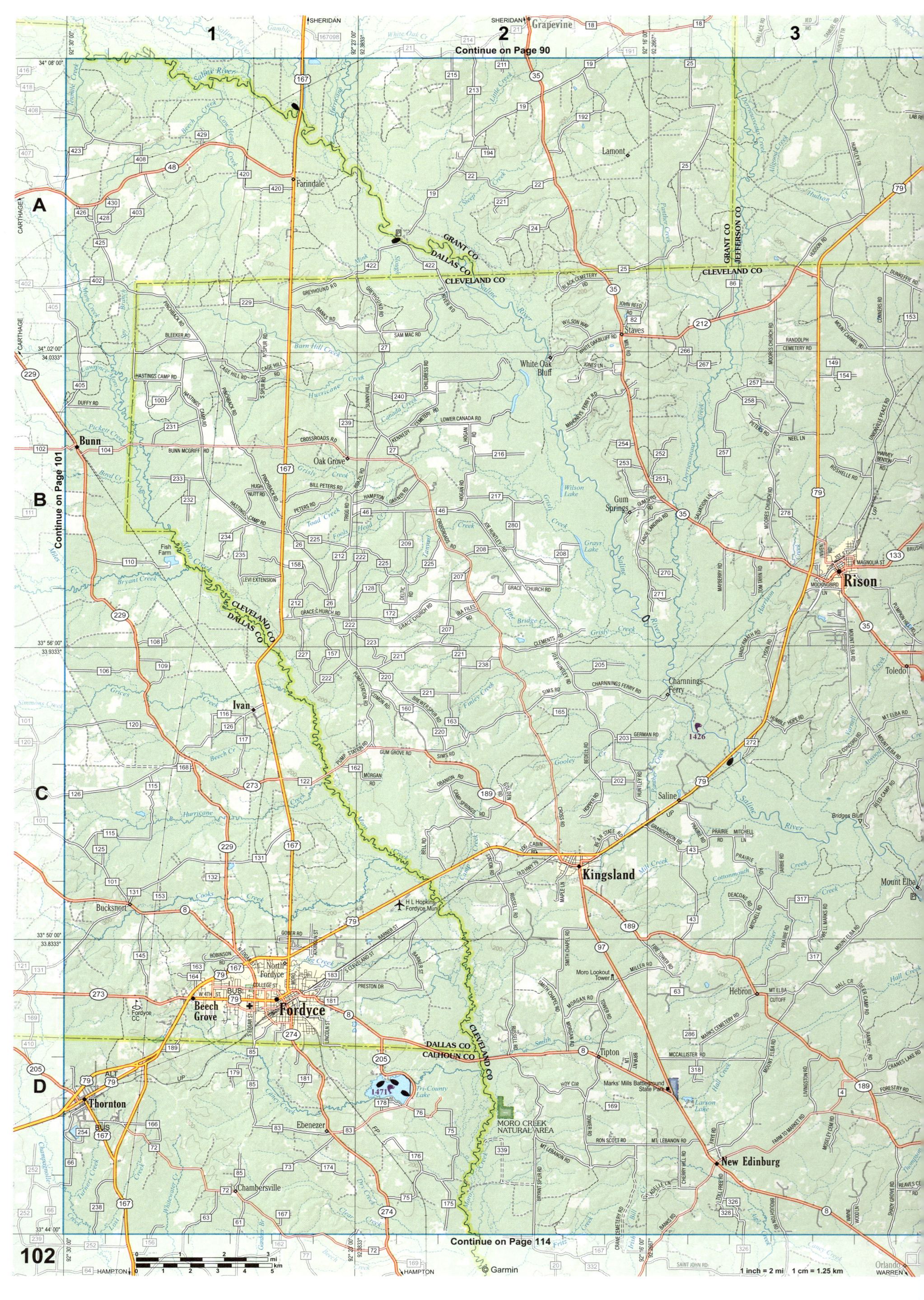

Continue on Page 90

Continue on Page 101

Continue on Page 114

102

1 inch = 2 mi   1 cm = 1.25 km

© Garmin

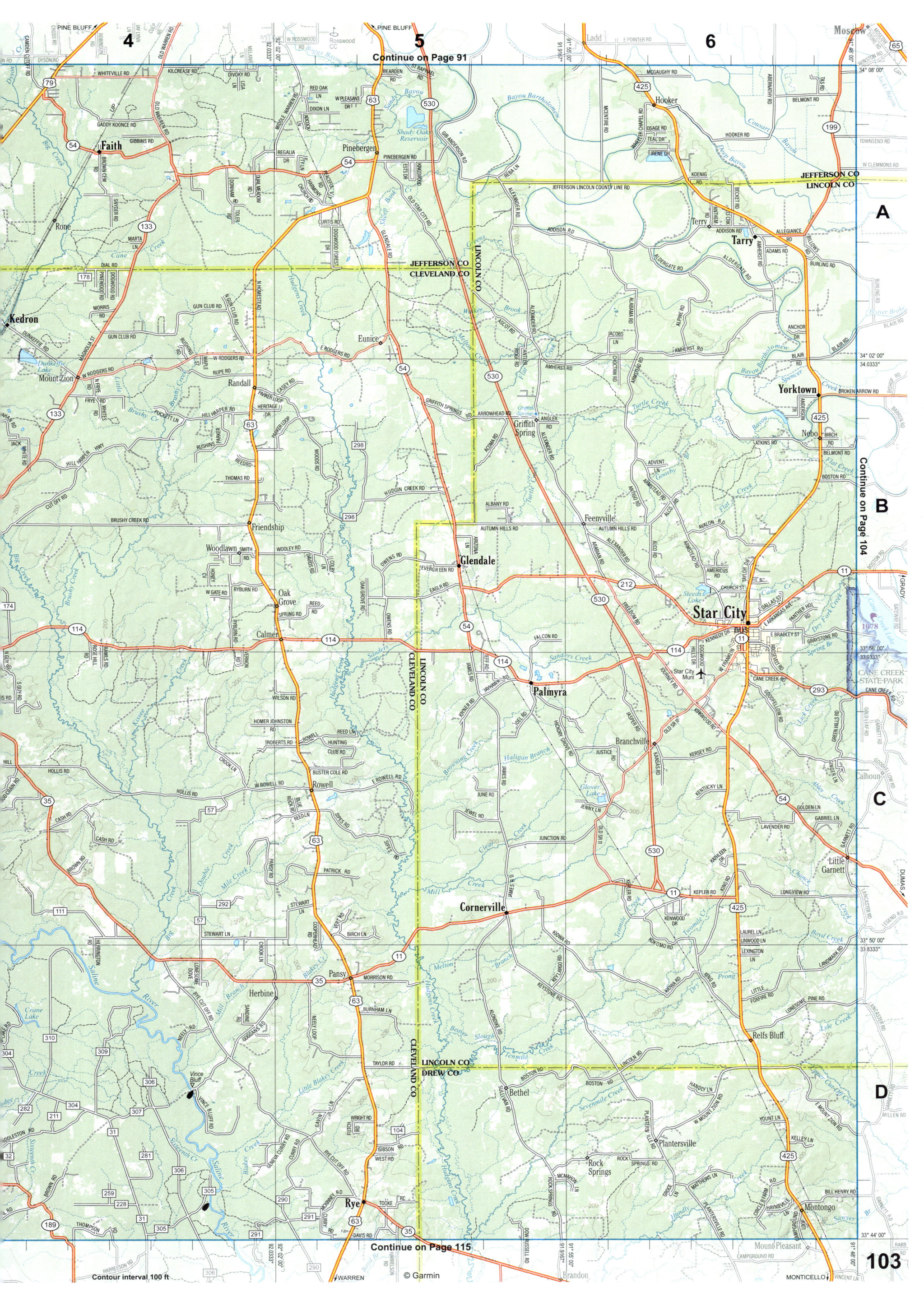

Continue on Page 91

Continue on Page 104

Continue on Page 115

4   **5**   **6**

A

B

C

D

Faith

Kedron

Mount Zion

Randall

Friendship

Woodlawn

Oak Grove

Calmer

Rowell

Cornerville

Pansy

Herbine

Rye

Pinebergen

Eunice

Glendale

Palmyra

Hooker

Terry

Tarry

Yorktown

Nebo

Feenyville

Star City

Branchville

Little Garnett

Relfs Bluff

Bethel

Plantersville

Rock Springs

Montongo

JEFFERSON CO / LINCOLN CO

JEFFERSON CO / CLEVELAND CO

LINCOLN CO

CLEVELAND CO

LINCOLN CO / CLEVELAND CO

LINCOLN CO / DREW CO

CANE CREEK STATE PARK

Contour interval 100 ft   © Garmin

103

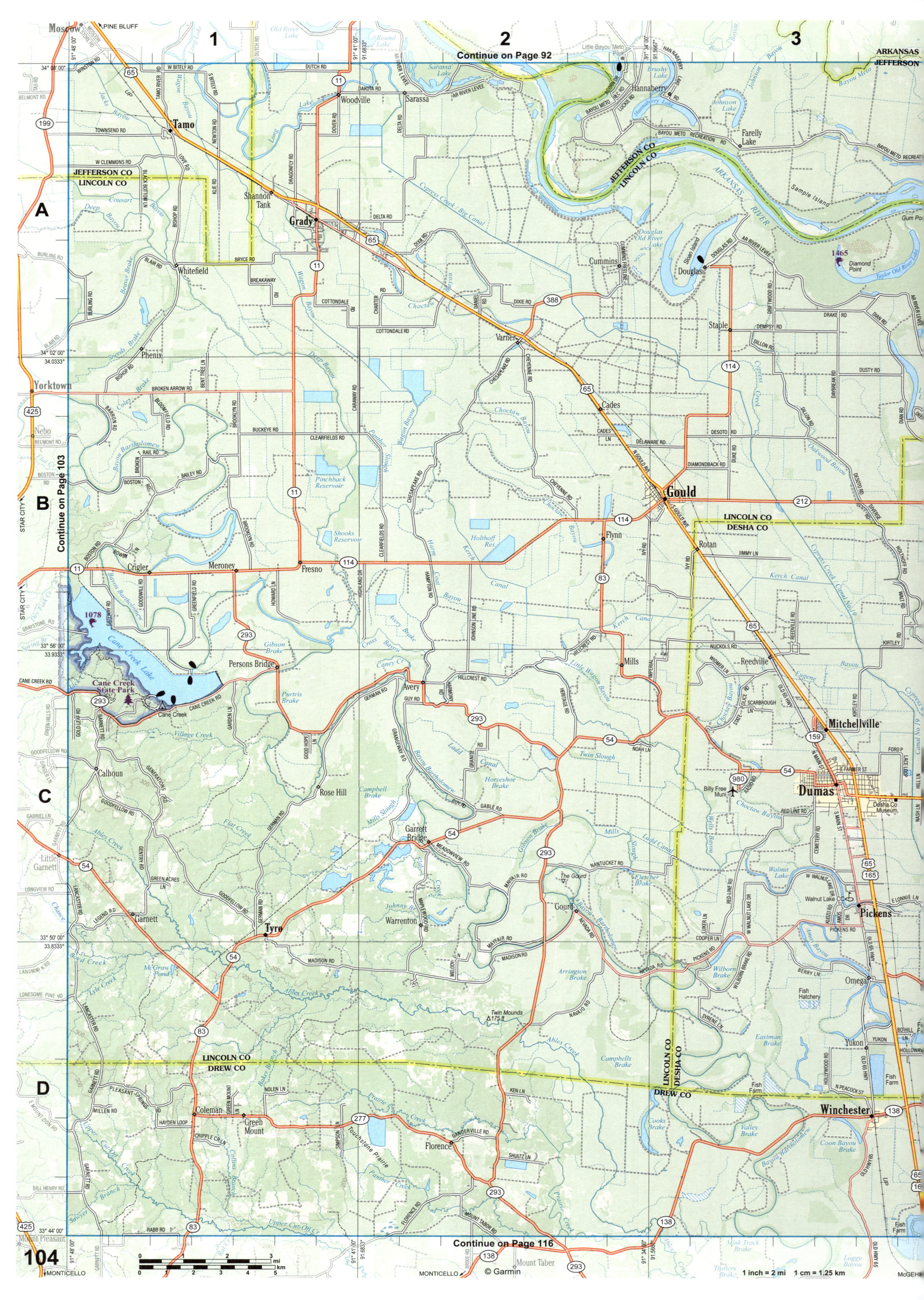

Continue on Page 92

Continue on Page 103

Continue on Page 116

ARKANSAS
JEFFERSON

1   2   3

A
B
C
D

104

JEFFERSON CO
LINCOLN CO

JEFFERSON CO
LINCOLN CO

LINCOLN CO
DESHA CO

LINCOLN CO
DREW CO

DREW CO
DESHA CO

Moscow   Pine Bluff
Tamo
Woodville   Sarassa
Grady
Whitefield
Phenix
Yorktown
Nebio
Crigler   Meroney   Fresno
Cane Creek State Park
Calhoun   Rose Hill
Garnett
Little Garnett
Tyro   Warrenton
Coleman   Green Mount
Florence

Hannaberry
Cummins
Douglas
Varner
Cades
Gould
Flynn   Rotan
Mills   Reedville
Avery
Mitchellville
Dumas
Gourd   Pickens
Omega
Yukon
Winchester

Staple

Persons Bridge
Garrett Bridge

1 inch = 2 mi   1 cm = 1.25 km

© Garmin

MONTICELLO   MONTICELLO   McGEHEE

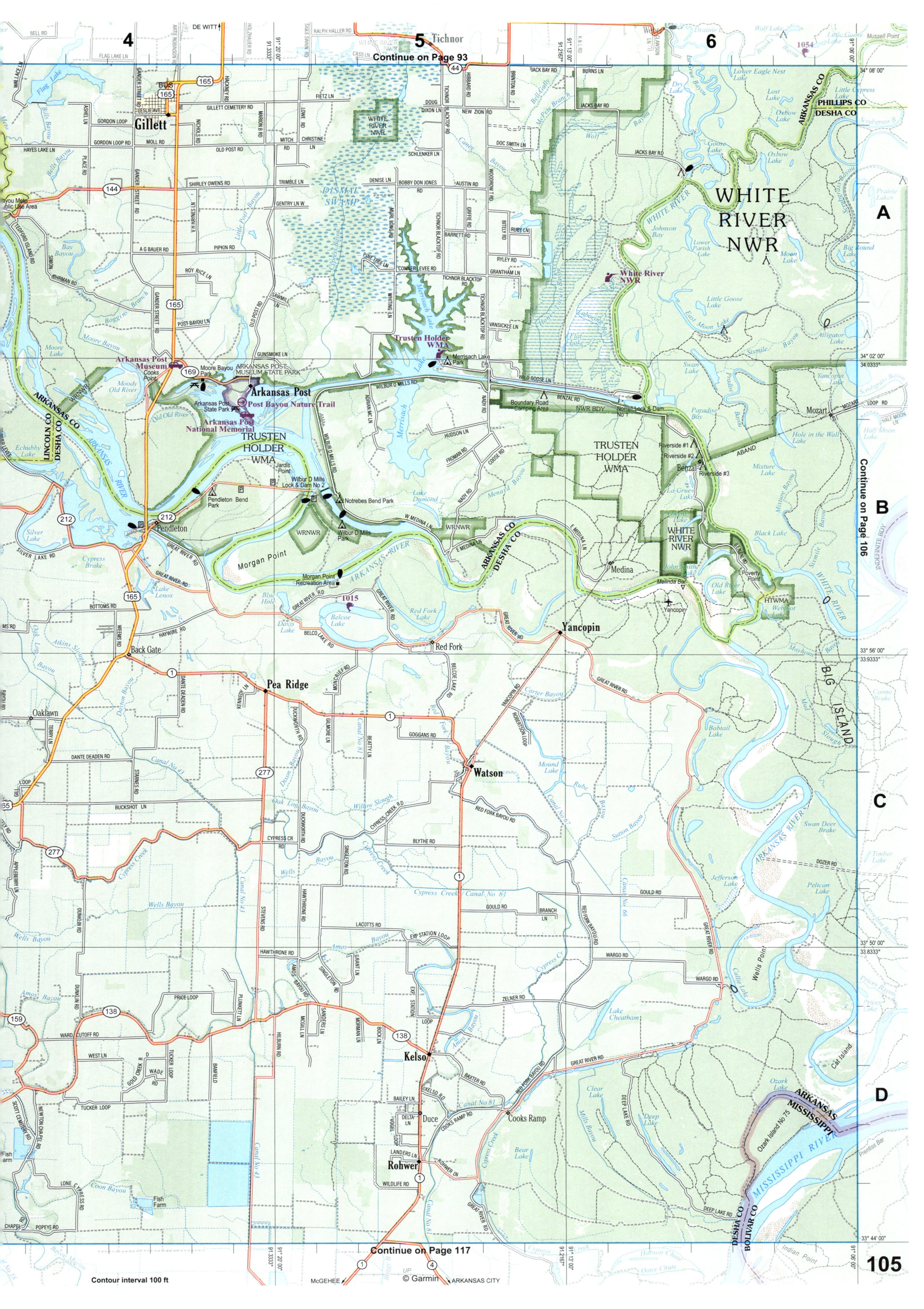

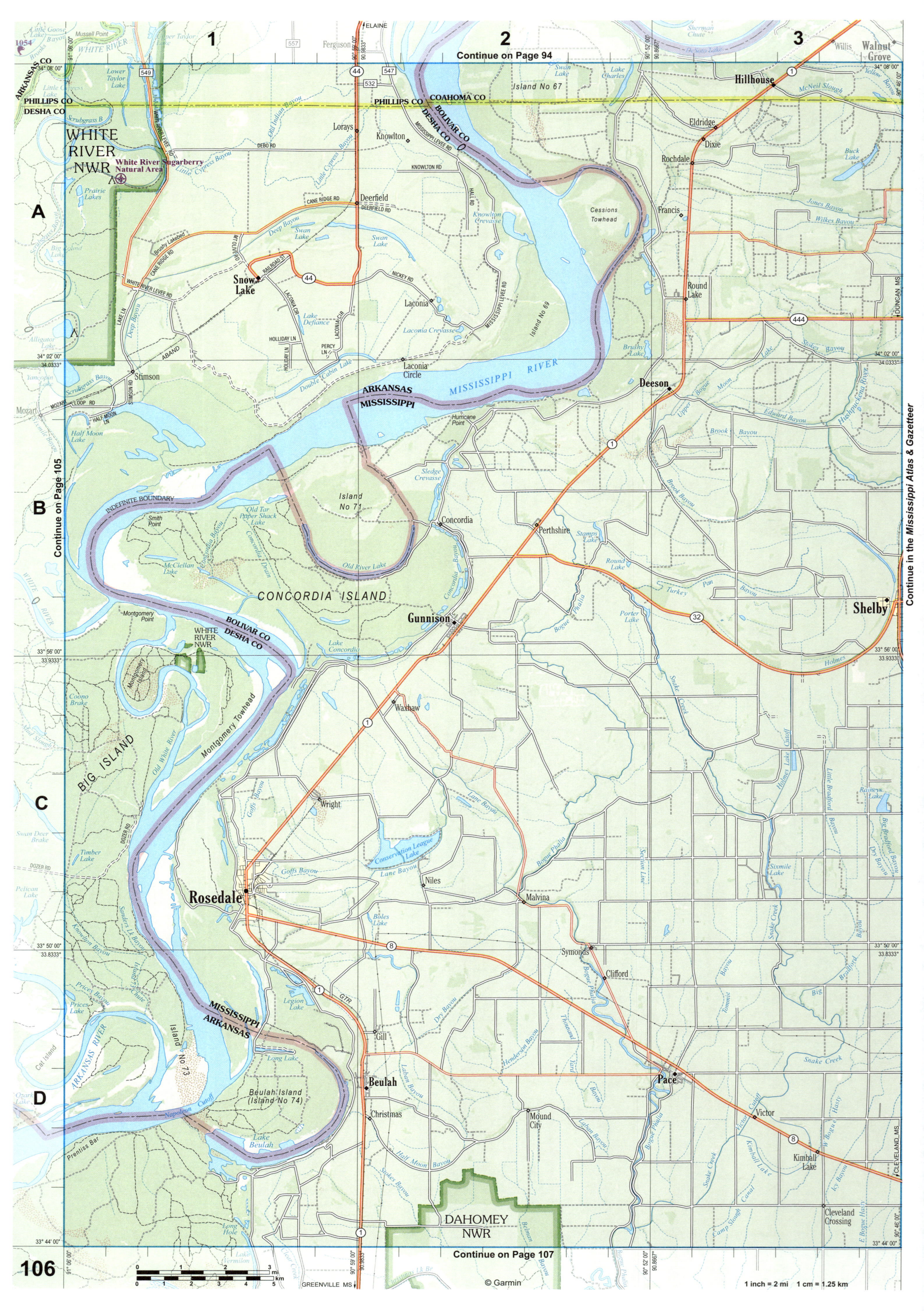

Continue on Page 94

Continue on Page 105

WHITE
RIVER
NWR

White River Sugarberry
Natural Area

PHILLIPS CO
DESHA CO

PHILLIPS CO
DESHA CO

COAHOMA CO
BOLIVAR CO

Island No 67

ELAINE

Ferguson

Willis   Walnut
Grove

Hillhouse

Eldridge

Dixie

Rochdale

Francis

Lorays

Knowlton

Deerfield

Snow
Lake

Laconia

Lake
Defiance

Laconia
Circle

Stimson

Mozart

Half Moon
Lake

Alligator
Lake

Prairie
Lakes

ARKANSAS
MISSISSIPPI

MISSISSIPPI RIVER

Hurricane
Point

Sledge
Crevasse

Island
No 71

Old Tar
Paper Shack
Lake

Old River Lake

Concordia

Perthshire

Round
Lake

Deeson

Round
Lake

Shelby

Smith
Point

McClellan
Lake

CONCORDIA ISLAND

Gunnison

Lake
Concordia

INDEFINITE BOUNDARY

Montgomery
Point

BOLIVAR CO
DESHA CO

WHITE RIVER
NWR

Montgomery
Island

Coono
Brake

BIG ISLAND

Montgomery Towhead

Waxhaw

Wright

Conservation League
Lake

Lane Bayou

Swan Deer
Brake

Timber
Lake

Pelican
Lake

Goffs Bayou

Niles

Malvina

Rosedale

Boles
Lake

Symonds

Clifford

Pace

Victor

Gill

Legion
Lake

MISSISSIPPI
ARKANSAS

Island
No 73

Beulah Island
(Island No 74)

Beulah

Christmas

Mound
City

Kimball
Lake

Long Lake

Lake
Beulah

Prentiss Bar

Cleveland
Crossing

Call Island

DAHOMEY
NWR

Continue on Page 107

GREENVILLE MS

© Garmin

1 inch = 2 mi   1 cm = 1.25 km

A

B

C

D

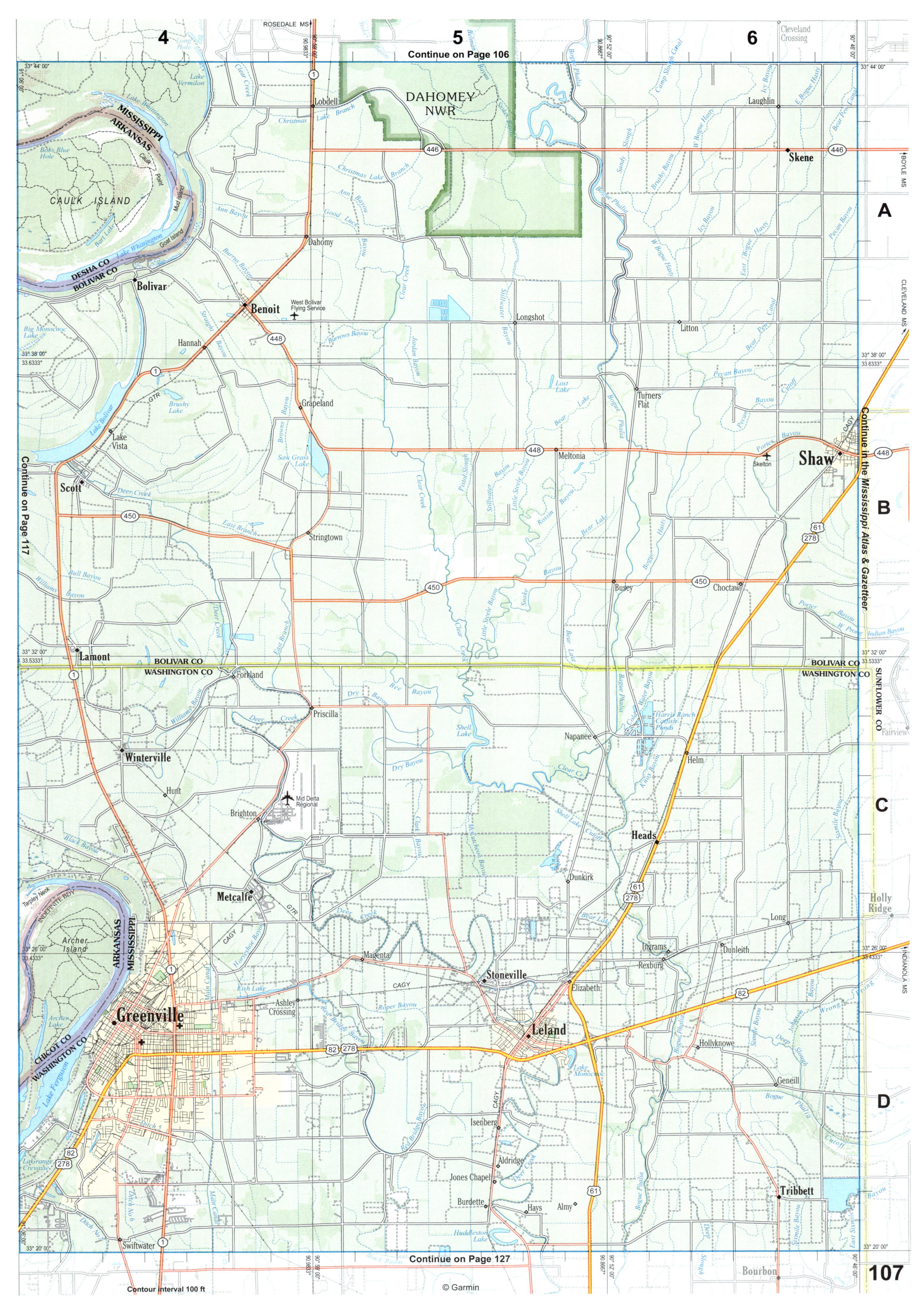

Continue on Page 106

4 5 6

ROSEDALE MS

Cleveland Crossing

DAHOMEY NWR

Laughlin

Skene

MISSISSIPPI
ARKANSAS

CAULK ISLAND

Lobdell

Christmas Lake Branch

Longshot

Litton

A

DESHA CO
BOLIVAR CO

Bolivar

Dahomy

Benoit
West Bolivar
Flying Service

Turners Flat

Lost Lake

Continue in the Mississippi Atlas & Gazetteer

Hannah

Grapeland

Meltonia

Shaw

Skelton

B

Continue on Page 117

Lake Vista

Scott

Stringtown

Busey

Choctaw

Lamont

BOLIVAR CO
WASHINGTON CO

Forkland

BOLIVAR CO
WASHINGTON CO

SUNFLOWER CO

Fairview

Priscilla

Napanee

Helm

Harris Ranch
Catfish Ponds

Winterville

Hunt

Shell Lake

Dry Bayou

C

Brighton

Mid Delta Regional

Heads

Dunkirk

Long

Holly Ridge

Metcalfe

Ingrams

Dunleith

ARKANSAS
MISSISSIPPI

Archer Island

Magenta

Stoneville

Rexburg

INDIANOLA MS

Greenville

Ashley Crossing

Leland

Elizabeth

Hollyknowe

Geneill

D

Lake Monoceo

Isenberg

Aldridge

Jones Chapel

Burdette

Hays

Almy

Tribbett

Swiftwater

Bourbon

Continue on Page 127

Contour interval 100 ft

© Garmin

OUACHITA NATIONAL FOREST

CHOCTAW NATION

Continue on Page 96

DE QUEEN

Foreman

GUM FLATS WMA

GUM FLATS WMA

Arden

Wallace

Wades Chapel

Palmetto Flats Natural Area WMA

Matteson Gin

Lanesport

RED RIVER

OKLAHOMA
ARKANSAS

TEXAS

Hamilton Lake

Grassy Lake

Choctaw Bayou

Horseshoe Slough

Walnut Bayou

Dunn Lake

Breedlove Lake

Bailey Cut-off

Sweet Island

BOWIE CO
McCURTAIN CO

Billy Hall Bend

New Lake

Gunn Lake

Josh Tom Island

Hurricane Bend Lake

Gano Island

Paul Moore Island

New Lake

Brushy Lake

Woodstock

Spanish Bluff

Hudson Lake

Hudson Bow

Applewhite Cutoff Lake

Whaley Lake

Little Red Lake

Smith Hill

LITTLE RIVER CO
BOWIE CO

Smith Club Lake

Crutchell's Lake

Black Bottom

Redbank

Burns

De Kalb

Malta

Old Salem

EXIT 199
EXIT 198

EXIT 201

EXIT 206

EXIT 208

Hooks

New Boston

Boston

SPUR 86

Whaley

RED RIVER ARMY DEPOT

Little Prairie

Rea Hill

Old Boston

College Hill

EXIT 192

Siloam

Simms

Old Union

Calvin Creek Reservoir

Elliott Cr Reservoir

Redwater

Maud

Corley

Continue in the *Texas Atlas & Gazetteer*

© Garmin

1 inch = 2 mi 1 cm = 1.25 km

A
B
C
D

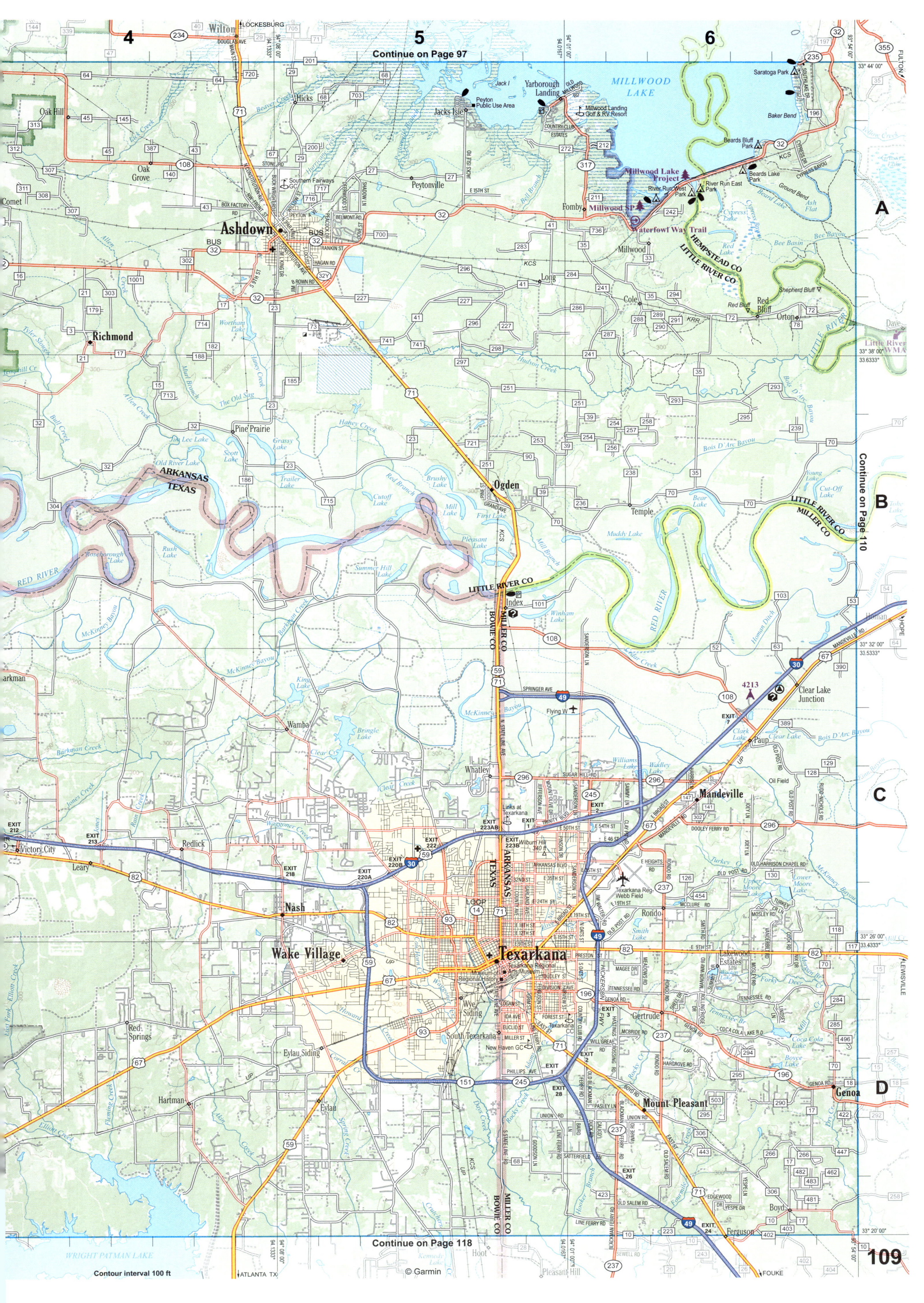

Continue on Page 97

Continue on Page 110

Continue on Page 118

Contour interval 100 ft

© Garmin

109

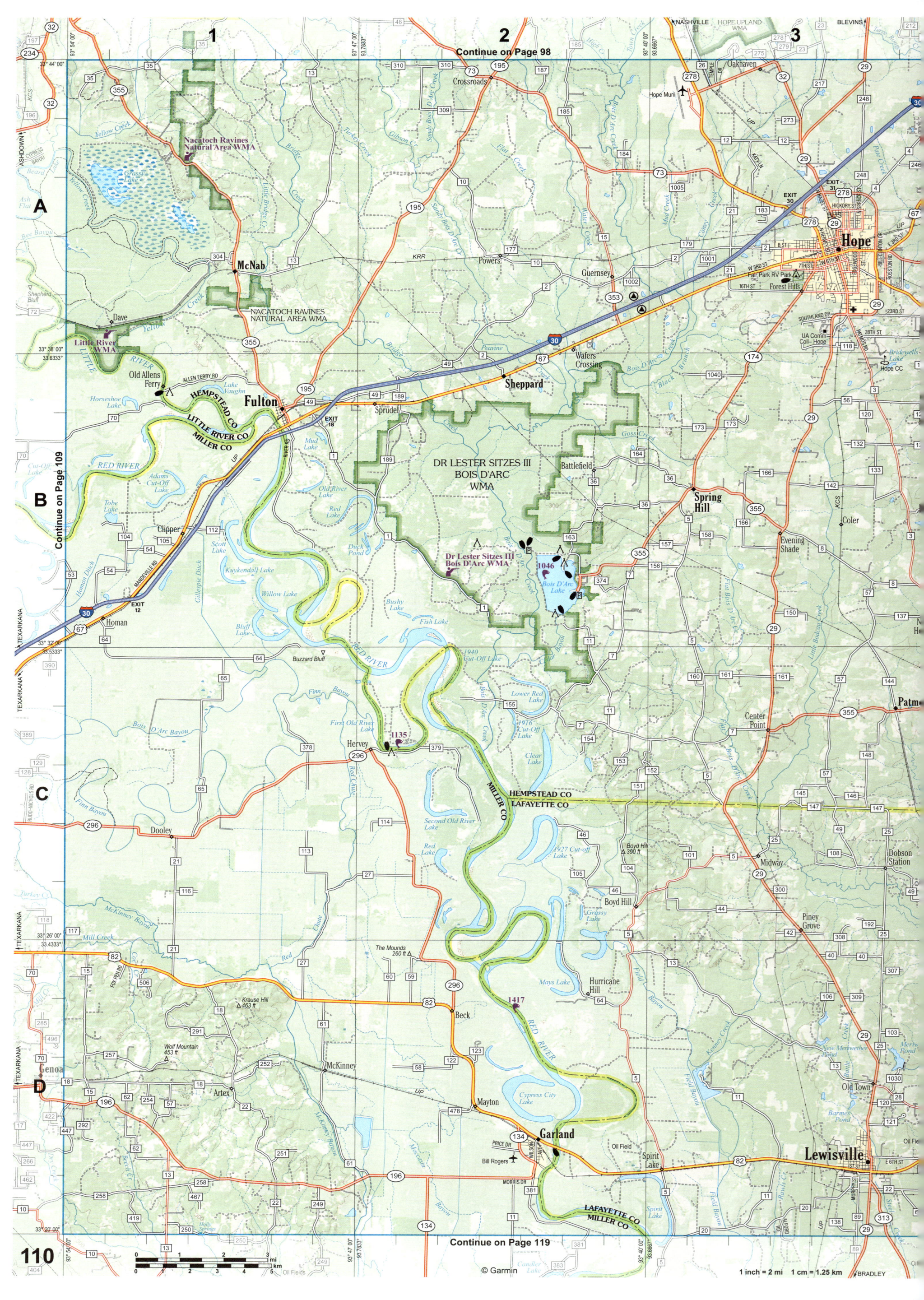

Continue on Page 109

Continue on Page 119

© Garmin

1 inch = 2 mi   1 cm = 1.25 km

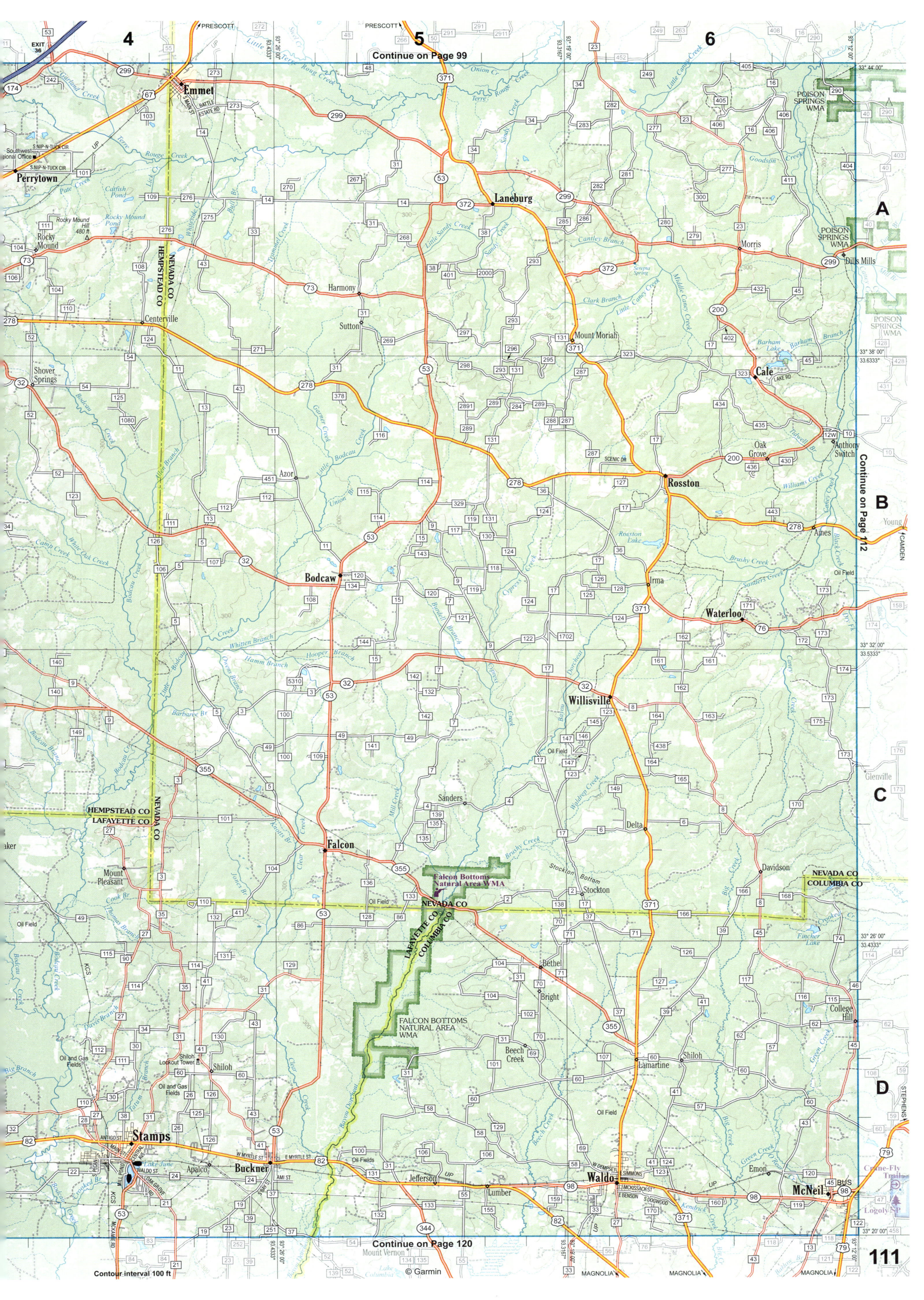

Continue on Page 99

Continue on Page 112

Continue on Page 120

A

B

C

D

Emmet

Perrytown

Rocky Mound

Laneburg

Morris

Dills Mills

POISON SPRINGS WMA

POISON SPRINGS WMA

Harmony

Centerville

Sutton

Mount Moriah

Cale

Shover Springs

Azor

Oak Grove

Anthony Switch

Rosston

Irma

Ames

Bodcaw

Waterloo

Willisville

Sanders

Delta

Davidson

HEMPSTEAD CO
LAFAYETTE CO

Falcon

Mount Pleasant

Falcon Bottoms
Natural Area WMA

Stockton

NEVADA CO
COLUMBIA CO

NEVADA CO
LAFAYETTE CO
COLUMBIA CO

FALCON BOTTOMS
NATURAL AREA
WMA

Bethel

Bright

College Hill

Shiloh

Beech Creek

Lamartine

Shiloh

Shiloh Lookout Tower

Stamps

Buckner

Jefferson

Lumber

Waldo

Emon

McNeil

Logoly SP

Contour interval 100 ft

© Garmin

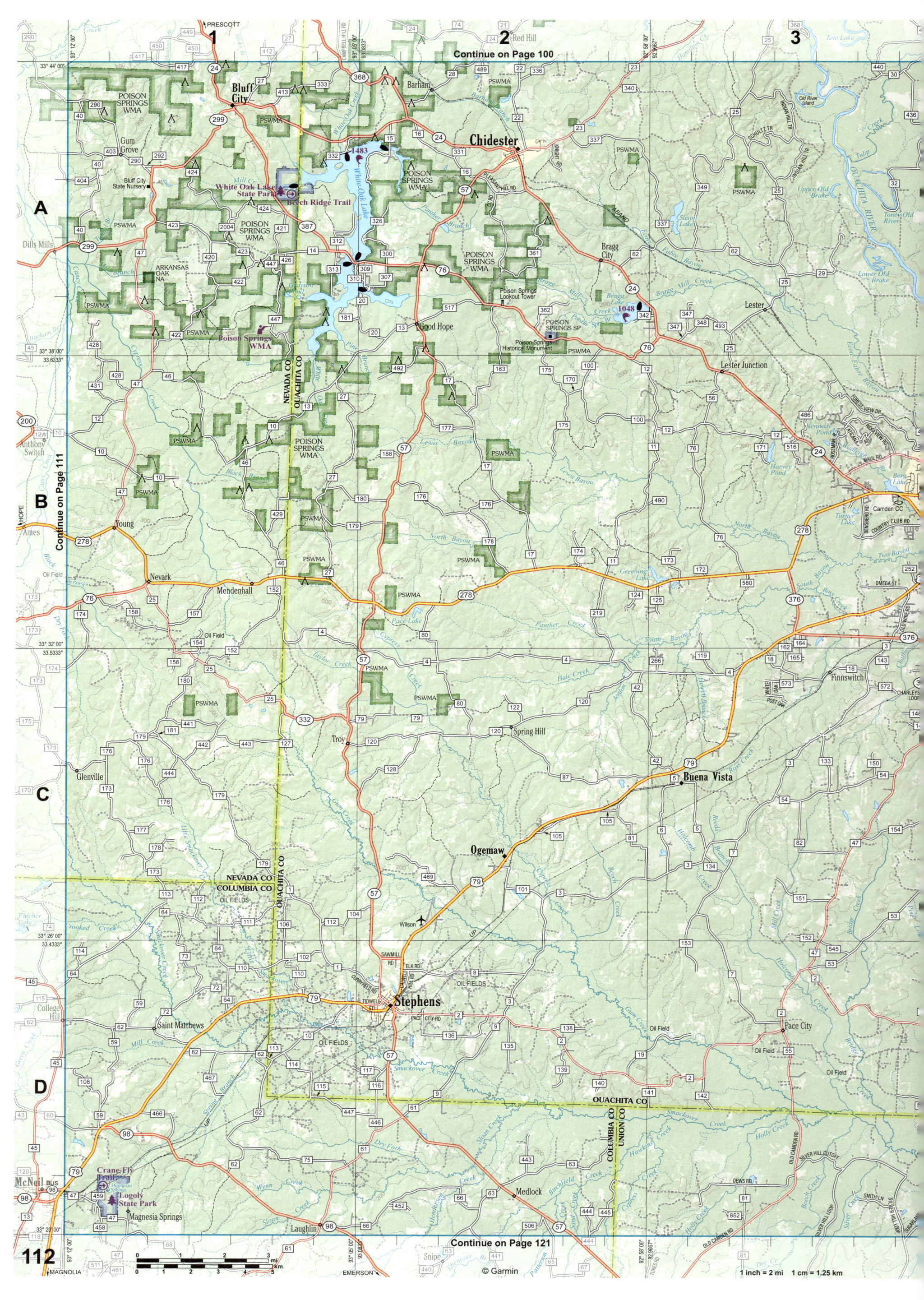

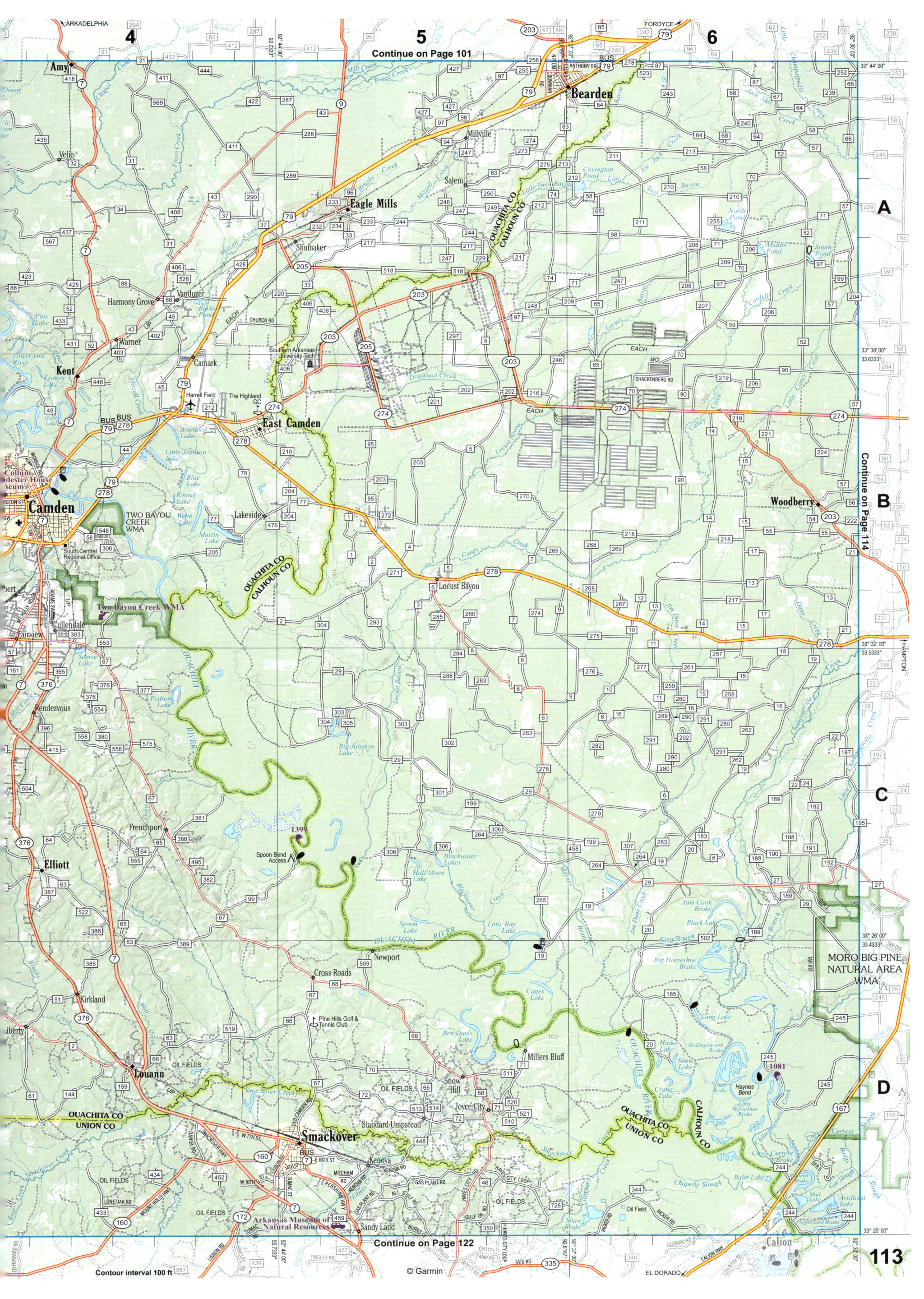

Continue on Page 101

Continue on Page 114

Continue on Page 122

© Garmin

Contour interval 100 ft

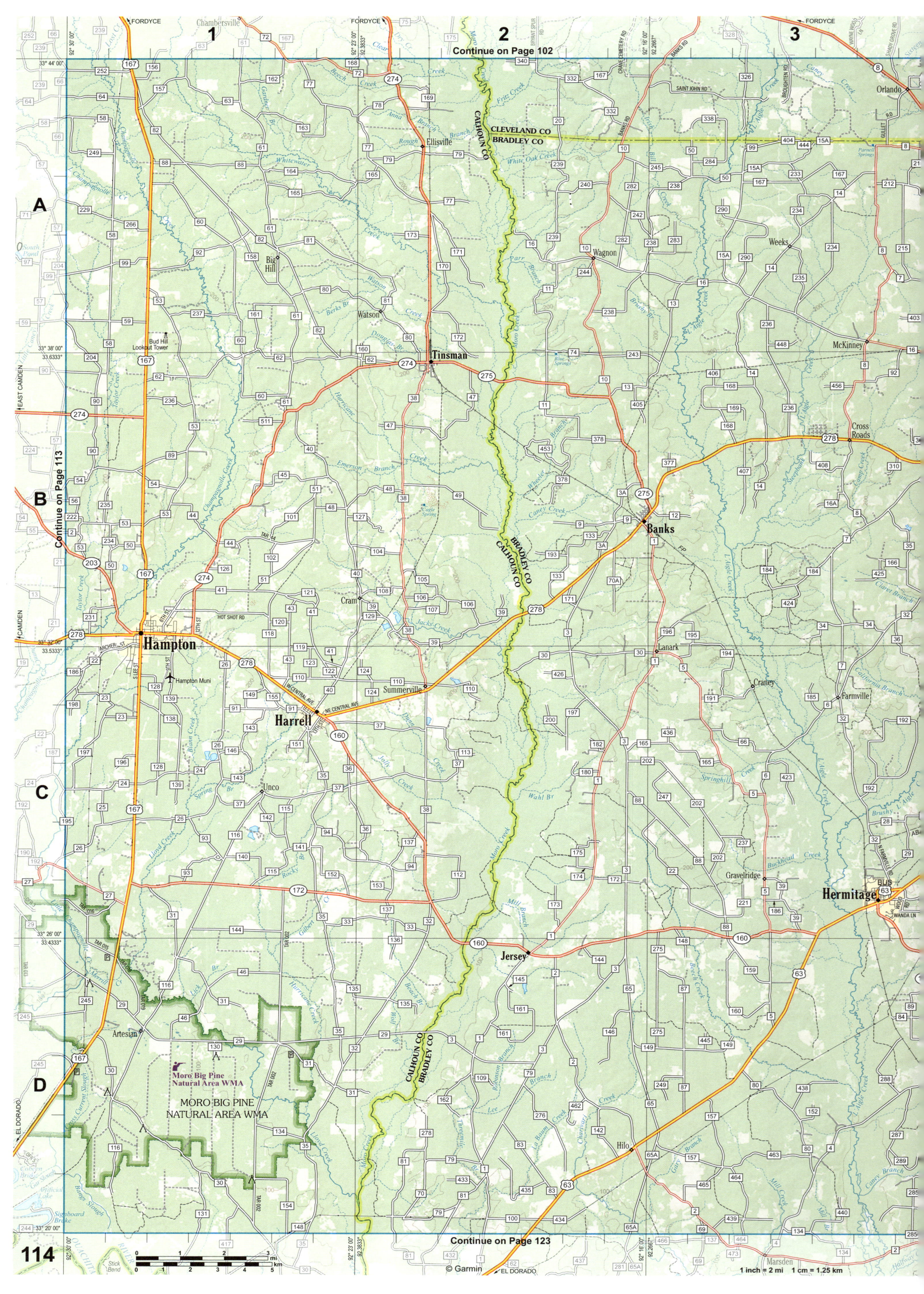

Continue on Page 113

MORO BIG PINE
NATURAL AREA WMA

Moro Big Pine
Natural Area WMA

1 inch = 2 mi   1 cm = 1,25 km

© Garmin

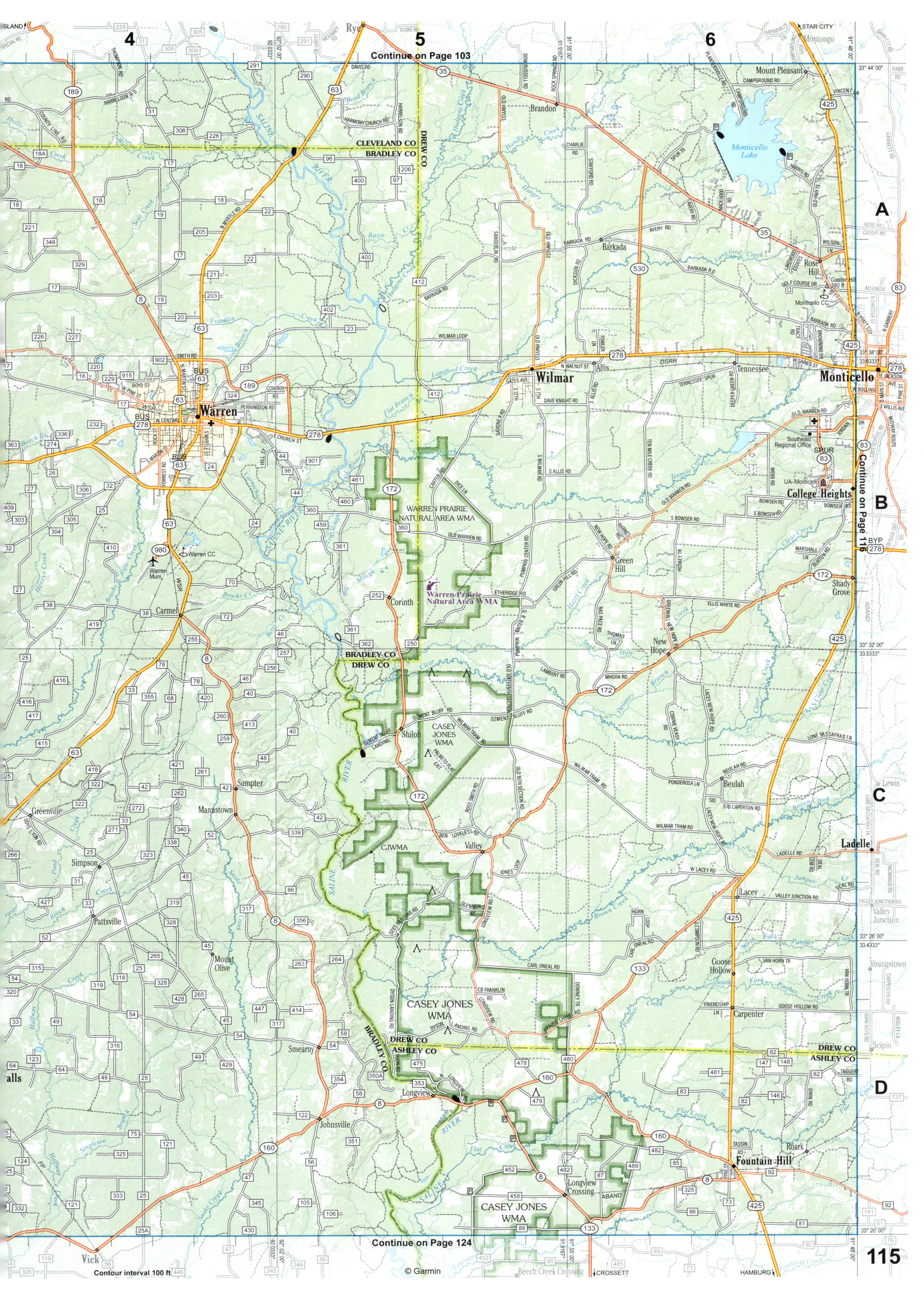

Continue on Page 116

Contour interval 100 ft

© Garmin

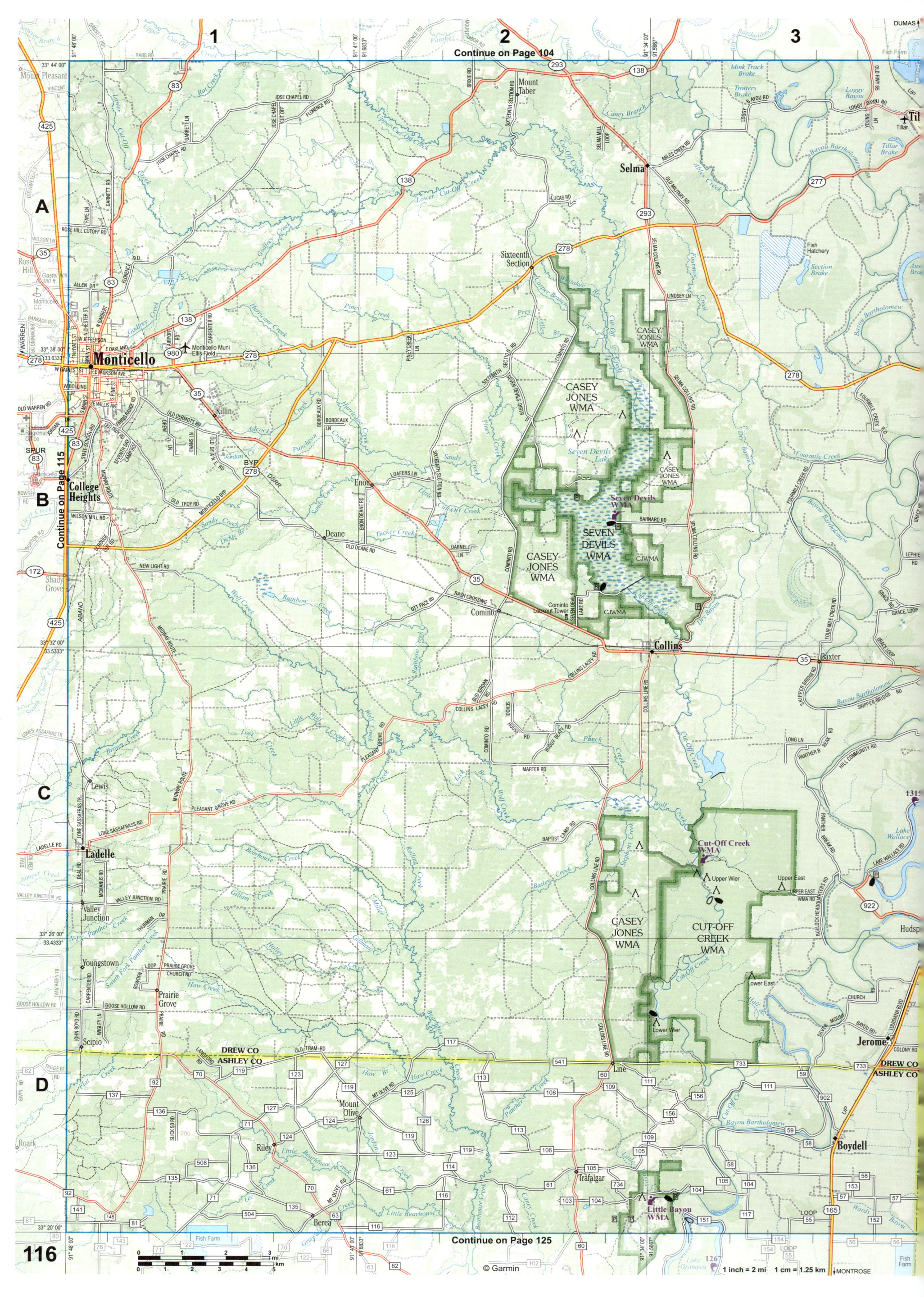

Continue on Page 104

Continue on Page 115

Continue on Page 125

© Garmin

1 inch = 2 mi   1 cm = 1.25 km

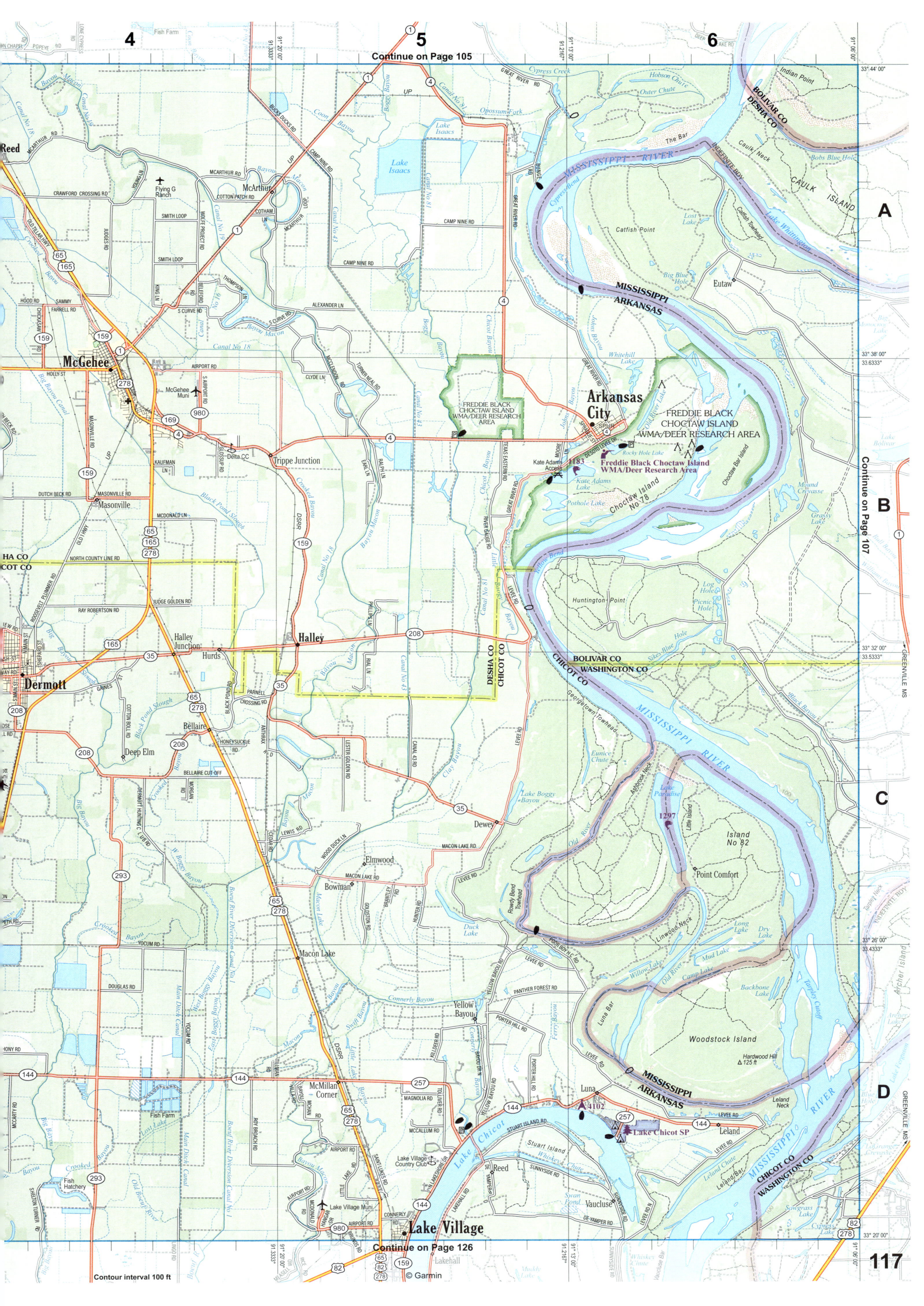

Continue on Page 107

Contour interval 100 ft

© Garmin

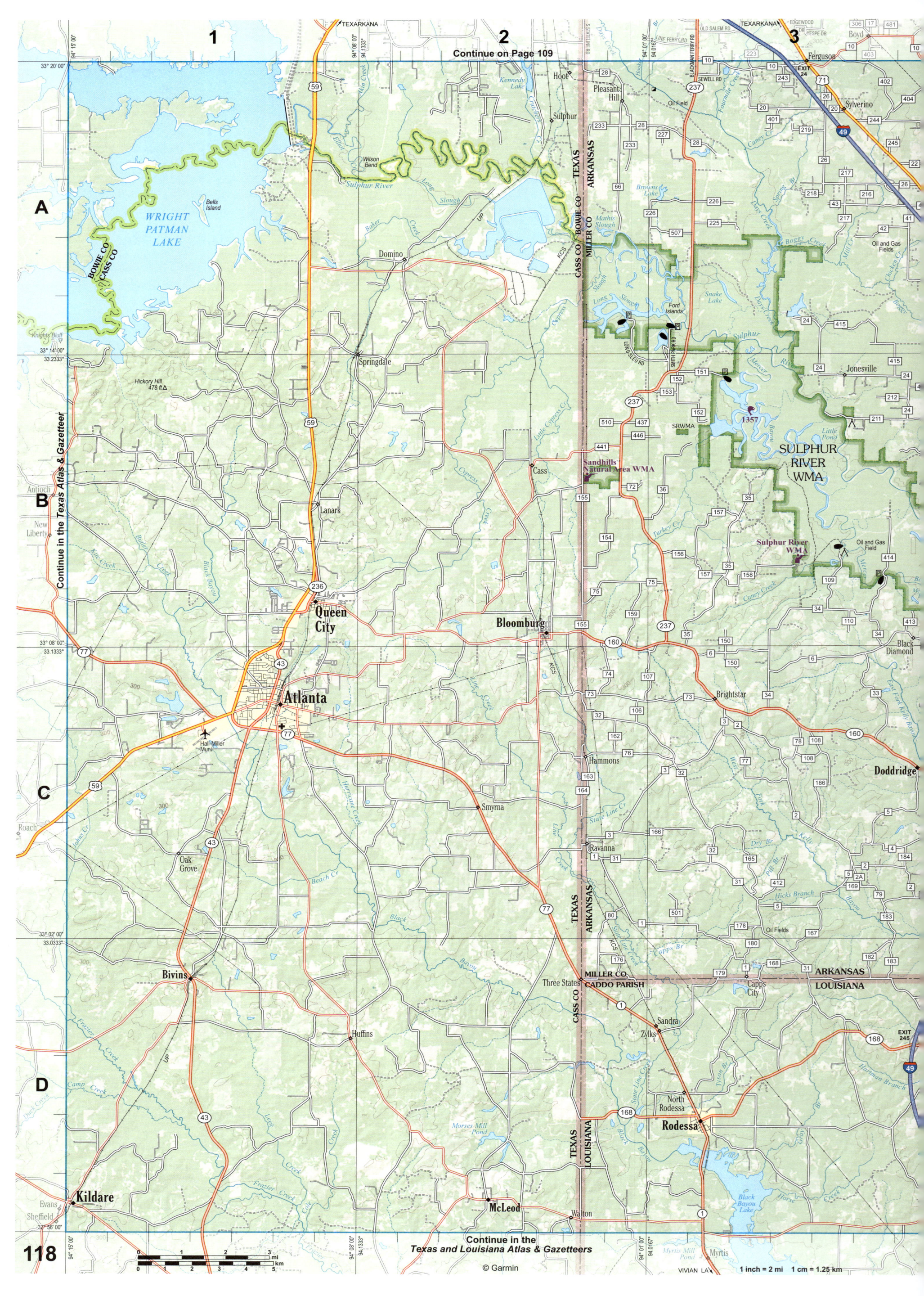

1 2 3

A

B

C

D

118

TEXARKANA

WRIGHT
PATMAN
LAKE

BOWIE CO
CASS CO

Bells
Island

Knights Bluff

Kennedy
Lake

Hoot

Sulphur

Pleasant
Hill

Oil Field

Wilson
Bend

Sulphur River

Long
Slough

Domino

TEXAS
ARKANSAS

CASS CO / BOWIE CO
MILLER CO

Bryans
Lake

Mathis
Slough

Long
Slough

Snake
Lake

Ford
Islands

Sulphur

Mercer
Bayou

Jonesville

SULPHUR
RIVER
WMA

Oil and Gas
Fields

Springdale

Hickory Hill
478 ft △

Lanark

Cypress

Little Cypress Cr

Cass

Sandhills
Natural Area WMA

SRWMA

Little
Pond

Sulphur River
WMA

Oil and Gas
Field

Antioch

New
Liberty

Queen
City

Atlanta

Half-Miller
Muni

Bloomburg

Turkey Cr

Caney Creek

Black
Diamond

Brightstar

Doddridge

Smyrna

Oak
Grove

Roach

Hammons

Ravanna

Dry Br

Three States

Bivins

Huffins

MILLER CO
CADDO PARISH

Capps
City

ARKANSAS
LOUISIANA

TEXAS
ARKANSAS

CASS CO / MILLER CO

Oil Fields

Sandra

Zylks

EXIT
245

North
Rodessa

Rodessa

Kildare

Evans
Sheffield

TEXAS
LOUISIANA

Morses Mill Pond

McLeod

Walton

Myrtle Mill
Pond

Myrtis

VIVIAN LA

Black
Bayou
Lake

© Garmin

1 inch = 2 mi   1 cm = 1.25 km

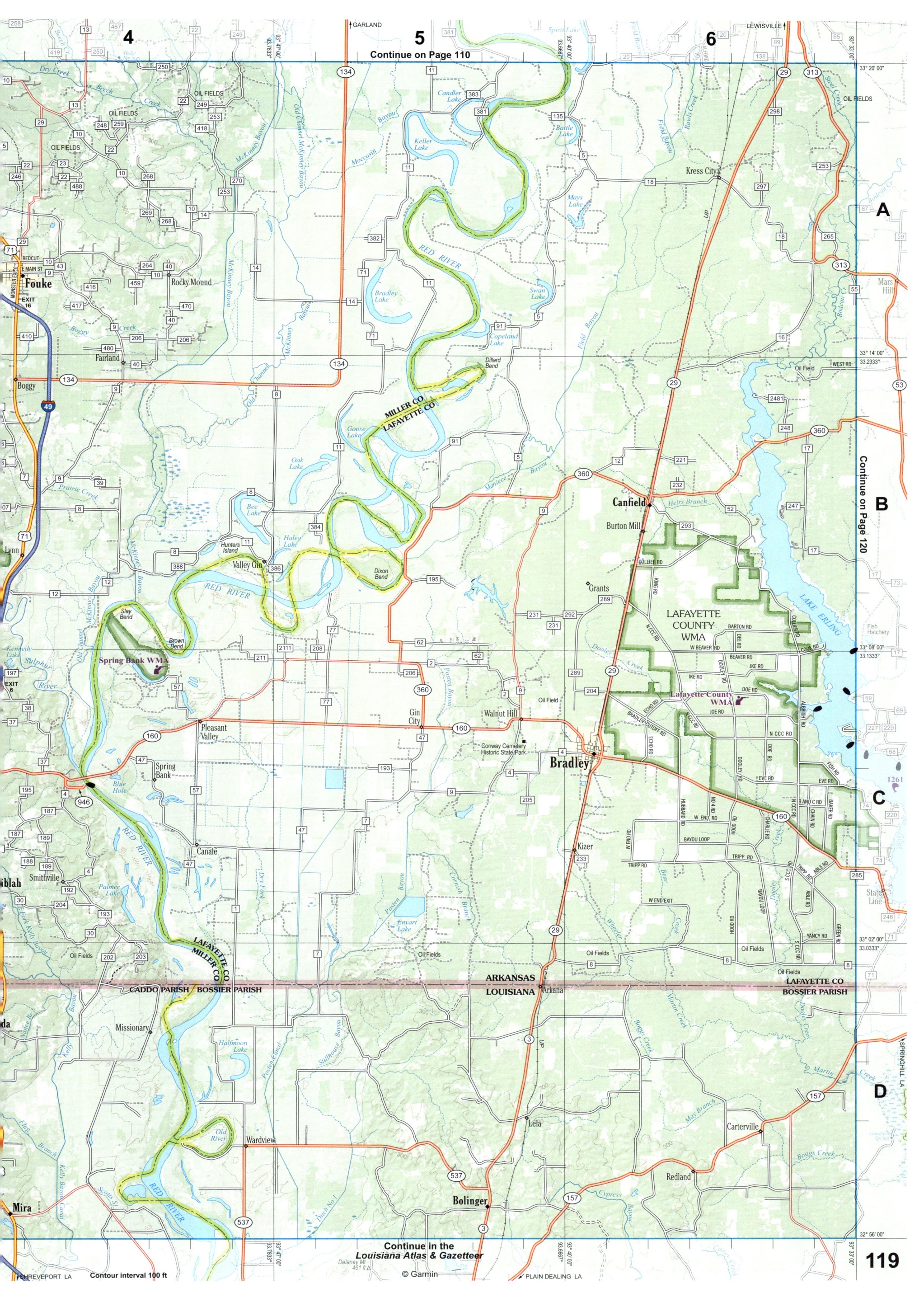

GARLAND

Fouke
EXIT 16

Rocky Mound

Fairland

Boggy

134

Lynn

Smithville

Mira

Kress City

Candler Lake
Keller Lake
Battle Lake
Mays Lake
Bradley Lake
Swan Lake
Copeland Lake

RED RIVER

Dillard Bend

MILLER CO
LAFAYETTE CO

Goose Lake

Oak Lake

Bee Lake

Haley Lake

Hunters Island
Valley Gin

Dixon Bend

RED RIVER

Slay Bend

Brown Bend

Spring Bank WMA

Pleasant Valley

Spring Bank

Blue Hole

Canale

Palmer Lake

LAFAYETTE CO
MILLER CO

CADDO PARISH / BOSSIER PARISH

Missionary

Halfmoon Lake

Wardview

Old River

RED RIVER

Canfield
Burton Mill

Grants

LAFAYETTE COUNTY WMA

Lafayette County WMA

LAKE ERLING

Fish Hatchery

Gin City
Walnut Hill
Oil Field

Conway Cemetery Historic State Park

Bradley

Kizer

ARKANSAS
LOUISIANA
Arkana

Lela

Bolinger

Carterville

Redland

Continue in the
Louisiana Atlas & Gazetteer

Contour interval 100 ft

© Garmin

PLAIN DEALING LA

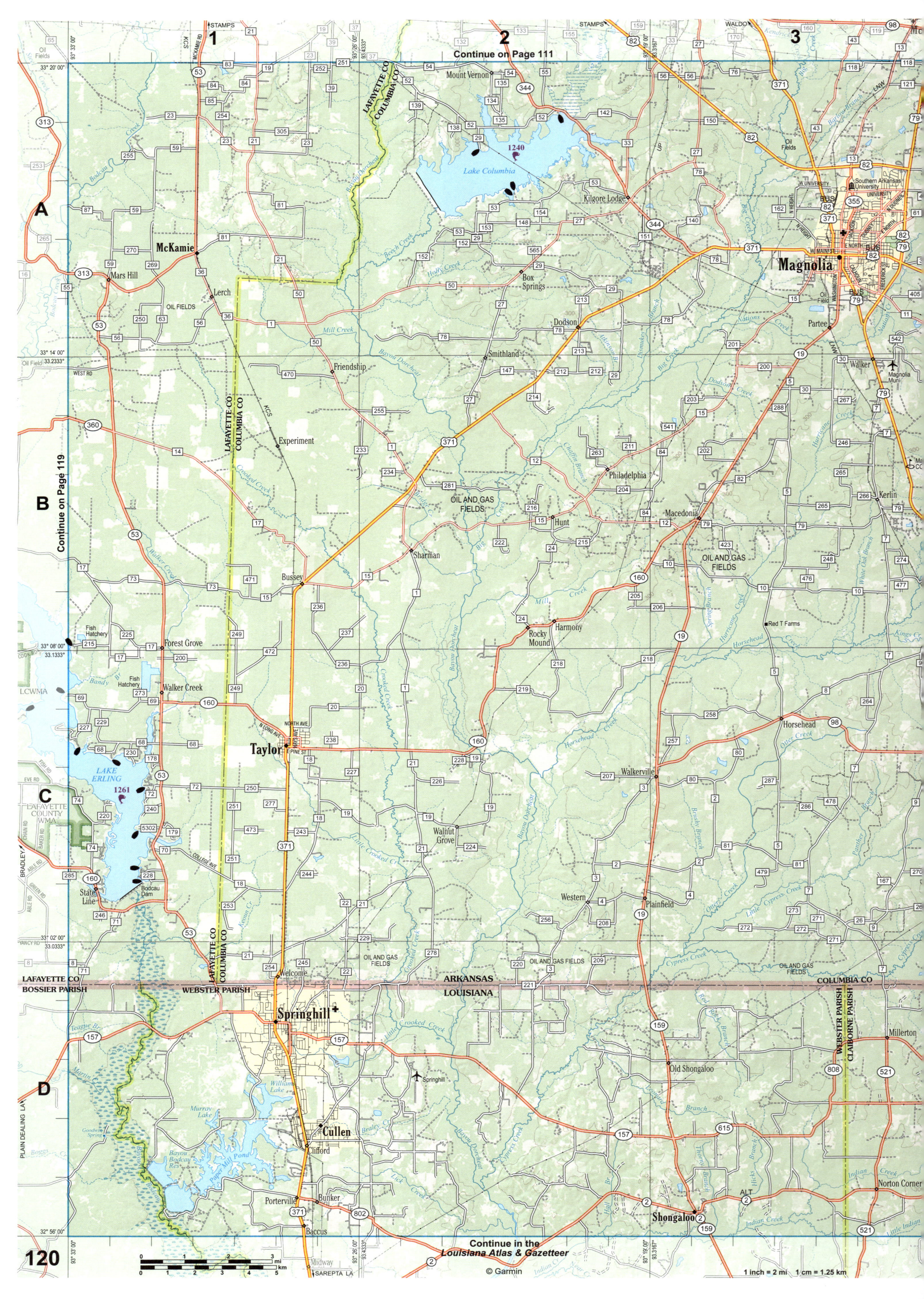

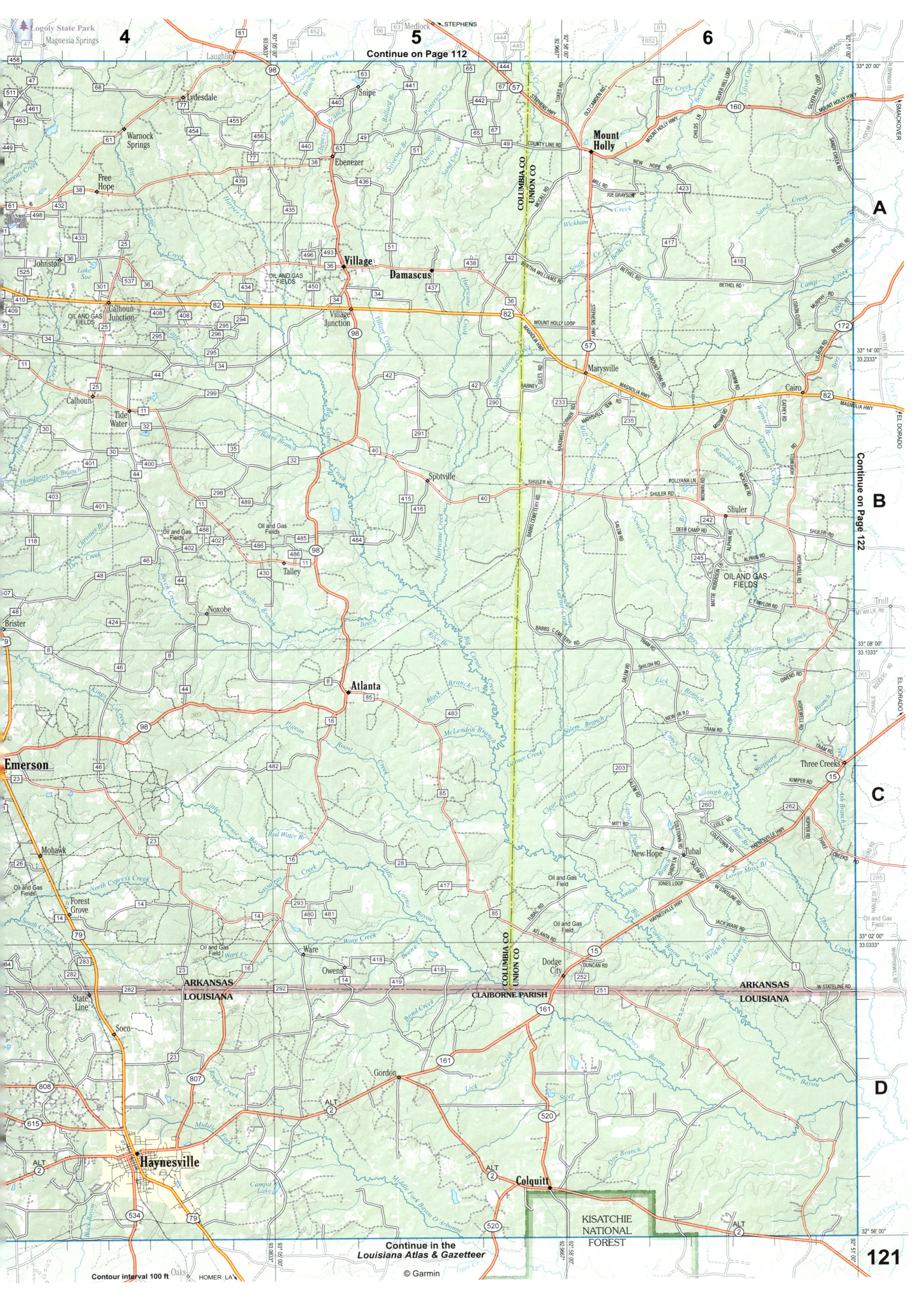

Continue on Page 112
Continue on Page 122
Continue in the
Louisiana Atlas & Gazetteer

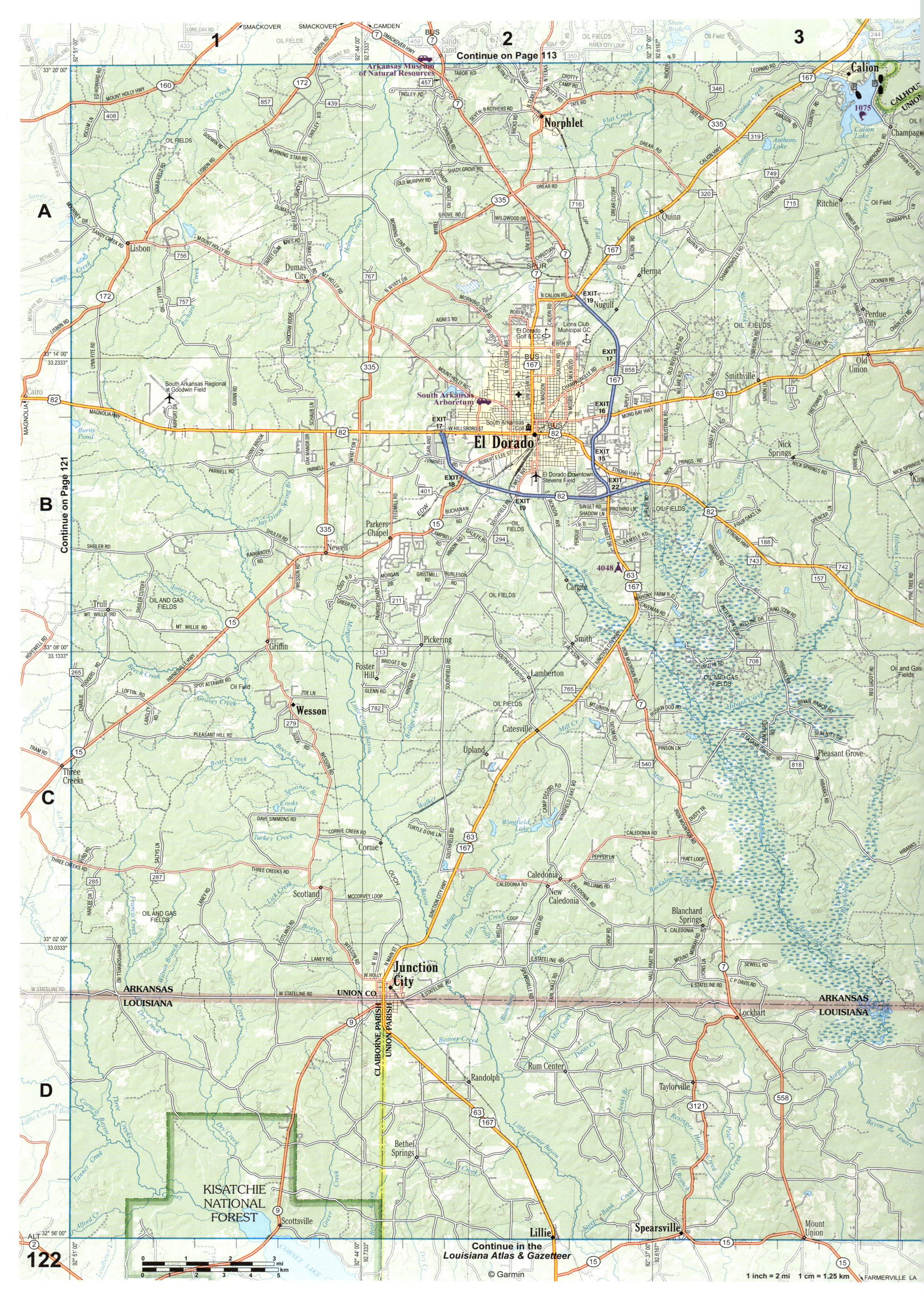

Continue on Page 113

Continue on Page 121

A

B

C

D

SMACKOVER   SMACKOVER   CAMDEN

Calion

CALHOUN

UNION

Norphlet

Lisbon

Dumas City

SPUR

Nugull

Quinn

Herma

EXIT 19

EXIT 17

EXIT 16

Smithville

Old Union

South Arkansas Regional at Goodwin Field

Arkansas Museum of Natural Resources

South Arkansas Arboretum

El Dorado

EXIT 17

EXIT 15

EXIT 18

EXIT 22

EXIT 19

El Dorado Downtown Stevens Field

Nick Springs

Parkers Chapel

Newell

Buchanan

Oil Fields

Carette

Oil and Gas Fields

Trull

Oil and Gas Fields

MT. WILLIE RD

Griffin

Pickering

Smith

Lamberton

Foster Hill

Wesson

Catesville

Upland

Oil Fields

Oil and Gas Fields

Pleasant Grove

Three Creeks

Cornie

Scotland

Caledonia

New Caledonia

Blanchard Springs

S. Caledonia

Junction City

ARKANSAS
LOUISIANA

UNION CO.

CLAIBORNE PARISH   UNION PARISH

Lockhart

ARKANSAS
LOUISIANA

Randolph

Rum Center

Taylorville

Bethel Springs

KISATCHIE NATIONAL FOREST

Scottsville

Lillie

Spearsville

Mount Union

Continue in the
Louisiana Atlas & Gazetteer

0 1 2 3 mi
0 1 2 3 4 5 km

© Garmin

1 inch = 2 mi   1 cm = 1.25 km   FARMERVILLE LA

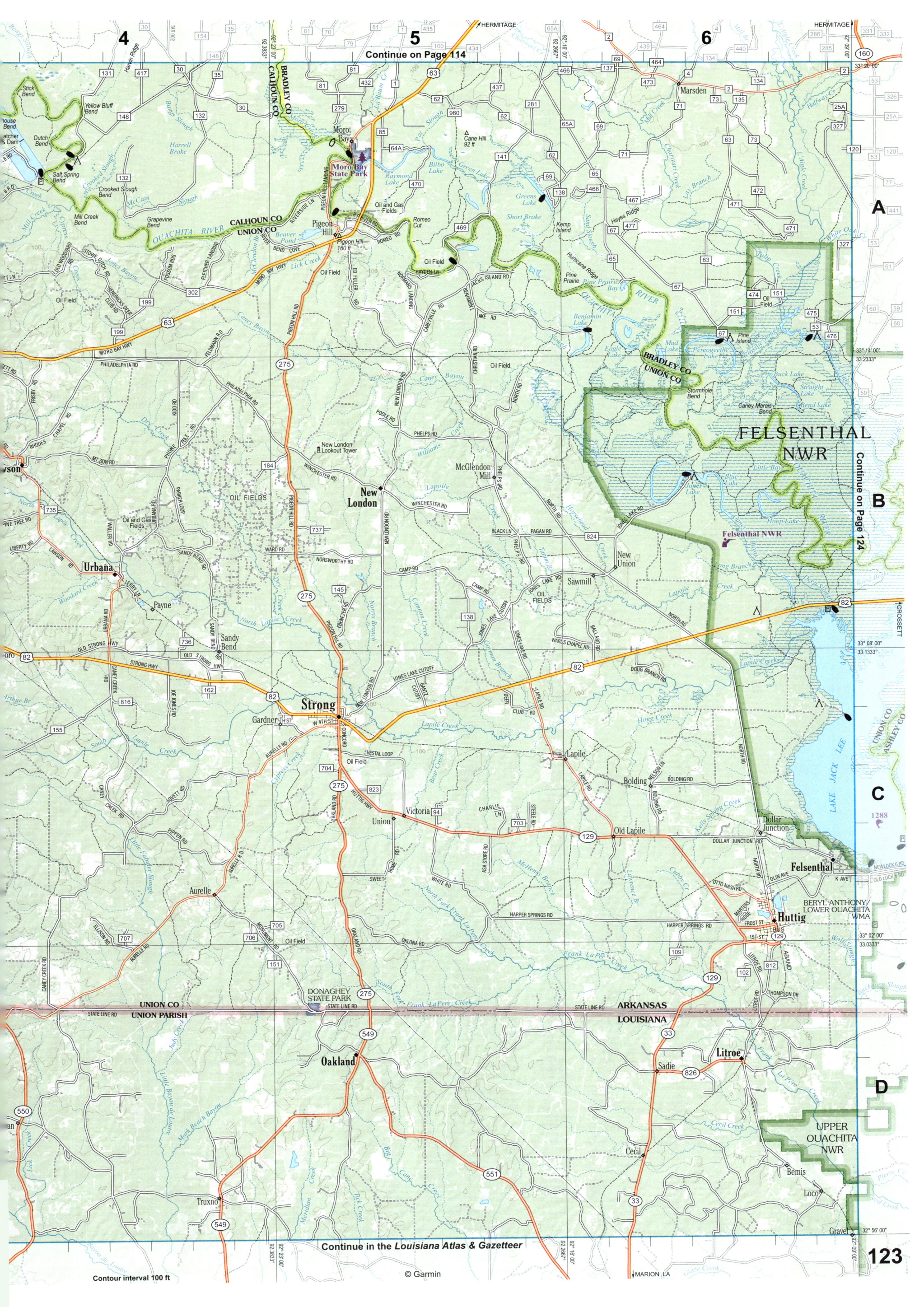

Continue on Page 124

FELSENTHAL
NWR

BRADLEY CO
UNION CO

CALHOUN CO
UNION CO

Moro Bay
State Park

Pigeon Hill

New London

McGlendon Mill

New Union

Sawmill

Urbana

Payne

Sandy Bend

Strong

Gardner

Lapile

Bolding

Victoria

Union

Old Lapile

Dollar Junction

Felsenthal

Aurelle

Huttig

BERYL ANTHONY/
LOWER OUACHITA WMA

DONAGHEY
STATE PARK

UNION CO
UNION PARISH

ARKANSAS
LOUISIANA

Oakland

Litroe

Sadie

Cecil

Truxno

UPPER
OUACHITA
NWR

Bemis

Loco

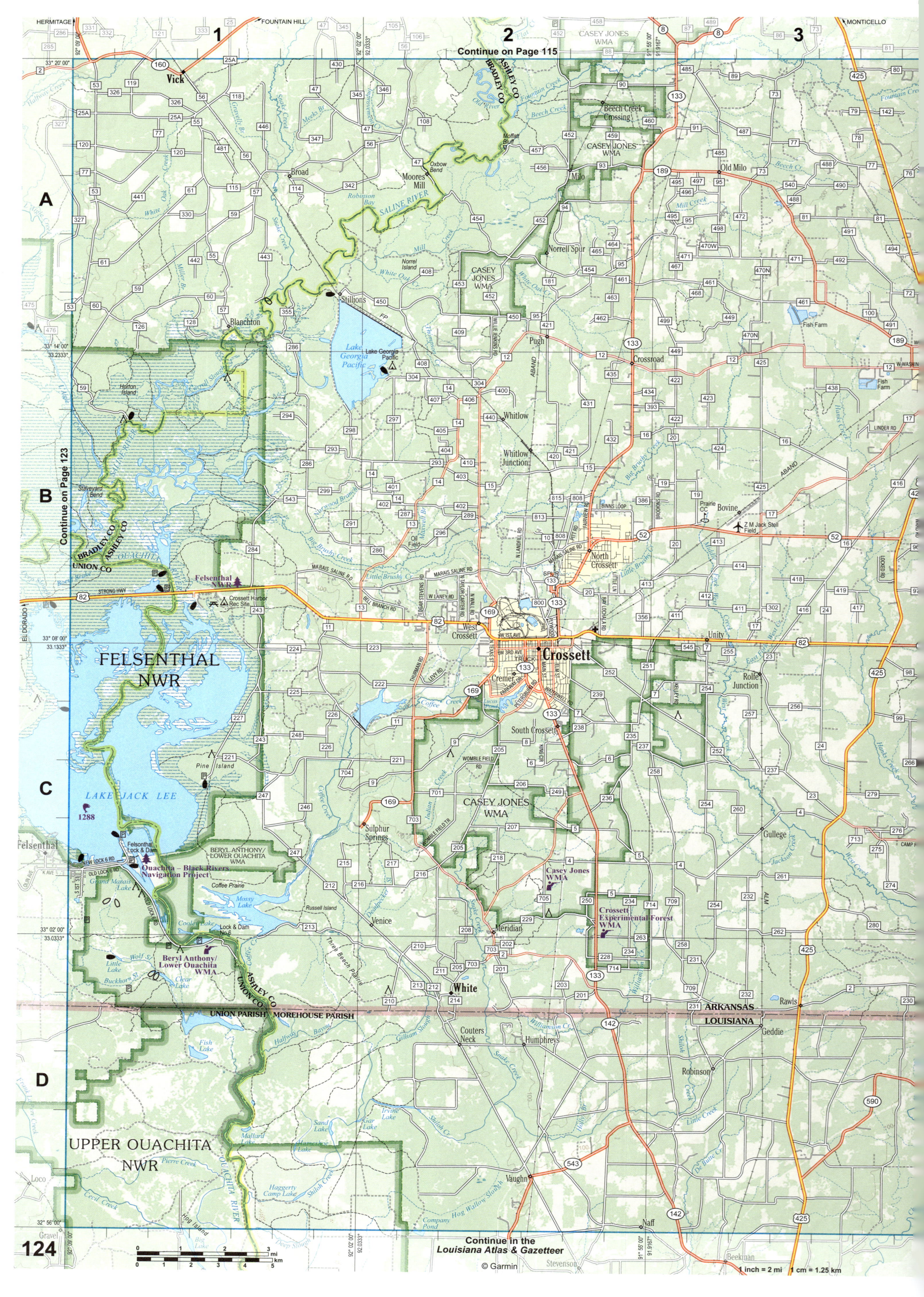

Continue on Page 115

Continue on Page 123

FELSENTHAL
NWR

LAKE JACK LEE

UPPER OUACHITA
NWR

Crossett

Felsenthal
NWR

CASEY JONES
WMA

© Garmin

1 inch = 2 mi   1 cm = 1.25 km

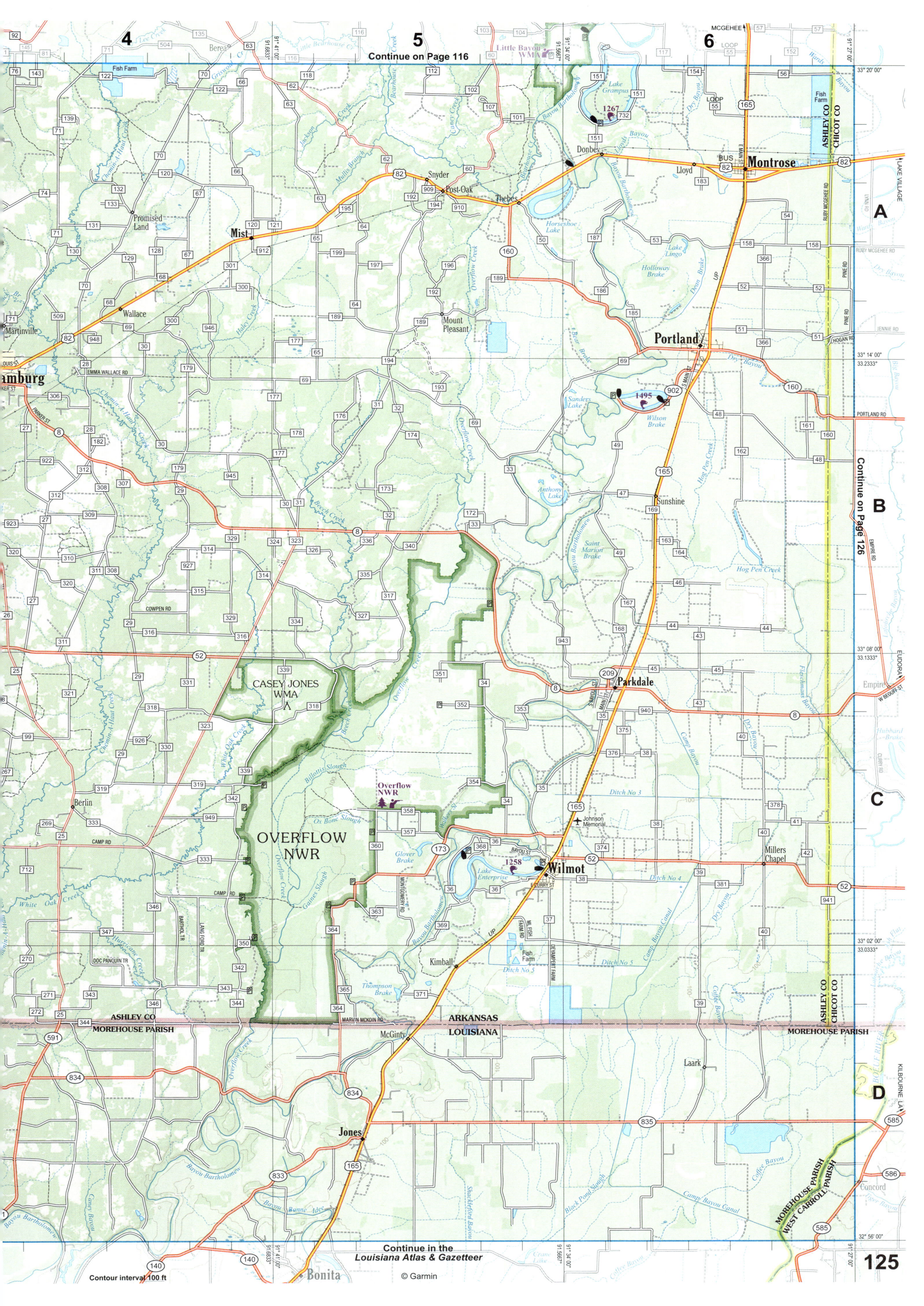

Continue on Page 116

Continue on Page 126

A

B

C

D

McGinty

OVERFLOW
NWR

CASEY JONES
WMA

Overflow
NWR

Portland

Montrose

Parkdale

Wilmot

Kimball

Jones

Bonita

Mist

Wallace

Martinville

Berlin

Promised
Land

Snyder
Post-Oak
Thebes
Donbey
Lloyd

Mount
Pleasant

Sunshine

Millers
Chapel

ARKANSAS
LOUISIANA

ASHLEY CO
MOREHOUSE PARISH

ASHLEY CO
CHICOT CO

ASHLEY CO
CHICOT CO

MOREHOUSE PARISH

MOREHOUSE PARISH
WEST CARROLL PARISH

Laark

Concord

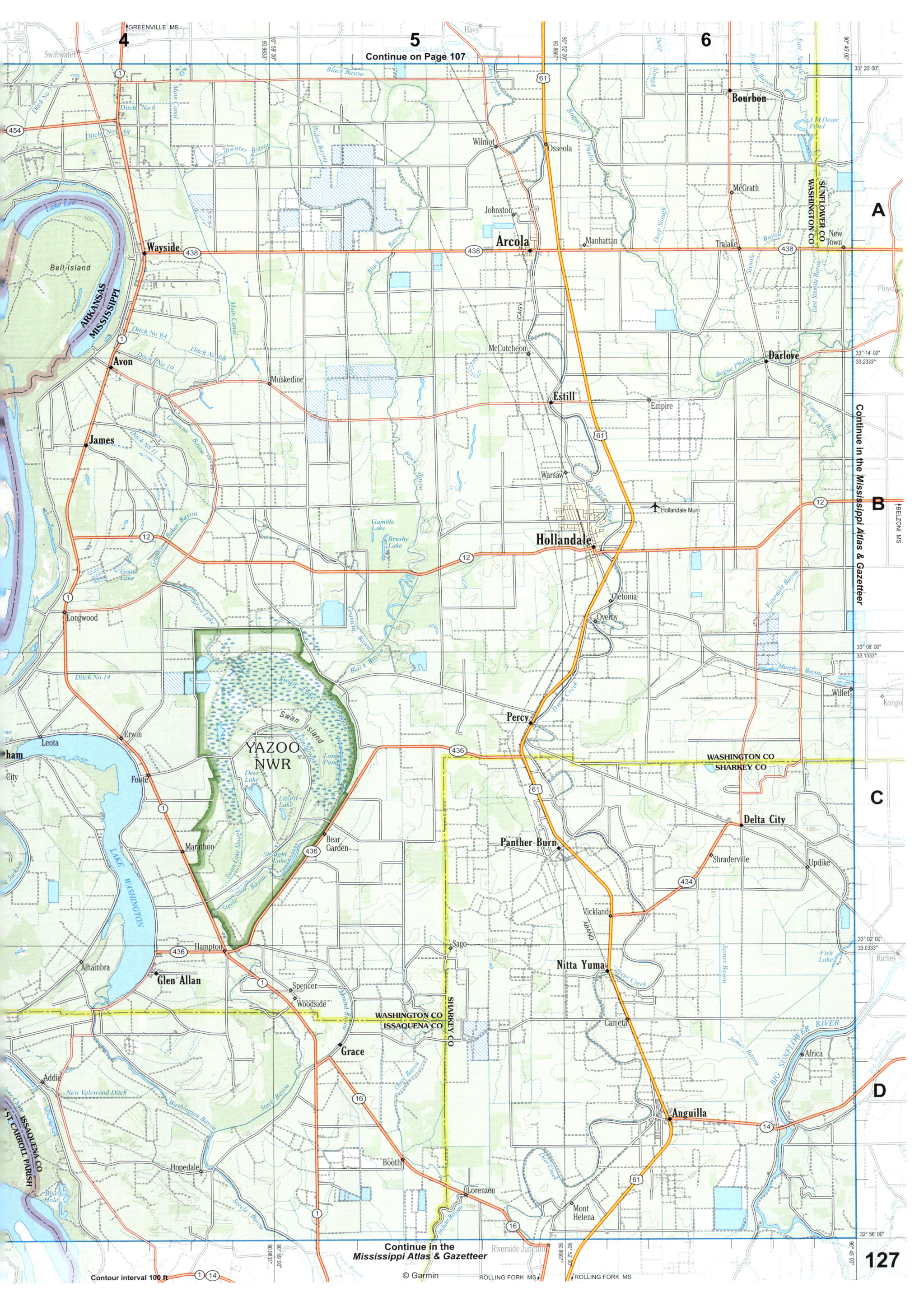

Continue on Page 107

A
B
C
D

GREENVILLE MS

Swiftwater

ARKANSAS
MISSISSIPPI

Bell Island
Lake Lee

Wayside

Avon

Muskedine

James

Longwood

Erwin

Leota

Foote

ham
City

Marathon

LAKE
WASHINGTON

Hampton

Alhambra

Glen Allan

Spencer

Woodside

Grace

Addie

Hopedale

Blue
Hole

New Valewood Ditch

ST CARROLL PARISH

ISSAQUENA CO

Black Bayou

Main Canal

Ditch No 6
Ditch No 8

Swiftwater Bayou

Widow Bayou

Ditch No 9A
Ditch No 9B

Ditch No 10

Ditch No 11

Ditch No 14

Gamble
Lake

Brushy
Lake

Grand Redex Bayou

Silver Lake

Goose
Lake

YAZOO
NWR

Swan Lake

Swan Island

Deer Lake

Long
Pond

Lizard
Lake

Bear
Garden

Steele

Swan Lake Slough

Steele Bayou

Black Bayou

Mound Bayou

Steele Bayou

Booth

Lorenzen

Wilmot

Osceola

Johnston

Arcola

Manhattan

McCutcheon

Estill

Empire

Warsaw

Hollandale Muni

Hollandale

Cletonia

Overby

Percy

Panther Burn

Sago

Nitta Yuma

Cameta

Africa

Anguilla

Mont
Helena

Hays

Deer Creek

Bogue Phalia

Black Bayou

Gamble
Bayou

Black Bayou

Deer Creek

Deer Creek

Murphy Bayou

Steele Bayou

Bourbon

J M Dean
Pond

McGrath

Tralake

New
Town

Floyd

Darlove

WASHINGTON CO
SUNFLOWER CO

BELZONI MS

Fontaine Bayou

Fontaine Bayou

Willet

Kongo

WASHINGTON CO
SHARKEY CO

Delta City

Shraderville

Updike

Vickland

ABAND

James Bayou

Deer Creek

Fish
Lake

Richey

BIG SUNFLOWER RIVER

County Bayou

SHARKEY CO
ISSAQUENA CO

WASHINGTON CO
ISSAQUENA CO

Riverside Junction

Continue in the
Mississippi Atlas & Gazetteer

Continue in the Mississippi Atlas & Gazetteer

33° 20' 00"

33° 14' 00"
33.2333°

33° 08' 00"
33.1333°

33° 02' 00"
33.0333°

32° 56' 00"

90° 45' 00"

90° 59' 00"
90.9833°

90° 25' 06"

90° 45' 00"

Contour interval 100 ft

© Garmin

ROLLING FORK MS

ROLLING FORK MS

Recreation Areas

Administration Legend
ARSP=Arkansas State Parks   NPS=National Park Service
DARH=Dept. of Arkansas Heritage   USACE=US Army Corps of Engineers
USFS=USDA Forest Service   USFWS= US Fish & Wildlife Service

Name, Location	Page & Grid	Acreage/Mileage	Administration	Concessions	Dumping Sta	Lodging	Marina	Picnic Area	Playground	Visitor Center	Boating	Camping	Fishing	Hiking	Hunting	Swimming
Arkansas River Navigation System, Pine Bluff	91 C5	445	USACE					•			•		•	•	•	
Baker Prairie Natural Area, Harrison	19 C4	30	DARH											•		
Bald Knob National Wildlife Refuge, Bald Knob	66 A2	13,900	USFWS								•		•		•	
Beaver Lake Project, Busch	17 B4	41,700	USACE	•	•			•	•		•	•	•	•	•	•
Big Creek Natural Area, Wilburn	49 C6	1,188	ANHC										•	•	•	
Big Lake National Wildlife Refuge, Manila	40 C3	11,038	USFWS								•		•		•	
Black Fork Mountain Wilderness, Ouachita National Forest	72 C2	7,568	USFS										•	•	•	
Blue Mountain Lake Project, Waveland	58 C3	17,019	USACE		•			•	•		•	•	•		•	•
Buffalo National River, Woolum	32 B3	95,730	NPS	•				•		•	•	•	•	•	•	•
Bull Shoals–White River State Park, Bull Shoals	20 B3	732	ARSP		•		•	•			•	•	•			•
Bull Shoals Lake Project, Bull Shoals	20 B3	101,196	USACE	•	•			•			•	•	•	•	•	•
Byrd Lake Natural Area, Pine Bluff	91 D5	144	DARH											•		
Cache River National Wildlife Refuge, Dixie	67 C4	56,000	USFWS								•		•		•	
Cane Creek State Park, Star City	104 C1	2,053	ARSP		•			•			•	•	•	•		
Caney Creek Wilderness, Ouachita National Forest	85 C4	14,460	USFS										•	•	•	
Chalk Bluff Natural Area, St Francis	27 A6	55	DARH											•		
Cossatot River State Park–Natural Area, Vandervoort	85 C4	4,470	ARSP					•		•			•	•		
Crater of Diamonds State Park, Murfreesboro	98 A2	888	ARSP	•	•			•			•	•	•	•		•
Crowleys Ridge State Park, Walcott	39 A4	271	ARSP	•	•			•	•			•	•	•		•
Daisy State Park, Daisy	86 D2	5,000	ARSP	•	•			•			•	•	•	•		•
DeGray Lake Project, Caddo Valley	88 D1	13,800	USACE		•		•	•			•	•	•			•
DeGray Lake State Park, Caddo Valley	88 C1	1,000	ARSP	•	•		•	•	•		•	•	•	•		•
De Queen Lake Project, De Queen	96 A2	8,100	USACE		•			•			•	•	•		•	•
Devil's Den State Park, Winslow	29 D4	1,954	ARSP	•	•			•	•		•	•	•	•		•
Dierks Lake Project, Dierks	85 D5	8,100	USACE	•	•		•	•			•	•	•		•	•
Dry Creek Wilderness, Ouachita National Forest	58 D2	6,300	USFS										•	•	•	
East Fork Wilderness, Ozark–St Francis National Forest	46 B3	10,700	USFS										•	•	•	
Felsenthal National Wildlife Refuge, Felsenthal	124 B1	64,000	USFWS								•	•	•		•	
Flatside Wilderness, Ouachita National Forest	76 A3	10,105	USFS										•	•	•	
Gilman Lake Project, Gillham	85 D4	9,000	USACE		•			•			•	•	•		•	
Greers Ferry Lake Project, Heber Springs	49 C5	40,914	USACE	•	•			•	•		•	•	•		•	•
Henry Koen Experimental Forest, Ozark–St Francis National Forest	32 A1	600	USFS												•	
Hobbs State Park–Conservation Area, War Eagle	16 C3	12,056	ARSP							•				•	•	
Holla Bend National Wildlife Refuge, Dardanelle	60 B2	7,055	USFWS					•			•		•	•	•	
Hot Springs National Park, Hot Springs	88 A2	5,839	NPS	•				•		•		•		•		
Hurricane Creek Wilderness, Ozark–St Francis National Forest	31 D6	15,100	USFS										•	•	•	
Kings River Falls Natural Area, Boston	30 C3	946	DARH											•		
Lake Catherine State Park, Diamondhead	88 A3	2,180	ARSP	•	•	•	•	•			•	•	•	•		•
Lake Charles State Park, Powhatan	37 A6	14,000	ARSP		•			•			•	•	•	•		•
Lake Chicot State Park, Lake Village	117 D6	200	ARSP	•	•	•	•	•			•	•	•	•		•
Lake Dardenelle Project, Russellville	60 A1	40,000	USACE		•		•	•			•	•	•		•	•
Lake Dardanelle State Park, Russellville	59 A6	34,000	ARSP	•	•		•	•	•		•	•	•			•
Lake Ft Smith State Park, Maddux Spring	43 A5	650	ARSP				•	•				•		•		•
Lake Frierson State Park, Lorado	39 B4	135	ARSP	•				•					•	•		
Lake Greeson Project, Murfreesboro	86 D2	15,842	USACE		•		•	•			•	•	•		•	•
Lake Ouachita Project, Mountain Pine	76 D1	82,373	USACE		•		•	•			•	•	•		•	•
Lake Ouachita State Park, Mountain Pine	76 D1	360	ARSP	•	•		•	•			•	•	•	•		•
Lake Poinsett State Park, Harrisburg	53 C4	120	ARSP	•	•			•			•	•	•			•
Leatherwood Wilderness, Ozark–St Francis National Forest	34 A2	16,956	USFS										•	•	•	
Logoly State Park, McNeil	112 D1	345	ARSP	•				•		•				•		
Lorance Creek Natural Area, Bingham	78 D3	294	DARH											•		
Lower Buffalo Wilderness, Buffalo National River	33 A6	22,500	NPS								•		•	•	•	
Mammoth Spring State Park, Mammoth Spring	23 A6	10	ARSP	•				•	•	•			•			
Millwood Lake Project, Ashdown	109 A6	6,500	USACE		•			•			•	•	•	•	•	•
Millwood State Park, Ashdown	109 A6	824	ARSP		•		•	•			•	•	•		•	
Mississippi River State Park, Mariana	83 D4	548	ARSP		•			•					•	•		•
Moro Bay State Park, New London	123 A5	110	ARSP	•	•		•	•			•	•	•			
Mount Magazine State Park, Havana	58 B3	2,234	ARSP	•		•		•				•		•		
Mount Nebo State Park, Dardanelle	59 B6	3,783	ARSP	•		•		•				•		•		
Nimrod Lake Project, Fourche Junction	59 D6	25,000	USACE		•			•			•	•	•		•	•
Norfork Lake Project, Salesville	21 C6	54,000	USACE	•	•			•			•	•	•		•	•
Ouachita – Black Rivers Navigation Project, Felsenthal	124 C1	40,000	USACE		•			•			•	•	•		•	
Ouachita National Forest, Mt Ida	74 D3	1,700,000	USFS					•			•	•	•	•	•	•
Overflow National Wildlife Refuge, Wilmot	125 C5	12,000	USFWS												•	
Ozark Lake Project, Ozark	44 C1	10,600	USACE		•			•			•	•	•		•	
Ozark–St Francis National Forest, Hector	46 C3	1,222,000	USFS		•			•			•	•	•	•	•	•
Petit Jean State Park, Pontoon	60 C3	3,471	ARSP	•	•	•		•	•		•	•	•	•		•
Pianncle Mountain State Park, Pinnacle	78 A1	1,770	ARSP	•				•		•	•		•	•		
Ponca Wilderness, Ponca	31 A5	11,300	NPS										•	•	•	
Pond Creek National Wildlife Refuge, Winthrup	97 C4	27,000	USFWS								•		•		•	
Poteau Mountain Wilderness, Ouachita National Forest	56 D3	10,884	USFS										•	•	•	
Queen Wilhelmina State Park, Rich Mountain	72 C2	640	ARSP	•		•		•				•		•		
Richland Creek Wilderness, Ozark-St Francis National Forest	32 D2	11,800	USFS										•	•	•	
Stone Road Glade Natural Area, Center Point	97 A6	108	DARH											•		
Table Rock Lake Project, Beaver	17 A5	43,070	USACE			•	•	•		•	•	•	•			•
Toad Suck Ferry and Murray Locks & Dams Project, Toad Suck	61 C6	9,700	USACE					•	•		•	•	•		•	
Upper Buffalo Wilderness–NPS, Buffalo National River	31 C5	10,819	NPS										•	•	•	
Upper Buffalo Wilderness–USFS, Ozark-St Francis National Forest	31 C5	11,094	USFS										•	•	•	
Village Creek State Park, Newcastle	69 B4	7,000	ARSP	•	•		•	•	•	•	•	•	•	•		•
Wapanocca National Wildlife Refuge, Turrell	54 D2	5,485	USFWS								•		•		•	
White Oak Lake State Park, Bluff City	112 A1	725	ARSP	•	•			•			•	•	•		•	
White River National Wildlife Refuge, Mellwood	94 D1	155,126	USFWS								•	•	•		•	
Withrow Springs State Park, Forum	17 D5	786	ARSP	•	•			•			•	•	•	•		•
Woolly Hollow State Park, Greenbrier	62 A2	440	ARSP	•	•			•	•		•	•	•	•		•